WOMEN'S HISTORY

AND

ANCIENT HISTORY

WOMEN'S HISTORY

AND

ANCIENT HISTORY

EDITED BY

SARAH B. POMEROY

The University of North Carolina Press

Chapel Hill and London

© 1991 The University of North Carolina Press

Library of Congress Cataloging-in-Publication Data

Women's history and ancient history / edited by
Sarah B. Pomeroy.
   p.   cm.
Includes bibliographical references and index.
ISBN 0-8078-1949-2 (cloth : alk. paper).—ISBN 0-8078-4310-5
(pbk. : alk. paper)
   1. Women—History—To 500.   2. Women—Greece—
History.   3. Women—Rome—History.   I. Pomeroy,
Sarah B.
HQ1127.W6525   1991
305.4'09—dc20   90-24488
                                             CIP

Manufactured in the United States of America
95 94 93 92 91   5 4 3 2 1

TO

———

Dorothy O. Helly

Susan Lees

Jo Ann McNamara

Sue Rosenberg Zalk

esteemed colleagues

and dear friends

CONTENTS

———

Contents ix

SARAH B. POMEROY

Preface

The predominant theme of the papers collected in this volume is the relationship between public and private in the lives of women in antiquity. For example, the first article in the collection, Jane McIntosh Snyder's study of Sappho, describes the ways in which the poet gave public voice to personal emotion. Cynthia B. Patterson and Mireille Corbier discuss the intrusion of politics and the state into the sexual and reproductive lives of women. Shaye J. D. Cohen examines the imposition of Jewish and Christian taboos connected with women's sexual and reproductive functions. In articles on the Hippocratic corpus Ann Ellis Hanson and Lesley Dean-Jones investigate the dissemination of knowledge and opinion about the interior of women's bodies and the most intimate gynecological matters.

For women, private preceded public: when public roles existed, they developed from family relationships. Claude Mossé demonstrates that Spartan queens exercised a decisive influence in politics but came to their position as mothers, wives, and widows of kings. They used their property (which they had taken as daughters through dowry and inheritance) to foster or defeat political change. Mary Taliaferro Boatwright shows that Plancia Magna also gained her wealth and public prominence as daughter, and then wife, of wealthy and distinguished men. Likewise, as Diana Delia argues, Fulvia gained a reputation for being manipulative in politics by virtue of her marriages to politicians. Most Hellenistic queens also attained their position as wives or, in fewer cases, as daughters of kings. Unlike Spartan queens, or the aristocratic women of Rome, some Hellenistic queens in the new monarchies created by Alexander and his successors exercised legitimate political authority. Elizabeth Carney's study of the emergence of a title for these queens traces the expansion of the queens' activities in the political sphere and the development of the mon-archy as an institution that might include women. The various articles on Spartan, Hellenistic, and Roman women are linked in their focus on the radical effect of war and revolution on women's lives. They document the ways in which the status of upper-class women changed over time. Politi-cal upheaval created opportunities for Spartan and Hellenistic queens and upper-class Roman women to exercise powers previously reserved for men. In most cases control of enormous amounts of wealth was a signifi-cant factor in securing a public role for royal and elite women.[1]

Despite the public roles that some upper-class Greek and Roman women played, they maintained their female identity. According to Diana Delia's revisionist view, Fulvia was primarily a wife and mother, not the androgyne and virago depicted in propaganda manufactured by her hus-bands' enemies. Mireille Corbier's survey suggests that Fulvia's serial monogamy was typical of the marital behavior of upper-class women in the late Republic. The role of women—even of those active in the public sphere—generally remained complementary to that of men. Although Julia Domna did not confine her activities to the domestic sphere, Roman propaganda associated the empress with reproduction and dynastic con-tinuity. As Natalie Boymel Kampen shows, the empress's antithesis on the social scale, the captive barbarian woman, symbolized sterility and hence the total extinction of Rome's rivals. Their function as wives and producers of legitimate children indicates that—with the exception of a few *hetairai* who commissioned Nossis to write epigrams for them—the women discussed in this collection were respectable. The upper-class women who crossed the boundaries from private to public sacrificed neither their femininity nor their respectability.

Historians of women nowadays applaud the study of women of op-pressed groups, rather than "great" women. Paradoxically, "great" has become almost a term of denigration. However, the royal and elite women of antiquity are deserving of our scrutiny. First of all, there is usually more than one primary source of information about them, whereas women of the lower classes are often known only through a single funerary inscrip-tion. Sufficient reliable historical data exist on elite Roman women for Mireille Corbier to be able to distinguish the marriage patterns of aristo-crats from those of the imperial family. Second, elite women served as models for other women. Hellenistic queens provided new paradigms, not only for Greek women but for some Roman women of the upper class and the demimonde as well. Thus Mary Taliaferro Boatwright sets the phenomenon of Plancia Magna in the context of public benefactions by Hellenistic Greeks. By contrast, articles such as those on the gynecological treatises, on Athenian marriage, on women in Roman sculpture, and on menstrual taboos explore cultural, political, iconographic, and religious constructs that cut across classes.

The articles illuminate aspects of the full range of ancient history from archaic Greece to late antiquity. That more pages are devoted to Greek than to Roman women is a reflection of the state of contemporary scholarship on women in antiquity. The articles deal with women of a variety of ethnicities who lived in widespread geographical areas. Thus, although they are presented in a chronological arrangement, they are not intended to show a continuous line of historical development or progression. Indeed, the last article in the collection, Shaye J. D. Cohen's study of Jewish and Christian women, demonstrates that personal and domestic concerns (especially motherhood and sexuality) continued to be viewed as the most important foci of women's lives: works such as the gynecological treatises indicate that the same concerns had been central for pagan women in earlier periods of antiquity. Interestingly enough, the Hippocratic corpus, like the rest of Greek literature—but unlike the later Jewish and Christian texts—does not refer to menstruation or childbirth as inherently polluting. Lesley Dean-Jones explains that these natural processes served to endorse the Greeks' belief that women and men were vastly different creatures. Perhaps because women and men were already segregated by sex in Greece, with women living upstairs in women's quarters and men downstairs in men's quarters, there was no need for taboos to keep them apart. Within their separate domains, some women—at least those of the upper class—created their own culture and society. Jane McIntosh Snyder and Marilyn B. Skinner offer close and sympathetic studies of the relationships between women described by women poets. Perhaps some Roman women as well were conscious of their ties to other women. It is relevant that the arch of Plancia Magna displayed more representations of women than of men.

Unlike other collections of articles on women in antiquity, this group of essays includes purely literary studies only when the ancient authors are female, as is the case in the articles on Sappho and Nossis. Of course, in antiquity very few women wrote literature. The confinement of the majority of women to the domestic realm was a significant cause of their illiteracy. However, as the articles by Ann Ellis Hanson and Shaye J. D. Cohen suggest, women's oral tradition may be assimilated and transmitted in male-authored works such as the gynecological treatises and Jewish legal texts. Aside from the articles in which poetry written by women is examined, the work in this volume is based on traditional sources employed by ancient historians, namely coins, inscriptions, historical relief sculpture, and prose texts including works by Xenophon, Aristotle, Polybius, Plutarch, Cicero, Livy, the Hippocratic corpus, Roman Law, the Bible, and the Talmud. The scholarship displayed in this collection is firmly based in close and critical examination of such sources, rather than in the wholesale application of currently popular theories of analysis such as structuralism or psychoanalysis to images of women in myth-based literature. For example, Diana Delia analyzes contemporary sources of information about Fulvia and concludes that they were biased.[2] In the first historical survey in English of menstrual taboos in Judaism, Shaye J. D. Cohen relies primarily on Jewish and Christian legal texts.

The articles are feminist in that women are at the center of each author's inquiry. In the tradition of feminist scholarship, the collection has been turned into a collaborative effort by pairing some of the naturally related articles, such as those on Sappho and Nossis, the two on the Hippocratic corpus, those on Athenians and Spartans, and those on women in Roman art and Plancia Magna: each member of the pair of authors commented on the work of the other and refers to it when appropriate. Of course, the pairs of authors do not always agree, but they alert the reader to additional examples or to places where another perspective on similar material can be found in the present volume.

Seven of the twelve articles appearing in this volume were first delivered as papers at either the seventh Berkshire Conference on the History of Women at Wellesley College in June 1987 or at the Summer Seminar for College Teachers on "The Family in Classical and Hellenistic Greece" sponsored by the National Endowment for the Humanities that I directed in 1987 at the Graduate School of the City University of New York.[3] As the member of the Program Committee of the Berkshire Conference with responsibility for the sessions on classical antiquity and as the director of the Summer Seminar on "The Family in Classical and Hellenistic Greece," I endeavored to create a cordial atmosphere in which colleagues could readily exchange information and constructive criticism on their work in progress. The papers have benefited from the comments of participants at the conference and the seminar. It would be impossible to mention them all by name, but I would like to thank Phyllis Culham for her incisive comments on two of the articles and Keith R. Bradley for suggesting the title of this volume. Thus this collection has been assembled as a new chapter in the ongoing dialogue about women in classical antiquity.

The objective stance of most of the authors included in this collection is characteristic of scholars of women in antiquity in the late 1980s. Historiographically this stance should be compared to the outspoken (and, in my view, correct) judgments of scholars of the 1970s about the subordination and oppression of women in antiquity. Although, as Jane McIntosh Snyder found, it is still necessary to correct the androcentric views of previous generations of classical scholars, it is no longer necessary to argue, in general, that the status of women was inferior to that of men in patriarchal societies and religions such as those of Greece and Rome and to emphasize that even upper-class women were valued primarily for their reproductive capacity and for their use in marriages that would create alliances between men. Some authors, such as Ann Ellis Hanson, Cynthia B. Patterson, and Mireille Corbier, have been primarily interested in describing and explaining the functioning of traditional systems of thought or of politics. More than the other articles, Shaye J. D. Cohen's study of the history of menstrual taboos deals directly with a subject of current concern to numerous Jewish and Christian women and men. None of the articles is propagandistic: readers are free to draw their own conclusions.

This volume should be influential in determining the future directions of the historical study of women in antiquity. Nowadays, scholars in the mainstream are moving on to the painstaking work of recovering the diverse lives of ancient women. Women did have a history, often different from the history of men. But women's history cannot always be subsumed under social history. Queens and aristocrats and laws about sexuality and reproduction constitute subject matter for women's history, but they should not be excluded from political and economic history. Thus it is to be hoped that this book will serve to expand the paradigms of ancient history to include women.

Sarah B. Pomeroy
Hunter College and the
Graduate School, C.U.N.Y.

Notes

1. See further Sarah B. Pomeroy, *Women in Hellenistic Egypt from Alexander to Cleopatra* (paperback reprint, Detroit: Wayne State University Press, 1990), 14–16.

2. It is perhaps no accident that Cicero, one of the principal authors of the calumny against Fulvia, was also critical of Spartan women and of Cleopatra VII. See *Tusc. Disp.* 2.15.36, *Ad Att.* 14.8, 14.20, 15.4, 15.15.

3. The essays in this collection were substantially completed in 1989.

WOMEN'S HISTORY
AND
ANCIENT HISTORY

JANE MCINTOSH SNYDER

Public Occasion and Private Passion

in the Lyrics of Sappho of Lesbos

Part of the problem faced by literary critics and historians in interpreting the poetry of Sappho has to do with the imposition of a "public" audience onto poems which seem designed for a "private" hearer—or at least for a hearer who understands the special language of women speaking to other women in a context not considered "public" according to prevailing male standards of social organization. The problem is in many ways analogous to the difficulty an ethnographer has in studying women in a particular society using a model of that society which is derived only from the male portion of the population. As the anthropologist Edwin Ardener has observed, the ethnographer who interviews women in a certain society must be aware that the women "will not necessarily provide a model for society as a unit that will contain both men and themselves. They may indeed provide a model in which women and nature are outside men and society."[1] As I hope to demonstrate, Sappho's poetry covers the full spectrum of models—and it is those fragments at the women-and-nature end of the spectrum which have been the most puzzling over the centuries to male-oriented critics of her work.

I

Many of the fragments of Sappho's poems seem to have been intended for presentation in connection with some social occasion—most often a wedding—which was part of the larger social structure in which Sappho lived, namely the presumably male-dominated aristocracy of late seventh- and early sixth-century B.C. Lesbos.[2] We can recognize the genre of these songs by comparing them with similar lyrics in, for example, later Athenian comedy, which often contain nuptial scenes. The characteristics of these wedding songs (or epithalamia, as they are called in Greek, literally "bed-chamber songs") generally include ribald jokes and mock criticism of the groom, often with specific reference to his size or physical appearance. Two examples among Sappho's fragments are 110a and 111:

θυρώρῳ πόδες ἐπτορόγυιοι,
τὰ δὲ σάμβαλα πεμπεβόηα,
πίσσυγγοι δὲ δέκ᾽ ἐξεπόναισαν. (110a)

[At the wedding]
the door-keeper's feet are seven fathoms long,
and his sandals are made of five ox-hides,
and ten shoemakers worked away to make them.

ἴψοι δὴ τὸ μέλαθρον,
ὑμήναον,
ἀέρρετε, τέκτονες ἄνδρες·
ὑμήναον.
γάμβρος † (εἰσ)έρχεται ἴσος † Ἄρευι,
ἄνδρος μεγάλω πόλυ μέσδων.

Raise high the roof-beams!
    Sing the Hymeneal!
Raise it high, O carpenter men!
    Sing the Hymeneal!
The bridegroom enters, like to Ares,
by far bigger than a big man.

In 110a the groom's attendant seems to suffer from excessively large feet, which require enormous sandals made from a ridiculous amount of leather. In 111, whose strains may be familiar to the reader from J. D. Salinger's use of them in the title of his long short story "Raise High the Roofbeam, Carpenters," the emphasis is instead on the extreme height of the groom, with a probable allusion in the last line to his ithyphallic state of excitement.[3] (Fragment 44, which describes the wedding of Hektor and Andromache, may offer evidence of a more serious type of wedding song, if we assume that the mythological bride and groom were linked elsewhere in the poem to a contemporary couple.)

These are examples, then, of a genre which is recognizable to us from comparative material elsewhere in Greek literature and in the literature of other cultures as well. Even without their surrounding material such fragments offer no great difficulty in interpretation, as we can imagine the context from which they come. These are songs which are basically intelligible to a "public" audience, even one removed from Sappho's world by the passage of 2,600 years.

II

A second group of the fragments of Sappho's poetry includes many which have some sort of "shape" which renders them familiar in their patterns on the basis of our knowledge of other Greek lyric poetry and of other lyric poetry in general. In this intermediate group, although the content of the poems is generally far different from the comparable works by male lyric poets, the *form* (or apparent form, I should say, as all but one of Sappho's poems are in a fragmentary state) is relatively conventional. Even though we may not want to go so far as to say that these songs were meant to be performed at some specific occasion, they nevertheless seem in some way connected with familiar rituals of a public character. Here let me mention three examples—one a hymn to Aphrodite (which is in fact our only complete poem), another a prayer for the epiphany of the same goddess, and the third a traditional type of catalogue called a "priamel."

The first example, the Hymn to Aphrodite (fragment 1), is written in imitation of the standard form of a Greek prayer:

ποικιλόθρον᾽ ἀθανάτ᾽ Ἀφρόδιτα,
παῖ Δίος δολόπλοκε, λίσσομαί σε,
μή μ᾽ ἄσαισι μηδ᾽ ὀνίαισι δάμνα,
πότνια, θῦμον,

ἀλλὰ τυίδ᾽ ἔλθ᾽, αἴ ποτα κἀτέρωτα
τὰς ἔμας αὔδας ἀίοισα πήλοι
ἔκλυες, πάτρος δὲ δόμον λίποισα
χρύσιον ἦλθες

ἄρμ᾽ ὑπασδεύξαισα· κάλοι δέ σ᾽ ἆγον
ὦκεες στροῦθοι περὶ γᾶς μελαίνας
πύκνα δίννεντες πτέρ᾽ ἀπ᾽ ὠράνωἴθε-
ρος διὰ μέσσω,

αἶψα δ' ἐξίκοντο˙ σὺ δ', ὦ μάκαιρα,
μειδιαίσαισ' ἀθανάτῳ προσώπῳ
ἤρε' ὄττι δηὖτε πέπονθα κὤττι
δηὖτε κάλημμι,

κὤττι μοι μάλιστα θέλω γένεσθαι
μαινόλᾳ θύμῳ˙ τίνα δηὖτε πείθω
ἄψ σ' ἄγην ἐς Fὰν φιλότατα; τίς σ', ὦ
Ψάπφ', ἀδικήει;

καὶ γὰρ αἰ φεύγει, ταχέως διώξει˙
αἰ δὲ δῶρα μὴ δέκετ', ἀλλὰ δώσει˙
αἰ δὲ μὴ φίλει, ταχέως φιλήσει
κωὐκ ἐθέλοισα.

ἔλθε μοι καὶ νῦν, χαλέπαν δὲ λῦσον
ἐκ μερίμναν, ὄσσα δέ μοι τέλεσσαι
θῦμος ἰμέρρει, τέλεσον˙ σὺ δ' αὔτα
σύμμαχος ἔσσο.

O immortal Aphrodite of the many-colored throne,
child of Zeus, weaver of wiles, I beseech you,
do not overwhelm me in my heart
with anguish and pain, O Mistress,

But come hither, if ever at another time
hearing my cries from afar
you heeded them, and leaving the home of your father
came, yoking your golden

Chariot: beautiful, swift sparrows
drew you above the black earth
whirling their wings thick and fast,
from heaven's ether through mid-air.

Suddenly they had arrived; but you, O Blessed Lady,
with a smile on your immortal face,
asked what I had suffered again and
why I was calling again

And what I was most wanting to happen for me
in my frenzied heart: "Whom again shall I persuade

to come back into friendship with you? Who,
O Sappho, does you injustice?

"For if indeed she flees, soon will she pursue,
and though she receives not your gifts, she will give them,
and if she loves not now, soon she will love,
even against her will."

Come to me now also, release me from
harsh cares; accomplish as many things as my heart desires
to accomplish; and you yourself
be my fellow soldier.

The form of this poem is well documented from sources such as the many prayers to the gods in Homer's *Iliad* and *Odyssey*. The deity, in this case Aphrodite, is first addressed and identified, then reminded of a past relationship with the speaker, and finally called upon to perform a particular service. Here Sappho calls upon the goddess to come to her aid in the fulfillment of a conquest she hopes to make on the "battlefield" of love—to borrow from Sappho's metaphor of address to Aphrodite as a "fellow soldier."

One of the notable characteristics of Sappho as a writer is her ability to adapt traditional forms—such as the prayer—to suit her own purposes. Here Sappho brings Aphrodite to life by reducing the first and last parts of the prayer formula—the invocation and the request—in such a way that they occupy only the first and last stanzas of the poem. The middle part of the formula—the description of the past relationship—then is filled out in elaborate detail so that it occupies five full stanzas. The goddess's presence is made remarkably vivid through this central description of her visit to Sappho at some indefinite time in the past. The report of the goddess's words within the description, first indirectly and then directly (through quotation) not only pays tribute to Aphrodite's wonderful power but also implies (through repetition of the word "again") that she has exerted that power on Sappho's behalf many times in the still more distant past. Oddly then, the direction of the poem is continually backward into the past, and yet the vividness of the description evokes the image of the goddess as a real force in the immediate present, who is being called upon to assist Sappho *now*. As in the past, so now Aphrodite has absolute power to transform a situation: to change flight into pursuit, refusal into desire, rejection into love. The woman who runs away from the Sappho-narra-tor's overtures will not just stop running away—she will actually run *toward* the Sappho-narrator instead.[4]

Whether this piece was actually offered up as a prayer is debatable, especially in view of the artfulness in emphasizing the past relationship by making it occupy the bulk of the poem. But the point to be noticed here is that Sappho has encoded her message within a perfectly traditional form which was clearly part of the public consciousness and one with which her readers were all completely familiar—a prayer to one of the Olympian deities. However novel and striking the contents of the poem may be, the outward appearance and general shape of the poem are completely predictable on the basis of both earlier and later material within Greek sources, not to mention sources from outside the Greek tradition. It is not surprising, then, that critics over the centuries (most of them male) have had no particular difficulty in interpeting this poem, with the possible exception of several translators in the eighteenth century who were so uncomfortable with the issue of gender within the poem that they changed the "she's" to "he's."[5]

Another example of a poem of familiar shape is fragment 2, often referred to as the "epiphany" fragment:

δεῦϱύ μ' ἐκ Κϱήτας ἐπ[ὶ τόνδ]ε ναῦον
ἄγνον, ὅππ[ᾳ τοι] χάϱιεν μὲν ἄλσος
μαλί[αν], βῶμοι δὲ τεθυμιάμε-
νοι [λι]βανώτῳ·

ἐν δ' ὕδωϱ ψῦχϱον κελάδει δι' ὕσδων
μαλίνων, βϱόδοισι δὲ παῖς ὁ χῶϱος
ἐσκίαστ', αἰθυσσομένων δὲ φύλλων
κῶμα κατέϱϱει·

ἐν δὲ λείμων ἱππόβοτος τέθαλεν
ἠϱίνοισιν ἄνθεσιν, αἱ δ' ἄηται
μέλλιχα πνέοισιν [
[   ]

ἔνθα δὴ σὺ . . . . ἔλοισα Κύπϱι
χϱυσίαισιν ἐν κυλίκεσσιν ἄβϱως
ὀμμεμείχμενον θαλίαισι νέκταϱ
οἰνοχόαισον

Hither to me from Crete, to this holy
temple, where your lovely grove
of apple trees is, and the altars
smoke with frankincense.

Herein cold water rushes through
apple boughs, and the whole place is shaded
with roses, and sleep comes down
from rustling leaves.

Herein a meadow where horses graze
blooms with spring flowers, and the winds
blow gently . . .

Here, O Cyprian, taking [garlands],
in golden cups gently pour forth
nectar mingled together with our
festivities. . . .

Like the Hymn to Aphrodite, which we have just examined, fragment 2 is
cast in the form of a request that Aphrodite come from afar and make
herself present. This time, however, the request is tied to description not
of past assistance but of present ritual, whose setting at springtime in a
temple in the middle of a meadow becomes the focus of the extant portion
of the poem. The poem resembles others of the period in which Sappho
lived which ask for the epiphany of some deity or deities, as, for example,
Alcaeus' request (his fragment 34a) that Castor and Pollux make an appearance to aid (real or metaphorical) sea-voyagers. What distinguishes
Sappho's piece is its delightful sensuality in the way that it appeals to our
senses of sight (the temple and its altars, the grove of apple trees, etc.),
smell (the frankincense), touch (the coldness of the water and the cool-
ness of the shade), and sound (the rushing of water, the rustling of leaves,
the whispering of the breeze). The effect is hypnotic; Sappho transports
the audience to a place where the magic of sleep descends from the
rustling leaves of trees, the sound of which is echoed through the prepon-
derance of *s* sounds in the original Greek. Unfortunately the fragment
breaks off just as the speaker of the poem invites Aphrodite to join in the
ritual being celebrated. But even without its ending we can conclude on
the basis of the poem's opening that it probably followed the usual pattern
of other epiphany poems in describing in further detail the place or

occasion at which the divine presence is asked to manifest itself, along with the reason for the petitioner's request. We should note that despite its arrestingly sensual qualities, there is evidently nothing particularly unusual in the outward *form* of this poem, so far as we can tell from what remains of it.

Fragment 16, apparently a nearly complete piece, provides yet another example of a poem that is purely conventional in its outward shape yet contains a shift of perspective that renders it uniquely Sapphic in its treatment:

o]ἰ μὲν ἰππήων στρότον οἰ δὲ πέσδων
οἰ δὲ νάων φαῖσ᾽ ἐπ[ὶ] γᾶν μέλαι[ν]αν
ἔ]μμεναι κάλλιστον, ἔγω δὲ κῆν᾽ ὄτ-
τω τις ἔραται˙

πά]γχυ δ᾽ εὔμαρες σύνετον πόησαι
π]άντι τ[ο]ῦτ᾽, ἀ γὰρ πόλυ περσκέθοισα
κάλλος [ἀνθ]ρώπων Ἐλένα [τὸ]ν ἄνδρα
τὸν [πανάρ]ιστον

καλλ[ίποι]σ᾽ ἔβα 'ς Τροΐαν πλέοι[σα
κωὐδ[ὲ πα]ῖδος οὐδὲ φίλων το[κ]ήων
πά[μπαν] ἐμνάσθη, ἀλλὰ παράγαγ᾽ αὖταν
                    ]σαν

            ]αμπτον γὰρ]
        ] . . . κούφως τ[   ]οησ[.]ν
. .]με νῦν Ἀνακτορί[ας ὀ]νέμναι-
σ᾽ οὐ] παρεοίσας˙

τᾶ[ς κε βολλοίμαν ἔρατόν τε βᾶμα
κἀμάρυχμα λάμπρον ἴδην προσώπω
ἤ τὰ Λύδων ἄρματα κἀν ὄπλοισι
πεσδομ]άχεντας.

Some say that the most beautiful thing
upon the black earth is an army of horsemen;
others, of infantry, still others, of ships;
but I say it is what one loves.

It is completely easy to make this
intelligible to everyone; for the woman

who far surpassed all mortals in beauty,
Helen, left her most brave husband

And sailed off to Troy, nor did she
remember at all her child
or her dear parents; but [the Cyprian]
led her away. . . .

[All of which] has now reminded me
of Anaktoria, who is not here.

Her lovely walk and the bright sparkle of her face
I would rather look upon than
all the Lydian chariots
and full-armed infantry.

The description (in what is evidently the final stanza) of the speaker's overwhelming preference for the sight of Anaktoria's "lovely walk and the bright sparkle of her face" forms part of the "cap" for the preceding list of other sights which someone other than the narrator might prefer to behold. This pattern—a catalogue or list of items rejected capped at the end by one item accepted as being of special significance—is a familiar one in Greek and Latin literature and can be found in other Archaic and later authors ranging from Tyrtaeus, Solon, and Pindar to Lucretius and others. Such a rhetorical device is generally referred to now by the term "priamel," after the name for a genre of medieval German poetry that features the device of the catalogue.[6]

At the most basic level, the poem simply follows the form of the traditional catalogue. The speaker offers a list of items that some would consider the most beautiful thing in the world; cavalry, infantry, and naval forces are all rejected, and then one item is set forth as the only valid one: "what one loves." The accepted item is then illustrated first by an example from myth and then by the example of the narrator's own personal preference, with a return in the last extant lines to the opening military motifs. To one versed in ancient rhetorical devices frequently used by the lyric poets, the piece has at least a superficial ring of a familiar narrative pattern.

As in the Hymn to Aphrodite, however, Sappho has molded the traditional form to suit her own purposes, so that one must look beneath the familiar pattern to discover what she is really trying to present. Some scholars have searched for stark logic in the poem's examples, and, finding it wanting, have criticized the poem as too loosely tied together. After all, they say, how does the fact that Helen left her husband and child and went off to Troy prove the narrator's thesis that what is most beautiful is what one loves?[7] If we look for association of ideas and images, rather than strict logic, however, we can see the poem as highly coherent. The emphasis of the song is on the concept of *kalliston* (line 3)—the power of whatever is "most beautiful"—and Helen, as the most beautiful woman in the world, is the supreme exemplum of *kallos* (line 7, the corresponding line in the next stanza). Although the gap in the text of stanza 4 prevents us from seeing the exact connection, it appears to be the thought of Helen that reminds the narrator of the absent Anaktoria (lines 15–16). Even if Helen represents par excellence what is "most beautiful," to the narrator the most beautiful thing in the world is the sight of Anaktoria. And again through association and implication, the epic-scale naval expedition and displays of military might connected with the abduction of Helen pale in significance to the splendor of one face—the face that by the narrator's standard is the most beautiful.

Thus the myth of Helen, while it does not "prove" the thesis of the song, incorporates all of the elements of the catalogue—ships, foot-soldiers, cavalry, and an object of love, Helen herself—and at the same time provides the poem with a foil for the speaker's own redefinition of *kalliston*. The most beautiful thing in the world is not Helen, but Anaktoria, who represents for the narrator "what one loves." Beauty is defined not in a cosmic way in mythical terms, but in a particular way in terms of a single individual's perception. Through that perception the myth of Helen has been transformed, for Helen is no longer a passive object of others' attentions. Like the narrator, who actively seeks the sight of Anaktoria, Helen evidently chooses to leave behind her husband and forget her child and parents. Just as the narrator seeks Anaktoria, so Helen here seeks her voyage to Troy to be with Paris.[8]

III

We come now to the final type of poem: the women-and-nature songs that do not seem to follow, even outwardly, the conventional forms of public poetry. I choose to focus here on the two most obvious examples among the fragments (31 and 94), although certainly others could be cited as well.

To those versed in the classical tradition, Sappho 31 seems somehow familiar, for it was widely imitated among ancient writers:

φαίνεταί μοι κῆνος ἴσος θέοισιν
ἔμμεν’ ὤνηρ, ὄττις ἐνάντιός τοι
ἰσδάνει καὶ πλάσιον ἆδυ φωνεί-
σας ὐπακούει

καὶ γελαίσας ἰμέροεν, τό μ’ ἦ μὰν
καρδίαν ἐν στήθεσιν ἐπτόαισεν·
ὡς γὰρ ἔς σ’ ἴδω βρόχε’, ὤς με φώναι-
σ’ οὐδ’ ἒν ἔτ’ εἴκει,

ἀλλὰ κὰμ μὲν γλῶσσά ⟨μ’⟩ ἔαγε, λέπτον
δ’ αὔτικα χρῷ πῦρ ὐπαδεδρόμηκεν,
ὀππάτεσσι δ’ οὐδ’ ἒν ὄρημμ’, ἐπιρρόμ-
βεισι δ’ ἄκουαι,

κὰδ δέ μ’ ἴδρως κακχέεται, τρόμος δὲ
παῖσαν ἄγρει, χλωροτέρα δὲ ποίας
ἔμμι, τεθνάκην δ’ ὀλίγω ’πιδεύης
φαίνομ’ ἔμ’ αὔτ[ᾳ.

ἀλλὰ πὰν τόλματον, ἐπεὶ †καὶ πένητα†

He seems to me to be like the gods
—whatever man sits opposite you
and close by hears you
talking sweetly

And laughing charmingly; which
makes the heart within my breast take flight;
for the instant I look upon you, I cannot anymore
speak one word,

But in silence my tongue is broken, a fine
fire at once runs under my skin,
with my eyes I see not one thing, my ears
buzz,

Cold sweat covers me, trembling
seizes my whole body, I am more moist than grass;

I seem to be little short
of dying. . . .

But all must be ventured. . . .

Catullus 51 is the most obvious adaptation, but similar echoes may be
found, for example, in Theocritus 2.106–10 and Lucretius 3.152–58. But if
we look at the poem in the light of earlier Greek literature, the closest kind
of parallel in the *Iliad* is mild by comparison; for example, in the lull before
the storm of battle, the Greek troops feast outside the walls of Troy all
night long, and "green fear took hold of them" (*Il.* 7.479: *tous de chlōron
deos heirei*). In Sappho, it is not some external force like fear that is "green"
(or "pale" or "moist"—the word carries all three meanings), but the narrator herself.[9] Indeed there is nothing in Greek epic or lyric poetry that even
remotely matches the power of this description of the narrator's intense
emotional and physical reaction to the sight of the woman for whom she
feels desire.

Precisely because this fragment is so outside the conventional forms of
its time—being neither prayer nor invocation nor ribald nuptial song nor
priamel—it has been subject to gross misinterpretation by critics who
wish to make it fit the narrative structure of public, that is, male, discourse. The man of the opening line has been magnified in importance
ever since the publication in 1913 of a book on Sappho by Ulrich von
Wilamowitz-Moellendorff; he was an enormously influential scholar, and
rightly so, but his blindness with repect to Sappho has profoundly dis-
torted the modern view of her and particularly of this fragment. To paraphrase his interpretation:

> The woman sits opposite a man and jokes and laughs with him. Who
> can he be other than her bridegroom? The wedding guests enter, and
> Sappho takes up the barbitos and sings a song similar to the ones she
> has composed for the weddings of so many of her pupils. This time
> she sings of her passionate love for the bride. But, contrary to the
> remark in the *Suda* about Sappho's "shameful friendships," this love
> is completely honorable because a) she is not embarassed to mention
> it openly and b) she sings of it in the context of a wedding.[10]

So Wilamowitz "proves"—by mere assertion—that fragment 31 is a wedding song! And thus Sappho's homoeroticism is diluted and placed into a
context that offers no offense to the Victorian morality of Wilamowitz's
day.

The absurdity of Wilamowitz's explanation of fragment 31 has been amply noted in recent years and the obvious pointed out—that a wedding song must have chiefly to do with the bride and groom, not with the speaker's passion for one of them. Yet the wedding-song theory persists. Max Treu, for example (following Bruno Snell), thinks the poem is "in all probability" a wedding song, albeit of a "personal" nature, since it begins with a praise of the "groom"; Hermann Fränkel likewise dubs the poem a "personal" marriage song; and in an interesting recent twist on the theme, Thomas McEvilley proposes that the poem is an intentional distortion of the genre, in which Sappho wants the audience to think at first that they are about to hear a marriage song, which she then transforms, in a deliberate upsetting of the audience's expectations, into a description of her own inner feelings.[11] Thus many scholars fail to note the relative unimportance of the man of the first line of the poem, except as part of the background for the poem's setting and as a foil for the exposition of the speaker's feelings; he is calmly "godlike" in response to the woman's sweet talk and charming laugh, whereas the speaker, in the same situation, is instantly struck dumb.

Much more could be said about the range of interpretations of this poem in the twentieth century, but let me mention only one other of the more novel readings. According to George Devereux, the poem is primarily about jealousy, and the symptoms enumerated constitute a clinical description of what Devereux labels a homosexual "anxiety attack."[12]

We might more usefully take note of the female language of the song. For example, the emphasis in the description of the woman is on her activity, not on specific physical characteristics (height, hair color, etc.). Instead the speaker focuses on the woman's speaking and laughing, much in the same way that the narrator of fragment 16 calls to her mind Anaktoria's "lovely walk and the bright sparkle of her face." In addition the detailed, introspective picture of the narrator's feelings on seeing and hearing the beloved woman concludes—just before the narrator's illusion of near-death—with a comparison drawn from nature. The speaker is *chlōrotera de poias*, "paler" or "moister" than grass. (The phrase is usually translated as "*greener* than grass" by those who want to read the poem as one about envy and jealousy.) In Greek the adjective *chlōros* is often used of young shoots and also describes wood, honey, and the pale yellow-green band in the spectrum of a rainbow. Thus the word is connected with youth and life—not the death seemingly experienced by the speaker in the very next line. The death is only apparent—as emphasized in the opening word of line 16, "*I seem* to myself. . . ." Far from being an absurd exaggeration, as many have taken the phrase, *chlōrotera de poias* anchors the speaker's experience firmly in the natural world, a world of freshness, growth, and moisture. Just as nature quickens with the advent of spring, so the speaker quickens even as she seems to die.

The final fragment of Sappho's poetry that I would like to consider (fragment 94) is one that has suffered perhaps the most misinterpretation by critics who wish to make its tattered remains conform to the image of the "respectable" Sappho who always wrote conventional, public poetry:

τεθνάκην δ' ἀδόλως θέλω·
ἄ με ψισδομένα κατελίμπανεν

πόλλα καὶ τόδ' ἔειπέ [μοι·
'ὤιμ' ὡς δεῖνα πεπ[όνθ]αμεν,
Ψάπφ', ἦ μάν σ' ἀέκοισ' ἀπυλιμπάνω.'

τὰν δ' ἔγω τάδ' ἀμειβόμαν·
'χαίροισ' ἔρχεο κἄμεθεν
μέμναισ', οἶσθα γὰρ ὥς σε πεδήπομεν·

αἰ δὲ μή, ἀλλά σ' ἔγω θέλω
ὄμναισαι [. . .].[. . .]. . αι
. .[   ]καὶ κάλ' ἐπάσχομεν.

πό[λλοις γὰρ στεφάν]οις ἴων
καὶ βρ[όδων κρο]κίων τ' ὔμοι
κα . . [   ] πὰρ ἔμοι περεθήκαο,

καὶ πό[λλαις ὐπα]θύμιδας
πλέκ[ταις ἀμφ' ἀ]πάλαι δέραι
ἀνθέων ἔ[βαλες] πεποημμέναις,

καὶ πολλῳι[   ] . μύρωι
βρενθείωι. [   ]ρυ[. .]ν
ἐξαλείψαο κα[ὶ βασ]ιληίωι,

καὶ στρώμν[αν ἐ]πὶ μολθάκαν
ἀπάλαν πα . [   ] . . . ων
ἐξίης πόθο[ν   ] . νίδων,

κωὔτε τις[οὔ]τε τι
ἶρον οὐδυ[   ]

ἔπλετ᾽ ὄππ[οθεν ἄμ]μες ἀπέσκομεν

οὐκ ἄλσος . [χ]όρος
           ]ψόφος
           ] . . . οιδιαι

"Honestly, I wish I were dead!"
Weeping many tears she left me,

Saying this as well:
"Oh, what dreadful things have happened to us,
Sappho! I don't want to leave you!"

I answered her:
"Go with my blessings, and remember me,
for you know how we cherished you.

"But if you have [forgotten], I want
to remind you . . .
of the beautiful things that happened to us:

"Close by my side you put around yourself
[many wreaths] of violets and roses and saffron . . .

"And many woven garlands
made from flowers . . .
around your tender neck,

"And . . . with costly royal
myrrh . . .
you anointed . . . ,

"And on a soft bed
. . . tender . . .
you satisfied your desire . . .

"Nor was there any . . .
nor any holy . . .
from which we were away,

. . . nor grove. . . ."

Denys Page, in his edition of 1955, nervously comments concerning fragment 94 that "there are obvious indications that it contained matter in-

compatible with the modern theory of Sappho's character," by which he means Sappho as schoolmistress offering moral lessons to her girl pupils.[13] (The stanza he is most nervous about is the one beginning "And on a soft bed. . . .") Despite the gaps in the text of the poem, the general character of the imagery is clear enough: flowers and garlands and oils, and at the end, a grove of trees. It is a world permeated with the sensuous sights and smells of nature.

The first extant line of the fragment has often been taken as a *cri du coeur* on the part of the narrator of the poem, who is accordingly viewed as a desperately bitter figure looking back on a painful scene of breaking up. Anne Pippin Burnett, however, has demonstrated that the piece focuses on the power of memory to recapture past pleasures.[14] She takes the opening line as belonging to the departing friend, whose "raw emotion" is set against the "perfected meditation" of the calmer Sappho-narrator. Far from being a confessional lament, the piece through this reading becomes a celebration of shared experience. The departing woman weeps and bewails the impending separation, while the Sappho-narrator counters with a gentle exhortation to remember the past. What the departing woman sees as "terrible" experiences (line 4), the Sappho-narrator transforms into "beautiful" experiences (line 11).

The next four stanzas elaborate the remembered experience as the narrator recreates the shared delights, their mutuality emphasized in the juxtaposition at the end of the first of these stanzas (line 14) of *emoi* and *perethēkao* ("beside *me you* placed . . ."). The same pattern emerges in the succeeding stanzas as the narrator describes various sensual experiences, evidently always with a second-person singular verb in the final line of the stanza. Then the narrator returns to the first-person plural, apparently emphasized in the restored pronoun in line 26, *am]mes* ("we").

The imagery in the second half of the fragment is worthy of May Sarton: violets, roses, and, if the Greek is correctly restored in *kro]kiōn* (line 13), saffron (a type of crocus with purple flowers). The female associations of flowers in Sappho's poetry are well established through references in other fragments to a woman who is like a mountain hyancinth trampled by shepherds (105c), the roses around Aphrodite's temple (2), the many-flowered fields in Lydia where Atthis' departed friend roams (96, line 11), the wreaths of flowers worn by the yellow-haired girl of fragment 98, and the golden flowers connected with Kleis (132). The predominance of such flower imagery in Sappho is all the more striking when we note its rarity in her compatriot, Alcaeus, whose favorite imagery involves the sea. The anthological list here in Sappho 94 is filled out by further references to natural beauty in the form of myrrh, a resin produced by certain trees and shrubs, and the grove alluded to (line 27) as the fragment breaks off. Just as the departed woman in fragment 96 (another poem concerned with the theme of separation) is described through a simile involving the moon, flowery fields, the sea, and dew, so here the past relationship between the two women is depicted through recollection and recreation of their mutual enjoyment of especially sensuous aspects of nature—her flowers and her exotic perfumes. Like fragment 96, this fragment too is primarily concerned with private human emotions set within the context of selected aspects of the natural environment. It lies outside the established patterns within Greek literature for public, male discourse, and any attempts to read into the poem some kind of institutional framework only result in the sort of ludicrous interpretation offered by Wilamowitz when he said that the phrase *exiēs potho[n,* "you satisfied your desire," means "you stilled your need for rest," a need which he takes to have been brought on among the pupils in Sappho's school by excessive dancing.[15]

I have tried to demonstrate that Sappho, who served as an important model for subsequent generations of women poets such as Nossis and Erinna, had at her command a wide repertory of approaches in directing her songs to an audience. Sometimes the audience is clearly a public one including both men and women, as in the various sorts of occasional poetry such as the wedding song that jokes about the attendant's oversized feet. In other cases the outward form resembles what we know as public poetry from roughly contemporary sources, as, for example, in Sappho's Hymn to Aphrodite, where she plays with the traditional form of a Greek prayer. Finally, in still other examples, she seems to depart altogether from the established mode of public discourse to a private, female-oriented world infused with the sights and smells of nature. Although the fragmentary state of Sappho's poetry makes it impossible to insist on a rigid classification here, both fragment 31 and fragment 94 (and 96 as well) appear to focus on matters generally not addressed by the male writers of Sappho's time—as, for example, detailed descriptions of the inner emotions of love and desire and the role of memory in assuaging the pain of separation, all couched in language that is imbued with the imagery of myrrh, flowers, trees, grass, dew, and moonlight. It is a female setting unencumbered with the public conventions of weddings and the expected structures of public discourse. Instead we find ourselves in a private world in which the female, closely identified with the beautiful and gentle side of nature, is entirely self-defined.

Notes

This paper is partially based on my larger study of women writers in the ancient world, *The Woman and the Lyre: Women Writers in Greece and Rome* (Carbondale: Southern Illinois University Press, 1989), from which the translations here (my own) are taken. I am indebted to several scholars for their comments and assistance as I revised this paper for publication, among them Marilyn B. Skinner, Deborah Boedeker, Sarah B. Pomeroy, Hugh Lloyd-Jones, and Joseph Russo. I would like to thank Susan Hartmann and Marcia Dalbey for their support, and I am also grateful for the suggestions of the two referees for the University of North Carolina Press.

1. Edwin Ardener, "Belief and the Problem of Women," in *Perceiving Women*, ed. Shirley Ardener (New York: John Wiley, 1975), 3. See also Jack Winkler, "Gardens of Nymphs: Public and Private in Sappho's Lyrics," *Women's Studies* 8 (1981): 71, reprinted in *Reflections of Women in Antiquity*, ed. H. P. Foley (New York: Gordon & Breach, 1981), 63–89: "Because men define and exhibit their language and manners as *the* culture and segregate women's language and manners as a subculture . . . women are in the position of knowing two cultures where men know only one." Winkler focuses on Sappho's reactions to Homer (as the representative of male-centered public culture) and on what he identifies as her sexual images (representing a mixture of public concern for fertility and private allusions to a woman-centered eroticism).

2. The Greek text of Sappho printed here is that of David A. Campbell, *Greek Lyric*, vol. 1 (Cambridge: Harvard University Press, 1982).

3. G. S. Kirk, "A Fragment of Sappho Reinterpreted," *Classical Quarterly* 13 (1963): 51–52.

4. For an alternative interpretation of the stanza see Anne Giacomelli, "The Justice of Aphrodite," *Transactions of the American Philological Association* 110 (1980): 135–42. She argues that the transformation prayed for is that "the unresponsive beloved will one day grow up and become a lover . . . herself, and in the role of lover will pursue an unresponsive beloved."

5. Examples are collected in *Sappho: Memoir, Text, Selected Renderings, and a Literal Translation*, ed. Henry Thornton Wharton (Amsterdam: Liberac, 1974; reprinted from the edition of 1898), 51–64.

6. See William H. Race, *The Classical Priamel from Homer to Boethius, Mnemosyne,* suppl. 74 (Leiden: E. J. Brill, 1982).

7. See, for example, Garry Wills, "The Sapphic 'Umvertung aller Werte,' " *American Journal of Philology* 88 (1967): 434–42. Cf. Denys Page, *Sappho and Alcaeus* (Oxford: Clarendon Press, 1959), 53: "The sequence of thought might have been clearer." In Winkler's view, "There is a charming parody of logical argumentation in these stanzas" ("Gardens of Nymphs," 74).

8. On Sappho's emphasis on the active choices made by Helen see Page duBois, "Sappho and Helen," *Arethusa* 11 (1978): 89–99. Cf. Leah Rissman, *Love as War: Homeric Allusion in the Poetry of Sappho* (Königstein: Hain, 1983), 42–43.

9. On *chlōros* see Eleanor Irwin, *Colour Terms in Greek Poetry* (Toronto: Hakkert, 1974), 31–78.

10. Ulrich von Wilamowitz-Moellendorff, *Sappho und Simonides* (Berlin: Weidmann, 1913), 58–59.

11. Max Treu, *Sappho* (Munich: Ernst Heimeran, 1954), 178–79; Hermann Fränkel, *Early Greek Poetry and Philosophy,* trans. Moses Hadas and James Willis (New York: Harcourt Brace Jovanovich, 1973), 176; Thomas McEvilley, "Sappho, Fragment Thirty-One: The Face behind the Mask," *Phoenix* 32 (1978): 1–18.

12. George Devereux, "The Nature of Sappho's Seizure in Fr. 31 LP as Evidence of Her Inversion," *Classical Quarterly* 20 (1970): 17–34. For opposing views see M. Marcovich, "Sappho: Fr. 31: Anxiety Attack or Love Declaration?" *Classical Quarterly* 22 (1972): 19–32, and G. L. Koniaris, "On Sappho, Fr. 31 (L.-P.)," *Philologus* 112 (1968): 173–86. See also Mary R. Lefkowitz, "Critical Stereotypes and the Poetry of Sappho," *Greek, Roman and Byzantine Studies* 14 (1973): 113–23.

13. Page, *Sappho and Alcaeus,* 80.

14. Anne Pippin Burnett, "Desire and Memory (Sappho Frag. 94)," *Classical Philology* 74 (1979): 16–27. On the importance of memory and of mutuality see also Eva Stehle Stigers, "Sappho's Private World," *Women's Studies* 8 (1981): 54–56, reprinted in *Reflections of Women in Antiquity,* ed. H. P. Foley (New York: Gordon & Breach, 1981), 45–61.

15. Wilamowitz-Moellendorff, *Sappho und Simonides,* 51.

MARILYN B. SKINNER

Nossis *Thēlyglōssos*:

The Private Text and the Public Book

Eleven quatrains accidentally preserved in the *Greek Anthology* comprise the literary remains of the woman epigrammatist Nossis, a native of the Greek colony of Locri Epizephyrii in southern Italy active around the beginning of the third century B.C.[1] Together with her predecessors Sappho and Erinna, both of whom situated their poetry within the sphere of women's religious and domestic lives and proclaimed their own deep emotional attachments to other women, Nossis may be one of the earliest Western European exemplars of the recognizably female literary voice.[2] Certainly her slight body of texts gives the impression of a forthright personality with an idiosyncratic point of view that upon close reading emerges as strongly woman-identified.[3]

For anyone planning to demonstrate the peculiarly female timbre of Nossis' poetic voice, however, the fact that she chose to work within the epigrammatic tradition presents an initial interpretative difficulty. The majority of her surviving quatrains are dedicatory, honoring gifts made by women to goddesses. There is nothing particularly unusual in her subject matter, for male poets also wrote about women's offerings to female divinities. Moreover, the dedicatory epigram is by its very nature a public and impersonal mode of poetic discourse.[4] Destined to commemorate a votive offering, usually by being affixed to a temple wall alongside the donor's present, such testimonial verses necessarily addressed the world at large, and their preoccupation with the votive object itself left scant room for authorial subjectivity. Then too, most dedicatory epigrams were probably commissioned from professional writers. Although dedicants might have hoped for some share of literary immortality in having their individual offerings memorialized by a Callimachus or a Leonidas of Tarentum, what they surely expected from any poet, no matter how talented, was no more than a new and clever way of dealing with mandatory formulaic elements—the donor's piety, the gift's value, the god's consequent obligation. The work of another epigrammatist, Anyte, in whose quatrains Wilamowitz observed "nothing at all personal, not even anything feminine," indicates how conventional such verse could be, even when composed by a woman.[5]

By contrast with Anyte's verse, and with similar verse produced by male epigrammatists, Nossis' dedicatory epigrams display some unconventional features. First, the speaker is not a detached observer: she invariably expresses warm personal feeling for the dedicant conveyed in familiar, in fact intimate, tones. Again, she speaks explicitly to an audience of women companions who are themselves presumed to know the donors in question. Finally, in the course of describing the dedicated object, she sometimes articulates sentiments decidedly at variance with the values inscribed in the mainstream poetic tradition. Thus, despite the overtly "public" character of Nossis' chosen subgenre, we receive the distinct impression of writing directed exclusively toward a relatively small, self-contained female community. The paradox can be explained if we postulate that these quatrains were intended to operate as literary texts abstracted from their original commemorative function. Though they record actual donations, they would have been written for private circulation among the members of a tightly knit circle rather than for public display in a temple; and they must accordingly have served a poetic purpose far more complex than merely preserving a dedicant's name. We shall see that the author herself ultimately issued these pieces in book form accompanied by prologue and epilogue poems: to that extent, at least, she did treat her dedicatory epigrams as purely literary documents.

The use of a quasi-public verse form for poetic statements really designed for a private female readership would draw attention to the culturally meaningful distinction between the sheltered domestic interior and the much more accessible temple precinct.[6] That tension would then be augmented by book publication, with its corresponding change in readership from a coterie of women friends to a bigger, predominantly male audience dwelling beyond the confines of Locri. Consequently Nossis may be important not only as an ancient embodiment of the "private" female voice but as an illustration of how that voice might subsequently have been heard by the larger "public" world. I shall return to the latter question after we have had the opportunity to examine Nossis' poetry.

One of the few references to this author in later Greek literature furnishes evidence that ancient readers regarded her as an intensely woman-centered poet. By the beginning of the Christian era, Alexandrian literary scholarship had already constructed a roster of major women writers.[7] These figures, nine in number by a predictable analogy with the nine Muses, are listed by Antipater of Thessalonica in his declamatory epigram *Anth. Pal.* 9.26. There Nossis is characterized by the lone adjective *thēlyglōssos*. Because the word does not occur elsewhere, its exact meaning is uncertain, but it is generally thought to denote "one who spoke like a woman"—a curiously redundant epithet for a canonical woman poet.[8] Alternatively, *thēlyglōssos* may be translated as "one who spoke specifically to women." So construed, it would imply that ancient readers perceived Nossis' poetry as oriented toward her own sex to a degree unusual even for female writers. This interpretation of *thēlyglōssos* can be supported by a detailed examination of her most typical productions, the dedicatory epigrams 3 through 9, where analysis quickly reveals the extent of her interest not only in women's religious activities but also in women as subjects of representative art.

In form a commemoration of a gift to Hera Lacinia, poem 3 (*Anth. Pal.* 6.265) is in reality an autobiographical *sphragis* or "signature-poem":

Ἥρα τιμάεσσα, Λακίνιον ἃ τὸ θυῶδες
  πολλάκις οὐρανόθεν νισομένα καθορῇς,
δέξαι βύσσινον εἶμα τό τοι μετὰ παιδὸς ἀγαυᾶς
  Νοσσίδος ὕφανεν Θευφιλὶς ἁ Κλεόχας.

Most reverend Hera, you who often descending from heaven
  behold your Lacinian shrine fragrant with incense,
receive the linen wrap that with her noble child Nossis
  Theophilis daughter of Cleocha wove for you.

The first distich tactfully reminds the goddess of the constant honors paid her at her temple on the Lacinian promontory near Croton—the most celebrated shrine in southern Italy, known for its wealth no less than its sanctity (Livy 24.3.6). Hera is then requested to accept a textile produced by the author's mother, Theophilis, with the help of her daughter. This robe is no ordinary piece of homespun: its imported material, linen, singles it out as a costly garment.[9] The central ritual event of the Panathenaic festival at Athens, immortalized in the processional frieze from the Parthenon, was the presentation to Athena of a peplos woven by the leading women of the polis; and fifth-century votive tablets indicate that at Locri itself a similar practice obtained for the cults of the great goddesses Persephone and Aphrodite.[10] Nossis' epigram may memorialize just such a solemn public offering to Hera. If so, the dedicants would certainly have been of prominent social rank. The adjective *agaua*, "noble," with which the poet modifies her own name, validates that inference: infused with Homeric associations of antique eminence, it testifies to her membership in one of the old aristocratic families of the geographical region served by Hera's temple.[11]

At the conclusion of the epigram Nossis identifies her mother as *Theuphilis ha Kleochas*, tracing her elite ancestry back two generations through the female line. The phrase cannot be used as evidence for an exceptional public custom of matrilineal descent-reckoning at Locri, as W. A. Oldfather argued, for it was common practice for Greek women in general to designate each other by metronymics, rather than patronymics, when speaking privately among themselves.[12] Accordingly, the poet calls her mother "daughter of Cleocha" to show that she is addressing an audience composed of her female companions. By stressing her grandmother's name, she directs attention to Cleocha's distinguished position within that Locrian community. The ceremonial gift of a choice piece of women's handiwork to Hera, queen of the gods, has already established her mother's consequence and her own. Furthermore, the conventional metonymic association between weaving and poetry also allows Nossis, in casting herself as apprentice to Theophilis the dominant artisan, to pay loving tribute to her mother as her earliest creative mentor.[13] This epigram is therefore a comprehensive statement of personal identity in which a woman writer "thinks back through her mother" both biologically and artistically. At the same time, it provides a glimpse of an alternative cultural environment set apart, to some degree, from the male-dominated public order, a milieu in which religious observance, social position, and creative self-consciousness all find expression in activities and language derived from women's domestic experience.

Poems 4 and 5, describing two dedications to Aphrodite, touch upon those aspects of her divine personality that were apparently the particular concerns of her cult at Locri: sexuality as a cosmic principle, and the realm of sexual activities not institutionalized within marriage, "its illicit and 'aberrant' forms which do not serve society."[14] In the first epigram (*Anth. Pal.* 9.332), Nossis summons her companions to go and view a statue of Aphrodite set up by the courtesan Polyarchis:

ἐλθοῖσαι ποτὶ ναὸν ἰδώμεθα τᾶς Ἀφροδίτας
τὸ βρέτας ὡς χρυσῷ δαιδαλόεν τελέθει.
εἵσατό μιν Πολυαρχὶς ἐπαυρομένα μάλα πολλάν
κτῆσιν ἀπ᾿ οἰκείου σώματος ἀγλαΐας.

Let us go to Aphrodite's temple to see her statue,
    how finely it is embellished with gold.
Polyarchis dedicated it, having made a great fortune
    out of the splendor of her own body.

Placed for emphasis as the opening word, *elthoisai*, the participle denoting
the act of departure, is grammatically feminine. Once again the sex of the
addressees is specified as exclusively female; meanwhile the hortatory
idōmetha, "let us see," imposes a shared viewpoint upon the entire group
of observers. We readers are welcomed into the circle of women surrounding the speaker and invited to discover in Polyarchis' statue what that
speaker herself beholds: we are to confront it, that is, from a woman-
oriented perspective. Elaborately crafted and gilded, obviously very expensive, the figure testifies not only to the dedicant's wealth but also to its
source in her physical perfections. The overtones of metallic brightness in
the word "splendor," *aglaïas*, combine with the prior description of the
statue as *chrysōi daidaloen* ("embellished with gold") to create an impression of exact correspondence between gift and donor: like her offering,
the lovely Polyarchis was herself an exquisitely wrought artifact. Mention
of her great fortune recalls the literary stereotype of the mercenary courtesan.[15] Yet the speaker's undeniable admiration for Polyarchis finally coun-
teracts any censorious implications. We are left with the conviction that
her riches, themselves no more than her elegance deserved, were put to
good use in the creation of a votive image as elegant as herself. This is not
the only epigram in which we find Nossis pointedly correcting misogynistic or androcentric tenets embedded in the patriarchal literary tradition.

Whereas poem 4 conveys a female observer's response to a dedicated
object, poem 5 (*Anth. Pal.* 6.275) attempts to voice the reaction of its divine
recipient:

χαίροισάν τοι ἔοικε κομᾶν ἄπο τὰν Ἀφροδίταν
    ἄνθεμα κεκρύφαλον τόνδε λαβεῖν Σαμύθας·
δαιδάλεός τε γάρ ἐστι καὶ ἁδύ τι νέκταρος ὄσδει·
    τούτῳ καὶ τήνα καλὸν Ἄδωνα χρίει.

Joyfully indeed, I think, Aphrodite receives this gift,
   a headdress from Samytha's own hair.
For it is elaborate, and smells sweetly in some way of nectar.
   With this she too anoints the beautiful Adonis.

Like Polyarchis' statue, Samytha's headdress is sumptuously worked
(*daidaleos*), but it is also redolent of the pomade with which its former
owner scented her hair. Use of rich balms and incenses was intrinsic to the
cult of the dying god, Aphrodite's consort, and we may therefore assume
that Samytha has recently participated in the yearly Adonia.[16] Nossis
calls attention to the similarity of interests between goddess and mortal
woman by dwelling upon their mutual pleasure in Samytha's perfume, by
investing that perfume with associations of divine nectar, and by concluding the poem with a subtle ambiguity: the antecedent of the rhetorically
and metrically accentuated "she too" (*kai tēna*) could be either Aphrodite
or Samytha herself.[17] Although we are given no explicit indication of
Samytha's social position, passages in Middle and New Comedy show
hetairai observing the Adonia in a particularly lavish manner, and later
authors depict them playfully using "Adonis" as a nickname for their
lovers.[18] Perfumed oils, too, have an erotic as well as a ritual significance.
Nossis thus sets up a sly correlation between Aphrodite and Samytha:
both derive sensual enjoyment from unguents—and from the company of
a young male friend. This flattering analogy finds a parallel in poem 4,
where we must understand Polyarchis to have served as the actual model
for the statue ostensibly dedicated as an effigy of the divinity. Aphrodite
accordingly looks with favor upon the two dedicants Polyarchis and
Samytha because their physical allure and sexual expertise bear compelling witness to her own divine power. Though herself of aristocratic birth,
Nossis does not patronize or condemn either woman; on the contrary, her
poetic statements reflect a positive attitude toward sexuality and a keen
awareness of the pleasures to be gained from the skilled gratification of
sight, smell, and touch.

   Poems 6 through 9 belong to the venerable tradition of *ekphrasis*, the
verbal reproduction of a work of plastic art.[19] All four deal with paintings
in encaustic, the regular medium of ancient portraiture.[20] Descriptions of
art objects recur with unusual frequency in the small number of extant
epigrams written by ancient Greek women. Erinna 3 (*Anth. Pal.* 6.352),
which insists upon the lifelikeness of a girl's painted countenance, seems

to have furnished a prototype for the next generation of women poets: Moero 1 (*Anth. Pal.* 6.119) must have accompanied a picture of a grape cluster, and, of Anyte's twenty-one genuine epigrams, two are obviously ecphrastic.[21] In one respect, though, Nossis' quatrains differ strikingly from those of most other female and male poets working within the same tradition: she is preoccupied not so much with the painter's success in effecting a physical likeness as with his ability to capture distinctive traits of the sitter's personality. Her ecphrastic poems thus become brief character sketches of members of the Locrian community—relatives and acquaintances of her original audience. Like the very portraits she affects to describe, these quatrains were apparently designed to put her readers in the imagined presence of a known individual.

The only one of these *pinakes*, or wooden panels, clearly designated as a temple offering is that of Callo, who in poem 6 (*Anth. Pal.* 9.605) dedicates her picture to Aphrodite:

τὸν πίνακα ξανθᾶς Καλλὼ δόμον εἰς Ἀφροδίτας
   εἰκόνα γραψαμένα πάντ' ἀνέθηκεν ἴσαν.
ὡς ἀγανῶς ἕστακεν· ἴδ' ἁ χάρις ἁλίκον ἀνθεῖ.
   χαιρέτω, οὔ τινα γὰρ μέμψιν ἔχει βιοτᾶς.

This tablet Callo set up in the house of blonde Aphrodite,
   a portrait she had painted, like her in every way.
How tenderly she stands! See how her charm blooms!
   May she fare well: her way of life is blameless.

Here, as in poems 4 and 5, the text insists upon a mysterious affinity between goddess and worshiper. The proper name Callo at once recalls *kallos*, "beauty," the distinguishing hallmark of Aphrodite's darlings (*Il.* 3.54–55). Though common in inscriptions, as Gow and Page observe, the name still gives the impression of being carefully chosen. At any rate, it is very appropriate for a young woman whose tender, blooming appearance elicits the speaker's warm approval. Furthermore, we are told that the painted image is *pant'* . . . *isan*, "wholly like," with no object specified; this portrait, then, could be either like the sitter or like the divinity who receives it. Remembering the provenance of those other dedications to Aphrodite mentioned in poems 4 and 5, we may conclude that the subject of the present epigram is quite probably another *hetaira*. If so, its last line must be construed as a bold defense of her way of life, the forthright proclamation of a judgment already implicit in the two quatrains we have previously examined. In addition, the express identification of Polyarchis, Samytha, and now Callo with the Locrian Aphrodite transforms all three women into avatars of a goddess honored as the demiurgic principle of sexuality operating outside the sphere of marriage.

Nossis' eulogies of courtesans and their profession are remarkable. It is tempting to speculate that poems 4, 5, and 6 were commissioned and that such sentiments were intended to gratify a paying clientele.[22] Yet similar views are not expressed in epigrams written by male poets, where verses commemorating actual dedications by *hetairai* limit themselves, discreetly, to a bare inventory of votive objects. Although fictive dedications by notorious courtesans do provide the occasion for gnomic pronouncements, the speaker always elects to moralize upon the ephemerality of physical beauty rather than the might of *erōs*. Nossis' quatrains indicate that her original female audience was not at all disposed to object to frank praise of *hetairai*. The hypothesis of commissioned verses thus casts an intriguing light upon respectable women's attitudes toward nonrespectable women and also suggests the possibility of some degree of acquaintance between the two groups. Apart from their literary merits, these texts are therefore of considerable importance as cultural documents, for they raise provocative questions about the possible relaxation of rigid caste distinctions between respectable and nonrespectable women in third-century B.C. Locri.

In two other ecphrastic epigrams Nossis addresses the problem of how female selfhood is achieved and manifested. Poem 7 (*Anth. Pal.* 9.604) conveys a vivid impression of an adolescent girl's personality through sharp verbal dissonances combined with subtle humor:

Θαυμαρέτας μορφὰν ὁ πίναξ ἔχει· εὖ γε τὸ γαῦρον
τεῦξε τό θ᾽ ὡραῖον τᾶς ἀγανοβλεφάρου.
σαίνοι κέν σ᾽ ἐσιδοῖσα καὶ οἰκοφύλαξ σκυλάκαινα,
δέσποιναν μελάθρων οἰομένα ποθορῆν.

This tablet shows Thaumareta. Well indeed it portrayed
the pride and the ripeness of the tender-eyed girl.
Even your house-guarding puppy would wag her tail on seeing you,
thinking she gazed on the mistress of the mansion.

Although young (we should recall that Greek girls frequently married in their early teens), Thaumareta is already installed as manager of a great household. Her portrait reveals a piquant combination of character traits:

endowed with the ripe physical charm of youth, she is also arrogant, doubtless because of her recent accession to that position of responsibility.[23] The young woman's underlying vulnerability—intimated by the descriptive adjective *aganoblepharos*, "tender-eyed"—betrays itself in her attachment to her pet dog, an emotion somewhat unsuited to a haughty *despoina melathrōn*. With arch magniloquence, Nossis calls this animal an *oikophylax skylakaina*, a "house-guarding female puppy" that would wag its tail in greeting were it to see its mistress's picture.[24] The oxymoron draws a shrewd parallel between dog and owner, insinuating that the latter ought to refrain from giving herself airs inappropriate to her age; and the final hyperbole, a neat reminiscence of Odysseus' encounter with the aged dog Argos (*Od.* 17.301–04), lightly mocks Thaumareta's pretensions to authority and so completes the process of genial deflation.

In a more serious vein, poem 8 (*Anth. Pal.* 6.353) addresses the biological and psychological complexities of the mother-daughter relationship:

> Αὐτομέλιννα τέτυκται· ἴδ' ὡς ἀγανὸν τὸ πρόσωπον.
> ἁμὲ ποτοπτάζειν μειλιχίως δοκέει.
> ὡς ἐτύμως θυγάτηρ τᾷ ματέρι πάντα ποτῴκει·
> ἦ καλὸν ὅκκα πέλῃ τέκνα γονεῦσιν ἴσα.

Melinna herself is fully wrought. See how tender her face is.
    She seems to gaze upon us benignly.
How truly the daughter resembles her mother in all things!
    Indeed it is good when children are like their parents.

Into the verb *tetuktai*, "fully wrought," ostensibly predicated of Melinna's painted representation, Nossis retrospectively inscribes a startling biological analogy: like the painter, the girl's mother has created a likeness by reproducing her own self in her daughter's flesh. While the speaker marvels at the wonderful physical similarity of mother and daughter, the text meanwhile underscores the fundamental tension between "Melinna herself," *automelinna*, and Melinna as the genetic reincarnation of her parent: by juxtaposing those two contradictory notions without reconciling them, it hints at the struggle over the daughter's autonomy latent in the mother-daughter dyad. At the same time, the epigram ingeniously appropriates the patriarchal tenet that sons should resemble fathers as proof of their legitimacy and converts it into a confirmation of the hereditary bond between female parent and female child.[25]

In contrast to Thaumareta and Melinna, Sabaethis, the subject of poem 9 (*Anth. Pal.* 6.354), is definitely a mature woman:

γνωτὰ καὶ τηλῶθε Σαβαιθίδος εἴδεται ἔμμεν
ἅδ᾽ εἰκὼν μορφᾷ καὶ μεγαλειοσύνᾳ.
θάεο᾽ τὰν πινυτὰν τό τε μείλιχον αὐτόθι τήνας
ἔλπομ᾽ ὁρῆν. χαίροις πολλά, μάκαιρα γύναι.

Even from far off this image is known as Sabaethis'
    because of its beauty and stature.
Look! From this spot I observe, I think, her wisdom and kindness.
    Fare you very well, blessed lady.

The language of this quatrain is charged with religious nuances, for Sabaethis' external and internal qualities are elsewhere associated either with female deities or with heroines singularly favored by the gods.[26] Conspicuous in her picture and making recognition possible even at a distance, her shapely form and stature (*morpha kai megaleiosyna*) are distinctive attributes of the goddess who reveals herself to human eyes. Her prudence, observable at close quarters, is a gift bestowed upon divine protégées, most notably the virtuous Penelope, and the benevolence that accompanies it informs the relationship of gracious divinity to pious mortal. The transition from external appearance to internal character is marked by adverbs of place that seem to designate two separate planes of existence, the transcendent (*tēlōthe*, "from afar off") and the mundane (*autothi*, "on this spot").[27] Nossis' parting salute to Sabaethis, *chairois polla, makaira gynai*, is therefore a studied equivocation: although the use of such heightened language is not unusual in encomiastic contexts, the epithet *makaira*, "blessed," here eradicates the boundary between mortal and immortal already blurred by the preceding description. Surrounding this older woman, clearly a person of some standing, with an awesome numinosity, the *ekphrasis* of her portrait approximates a divine epiphany.

This cursory examination of poems 3 through 9 has attempted to show that Nossis was in actual fact *thēlyglōssos*, a woman who chose to speak specifically to members of her own sex. As I have previously said, her identification with women extends far beyond the mere celebration of their dedications to female divinities. It manifests itself most conclusively in the assumption of a purely female audience to whom the speaker can identify herself both as artist and as artist's daughter, employing a private, gender-linked form of speech common to the women's quarters. The ecphrastic epigrams then attempt to recreate the experience of living within a closely affiliated female community by evoking the essential personality of each sitter insofar as it was known to her companions and has now received enduring visual expression. Nossis' value system also differs in noteworthy ways from that reflected in the androcentric public culture. Her candid tributes to the physical charms of *hetairai*, which betray no consciousness of her own social or moral superiority, may be contrasted with the presumed hostility of respectable Athenian women toward the former courtesan Neaera, as alleged by the male speaker of [Demosthenes] 59.110–11.[28] Similarly, her personal interest in the transmission of skills and attributes from mother to daughter, glanced at in the quasi-autobiographical poem 3, surfaces again in poem 8, which implicitly repudiates the very structures of patriarchy by transforming the evidential basis for claims of paternity into a proof of the mother's vital role in the reproductive process.

While those seven poems dealing with women constitute the majority of Nossis' surviving pieces, two other quatrains indicate that she also devoted some attention to traditional epigrammatic themes. Despite their surface preoccupation with male pursuits and ostensible adoption of a conventional masculine stance, these texts can also be read as the expression of a markedly idiosyncratic point of view. Poem 2 (*Anth. Pal.* 6.132) is a patriotic commemoration of a Locrian victory over the Bruttians, an indigenous tribe that had long posed a threat to Greek settlements in southern Italy:

ἔντεα Βρέττιοι ἄνδρες ἀπ' αἰνομόρων βάλον ὤμων
    θεινόμενοι Λοκρῶν χερσὶν ὕπ' ὠκυμάχων,
ὧν ἀρετὰν ὑμνεῦντα θεῶν ὑπ' ἀνάκτορα κεῖνται,
    οὐδὲ ποθεῦντι κακῶν πάχεας οὓς ἔλιπον.

These shields the Bruttians cast from doomed shoulders
    as they fell by the hands of the battle-swift Locrians.
Hung beneath temple roofs, the shields praise the Locrians' valor
    and do not long for the arms of the cowards they deserted.

Anyte's epigrams prove that it was not unthinkable for a woman to celebrate martial prowess, but the austere solemnity of her dedication poem for Echecratidas' spear and of her epitaphs for fallen combatants, human and equine, has no echo in Nossis.[29] Finding blame more congenial than praise, the Locrian poet applies her energies to reviling the defeated enemy. Initially she alleges that the Bruttians had thrown away their shields in flight—for a soldier, the ultimate act of cowardice. In the last line, however, she reverses herself, claiming that the shields themselves chose to desert their unworthy masters and do not, even now, miss them. This statement negates the sentimental conceit whereby a warrior's horses or personified weapons grieve for him, a topos already present in Homer and popular with composers of dedicatory epigrams.[30] Meanwhile the reiterated motif of defection invokes the supposed etymological derivation of the tribal name *Brettioi* from an Italian dialect word for "runaway slave" or "rebel."[31] This allusion to their unsavory origins defames the Bruttians, but it also undercuts the ethical posture of the shields, whose condemnation of their former masters' pusillanimity is itself tainted by implications of having abandoned a comrade in the heat of battle. In contrast to Anyte's idealization of the warrior and his deeds of valor, Nossis tenders an undeniably patriotic, but still wry, comment upon the equivocal operations of the heroic code.

On the other hand, poem 10 (*Anth. Pal.* 7.414) does convey strong partisan admiration, but for a literary product—the work of Rhinthon, composer of *phluakes*, or parodies of classic tragedy:

καὶ καπυρὸν γελάσας παραμείβεο καὶ φίλον εἰπών
  ῥῆμ' ἐπ' ἐμοί. 'Ρίνθων εἴμ' ὁ Συρακόσιος,
Μουσάων ὀλίγα τις ἀηδονίς, ἀλλὰ φλυάκων
  ἐκ τραγικῶν ἴδιον κισσὸν ἐδρεψάμεθα.

Laugh, and loudly. Then pass by, saying a kind word
  over me. I am Rhinthon of Syracuse,
a small nightingale of the Muses, but from my tragic burlesques
  I plucked for myself a personal ivy crown.

In this quatrain Nossis assumes a masculine persona as she makes use of the poetic convention that permits the dead man's gravestone to speak for him in his own voice. By attaching the superfluous feminine suffix *-onis* to *aēdon*, "nightingale," however, she emphasizes the grammatical gender of that noun and so appears to call attention to the female poetic presence behind the male mask.[32] Metaphorically, the epigram pleads the necessity of evaluating any literary composition on its own proper merits, independent of genre—for the sacred ivy garland earned by the successful dramatic poet is owed to the parodist Rhinthon no less than to his illustrious tragic forebears Aeschylus, Sophocles, and Euripides. In true Hellenistic fashion Nossis affirms the possibility of extraordinary accomplishment within an "inferior" poetic form and so challenges the time-honored Greek conception of an objective literary hierarchy with the sober genres of tragedy and epic poised at its apex.[33] This defense of Rhinthon has obvious relevance for Nossis' own painstaking efforts in the slighter genre of epigram; but it would have been inherently applicable to all literary production by women, who, because of the exigencies of their private lives, were less likely to attempt the *mega biblion* or "weighty masterpiece" that Callimachus, a generation later, would magisterially condemn. Nossis 10 is therefore a literary manifesto in which the figure of Rhinthon, the hyperfeminine *aēdonis*, fronts for the author, who tacitly professes her own allegiance to that emerging principle of Hellenistic taste that renounces magnitude and high seriousness in favor of a deft and playful textual finesse.

In reviewing Nossis' surviving epigrams I have reserved poems 1 and 11 (*Anth. Pal.* 5.170 and 7.718) for last, as both quatrains pose special textual and interpretative problems.[34] Their unique literary purpose also sets them apart, for they are Nossis' only two demonstrably public poems—"public" insofar as they patently speak to an audience larger than her coterie of women friends. It was a standard Hellenistic poetic convention to preface and end a book-length verse collection with programmatic pieces identifying the author and commenting directly or indirectly upon the contents of the volume.[35] Nossis 1 and 11 exhibit many of the formal generic elements that characterize such studied manifestos: each mentions the author's name, and 11 also informs us of her birthplace; each invokes a primary literary model—in this case, Sappho—either forthrightly or through carefully deployed reminiscences; and each claims the patronage of a presiding deity, Aphrodite or the Muses. Scholars have reasonably concluded that 1 and 11 were designed to perform the respective functions of preface and epilogue for Nossis' epigram collection.[36] The poet herself, then, would have prepared her quatrains for broader circulation. Consequently her introductory and concluding statements may be examined as a twofold attempt to communicate her artistic intentions to a new, overwhelmingly male reading audience that would have known little, if anything, about her.

Poem 1 begins with a blunt pronouncement that the joys of *erōs* are supreme:

ἅδιον οὐδὲν ἔρωτος· ἃ δ' ὄλβια, δεύτερα πάντα
ἐστίν· ἀπὸ στόματος δ' ἔπτυσα καὶ τὸ μέλι.
τοῦτο λέγει Νοσσίς· τίνα δ' ἁ Κύπρις οὐκ ἐφίλασεν,
οὐκ οἶδεν τήνας τἄνθεα, ποῖα ῥόδα.

Nothing is sweeter than desire. All other delights are second.
    From my mouth I spit even honey.
Nossis says this. Whom Aphrodite does not love,
    knows not her flowers, what roses they are.

This gnomic utterance is arrestingly programmatic in two quite different ways. First, it proclaims that *erōs* is the controlling theme of the book and the crucial ingredient of the poems to follow. Second, and more audaciously, it contradicts Sappho's archetypal personification of desire as paradoxically both sweet and bitter, *glukypikros*, and intimates the possibility of an alternative construction of human sexual experience in which love can offer absolute pleasure untempered by any concomitant suffering.[37] From that initial urgent pitch the rhetoric becomes still more impassioned, rising through a sweeping dismissal of "all other goods" to culminate in a bold conflation of metaphorical and literal "sweetness": by comparison with the lusciousness of *erōs*, honey itself is spat out. Yet this paratragic expression, *apo stomatos d' eptusa*, with its intertextual echoes of violent and horrified repudiation, introjects an unexpected note of bathos, allowing the speaker to mock her own rhetorical ardor.[38] Just as we have begun to relate to this engaging authorial voice, however, it switches abruptly to the impersonal mode: in the next line the poet formally identifies herself with *touto legei Nossis*, a third-person *sphragis* that distances her psychologically from her earlier proclamation even as it endows that proclamation with objective authority. She then concludes with the almost apologetic assertion that those not in Aphrodite's favor cannot know her *anthea*—in programmatic terms, her poems—for the Sapphic roses they are.[39] It appears that Nossis has confronted the possibility that the erotic element in her art might well be misunderstood and is therefore attempting to forestall the censure of a hostile reading public.

Poem 11, however, assumes a much more trusting posture toward the general reader, for it adapts a motif common in funerary epigram, the request to a passer-by to bear a farewell message to the dead person's homeland:[40]

ὦ ξεῖν', εἰ τύ γε πλεῖς ποτὶ καλλίχορον Μιτυλήναν
  τᾶν Σαπφοῦς χαρίτων ἄνθος ἐναυσόμενος,
εἰπεῖν ὡς Μούσαισι φίλαν τήνᾳ τε Λοκρὶς γᾶ
  τίκτε μ'· ἴσαις δ' ὅτι μοι τοὔνομα Νοσσίς, ἴθι.

Stranger, if you sail to Mytilene of the lovely dances
  to be inspired with the flower of Sappho's graces,
say that the Locrian land bore me, one dear to the Muses
  and to her. Having learned that my name is Nossis, go.

In all other instances of the motif, the subject feels nostalgia for his or her own native land; this speaker, though, directs her thoughts across time and space to Sappho's city-state, Mytilene. Sappho plainly served as Nossis' sovereign literary model: poem 1 is a tissue of Sapphic allusions, and several other epigrams contain unmistakable echoes of her language.[41] In the epilogue to her collection Nossis accordingly represents herself as a lost companion of Sappho yearning hopelessly for her mistress, like Atthis' beloved in *LP* 96, homesick in far-off Lydia. By asking a *xenos* bound for Mytilene to inform its citizens of her literary ties with their great countrywoman, Nossis admits to a sense of creative isolation caused by her temporal and spatial distance from her predecessor: in death she will have to rely on a male stranger/friend, her one last addressee, to effect a tenuous affiliation between Sappho and herself. Thus the *envoi* sounds a final chord of lingering uncertainty, for the dead speaker will never know whether her message was received, her connection with her model fully understood. It is not an auspicious note on which to end a book and send it forth into the world.

These two authorial statements are self-conscious attempts to gain the goodwill of an anticipated reader and explain those features of Nossis' poetry that he, the *xenos*, might find exceptional or even shocking. The prologue singles out her eroticism as problematic, and rightly so: it would have been unusual, to say the least, for a woman of Nossis' elite background to have written openly about sexual passion. Sappho, herself an aristocrat, is therefore brought forward in poems 1 and 11 as an enabling precedent.[42] Elsewhere I have suggested that that appeal to Sappho, taken together with certain homoerotic nuances in the surviving epigrams, must indicate that Nossis' texts would have looked to women rather than men as objects of desire.[43] At any rate succeeding generations certainly did categorize her as a love poet. Meleager, the first century B.C. anthologist who excerpted some of her pieces for his epigram collection, the *Garland*, states that he "wove in at random the myrrh-breathing, well-blooming iris of Nossis, for whose tablets Eros melted the wax" (Gow and Page 1 = *Anth. Pal.* 4.1.9–10). His selection of the iris as her flowery token surrounds her with a heady and exotic, yet refined, sensuality; and the conceit of Eros melting wax, a reference to the encaustic process and therefore to her ecphrastic quatrains, hints at an undercurrent of physical desire permeating those poems that claim to transmit the speaker's spontaneous reaction to a compelling graphic image.[44]

Meleager furnishes an example of the male reader well-disposed toward Nossis: an expert connoisseur of epigram, he savors the delicate sensuality of those pieces he has chosen to anthologize. But the only other recorded references to her are trivializing and prurient. Herodas, a writer about whom little is known but who was probably her much younger contemporary, composed *mimiambi*, sketches based on a popular dramatic form, for the amusement of the bookish intelligentsia of Alexandria.[45] In his sixth and seventh mimes he portrays middle-class housewives first discussing the merits of, and then shopping for, leather dildoes. The first of these two works gratuitously designates a "Nossis daughter of Erinna" as the illegitimate possessor of such an implement (6.20–36); the second, in which the running joke involves an analogy between dildoes and women's shoes, puns on Nossis' name and that of Baucis, Erinna's dead girlhood companion, as specific kinds of footwear (7.57–58). Nossis and Erinna have been singled out, then, as emblems of perverted female sexuality, given to practices either solitary or indulged in with another woman but in either case devoted to ends other than the gratification of a male partner. As the reference to Baucis indicates, it was Erinna's passionate attachment to her friend, expressed in both her epigrams and her greatly admired epyllion, the *Distaff*, that invited that insulting appropriation of her name.[46] Nossis must figure in Herodas' mimes for a very similar reason. The extended use made of her in mime 6 implies not only that her own name was known to an educated audience, as Erinna's certainly was, but that it could be relied upon to arouse salacious laughter. Since the initial mention of Nossis straightaway prompts a misogynistic attack upon women's disloyalty to one another, an attack tellingly placed in the mouth of a woman speaker, the Locrian poet's glorification of female community and absorption in female culture appear to have been targeted for coarse parody. These two mimes, featuring matrons outwardly priggish but grossly amoral in private, operate as a harsh male corrective to Nossis' woman-centered, erotically charged world.

Vastly different in their appreciation of Nossis, the reactions of Meleager and Herodas are nevertheless alike in one instructive way: both foreground and isolate her eroticism at the expense of all other components of her work. By the Hellenistic period, sensational literary portrayals of Sappho had already conditioned the general reading public to imagine a woman who had written about love as herself experienced in such matters, if not actually promiscuous.[47] Furthermore, and despite the evidence of Sappho's own lyrics, the Sappho figure of fourth-century comedy and sentimental legend is not attracted to women; rather, she is the beloved of a whole company of archaic male poets or, alternatively, the aggressive pursuer of the handsome youth Phaon. We see much the same tendencies present in subsequent representations of Nossis. Herodas' unsubtle devaluation looks back to that lurid popular notion of an "amorous Sappho" for its image of another woman poet rapaciously bent upon artificial penile stimulation. Meleager takes a vicarious delight in the sexual undercurrents pervading her ostensibly descriptive impressions of painted portraits. These reductionist readings detach the author from her female community, the milieu in which her texts were originally conceived and her woman-identified sensibility fostered. In a new and fundamentally unhospitable literary environment, Nossis thus became a stereotype of aberrant female sexuality, to be romanticized or denigrated as the reader saw fit, and at length to be as good as forgotten.

Ancient male readers' inability to comprehend Nossis' special woman-oriented poetic discourse seems to be shared by contemporary classical scholars, accounting for her continued neglect by historians as well as literary critics. As Snyder demonstrates in the preceding essay in this volume, absurdities of interpretation occur when commentators fail to perceive that a woman writer like Sappho, in speaking privately to members of her own sex, is making use of a semiotic code of emotional and sensual imagery—an evocative strategy better adapted to communication among women than to rational academic exchange.[48] Nevertheless, despite the hardships she poses for some readers, Sappho is still recognized as both a major poet and a key source for uncovering the realities of Greek women's lives. Nossis, however, has been utterly ignored: no one, to my knowledge, has ever cited her texts as evidence for a female perspective upon religious cult, visual art, sexuality, or personal relationships. Yet if my assumption of an original female audience for her poetry is correct, the sentiments expressed in her verses must largely mirror attitudes common to her circle of friends, for she would not have been moved to publish her works in book form had they not met with approval from her first readers. I submit, then, that the values she affirms—values, as we have seen, quite distinct from those found in mainstream Greek literature—furnish evidence for the existence of a relatively autonomous women's subculture at Locri, one in which such an alternative perspective could be generated, nurtured, and transmitted, notwithstanding the pressures toward androcentric conformity exerted by the dominant culture.[49] We cannot, of course, term this perspective "feminist" in any modern sense, but it does concur with modern feminist thought in advocating the transcendent importance of women's experience—of intimate bonding, especially the bonding of mother and daughter; of physical desire and sensual enjoyment; of affectionate contact with divinity; and, not least, of the immediate aesthetic pleasure imparted by the woven, sculpted, painted, or written artifact.

At this point some caveats should be issued. We have hardly any reliable data about the sociohistorical circumstances of Sappho's life, and none about Nossis'; nor do we know how closely the cultural systems of their respective city-states conformed to prevailing models of Greek social organization.[50] It would be rash, then, to draw general conclusions about the overall "status" and "emancipation" of Lesbian or Locrian women from their texts. Again, though it is obvious that the two authors share many poetic concerns, their statements should not be used to prove a historical continuity of thought among all Greek women (or even among all elite women) extending from sixth-century B.C. Lesbos in the eastern Mediterranean to southern Italy three hundred years later: indeed, the example of Anyte warns us that we cannot project a characteristically female point of view onto Greek womanhood as a whole.

What we can extrapolate from Nossis' epigrams is, instead, the impact of Sappho's poetry upon a later generation of trained women readers. Nossis assumes a learned audience capable of apprehending deft allusions and pointed modifications of standard poetic tropes. The fact that she could make such demands upon a female readership tells us something about literacy among women of her class at this period.[51] Her efforts to imitate Sappho in the epigrammatic genre must reflect a broad admiration for the archaic poet within her own community, and her appeal to that figure as ideal reader in the epilogue to her book implies that she speaks not only as an individual woman, Nossis daughter of Theophilis, but also as emissary for a group of friends who have discovered a literary prototype of themselves in the Sapphic circle of companions. Her objective in appropriating the age-old formulas of the dedicatory epigram and infusing them with an unwonted subjectivity then becomes more intelligible: like Sappho, she attempted to transpose the public literary discourse of her time into forms more palatable to women, here blending the cool monumentality of the traditional graven inscription with the emotive urgency of the lyric moment. The misreadings of her critics, ancient and modern, are partial proof that she succeeded in this project. In turn, my cursory overview of her poetry now attempts to restore to Nossis her own proper female audience, an audience more distant in time and space than the Sappho she envisioned as an ideal reader, but one no less attentive to her woman-identified art.

Notes

This paper has been considerably revised since its initial oral presentation on 21 June 1987 at the Seventh Berkshire Conference on the History of Women. I have therefore been able to incorporate many helpful comments of the other panelists and the listening audience. Those who have contributed something to the final form of the essay include Judith Hallett, Hugh Lloyd-Jones, Amy Richlin, Eva Stehle, and my fellow presenters Joseph Russo and Jane McIntosh Snyder; and I owe particular thanks to Deborah Boedeker for her excellent literary insights and her friendly encouragement. Sarah B. Pomeroy's editorial advice has greatly improved both style and argumentation. I also appreciate the suggestions of the two anonymous referees for the University of North Carolina Press. None of these persons is responsible in any way for the faults that may be detected in this paper.

    1. The standard commentary on all epigrams of Hellenistic date, which also established the present convention of numeration, is A. S. F. Gow and D. L. Page, *The Greek Anthology: Hellenistic Epigrams*, 2 vols. (Cambridge: Cambridge University Press, 1965), cited hereafter by the editors' names. All page references are to vol. 2, *Commentary and Indexes*. To facilitate references to texts, I provide the number of the poem first in Gow and Page and then in the Loeb Classical Library edition of the Palatine and the Planudean anthologies: *The Greek Anthology*, trans.

W. R. Paton, 5 vols. (Cambridge: Harvard University Press, 1918). Other epigrams are cited by *Greek Anthology* number only; pertinent commentary references are provided in footnotes. Unless otherwise indicated, abbreviations are the standard ones from *L'année philologique* and the second edition of the *Oxford Classical Dictionary*. For the Greek text of Nossis I follow the edition of D. L. Page, *Epigrammata Graeca* (Oxford: Clarendon Press, 1975). All translations are my own. For Nossis' generally accepted date see P. Maas, *RE* XVII.1 (1936): col. 1053. Although Nossis 12 (*Anth. Pal.* 6.273), a prayer to Artemis for a woman in labor, would furnish one additional example of the poet's interest in the female sphere, I prefer to exclude it from consideration here, as the attribution to Nossis may be erroneous (on the evidence against its authenticity see Gow and Page, 443).

2. My underlying postulate of a culturally constructed female consciousness and a corresponding female literary voice, extant in antiquity no less than in modern times, has largely been shaped by contemporary feminist literary criticism, especially J. F. Diehl, " 'Come Slowly—Eden': An Exploration of Women Poets and Their Muse," *Signs* 3 (1978): 572–87; S. M. Gilbert and S. Gubar, *The Madwoman in the Attic* (New Haven and London: Yale University Press, 1979); and E. Showalter, "Toward a Feminist Poetics," in *Women Writing and Writing about Women*, ed. M. Jacobus (London: Croom Helm, 1979), 22–41, and "Feminist Criticism in the Wilderness," *Critical Inquiry* 8 (1981): 179–205. On Sappho's woman-centered poetic vision see the important article by J. Winkler, "Gardens of Nymphs: Public and Private in Sappho's Lyrics," *Women's Studies* 8 (1981): 65–91, reprinted in *Reflections of Women in Antiquity*, ed. H. P. Foley (New York: Gordon & Breach, 1981), 63–89. For Erinna as a strongly woman-identified poet see M. B. Arthur, "The Tortoise and the Mirror: Erinna *PSI* 1090," *CW* 74 (1980): 53–65. M. L. West, "Erinna," *ZPE* 25 (1977): 95–119, hypothesizes that Erinna's masterpiece, the *Distaff*, was an elaborate literary forgery and denies the historical existence of the poet; but his arguments have been answered by Sarah B. Pomeroy, "Supplementary Notes on Erinna," *ZPE* 32 (1978): 17–22.

3. Nossis' work is briefly surveyed by G. Luck, "Die Dichterinnen der griechischen Anthologie," *MH* 11 (1954): 170–87, and by S. Barnard, "Hellenistic Women Poets," *CJ* 73 (1978): 204–13; the single comprehensive study of the poet is M. Gigante, "Nosside," *PP* 29 (1974): 22–39.

4. The essential nature and development of the dedicatory epigram are analyzed by A. E. Raubitschek, "Das Denkmal-Epigramm," in *L'épigramme grecque*, Entretiens sur l'antiquité classique, 14 (Geneva: Vandoeuvres, 1968), 3–26.

5. U. von Wilamowitz-Moellendorff, *Hellenistische Dichtung in der Zeit des Kallimachos* (Berlin: Weidmannsche Buchhandlung, 1924) 1:136. For Anyte's close affiliation with the mainstream literary tradition see the remarks of Gow and Page, 89–104, and the much fuller commentary by D. Geoghegan, *Anyte: The Epigrams* (Rome: Edizioni dell'Ateneo & Bizzarri, 1979).

6. The contrast of domestic and public space, with the particular significance of

each for women, is also a central concern in Theocritus 15, where the transition from surburban household to royal palace is marked by a vivid dramatic realization of the physical dangers of ancient city streets. F. T. Griffiths, "Home before Lunch: The Emancipated Woman in Theocritus," in *Reflections of Women in Antiquity*, ed. H. P. Foley (New York: Gordon & Breach, 1981), 247–73, provides a nice analysis of that contrast.

7. On the evidence for such a canon see M. J. Baale, *Studia in Anytes poetriae vitam et carminum reliquias* (Haarlem: Kleynenberg, 1903), 7–9. Barnard, "Hellenistic Women Poets," 204, believes the selection of names originated with Antipater himself; but it was much more in keeping with epigrammatic practice to versify lists already in circulation. A. S. F. Gow and D. L. Page supply several parallels for this epigram, which they list as Antipater 19 in *The Greek Anthology: The Garland of Philip and Some Contemporary Epigrams* (Cambridge: Cambridge University Press, 1968), 2:36.

8. Gow and Page, *Garland of Philip*, 37, observe that the adjective is "not very descriptive." For a parallel to the standard interpretation one could point to *theoglōssous*, "god-voiced," in line 1 of the same poem, where the meaning is obviously "who spoke *like* divinities [i.e., Muses]." But Hellenistic conventions of poetic wit would not only have sanctioned but in fact encouraged the proximate use of morphologically similar compounds with a different syntactical relationship of parts.

9. The word *byssos* can be used of other fabrics besides linen—see the discussion at *RE* III.1 (1897): cols. 1108–14—but retains its connotations of oriental luxury and expense.

10. On the evidence for such ritual dedications at Locri see H. Prückner, *Die lokrischen Tonreliefs* (Mainz am Rhein: Philipp von Zabern, 1968), 42–43, with Abb. 5. Barnard, "Hellenistic Women Poets," 213, cites the literary parallel at *Il.* 6.286–311, where the women of Troy, led by Queen Hecuba, offer a robe to Athena. For the well-known offerings of women's clothing to Artemis of Brauron see T. Linders, *Studies in the Treasure Records of Artemis Brauronia Found in Athens* (Stockholm: Svenska Institutet i Athen, 1972), passim (this reference was provided by one of the anonymous referees). Sarah B. Pomeroy reminds me that at Elis a group of elite women termed "the Sixteen" wove a robe for Hera every fourth year (Pausanias 5.16.2, 5.16.6, 6.24.10). Many other instances of private and public dedications of textiles by wealthy or prominent Greek women could be cited.

11. In the *Iliad*, *agauos* is a regular epithet for the Trojans and for heroes (for example, Tydeus at 5.277, Laomedon at 5.649 and 6.23, Achilles at 17.557, Nestor at 18.16). In the *Odyssey* it becomes the characteristic epithet for the suitors; it is also applied thrice to the goddess Persephone (11.213, 226, 635; cf. *Hymn. Hom. Cer.* 348 and *Orphei Hymni*[3] (Quandt) 41.5–6; my thanks to J. Henderson for his help with the latter reference). Thereafter it is rarely found, even in poetry. The noun-epithet combination *pais agauos*, "noble child," occurs just once, interestingly enough at

Od. 11.492, where Achilles in the Underworld desires to learn of his son and is informed that by his deeds of valor Neoptolemus has proved himself his father's successor. If Nossis has this famous passage in mind, she is neatly reversing gender roles.

12. Against the contentions of Oldfather, *RE* XIII.2 (1927): cols. 1345–46, I argue in "Greek Women and the Metronymic: A Note on an Epigram by Nossis," *AHB* 1 (1987): 39–42, that identification by mother and mother's mother is a gender-specific speech trait. For other arguments against Oldfather's thesis see S. Pembroke, "Locres et Tarante: le rôle des femmes dans la fondation de deux colonies grecques," *Annales E.S.C.* 25 (1970): 1240–70.

13. For more extensive discussion of this point see M. B. Skinner, "Sapphic Nossis," *Arethusa* 22 (1989): 5–18.

14. C. Sourvinou-Inwood, "Persephone and Aphrodite at Locri: A Model for Personality Definitions in Greek Religion," *JHS* 98 (1978): 101–21 (quotation is from 120). I regret that considerations of space do not allow me to examine the problematic evidence for ritual prostitution associated with the cult of Locrian Aphrodite (see especially Justin 21.3), though such a practice, if its actual existence could be demonstrated, might have important ramifications for our understanding of poems 4, 5, and 6. For very different evaluations of this evidence see Prückner, *Die lokrischen Tonreliefs*, 4–14; C. Sourvinou-Inwood, "The Votum of 477/6 B.C. and the Foundation Legend of Locri Epizephyrii," *CQ* 24 (1974): 186–98; and L. Woodbury, "The Gratitude of the Locrian Maiden: Pindar, *Pyth.* 2.18–20," *TAPA* 108 (1978): 285–99.

15. This familiar type is studied by E. Fantham, "Sex, Status, and Survival in Hellenistic Athens: A Study of Women in New Comedy," *Phoenix* 29 (1975): 44–74, and by A. Cameron, "Asclepiades' Girl Friends," in *Reflections of Women in Antiquity*, ed. H. P. Foley (New York: Gordon & Breach, 1981), 275–302.

16. For Samytha's likely association with the Adonis rites see Gow and Page, 438. M. Detienne, *Les jardins d'Adonis* (Paris: Editions Gallimard, 1972), trans. J. Lloyd as *The Gardens of Adonis* (Atlantic Highlands, N.J.: Humanities Press, 1977), regards the use of exotic perfumes and spices as one of the primary and essential ingredients of this cult. Theocritus 15.114 furnishes one well-known example of the practice.

17. On the divine and magical powers of nectar, imagined as a quintessentially sweet fragrance, see S. Lilja, *The Treatment of Odours in the Poetry of Antiquity*, Commentationes Humanarum Litterarum 49 (Helsinki: Societas Scientiarum Fennica, 1972), 19–30. I am grateful to R. Ridinger for calling my attention to this study.

18. For courtesans celebrating this feast see Menander *Sam.* 38–48; cf. Diphilus as given in Athenaeus 7.292d, 10.451b (Meineke, *FCG*⁴, pp. 394–95, 399). At Alciphron *Epist. Meret.* 14.8, a woman invited to just such a celebration is asked to bring along *ton son Adōnin*, "your own Adonis," and at Lucian *Dial. Meret.* 7.297 an

older courtesan scornfully refers to her daughter's boyfriend in virtually the same words. For discussion of these passages see Detienne, *Gardens of Adonis*, 64–66.

19. For a basic overview of *ekphrasis* as an ancient literary convention see G. Downey, "Ekphrasis," *Reallexicon für Antike und Christentum* 4 (Stuttgart: Anton Hiersemann, 1959), 921–44. G. Zanker has now provided a definitive account of the theory and practice of pictorial description in Hellenistic literature: *Realism in Alexandrian Poetry* (London: Croom Helm, 1987), 39–112.

20. On the encaustic technique see Pliny *HN* 35.149 and Vitruvius 7.9.3; M. Cagiano de Azevedo, "Encausto," *EAA* 3:331–35; M. H. Swindler, *Ancient Painting* (New Haven: Yale University Press, 1929), 319–24; E. Pfuhl, *Masterpieces of Greek Drawing and Painting*, trans. J. D. Beazley (New York: Macmillan, 1955), 124–25.

21. For Erinna 3 (*Anth. Pal.* 6.352) as our oldest ecphrastic epigram see Luck, "Dichterinnen," 171, and U. W. Scholz, "Erinna," *A&A* 18 (1973): 21, with earlier bibliography. On Anyte 13 and 14 (*Anth. Pal.* 6.312, 9.745) as descriptions of artworks see Geoghegan, *Anyte*, 131, 137.

22. I am indebted to Sarah B. Pomeroy for the idea that these three epigrams were written to order for paying customers. Examples of poems by male authors apparently testifying to real offerings by *hetairai*, and so presumably also commissioned, include Leónidas 2 (*Anth. Pal.* 6.211) and Callimachus 20 (*Anth. Pal.* 13.24), both scarcely more than lists. Contrast the purely literary epigram, allegedly by Plato, which converts the courtesan Lais' presentation of her mirror to Aphrodite into an object lesson in mutability (*Anth. Pal.* 6.1); the topos is later taken up by Philetas 1 (*Anth. Pal.* 6.210) and Julianus (*Anth. Pal.* 6.18, 19, 20). In fragment 107 (Bowra), Pindar exempts from blame an entire troop of slave women sent to serve Aphrodite of Corinth as temple prostitutes, but his remarks are meant to dignify the male donor's generosity. For the primary patriarchal class distinction between "respectable women" living under a man's protection and "disreputable women" whose sexuality is public and commercial, see G. Lerner, *The Creation of Patriarchy* (New York and Oxford: Oxford University Press, 1986), 123–40.

23. Gow and Page, 439, propose that *to gauron* here means "sprightliness" rather than "insolence." But the latent notion of overweening pride in *gauron* would be brought to the surface by the bombastic expression *despoina melathrōn*. This phrase is a variant of the positive term *oikodespoina*, found at Babrius 10.5 and Plutarch *Quaest. conv.* 612f and etymologically analyzed by E. Fraenkel, "Zur griechischen Wortbildung," *Glotta* 32 (1952–53): 32 (I owe this reference to H. Lloyd-Jones). Gow and Page themselves note that *melathrōn* seems "a curiously stilted word to use of a house in such a context." Moreover, *despoina* can easily take on negative overtones; cf. Menander fragment 333.7, where the word is applied to the tyrannical wife Crobule.

24. Gow and Page, 440, observe that the form *skylakaina* does not occur elsewhere and that the feminine ending *-aina* furnishes the authors of Old Comedy with humorous material. At Aristophanes *Nub.* 658–67, the locus classicus, the

joke springs from Socrates' pedantic insistence upon constructing a distinct femi-nine form for the names of female domestic animals normally subsumed under the generic masculine. It is conceivable that Nossis is intentionally alluding to this passage, thereby giving the description of Thaumareta's puppy additional comic flavor. My reading of this line has benefited from the incisive comments of H. Lloyd-Jones and J. Russo.

25. For conventional expressions of the sentiment see the parallel passages cited by A. S. F. Gow, *Theocritus* (Cambridge: Cambridge University Press, 1952), 2:334, on 17.44 and by C. J. Fordyce, *Catullus* (Oxford: Clarendon Press, 1961), 253, on 61.214–18.

26. For the stature of a divinity manifest note especially *Hymn. Hom. Cer.* 275 and *Hymn. Hom. Ven.* 173–74; cf. the political trick played by Pisistratus at Herodo-tus 1.60. Agamemnon identifies Penelope's wisdom (*pinutē*) as her characteristic feminine trait at *Od.* 11.445–46; compare the remarks of Telemachus at 20.131 and 21.103 and of Odysseus at 23.361. We may also adduce Hera's gift to the daughters of Pandareus at 20.70–71.

27. If the original manuscript reading *tēnōthe*, "thence," is retained, the sugges-tion of an alternative plane of reality becomes even more pronounced: note the significance of the plausible conjecture *toutothen* at Erinna fragment 402.1 *Supp. Hell.* and cf. the phrase *ho ekeithen angelos* at Plato *Resp.* 619b.

28. W. K. Lacey, *The Family in Classical Greece* (Ithaca: Cornell University Press, 1968), 172–74, cites this statement as a factual illustration of Athenian women's domestic influence upon the public actions of male family members; but we should take into account the tendentious character of the oratorical passage.

29. On the epic tone and diction of Anyte 1, 4, 9, and 21 and their close thematic parallels with other epigrams see the discussions of Geoghegan, *Anyte*, ad loc., which show that in idealizing warfare she faithfully follows the dominant literary tradition. Luck, "Dichterinnen," 172–81, makes the same point.

30. The key Homeric passage is *Il.* 17.426–40, where the horses of Achilles weep for Patroclus; cf. 11.159–61, where runaway horses miss their fallen charioteers. Leonidas 35 (*Anth. Pal.* 6.131), Mnasalces 4 (*Anth. Pal.* 6.125) and Hegesippus 1 (*Anth. Pal.* 6.124) extend Homer's conceit by making dedicated weapons express devotion to their former owners.

31. For this etymology see Diodorus 16.15.1–2 and Strabo 6.255.

32. Gow and Page, 441, find the use of this form unusual; but it may have been in vogue among Hellenistic poets. Cf. Callimachus *Lav. Pall.* 94 and Theocritus 8.38.

33. Aristotle's *Poetics* epitomizes the classical notion of an inherent superiority of genres: see especially 1462b15, where the highest place is finally awarded to tragedy over epic. In contrast, Callimachus 57 (*Anth. Pal.* 9.565) counterposes the poetic immortality of Theaetetus, possibly an epigrammatist, to the brief moment of glory accorded victors in dramatic competitions. On Aristotle and Callimachus

as representative spokesmen for antithetical critical positions on measure and scale, see further J. Onians, *Art and Thought in the Hellenistic Age* (London: Thames & Hudson, 1979), 121–34. For the Hellenistic admiration of the "perfect small work" applied to poetry by women, note the praise of Erinna's *Distaff* by the anonymous author of *Anth. Pal.* 9.190, who pronounces her three hundred lines "equal to Homer," and the even more effusive celebration of her lasting fame in Antipater of Sidon 58 (*Anth. Pal.* 7.713).

34. Gow and Page, 435–36, provide an excellent summary of critical opinion on the crux involving the demonstrative pronoun *tēnas* in the final line of poem 1. Their suggestion that the pronoun may refer to Nossis herself, rather than to Aphrodite or to the implied antecedent of *tina*, seems the most economical and acceptable solution; for further discussion see note 38 below. On the textual difficulties in the last distich of poem 11 see the survey of scholarship by I. Cazzaniga, "Critica testuale ed esegesi a Nosside *A. P.* VII 718," *PP* 25 (1970): 431–45, along with the remarks of Gow and Page, 442; Luck, "Dichterinnen," 186–87; and Gigante, "Nosside," 38–39. A rationale for following the corrected text of Page is provided in Skinner, "Sapphic Nossis," 12.

35. For this convention see D. L. Clayman, "Callimachus' Thirteenth *Iamb*: The Last Word," *Hermes* 104 (1976): 29–35, and J. Van Sickle, "Poetics of Opening and Closure in Meleager, Catullus and Gallus," *CW* 75 (1981): 64–75; on the poetic *sphragis* see W. Kranz, "*SPHRAGIS*: Ichform und Namensiegel als Eingangs- und Schlussmotiv antiker Dichtung," *RhM* 104 (1961): 3–46, 97–124. That the convention was already in force in Nossis' lifetime is evident from a signature poem by her contemporary Posidippus: see H. Lloyd-Jones, "The Seal of Posidippus," *JHS* 83 (1963): 75–99.

36. The possibility that Nossis 1 was conceived as an introduction to a book-length epigram collection was first advanced by Luck, "Dichterinnen," 183. Long before, R. Reitzenstein, *Epigramm und Skolion* (Giessen: J. Ricker'sche Buchhandlung, 1893), 139, had proposed that Nossis 11 had once served to round off a book of poems, a suggestion that won the approval of Wilamowitz (*Hellenistische Dichtung*, 135). For the programmatic character of poem 1 see especially M. Gigante, "Il manifesto poetico di Nosside," in *Letterature comparate: problemi e metodo*, ed. V. Ussani et al. (Bologna: Pàtron Editore, 1981), 1:243–45.

37. Sappho *LP* 130.2, the famous description of the god as a "bittersweet irresistible crawling thing." Posidippus 1 (*Anth. Pal.* 5.134) and Meleager 61 (*Anth. Pal.* 12.109) employ Sappho's phrase in epigrams; Plutarch *Quaest. conv.* 681b indicates that by his time it had become proverbial. A. Carson has now traced out the complex psychological and literary resonances of the expression in a long meditative essay, *Eros the Bittersweet* (Princeton: Princeton University Press, 1986). My deep thanks to D. Boedeker for observing this direct allusion to Sappho and remarking upon its significance.

38. Figurative use of the verb *apoptuein* is frequent in tragedy, always with the suggestion of something abominable. Note Clytemnestra's horrified reaction to the news of Agamemnon's impending sacrifice of their daughter, *apeptus'*, *ō geraie*, *mython* (Euripides *IA* 874), and cf. these other instances: Aeschylus *Ag.* 1192, *Ch.* 197, *Eu.* 303; Euripides *Hec.* 1276, *Hel.* 664, *Hipp.* 614, *IT* 1161.

39. E. Degani, "Nosside," *GFF* 4 (1981): 51–52, follows Gow and Page in assuming that the poet's own name, emphatically stated one line above, is the immediate antecedent of *tēnas*; he then interprets *anthea* as a figurative expression for her poetic compositions. The metaphor of poems as flowers is as old as Pindar *Ol.* 6.105 and common in programmatic literary statements: we need look no further than the proem to Meleager's *Garland* (Gow and Page, 1 = *Anth. Pal.* 4.1). For the direct reminiscence of Sappho *LP* 55 in the last line see Gigante, "Il manifesto poetico di Nosside," 244–45.

40. On the funerary motif of "conveying the message" see S. L. Tarán, *The Art of Variation in the Hellenistic Epigram* (Leiden: E. J. Brill, 1979), 132–49; Nossis 11 is examined on pp. 146–48. Tarán observes that the epigram utilizes expressions and conceits regularly associated with this motif but differs from other fictitious epitaphs, even those composed by poets for themselves, in its general tone and intention.

41. Gigante, "Nosside," 25–26, lists a number of these reminiscences, claiming that Nossis' epigrams repeatedly attempt "l'emulazione di Saffo in chiave ellenistica" (25).

42. On the aristocratic rapport between Sappho and Nossis, shown especially in their joint assumption of an elite female audience, see Gigante, "Nosside," 25–26. The unconscious conviction that a woman who frankly affirmed the joys of love would not have been respectable may have induced Reitzenstein, *Epigramm und Skolion*, 142, to postulate that Nossis was herself a *hetaira*. Wilamowitz, *Hellenistiche Dichtung*, 135, objected to Reitzenstein's notion, which has since been decisively refuted by I. Cazzaniga, "Nosside, nome aristocratico per la poetessa di Locri?" *ASNP* 3a, ser. 2 (1972): 173–76.

43. Skinner, "Sapphic Nossis," 14.

44. Meleager's epithet *myropnoun* almost certainly points to the white iris (*Iris florentina*), which yields orris root, the principal ingredient of the unguent *myron irinon*: see Theophrastus *Hist. Pl.* 1.7.2, 9.7.3–4, and Athenaeus 15.689e. Pliny *HN* 21.19 states that this flower is not used in garlands; but see the references in Lilja, *Treatment of Odours*, 185. On the exotic origins of myrrh see Herodotus 3.107 and Theophrastus *Hist. Pl.* 9.4, along with the remarks of Detienne, *Gardens of Adonis*, 5–8; for its erotic aspects cf. Detienne, 60–66, and Lilja, 60–76. Because the process of encaustic painting involved laying pigmented wax onto a panel with a heated implement to fuse the colors, Greek epigrammatists hit upon the topos of the enamored painter whose heart is softened by desire for his sitter: for example, in

Anth. Plan. 16.80.5–6, *isa gar autōi / kērōi tēkomenōi tēketai hē kradiē*, "for his heart is melted like the melted wax itself." Meleager's capsule description of Nossis is unquestionably a clever variant of that conceit. *Deltos*, the standard Greek noun for the wooden writing tablet with a waxen interior surface, may also be applied, at least metaphorically, to the wooden panel that served as support for the image depicted in encaustic: see Aristophanes *Thesm.* 778.

45. On the spelling of Herodas' name, his likely *floruit* (the late 70s and early 60s of the third century B.C.), and the nature of his compositions see the introductory comments of I. C. Cunningham, *Herodas: Mimiambi* (Oxford: Clarendon Press, 1971), 1–17. G. Mastromarco, *The Public of Herondas* (Amsterdam: J. C. Gieben, 1984), establishes that he wrote for an educated audience.

46. O. Crusius, *Untersuchungen zu den Mimiamben des Herondas* (Leipzig: Teubner, 1892), 118, was the first to claim that 6.20–21 is a malicious slur upon both women poets, a suggestion that has won general acceptance. H. Lloyd-Jones is credited by I. C. Cunningham, "Herodas 6 and 7," *CQ* 14 (1964): 32 n. 3, with observing the sinister significance of Herodas' insertion of *Baukides* along with *Nossides* in the ostensible catalogue of footwear at 7.57–58. Taking a hint from Crusius, who supposed that Herodas was attacking these poets for their artistic failings, J. Stern, "Herodas' Mimiamb 6," *GRBS* 20 (1979): 247–54, theorizes that Erinna and Nossis are denounced for "taking the art of poetry in wrong directions." But it is hard to believe that either woman could have had that much influence upon the mainstream literary tradition, and ordinary misogyny seems to me a perfectly adequate explanation for Herodas' barbs.

47. Seneca *Ep.* 88.37 provides evidence that Sappho's alleged unchastity was a topic of scholarly debate; cf. the slanders mentioned by the biographer of *P. Oxy.* 1800 fragment 1, col. 1.16–19. For the tradition of portraying Sappho as the beloved of numerous male poets see K. J. Dover, *Greek Homosexuality* (London: Duckworth, 1978), 174. Menander fragment 258 alludes to the most famous Sapphic legend, that of her suicidal leap from the white rock at Cape Leukas in pursuit of the boatman Phaon. By the first century A.D. the tale had been incorporated into her biography; see Ovid *Her.* 15. For its likely mythic origins see G. Nagy, "Phaethon, Sappho's Phaon, and the White Rock of Leukas," *HSCP* 77 (1973): 137–77, and M. R. Lefkowitz, *The Lives of the Greek Poets* (Baltimore: The Johns Hopkins University Press, 1981), 36–37. On this later "heterosexualization" of Sappho's erotic life see J. P. Hallett, "Sappho and Her Social Context: Sense and Sensuality," *Signs* 4 (1979): 448–49.

48. Jane McIntosh Snyder, "Public Occasion and Private Passion in the Lyrics of Sappho of Lesbos," in this volume. Using examples of the critical reception of texts by Charlotte Perkins Gilman and Susan Keating Glaspell, A. Kolodny demonstrates in "A Map for Rereading: Or, Gender and the Interpretation of Literary Texts," *New Literary History* 11 (1980): 451–67, that readers accustomed to an exclu-

sively male-oriented conceptual system are often inadequate interpreters of literary products dealing with women's conceptual and symbolic worlds. For a hypothetical (and decidedly controversial) model of a "woman's poetics" see now L. Lipking, "Aristotle's Sister: A Poetics of Abandonment," *Critical Inquiry* 10 (1983): 61–81.

49. On female subcultures and their role in shaping the outlook of the woman writers who participate in them see E. Showalter, *A Literature of Their Own: British Women Novelists from Brontë to Lessing* (Princeton: Princeton University Press, 1977), 11. For the possibility that the domestic sphere of Greek women constituted a likely matrix for such a subculture see Skinner, "Greek Women and the Metronymic," 41–42.

50. Lefkowitz, *The Lives of the Greek Poets*, 36–37, notes that Sappho's ancient biography simply portrays her as conforming (or not conforming) to expected patterns of female behavior. Against those who conclude from her poetry that Lesbian women enjoyed high status and esteem M. B. Arthur contends in "Early Greece: The Origins of the Western Attitude toward Woman," *Arethusa* 6 (1973): 38–43, that Sappho's lyrics, like those of male poets of the same era, create an idealized, aristocratic fantasy world of refinement and romantic passion having little to do with reality. Even in antiquity there was some spirited argument about the foundation and customs of Italian Locri, as evidenced by the historian Timaeus' attack on Aristotle's account of its origins and Polybius' later polemic against Timaeus' assertions (Polybius 12.5–11). While Timaeus had apparently insisted that Locri was a normal Greek city, Polybius explicitly states that some of its usages were borrowed from the native Sicels (12.5.10); for an attempt to determine what Timaeus actually wrote see now L. Pearson, *The Greek Historians of the West: Timaeus and His Predecessors* (Atlanta: Scholars Press, 1987), 98–104. The supposed evidence for *Mutterrecht* at Locri as a remnant of indigenous Italian customs is laid out in Oldfather, *RE* XIII.2 (1927): cols. 1345–49; cf., however, the skeptical comments of T. J. Dunbabin, *The Western Greeks* (Oxford: Clarendon Press, 1948), 183–86.

51. On this topic see Sarah B. Pomeroy, "*TECHNIKAI KAI MOUSIKAI*: The Education of Women in the Fourth Century and in the Hellenistic Period," *AJAH* 2 (1977): 51–68, and S. G. Cole, "Could Greek Women Read and Write?" in *Reflections of Women in Antiquity*, ed. H. P. Foley (New York: Gordon & Breach, 1981), 219–45.

CYNTHIA B. PATTERSON

Marriage and the Married Woman

in Athenian Law

In the midst of describing the strange and exotic customs of the Egyptians, Herodotus pauses to note that the Egyptians, "like the Greeks," each have only one wife (2.92)—that is, that both the Greeks and the Egyptians are monogamous. That, at least, is what most readers of Herodotus (generally belonging to monogamous societies themselves) have very reasonably taken him to mean. Herodotus' exact wording is *gunaiki miē hekastos autōn sunoikeei*, literally "each of them lives together with one woman."[1] But was this marriage—to Herodotus or to an Athenian audience? In this essay I discuss the ways in which such "living together" of a man and woman was recognized and validated by classical Athenian law and custom, establishing what we can indeed call a marriage or marital relationship. I argue that although classical Athenian law concerned itself primarily with the identification of the wife as bearer of legitimate children and heirs, and secondarily (from at least the mid-fourth century) with prohibiting marital cohabitation of Athenians with non-Athenians,[2] significant aspects of the marital relationship, such as the celebration of the marriage and the setting up of the new household or *oikos*, were the domain of social ritual and custom. Marriage as an institution involved both kinds of validation, legal and social. Rather than search for a single formula for what constituted the legal *event* of "solemn marriage" (or "die rechtsgültige Ehe"),[3] we ought to see Athenian marriage as a multifaceted *process*,[4] comparable in this respect to the socially recognized processes of birth, coming of age, and death—which with marriage might be said to define the life of an ancient Athenian.

By what means or signs, then, did the Athenian community recognize that a marriage was a marriage and give validation to the "living together" (*sunoikein*) of a man and woman? And what does Aristotle's comment that the "yoking together" (*suzeuxis*) of man and woman had no special name[5] suggest about the formal status of the marriage relationship? For an attempt to answer these questions, the two most relevant parts of the process are the *enguē* (the "promising" or "pledging" of the bride) and the *gamos* (the wedding celebration itself); the central problem is the relative significance of the two. Although *gamos* is the term that most naturally calls to mind "marriage," *enguē* has received more attention from scholars engaged in the search for the legal form or formulae of Athenian marriage. So I turn first to the *enguē*.[6]

The verb *enguan* has the basic meaning "to pledge" or "to promise," with an etymological connection to a ritual gesture involving the hand or hands—either pledging by putting something into the hand of someone or promising with the seal of a handshake.[7] Wolff simply asserted the former view ("*ἐγγυᾶν* means *to hand over*; and *ἐγγυᾶσθαι* means *to receive into one's hand*"),[8] although Gernet had argued extensively on the basis of the first appearance of the term (*Odyssey* 8.351) for the latter view, that *enguan* originally referred to a solemn promise made by a family member on behalf of another family member, not to the actual transferral of object or person.[9] I find Gernet's interpretation inherently more convincing, and also more applicable to the role of the *enguē* in marriage. As the actual transfer of the bride was called the *ekdosis* (literally, the "giving out") and might but did not necessarily accompany the *enguē*,[10] it seems more reasonable to consider the *enguē* a promise or pledge rather than a transfer. (Also, if the woman was not present at the *enguē*, as often she may not have been, it is difficult to see this as an actual transfer.) Disagreement stems largely from the fact that in classical Athens *enguan* was used both for the procedure by which the creditor pledged a debtor to a guarantor and for that by which the father (or other male relative) pledged a woman to her future husband. (The guarantor and the husband receive the pledge in the middle voice; the woman and the debtor are pledged in the passive.)[11] Thus some have seen this usage as reflecting an essential similarity in the two transactions:[12] the wife is the passive "object" transferred, so that, we might say, she will pay her debt of "legitimate children," as the debtor is transferred to the custody of the guarantor to ensure the payment of his debt. But the parallel is not so neat and clear as it may seem at first glance. As already noted, the woman was not necessarily transferred at the moment of the *enguē*, and further, the children were "paid" not to the father who pledged but to the husband who accepted the pledged woman. It seems to me preferable to follow Gernet and consider both specialized uses of *enguan* as developing from a common basic meaning of "to make a promise or pledge about or on behalf of a family member."[13] In any case, however, the *enguē* resulted in the woman's becoming a *gunē enguētē* (a "pledged" or "promised" woman). What did this new description entail? Was the woman now "married"?

According to one interpretation, the *enguē* did formally and legally create marriage and the marital authority of husband over wife, the *kurieia*. The *gamos* and the "living together" of bride and groom were then necessary for, in Wolff's words, the "full effectiveness"[14] of that marriage and authority but were not themselves effective legal acts. The earliest specific reference to an Athenian marriage, the marriage of Megakles and Agariste reported by Herodotus 6.130, might be taken to support this view. After holding a Panhellenic contest for the hand of his daughter, Kleisthenes the tyrant of Sikyon chose the Athenian Megakles and said, according to Herodotus, "to Megakles son of Alcmaeon I pledge (*enguō*) my child Agariste by the laws of the Athenians (*nomoisi toisi Athenaiōn*)."[15] "When Megakles accepted the *enguē* (*phamenou enguasthai*)," said Herodotus, "the *gamos* was confirmed by Kleisthenes (*ekekurōto ho gamos Kleisthenei*)."[16] Then, he continued, from these two "living together" (*toutōn sunoikesantōn*) was born Kleisthenes the Athenian. The general implication of this story might seem to be that the *enguē* was the significant legal act (*kata nomous*) creating marriage, after which *gamos* and cohabitation (and a child) followed as a matter of course.[17]

There is, however, another well-known passage bearing upon the topic of the *enguē* which implies a different conclusion about the relative weighting of the elements of Athenian marriage and the legal effect of the *enguē*. In the second of Demosthenes' speeches against his guardians (for the embezzlement of his estate) the orator says that his father made a will, pledging (*enguōn*, 28.15) his mother to Aphobos (the defendant), and his sister, then only five years old, to Demophon (another of the corrupt guardians). But there were no marriages, and Demosthenes' sister eventually married another man. Demosthenes gives no indication that any sort of divorce was required to nullify the *enguē*—or that his mother and sister had any way of enforcing the promise or pledge through legal action or of receiving compensation for the broken "contract." Nor does it seem that his mother and sister were under the *kurieia* (legal authority or guardianship) of Aphobos and Demophon, respectively, rather than that of Aphobos, Demophon and Therippides, the joint guardians of the estate. And though Aphobos did receive Demosthenes' mother's dowry, Demosthenes insists that he owes interest on it (27.17). Aphobos did not yet have free use of the dowry, as he would if he were her husband.[18] Thus from the example of Demosthenes' family it seems that the *enguē* was simply a nonbinding betrothal, which neither created the marital state nor required a formal dissolution.[19]

For scholars caught between these two well-known *exempla* which seem each to imply a different legal significance for the *enguē*, a common solution has been a sort of compromise: the *enguē* was the only formal and legally necessary marriage transaction, but it required the completion of the *gamos* and *sunoikein* in order actually to become a valid and legal marriage.[20] Athenian marriage, on this view, was formally and legally complete without the presence of a wife, whose entry into the house of her husband occurred "whenever it was mutually convenient."[21] Her entry had no legal significance—apart from the fact that it was necessary to make that marriage a marriage.

Such a solution seems to me to make little sense, either legally or practically, and I suggest that the way out of this conceptual corner is to begin again with the particular interest of Athenian law in the marriage relationship and the nature of the *enguē*. First of all, although there is in discussions of Athenian marriage a tendency to treat the *enguē* as an official and public transaction,[22] it is clear that this was a private contract made between two adult males—very likely in the *andrōn* (male or "public" room of the house) of either the groom or the father of the bride. It was *kata nomon* and legally valid like other contracts; but, again like such contracts or agreements, there was neither public registration nor any required witnesses.[23] The origin of the belief in a more public, official character for the *enguē* transaction may lie in the frequency with which it is mentioned or appealed to in courtroom oratory. In speeches where family property and inheritance are at issue, the *enguē* of the claimant's mother to his or her father is regularly cited as proof of his or her legitimacy—and the lack of the *enguē* suggests illegitimacy (so in Isaeus 3, passim). Likewise, that the mother was *gunē enguētē* is commonly asserted by those attempting to establish their claim to both family and polis membership (see, e.g., Demosthenes 57.41, 43, 54). In contrast, the actual *gamoi* or marriage ceremonies are rarely mentioned.[24] The predominance of the *enguē* in the arguments of the orators does not, however, stem from its special suitability as legal proof of marriage.[25] It was not any more provable or verifiable than any other private contract for which witnesses were needed—needed, that is, not to validate, but to prove its completion, if that should be questioned. (A speech such as Isaeus 3 reveals that the existence of an *enguē* was not always particularly easy to prove or disprove.) Indeed, if it was simply a matter of witnesses, the *gamos*, celebrated over several days by friends and relatives and intended to attract the attention of neighbors and fellow citizens, was the more public and better witnessed event.

This brings me to my second and more positive point about the significance of the *enguē*. The emphasis on the *enguē* in courtroom oratory has to do with its purpose rather than its form. The *enguē* was the legal means (*kata nomon*) of establishing that a woman would be the mother of a man's legitimate heirs—and establishing legitimacy is precisely the concern of claimants to an inheritance. The connection between the *enguē* and the legitimacy of children is clear in the (Solonian?) law quoted in Demosthenes' speech "Against Leochares": (the woman) whom father or brother or grandfather entrusts (*enguēse*), from this woman are born legitimate children (*paidas gnēsious*) (44.49; cf. 46.18).[26] Although generally taken as a law concerned with marriage, this is better understood as about legitimacy. To the question "who is *gnēsios* [well born or legitimate] and heir to family property?" the law answers that the *gnēsios* is that child born from the *gunē enguētē*.[27] That this is the purpose of the *enguē* is suggested also by what seem to be the traditional words in which it was expressed: "I pledge (*enguō*) this woman to you for the purpose of [literally] the cultivation of legitimate children"[28]—apparently a contractual arrangement similar to leasing an agricultural field. The woman is the passive object here because the *enguē* is concerned not with her status and relationship to her husband (or his to her), but with the status and legitimacy of her children. When the *enguē* is taken as encapsulating the nature of Athenian marriage (as it often is) then the comment of a modern historian, "marriage did not create a new community of husband and wife; it was a means to provide heirs to the bridegroom's estate by continuing his line,"[29] follows naturally. But if the *enguē* is seen as a transaction with the specific and limited goal of establishing that one man's daughter (or sister or granddaughter) will be the recognized mother of legitimate heirs for another man's *oikos*, then the lack of interest in the woman herself or in her relationship with the children's father is less remarkable. Although she bore heirs (male and female), the wife never became part of her husband's *anchisteia*, those family members entitled to inherit.[30] In this sense, the wife remained always a *xenē* (a stranger or guest) in her husband's house, retaining rather her connection of *anchisteia* and *sungeneia* (kinship) to her natal family.

But though not his heir, the wife (at least ideally) was her husband's "yokemate" within the *oikos* and was related to him as one free member of the household to another. Husband and wife were *oikeioi*; indeed, according to Menander (fragment 647 Kock = 572 Koerte), nothing was *oikeion* so much as husband and wife.[31] This "yoking together" of man and woman within the *oikos* Aristotle termed a partnership or *koinōnia*, and although it had no name of its own, it was distinct (insisted Aristotle) from the other primary relationships of the household such as that between master and slave or between parent and child. Aristotle's analysis found that the rule of a master over a slave was despotic, of parent over child monarchic, of husband over wife political—in the sense that political rule is by citizens over fellow citizens.[32] The qualification was that in this last case the ruler (the husband) never left office, never gave up the "trappings" of authority (*Politics* 1259b8). If we want to understand more about how this "micropolitical" arrangement was entered into by husband and wife and validated by the community, we need to turn from the private contract of the *enguē* to the public celebration of the *gamos* or "wedding."

The public character of the ancient Greek *gamos* is clear in the first description we have of the social life of the polis. In book 18 of the *Iliad* Homer describes the city at peace which Hephaistos fashioned on the new shield he made for Achilles, and in this city *gamoi* are the first event noted:

> On it he wrought in all their beauty two cities of mortal
> men. And there were marriages (*gamoi*) in one, and festivals.
> They were leading the brides along the city from their maiden
>   chambers
> under the flaring of torches, and the loud bride song was arising.
>   (490–93 Lattimore)

One indication of the importance in Athens of this celebration—carried out by family, friends, and kin but clearly meant to engage the attention of the community as a whole—is the frequency with which scenes from the *gamos* appear on Athenian painted pottery (especially pots made either for feminine use or for the *gamos* itself).[33] In fact vase paintings are a prime source for the reconstruction of the Athenian *gamos* celebration, for which no complete literary description survives. Using the illustrations on vases plus numerous but scattered bits of literary evidence, it is possible to reconstruct the main elements of the *gamos*—if not always their sequence.[34] There were first of all sacrifices to the gods, including Zeus Teleios and Hera Teleia, the divine models and protectors of the new married state. Although in Homer, as Walter Burkert has noted, Hera seems "more a model of jealousy and marital strife than of connubial affection,"[35] her role in cult as Teleia and as Zugia (the "Yoker")[36] was precisely that of goddess of marriage, who with Zeus Teleios oversaw the initiation of bride and groom into their new married state or *telos*.[37] There were also sacrifices to Artemis and to Peitho, whose role presumably would have been to emphasize the relation of persuasion (rather than force) that obtained between husband and wife.[38] The bride and groom were each given nuptial baths and were dressed in the finest of clothes, and all gathered for a bridal dinner at (it seems) the house of the bride. After feasting together, at the rising of the evening star[39] the groom drove the bride off to her new home, amid a torch-lit parade of singing and dancing friends and relations. The couple spent the night together (the initiation of their "living together") and awoke to, it seems, another full day of feasting and celebration.

There was one additional element of the *gamos* which I have not yet mentioned, and that is the *anakaluptēria* or "unveiling." This seems to me to be the central moment of the *gamos*—conceptually if not temporally (there is dispute over just when it actually occurred).[40] The *anakaluptēria* denoted the moment when the bride lifted her veil, directly confronting and accepting her husband-to-be. At this time there was also an exchange of gifts, accordingly called *anakaluptēria*, "things given at the time of, or to celebrate, the unveiling of the bride." Alternatively, it seems, these gifts were called *prosphthenktēria* or *optēria*, from the verbs *prosphthengomai*, "address" or "salute," and *opteuō*, "see."[41] What is striking is that this ceremony directly involved the bride and groom together in a mutual exchange of glance, gifts, and perhaps words. By chance, there survives a description of one *anakaluptēria* which allows us to imagine what the silent images on vases might be saying.

One of the fragments of the writings of the sixth-century B.C.E. philosopher, or perhaps philosophical mythographer, Pherecydes of Syros is a description of the first *anakaluptēria* at which Chthonie or Ge (Earth) became the wife of Zas (Zeus).

His [Zas'] halls they make for him, many and vast. And when they had accomplished all these, and the furniture and manservants and maidservants and everything else necessary, when everything was ready, they hold the wedding (*gamos*). And on the third day of the wedding Zas makes a great and fair cloth and on it he decorates Ge and Ogenos and the halls of Ogenos. . . . "for wishing [*or some such word*] marriages to be yours, I honor you with this. Hail to you, and be my consort (σὺ δέ μοι χαῖρε καὶ σύνισθι)." And this they say was the first Anakalupteria: from this the custom arose both for gods and men. And she replies, receiving from him the cloth . . .[42]

And then, unfortunately, the fragment breaks off, without telling us just what she did say.

While Pherecydes is neither a classical nor an Athenian author, the *anakaluptēria* was part of the Athenian celebration,[43] and Pherecydes' fragment can help us understand the meaning of this ritual moment within the Athenian *gamos*. I suggest that the direct exchange of glance and perhaps words which accompanied the unveiling (the most likely interpretation of Pherecydes, although he does not mention the act of unveiling itself) was a symbolic indication of mutual consent to marriage. I emphasize "symbolic" here, for the bride in particular probably had little voice in the actual making of the decision; but it seems that, within the context of the *gamos* celebration, the gesture of *anakalupsis* symbolized the bride's giving herself to her husband.[44] Again, this has nothing to do with *actual* consent. The bride may or may not have been willing, just as husband and wife may or may not have loved one another. My concern is with social form, not affective reality.

Much later, Roman jurists recognized formal consent as a necessary element of marriage: *nuptias enim non concubitus sed consensus facit* (*Digest* 50.17, Ulpian). Here again, however, it should be emphasized that the woman's consent hardly guaranteed her emotional state of mind—a woman's consent was generally taken as given if she did not audibly or visibly refuse and as proper if her potential husband was not "morally unworthy or shameful" (*Digest* 23.1.12).[45] It has been said that Athenian marriage differed from Roman marriage on just this point; according to Sealey, "Athenian law did not ground marriage in the consent of the man and the woman, for it did not pay attention to the wishes of the woman."[46] This may indeed be true of Athenian law and the Athenian *enguē* (see above), but not necessarily of Athenian marital customs—*nomoi* in their larger sense.[47] Here again, emphasis on the *enguē*, which has seemed the only candidate for a formal and legal marriage act, has skewed perception of the nature of Athenian marriage. But Athenian marriage was more than the *enguē*—it was also the *gamos*, with resulting cohabitation within a common household (*sunoikein*) and eventual production of children (*paidopoiein*), as well. Although the *anakaluptēria* has left little trace in Athenian literary sources,[48] it can be seen as a ritual act within the *gamos* celebration signifying or symbolizing the mutual consent and intent of bride and groom, that is, their intent or determination to be husband and wife, or what the Roman jurists termed *affectio maritalis*, "marital intent."[49]

Athens, however, had no systematic corpus of civil law, no cadre of jurists to define just what marriage was. So we seem to have been left with the choice between taking the *enguē* as marriage or, in the absence of juristic definition, viewing Athenian marriage as a vague and ambiguous relationship, because Athenian marriage terminology (apart from *enguē*) seems vague and ambiguous. We hear, for example, that it is difficult to determine what constituted a "valid marriage,"[50] that "there were no formal requirements or practices to mark a difference between validly married couples and those living together on a permanent basis but without the possibility of transmitting citizen privileges to their offspring,"[51] and even that "Greek thought was not much concerned to distinguish between valid and invalid unions."[52] It is often noted, for example, that *gunē* ("woman") and *alochos* ("bedmate") are used to denote the wife but do not seem properly to describe her. *Alochos*, for instance, could be used of a concubine as well as a wife.[53] Even *damar*, the term usually thought to come closest to our (Anglo-Saxon) "wedded wife," appears in Sophocles' *Trachiniai* in reference to both the captured "war bride" Iole and Herakles' "wife" Deianeira, forcing one translator to render the word in both occurrences as "consort."[54] Similarly, Herakles in the same play is said to have "married" (*egēme*), or rather "mated with," many women (460). Without context, the noun *gamos*, like the verb *gamein*, has the essential meaning of sexual union of man and woman. In addition to the communally celebrated *gamoi* which Hephaistos fashioned on Achilles' shield, there were *methēmerinoi gamoi* (*gamoi* by day, or prostitution; Demosthenes 18.129), *Panos gamoi* ("marriages of Pan," or rape; Euripides *Helen* 190), or *hieroi gamoi* (ritual marriages, such as the *gamos* of the wife of the Athenian basileus and Dionysos).[55]

Herakles' noncivilized behavior, however, may be just Sophocles' point in the *Trachiniai*; Herakles is a hero who has violated ordinary human social conventions, most dramatically those of marriage (cf. Plato *Laws* 840e). It is against this violation that Deianeira, otherwise willing to tolerate Herakles' wanderings, objects when she says that in taking in Iole she has herself taken in not a girl (*korē*) but a "yoke-mate" (*ezeugmenē*) with whom she now must share her bed (536–40). Thus Sophocles' striking use of marriage terminology in reference to Deianeira and Iole may in fact show that despite the relative sexual freedom of Greek men (and especially Herakles), marriage was quite clearly and unambiguously understood in Athens to be properly a singular relation which linked (or yoked) two people, one husband and one wife.[56] The relation was not symmetrical, nor did it have the same impact on its two parties, male and female,[57] but it was nonetheless a recognized and, in the Athenian context, highly valued relationship, whose violation could bring on even Herakles' destruction. (Although Herakles eventually escapes both the human world and human mortality, entering Olympos as a god, Sophocles' play emphasizes rather the violence that the mortal Herakles precipitates within his human family.)

Furthermore, the lack of specificity in such words as *alochos* or similarly *akoitis* and, above all, *gunē*, need not necessarily imply an inability to recognize or distinguish a wife from a concubine or prostitute. Either the context or the addition of an adjective such as *kouridiē*—as in Agamemnon's preference for the daughter of Khryses over his *kouridiē alochos*, Klytemnestra (*Iliad* 1.114) or Herodotus' reference to *kouridiai gunaikes* in distinction to concubines (1.135, 6.138)[58]—can indicate the more precise status of the "bedmate." On this point the story of Briseis, although Homeric, is instructive. In book 9 of the *Iliad* Achilles refers to Briseis simply as his *alochos* (9.336). Later, in book 19, Briseis mourns Patroklos, in particular because he had promised to take her back to Phthia and make her Achilles' *kouridiē alochos* by celebrating the *gamos* among the Myrmidons (19.297–99). Marriage was thus fluid to the extent that Briseis could be "married" first by the spear and then with public feasting, but the use of *alochos* in both instances hardly proves that her status before and after the *gamos* in Phthia would have been indistinguishable. Rather, because Briseis was formerly a free and elite woman who became a slave when her city was captured and her family slaughtered by Achilles, the nature of her relationship to Achilles was inherently ambiguous. Patroklos, standing in for her dead parents, seems to have promised to treat her as the free woman she once was, and as a worthy spouse for Achilles.

In the nonheroic world of classical Athens the concubine or *pallakē* was also generally of slave or foreign origin, but her status was less fluid. No Patroklos could step in and give her (legally) as *kouridiē alochos* to an Athenian man. Even if free, she could not bear legitimate, citizen offspring to an Athenian man; she could not legally "live together with" an Athenian man.[59] And on the other side of the fence, that well-protected status distinction between citizen and noncitizen would discourage—although it did not prohibit—Athenians from taking an Athenian woman as a concubine. The Athenian wife brought her dowry into the joint household estate and bore children who would inherit that estate, as well as citizenship. The concubine brought nothing, and her children took nothing.[60] To give or take an Athenian woman as a concubine was thus to strip her and her children of both property and citizenship.[61]

Finally (in regard to terminology), that the Greeks most often used (and still use) the word for "woman" to indicate a "wife" is perhaps not so remarkable. It may in fact be English that is remarkable in using the special terms "husband and wife"—for which neither German nor Greek nor, until recently, French has any parallel. What is more significant is that *gunē* in some contexts could *only* mean wife, as in Isaeus 6, where the speaker insists on referring to the prostitute Alke as *hē anthrōpos* (e.g., 20, 21, 38), which might then be translated "that person." The proper social role of a mature woman was as a wife, thus making the terms interchangeable. The lack of what seems to us clear husband and wife "labels" does not indicate the lack of a clear idea of what marriage was or that marriage itself was without significance.

I return at last to the verb *sunoikein* as used by Herodotus in the passage quoted at the beginning of this essay. How might a word which literally means "to cohabit" come to denote a socially recognized marriage? As noted earlier, there were laws in Athens (by at least the mid-fourth century) prohibiting an Athenian man or woman from "living together" (*sunoikein*) with an alien woman or man, with stiff penalties for those who failed to comply—the guilty alien was sold into slavery ([Demosthenes]

59.16, 52).[62] Yet it is clear that neither prostitution nor concubinage was illegal in Athens. *Sunoikein* ought therefore to have been a legally as well as socially identifiable relationship—but in the absence of marriage licenses or parish records, how was it recognized and distinguished from concubinage, whether of the durable or less durable variety? Apollodorus, the speaker who cites these laws, in a speech prosecuting a woman named Neaira for usurping Athenian citizenship by the act of "living with" an Athenian, attempts an explanation: "for this is what *to sunoikein* is—when someone produces children (*paidopoiētai*) and introduces sons to phratry and deme and bestows daughters (*thugateras ekdidōi*) to husbands" (122).[63] Although some would again despair and see this as simply a de facto rather than de jure description, it does succeed in defining a relationship between a man and woman which has the primary goal of producing children and maintaining the identity of the *oikos* unit (the household) within the social and political community.

Similarly, in the *Oikonomikos* Xenophon begins his lecture to his wife on "How to Run a Household" by asking her why she supposes her parents had given her in marriage and why he, Xenophon, had taken her. It was, he answers, in order that they both would have the best possible partner in the household and in (the production of) children (*koinōnon beltiston oikou te kai teknōn*, 7.11). (Because they at this point have no children, Xenophon concentrates on what they do have already in common, the *oikos*, 7.13.)[64] This does not provide the kind of legal criterion some have been looking for, and it certainly does not define a legal moment or event; rather it describes something that occurs over time and is demonstrated to the community by appropriate behavior. I submit that it describes the substance of Athenian marriage.

From this point of view a recent summary of Roman marriage—"Roman marriage was made by two consenting parties who intended to be husband and wife"[65]—may not be completely inapplicable to Athenian marriage as well. The point is once again not that Roman and Greek marriages were essentially similar—although there are points of similarity, the institution of *manus* clearly distinguishes (early) Roman from Greek marriage—but that the lack of a comprehensive legal and juristic system in Athens meant that a general description of marriage, which was attempted by Roman jurists, was simply outside the scope of Athenian law. Athenian marriage law, as we know it, was concerned first with the identification of legitimate heirs, and second with restricting membership in Athenian families (or *oikoi*) to Athenians. Validation and recognition of the marriage itself was left to social and religious customs and rituals, of which, unfortunately, we have only fragmentary knowledge.[66] If it is true that Athenian descriptions of marriage seem to rely on the observed behavior and presumed intent over time of would-be husband and wife (and that such reliance could mean trouble when an inheritance or citizenship dispute called a marriage into question),[67] it is also true that when Roman jurists came to define the legal state of marriage, such behavior and intent were the basis of that definition. According to Modestinus, marriage "is the *coniunctio*, the joining together of a man and woman and the sharing of their entire life, the joint participation in rights human and divine."[68] As was the case for the Greek "yoking together" of husband and wife, no specific legal ceremony was necessary—or sufficient.

In conclusion I suggest that Athenian marriage be understood not as a simple legal event but as a composite process leading to or having as its goal the establishment of a new household or *oikos*, with the eventual production of children, introduction of children into appropriate civic and religious groups, marriage of children—and eventually the replacement of parents by children in new *oikoi* of their own which will continue or renew the life of the parents' *oikos*. The actions (and intentions) of *enguan*, *gamein*, and *sunoikein*, as well as *telein* (ritual "fulfillment") and *paidopoiein* ("production of children") are all part of the process, but not equally comprehended in Athenian law. Each could at times be taken to stand for the marriage as a whole, as a married woman might be called a *gunē enguētē* or *gametē*, as well as simply *alochos* or *akoitis*, that is, "bedmate," but any part or aspect should not be taken to *be* the whole. Likewise, omission of one element does not mean that there was no marriage. These are not the parts of a formal legal sequence but rather a cluster of ideas and actions associated with setting up a household. Marriage was nameless, I suggest, because there was no one term which encompassed its many aspects, just as there was no one legal rule sufficient to define it. Monogamy, in the sense of Herodotus' *sunoikei miē gunaiki*, which might now be translated "set up an *oikos* with one woman," was a central value and feature of Athenian society. As the *oikos* was the primary social and economic unit of Athenian society,[69] so marriage, the institution which created the central partnership of the *oikos* (and *oikeiotēs*) was also primary.

"Marriage," argued Aeschylus' Apollo at the opening of the *Eumenides* (using the marriage bed to represent the marriage institution),[70] is both "bigger than oaths" and "guarded by the right of nature" (217–22 Lattimore). By the end of the play (and trilogy), with Athena's vote for Orestes and her persuasion (and transformation) of the Furies, marriage has won a place among those "most dear" (*philtaton*, 608) familial bonds protected by the Furies. Instead of afflicting Athens with a destructive (*aphullos, ateknos*, 815) blight, the Furies accept Athena's offer of an honored place from which they will receive sacrifices *pro paidōn kai gamēliou telous*—in behalf of children and the *telos* ("fulfillment" or "rite") of marriage (835). In the civic, familial, and sexual reconciliation that marks the end of the *Oresteia* female power and authority is not so much appropriated by the male as subordinated with the male to the "yoke" of marriage and to the fostering of the *oikos*.[71] Outside the theater of Dionysos as well, Athenian marriage should not be considered simply as a transfer or "exchange" of women but as the multifaceted process through which a man and a woman set up a common household (*sunoikein*), whose purpose was a productive and reproductive *koinōnia*.

Notes

This essay was begun during a National Endowment for the Humanities summer seminar, "The Family in Classical and Hellenistic Greece," directed by Sarah B. Pomeroy, and finished at the Center for Hellenic Studies. I am grateful to the Endowment and the Center for their support, and to Richard Patterson, Sarah B. Pomeroy, Zeph Stewart, Herman Schibli, Susan Cole, Tom Gallant, David Halperin, Phyllis Culham, Adele Scafuro, Genevieve Edwards, and Rush Rehm for their criticism and comments. I cannot guarantee that I have satisfied all of the above critics in this short essay.

1. There is probably an implicit contrast here with the customs of the Persians described in book 1: γαμέουσι δὲ ἕκαστος αὐτῶν πολλὰς μὲν κουριδίας γυναῖκας, πολλῷ δ' ἔτι πλεῦνας παλλακὰς κτῶνται, "Each of them possesses many *kouridias gunaikas*, and still many more concubines" (135). For the significance of *kouridiē* see below, note 53. In beginning with this passage from Herodotus, I begin from the same point of reference as does R. Sealey in "On Lawful Concubinage in Athens," *Classical Antiquity* 3 (1984): 111–33. However, as will be seen, my interest and argument are quite different. For additional discussion of the issues raised by Sealey see my "Those Athenian Bastards," *Classical Antiquity* 9 (1990): 40–73.

2. So the laws on *sunoikein* in [Demosthenes] 59.16 and 52 are generally under-

stood. That the clause Ἐὰν δὲ ξένος ἀστῇ συνοικῇ τέχνῃ ἢ μηχανῇ ᾑτινιοῦν, "if a *xenos* 'lives together' with a citizen by any means or method," emphasizes deceit or misrepresentation of status and does not imply that the taking of a foreign wife "openly" was legal, but rather that deceit was expected in such circumstances. Note also that the use of *sunoikein* in the law and in the text of the speech establishes that this term does not denote simple cohabitation, for cohabitation with a non-Athenian, slave or free, was not at any time prohibited in Athens. Stephanos was charged not with keeping Neaira as a concubine but with unlawful marital cohabitation. For further comment on *sunoikein* see below.

3. The bibliography for Greek (and Athenian) marriage is long and, up until the middle of this century, predominantly in German. A. H. R. Harrison, *The Law of Athens*, vol. 1, *The Family and Property* (Oxford: Clarendon Press, 1968), 1–60, contains a thorough discussion with full references to earlier literature, of which the most influential today are W. Erdmann, *Die Ehe im alten Griechenland* (Munich: C. H. Beck, 1934), and H. J. Wolff, "Marriage Law and Family Organization in Ancient Athens," *Traditio* 2 (1944): 44–95. Of discussions published since Harrison, J.-P. Vernant, "Marriage," in *Myth and Society in Ancient Greece* (Atlantic Highlands, N.J.: Humanities Press, 1980), 45–70, and J. Redfield, "Notes on the Greek Wedding," *Arethusa* 15 (1982): 181–201 are particularly relevant to this paper. E. Craik, "Marriage in Ancient Greece," in *Marriage and Property*, ed. E. Craik (Aberdeen: University of Aberdeen Press, 1984), reviews the evidence for ancient Greek attitudes towards marriage.

4. An emphasis on the process of marriage is current practice among historians of the early modern family. See, for example, Christiane Klapisch-Zuber, *Women, Family and Ritual in Rennaisance Italy* (Chicago: University of Chicago Press, 1985), 178–212; cf. R. M. Smith, "Marriage Processes in the English Past," in *The World We Have Gained* (Oxford: Basil Blackwell, 1986), 43–99, who, using process in a somewhat different way than suggested here, emphasizes the social and demographic significance of marital or "cohabitational" habits rather than the moment or timing of the legal sanction of marital union. The latter has traditionally been the focus of modern discussion of ancient Greek marriage.

5. *Politics* 1253b9–10.

6. Much of the earlier discussion of Athenian marriage uses the term *enguēsis* rather than *enguē*, even though the latter is the regular term used by Attic authors and the former is used only once (Isaeus 3.53). This was apparently done in order to distinguish the marital from the surety transaction: see, for example, J. H. Lipsius, *Das Attische Recht und Rechtsverfahren* (Leipzig: O. R. Reisland, 1912), 468 n. 2; O. Schulthess, *RE* 19.2 (1938): col. 2042; Erdmann, *Die Ehe im alten Griechenland*, 225 n. 2. However, as the Athenians did not make this verbal distinction, it seems unnecessary and perhaps misleading for us to do so. Cf. Wolff, "Marriage Law," 44, n. 14.

7. For a discussion of the meaning and significance of the *enguē* see L. Gernet, "Hypothèses sur le contrat primitif en Grèce," *REG* 30 (1917): 249–93, 363–83. The issues are clearly presented by W. Wyse in *The Speeches of Isaeus* (Cambridge: Cambridge University Press, 1904), 289–93.

8. Wolff, "Marriage Law," 52. This is also the view of LSJ s.v. ἐγγυάω.

9. Gernet, "Hypothèses sur le contrat primitif."

10. On the meaning and significance of *ekdosis* and *ekdidonai* see Wolff, "Marriage Law," 46–49, who nonetheless holds to the meaning of *enguan* quoted above in the text. Cf. the comments of Harrison, *Law of Athens*, 1:6.

11. Wolff, "Marriage Law," 52. For the use of the middle see, for example, Herodotus 6.130 (which I quote just below in the text near notes 15–17) and Isaeus 3.70: ὁ ἀδελφιδοῦς ὑμῶν ἠγγυᾶτο τὴν μητέρα. For the passive use for the woman: Isaeus 6.14, τὴν Καλλίππην . . . ἐγγυηθεῖσαν κατὰ νόμον, and 8.29, δὶς ἐκδοθεῖσαν, δὶς ἐγγυηθεῖσαν. See Wyse, *Speeches of Isaeus*, 289, for further examples. Although LSJ cite Plato *Laws* 923d–e as an instance of the passive used in reference to the (prospective) husband (s.v. εγγυάω I.2), this is better read as the middle used without an object.

12. See Wolff, "Marriage Law," 52, and Sealey, "Lawful Concubinage," 120. The traditional expression of the *enguē* may be provided by Menander: ἐγγυῶ παίδων ἐπ᾽ ἀρότῳ γνησίων τὴν θυγατέρα (*Dyskolos* 842) and ἐγγυῶ ταύτην ἐμαυτοῦ θυγατέρα παίδων ἐπ᾽ ἀρότῳ γνησιῶν (P. Oxy. 2533, p. 300 Sandbach). Elsewhere in Menander (e.g., *Samia* 727, *Perik.* 1013–14) the father says *didōmi* instead of *enguō*. If the difference is significant, it may be because Menander's plays frequently collapse the distinction between the *enguē* and the *gamos*, as both occur together at the end of the play. (It may also be that Athenian social practice collapsed the distinction, as the two transactions are often referred to together.)

13. Gernet, "Hypothèses sur le contrat primitif." It can also be noted that Diodorus' comment on *enguē* (9.10.4), that the *sunthesis tou gamou* is called *enguē* by most Greeks, would seem to mean that the *enguē* was the arrangement or "putting together" of the marriage, at which time promises, not necessarily transfers, were made. Cf. the *impalmamento* of Rennaisance Florence, the first step in marriage negotiations between two families—after which "a father will say in his journal that he has *impalmato* his daughter" (Klapisch-Zuber, *Women, Family and Ritual*, 183).

14. Wolff, "Marriage Law," 52.

15. *Nomoi* here may be taken to mean "written laws" rather than simply "customs," particularly if it is recognized that marriage laws (for example, on heiresses) were a significant part of Solon's legislation or *nomothesia*. (See below, note 26, for the "Solonian" law on *enguē*.) In fourth-century orations the phrase *enguēsai kata nomous* or *enguētheisan kata ton nomon* (Isaeus 3.39, 6.14) would seem to indicate some kind of formal law. That the Greeks could use the same word, *nomos*, for both

statutory "law" and traditional "custom" is of course an important feature of their understanding of what law is or should be. For present purposes it is enough to say that the Athenians did recognize a distinction between *nomoi* as given by a lawgiver or voted by a community, and traditional custom—even if that distinction may sometimes be unclear to us. On the issue of marriage, for example, no one would be likely to think that the *nomos* Pisistratus violated in his relations with Megakles' daughter (Herodotus 1.61.1) was a statutory *nomos*; but those *nomoi* (by which parents are married and children are born) who appeal to Socrates in the *Crito*, 50d, might include both written rules such as formulated by Solon as well as traditional "customs." For a thorough discussion of the various uses and meanings of *nomos* see M. Ostwald, *Nomos and the Beginnings of the Athenian Democracy* (Oxford: Clarendon Press, 1969), 20–54.

16. For Herodotus' use of the pluperfect tense here, compare 6.110 (the battle of Marathon): προσγενομένης δὲ τοῦ πολεμάρχου τῆς γνώμης ἐκεκύρωτο συμβάλλειν. According to E. Abbott, *Herodotus, Books V and VI* (Oxford: Clarendon Press, 1893), 271, "the pluperfect means 'it was finally determined.' "

17. This view was developed most forcefully by E. Hruza in *Beiträge zur Geschichte des griechischen und römischen Familienrechtes* (Leipzig: Georg Bohme, 1892) and has some adherents. See Wyse, *Speeches of Isaeus*, 289–93, and Gernet "Hypothèses sur le contrat primitif," 275–76, who are not adherents, for clear summaries of the discussion.

18. On these last two points see Harrison, *Law of Athens*, 1:8 and (on the dowry) 45–60. Although the giving of a dowry was socially expected and might be very good proof that a marriage was made or intended, it did not per se contribute to the legal (as opposed to the social) standing of either marriage or wife or child. The topic is an important one, but one which I cannot address here. See note 61 below for a brief comment on the function of the dowry.

19. See also the less often cited passage in Isaeus 6 where Euktemon—in order to force his son to allow the recognition of, according to the speaker, a prostitute's sons as Euktemon's own legitimate sons (*gnēsioi*)—*enguatai* the sister of Demokrates of Aphidna (22). The point is that Euktemon thereby made arrangements to produce more heirs—but it is clear that there was no marriage and therefore no legal consequence to his action. When the son gave in, Euktemon simply "gave up the woman" (ἀπηλλάγη τῆς γυναικός, 24).

20. See, for example, Harrison, *Law of Athens*, 1:8–9, and Redfield, "The Greek Wedding," 188: "Gamos is the name, in its primary significance, not of a ceremony but of the sexual act itself—without which the marriage is not (as we say) consummated, actual. There was no legal requirement of a ceremony for gamos; the *engue is* the wedding, in the sense that no additional ceremonies are required to legitimate the children." As will be seen, Redfield's last qualifying phrase is an important one. It is, of course, somewhat odd to speak of a wedding with possibly no

bride. MacDowell's comments in *The Law in Classical Athens* (Ithaca: Cornell University Press, 1978)—"*Engye* was the giving of a woman to the prospective husband by her kyrios. . . . It was not legally necessary for the woman to be present or to consent or even to know that she was to be married" and "The legal difference between *engye* and *gamos* was, roughly, that *engye* was making a contract and *gamos* was carrying it out" (86)—seem to ride roughshod over the questions discussed in this paper. More helpful, if not definitive, is Clement of Alexandria's use of *enguēsamenos* in regard to the circumstances which exempt a man from service: if he has built a house but not lived in it, has worked a garden but not eaten its fruit, or *enguēsamenos* a woman but not "married" her (*ouk egēmen, Stromateis* 2.28.82). The formulation, however, goes back to the Old Testament (Deuteronomy 20), and the conception may be more Hebraic than Greek.

21. MacDowell, *Law in Classical Athens*, 86.

22. Thus Vernant, "Le mariage," 58: "L'engué les lie l'une à l'autre par un accord réciproque, public et solennel, scellé en présence de témoins qui peuvent s'en porter garant."

23. Harrison, *Law of Athens*, 1:18.

24. The *gamēlia* or feast presented to the husband's phratry on the occasion of the *gamos* is cited as evidence that a marriage took place in, e.g., Demosthenes 57.43, 69. The speaker of Isaeus 8 cites both the *gamēlia* and the (apparently more private) wedding dinner hosted by the groom (his father) for family and close friends (18, 20). A fragment of a speech by Lysias, "On the Anakalupteria," argues (apparently) that if gifts called *anakaluptēria* (see discussion below near note 42) were given, the woman was indeed *gamoumenē* (fragment 7, Thalheim) and her child *gnēsios*. The phrase *gunē gametē* is used in some versions of the oath with which a father introduced his son to his phratry and affirmed that son's legitimacy (e.g., Isaeus 12.10; *IG* II:1237.111). Although *gamos* by itself did not necessarily imply a legally or socially recognized marriage (see below), the adjective *gametē* and the participle *gamoumenē* do seem to imply just that. I do not follow Sealey, "Lawful Concubinage," 122, in seeing a significant distinction between the terms *enguētē* and *gametē* in these contexts.

25. As implied by Sealey, "Lawful Concubinage," 122.

26. For a discussion of this law as Solonian see J. Modrzejewski, "La structure juridique du mariage grec," *Scritti in onore di Orsolina Montevecchi* (Bologna: Editrice Bologna, 1981), 231–68, esp. 243–47. Others are less confident of Solonian authorship; for example, Harrison, *Law of Athens*, 1:5, considers the law "fairly early."

27. This point was recognized by Wolff, "Marriage Law," 75, but not by Sealey, "Lawful Concubinage," 119–20.

28. See discussion above and note 12, with comment on substitution of *didōmi* for *enguō*. As far as I know, this specific formula appears only in Menander, although the idea of woman as a field to be cultivated is certainly traditional. See,

e.g., Sophocles *Antigone* 569, *Trachiniai* 32–33, *Oedipous Tyrannos* 1256, 1485, 1497. For an interpretation of this metaphor along psychoanalytic lines see P. duBois, *Sowing the Body* (Chicago: University of Chicago Press, 1988), with the review of H. King, *LCM* 14, no.4 (1989): 63–64; and for the persistence of this idea in modern Mediterranean societies, Carol Delaney, "Seeds of Honor, Fields of Shame," in *Honor and Shame and the Unity of the Mediterranean*, ed. D. Gillmore, American Anthropological Association, Special Publication 22 (Washington, D.C.: American Anthropological Association, 1987), 35–48.

29. Sealey, "Lawful Concubinage," 121.

30. On the rules of intestate inheritance and the position of the wife see Harrison, *Law of Athens*, 1:142–49, and D. Schaps, *The Economic Rights of Woman in Ancient Greece* (Edinburgh: University of Edinburgh Press, 1979), 20–24. The essentially bilateral (and nonagnatic) character of the devolution of property in Athens is worth emphasizing, as its significance is often overlooked or underappreciated—e.g., J. Gould, "Law, Custom and Myth: Aspects of the Social Position of Women in Classical Athens," *JHS* 100 (1980): 44 n. 41 notwithstanding. For a recent discussion of the nature of ownership in Athens with particular attention to the relationship between private *oikos* and public *polis*, see L. Foxhall, "Household, Gender and Property in Classical Athens," *CQ* 39 (1989): 22–44.

Although a wife was not her husband's heir, her children might inherit through both the paternal and maternal line; for example, if a mother's only brother (by the same father) had no children, she and then her children were her brother's intestate heirs. This is in contrast to the way in which public and political identity was passed on through the father's line. There is potential conflict here, for one example of which see R. Osborne on the case of Euxitheos, in *Demos: The Discovery of Classical Attika* (Cambridge: Cambridge University Press, 1985), 146–51. Cf. Foxhall, "Household, Gender and Property," 26 n. 25.

31. *Oikeios* is an inclusive, expandable term for free persons who live together in, or are associated through, an *oikos*. (Slaves who belong to the *oikos* are generally termed *oiketai* rather than *oikeioi*.) The term *oikeios* implies not so much strict kinship as common interest and "face-to-face" interaction. *Oikeioi* are those who are expected to know about and care for the affairs of the household to which they are connected; thus they are the best witnesses for important events within that *oikos* (see, e.g., Isaeus 3.19, 6.15 and 9.7). On husband-wife and parent-child as first order *oikeioi* see Herodotus 3.119; for in-laws as *oikeioi* see [Demosthenes] 59, "Against Neaira." Cf. Euphiletos' comment that after his child was born he trusted his wife completely, ἡγούμενος ταύτην οἰκειότητα μεγίστην εἶναι (Lysias 1.6–7).

32. Aristotle *Politics* 1.1259a37–b10; see also Xenophon *Oikonomikos* 3.15. In the *Nicomachean Ethics* and *Eudemian Ethics* Aristotle terms the rule of husband over wife "aristocratic" (*EE* 1241b30; *NE* 1160b33) in the course of discussing the nature of the friendship or *philia* between husband and wife.

33. R. Sutton, "The Interaction between Men and Women Portrayed on Attic Red-figure Pottery" (Ph.D. dissertation, University of North Carolina, 1981), chap. 3. Sutton notes (150) that he can find only one possible representation of the *enguē* on vases, an interesting reversal of the pattern in courtroom oratory. For further discussion of this illustration see Sutton "On the Classical Athenian Wedding: Two Red-figure Loutrophoroi in Boston," in *Daidalikon: Studies in Memory of Raymond V. Schoder, S.J.*, ed. R. Sutton (Wauconda, Ill.: Bolchazy-Carducci, 1989), 331–59.

34. See R. Hague, "Marriage Athenian Style," *Archaeology* 41, no. 3 (1988): 32–36, for one reconstruction.

35. W. Burkert, *Greek Religion*, trans. John Raffan (Oxford: Basil Blackwell, 1985), 132.

36. For this term and other aspects of Hera's role in premarital ritual see the recent discussion of R. Seaford, "The Eleventh Ode of Bacchylides: Hera, Artemis, and the Absence of Dionysos," *JHS* 108 (1988): 118–36. Seaford emphasizes the idea that the yoking of the young woman into marriage was conceived as similar to the yoking or taming of a wild animal. It is also true, as mentioned above, that the yoking of marriage was the "yoking together" of husband and wife. A wife left alone without her husband was, in Aeschylus' term, μονόζυξ (*Persians* 139). Though the iconography and ritual of Greek marriage focus on the experience of the bride and might be said to emphasize the trauma of her movement from one household to another or from childhood to adulthood (see below, note 38), the result of the *gamos* was the creation of a new *koinōnia* or partnership, under (to use Aristotle's term) one yoke.

37. For marriage as a *telos* (here "fulfillment" or "rite of passage") see, e.g., *Odyssey* 20.74, *telos thaleroio gamoio*; Aeschylus *Eumenidides* 834, *gamēliou telous*. For use of *teleō* in context of marriage see, e.g., the lines from an unmarried woman's epitaph, οὐδ ἐτέλεσσα νυμφίδιων θαλάμων εἰς ὑμέναια λέχη, *SEG* I:567; R. Lattimore, *Themes in Greek and Latin Epitaphs* (Urbana: University of Illinois Press, 1962), 192. In an inscription from Hellenistic Cos married women are referred to as *teleumenai, GDI* 3721. Cf. Erdmann, *Die Ehe im alten Griechenland*, 136 n. 3. On the initiatory character of the Greek wedding see especially V. Magnien, "Le mariage chez les grecs anciens: l'initiation nuptiale," *AC* 5 (1936): 115–38, and "Le mariage chez les grecs," *Annuaire de l'Institut de Philologie et d'Histoire Orientales et Slaves* 4 (1936): 305–20.

38. On Artemis and Hera as "complementary goddesses of marriage" see Seaford, "Eleventh Ode of Bacchylides," 120 and passim. The reluctance of the bride to leave her natal home is an enduring feature of Greek marriage traditions and rituals, as seen most starkly perhaps in the Spartan "seizure" (*harpagē*) of the bride (Plutarch *Lykourgos* 15.3; see the comments of Claude Mossé in this volume), but most movingly in ancient and modern Greek marriage "laments": see esp. M. Alexiou, *The Ritual Lament in Greek Tradition* (Cambridge: Cambridge University

Press, 1974), 120–22, and L. Danforth, *The Death Rituals of Rural Greece* (Princeton: Princeton University Press, 1982), 74–90. For further comment on the willingness or "consent" of the bride and on the metaphor of "marriage to death" see discussion below and note 45. These ritual motives, it seems to me, are an indication of the profound social significance of kinship (natal and marital) and of marriage, the process by which a woman, in leaving one kin group and being incorporated into another, joined together the two.

39. Hague, "Marriage Athenian Style," 34.

40. For a discussion of the *anakaluptēria* (with full reference to earlier scholarship) in relation to one vase painting (Beazley, *ARV* 1017.44) see J. Oakley, "The Anakalupteria," *AA* 8 (1982): 113–18. For a useful compilation of sources see R. Hague, *Hymenaios: The Ancient Greek Wedding and Its Songs* (forthcoming), appendix 2, "The Anakalypteria." Hague argues that the *anakaluptēria* took place at the groom's house "after the bride and groom had spent the night together" (26). Although there are real problems in reconciling the sources on this point, I prefer to connect the unveiling with the prenuptial feast. There may, of course, have been variation in marriage practices within Greece and even within classical Athens. For discussion of other wedding scenes depicting or evoking the moment of the *anakaluptēria* see Sutton, *Interaction*, 160–215. See also his "On the Athenian Wedding" for more argument on the *anakaluptēria* in reference to Beazley, *ARV* 1017.44.

41. Pollux 3.36; cf. LSJ s.v. προσφθέγγομαι.

42. G. S. Kirk, J. E. Raven, and M. Schofield, *The Presocratic Philosophers*, 2d ed. (Cambridge: Cambridge University Press, 1983), 61. The fragment is from a third-century C.E. papyrus; the translation includes some restoration. For discussion see H. Schibli, *Pherekydes of Syros* (Oxford: Oxford University Press, forthcoming), chap. 3.

43. See note 40. Note also the title of the speech by Lysias cited in note 24.

44. It should be noted that this gesture may have a different significance in other contexts; according to M. Mayo, "The Gesture of 'Anakalypsis,'" *AJA* (1973): Abstracts, p. 220, the gesture is used in scenes illustrating "rape or sexual attraction," where "it reveals the relationship between the male and female figures." As far as I know, this article has not been published in full.

45. On the role of consent in Roman marriage see S. Treggiari, "Consent to Roman Marriage: Some Aspects of Law and Reality," *EMG* 26, n.s. 1 (1982): 34–44, with references. It is true that one can see such "consent" as similar to that of the sacrificial animal taken to the altar (see, e.g., Burkert, *Greek Religion*, 56). Ritual in general can be understood as expression of consent to the social and natural order. For the motif of "marriage as sacrifice" or "marriage to death" see, most recently, R. A. S. Seaford, "The Tragic Wedding," *JHS* 107 (1987): 106–30; also H. Foley, "Marriage and Sacrifice in Euripides' *Iphigeneia in Aulis*," *Arethusa* 15 (1982): 159–80, and I. Jenkins, "Is There Life after Marriage?" *Bulletin of the Institute of Classical*

Studies 30 (1983): 137–46. The point to be emphasized here is not so much the identity of marriage and death (cf. Jenkins's answer to his question on p. 146) as the comparable significance and structure of the two "rites of passage." For further comment on this theme in modern Greece see Danforth, *Death Rituals*. One of his examples is a lament over the death of a young man: "Don't tell them that I am dead. Just tell them that I have married and taken a good wife. I have taken the tombstone as my mother-in-law, the black earth as my wife, and I have the little pebbles as brothers- and sisters-in-law" (81).

46. Sealey, "Lawful Concubinage," 132. Cf. the comments of MacDowell, *Law in Classical Athens*.

47. On *nomos* as both law and custom see above, note 15.

48. See note 24, above, for Lysias' argument that if *anakaluptēria* (gifts) have been given, the woman is definitely *gamoumenē*.

49. S. Treggiari, "Concubinae," *PBSR* 49 (1981): 59–81, esp. 61; J. Gardner, "Marriage," in *Women in Roman Law and Society* (Bloomington: University of Indiana Press, 1986), 45–50. I am using Roman terms and definitions here simply to provide a suggestion of what may have been the significance of traditional rituals and gestures within the Athenian *gamos*. Given that marriage is distinguished from rape by reference to the willingness or unwillingness of the "bride" and that Athenians did distinguish between the two, it seems reasonable to argue for a ritual moment of "consent" within the *gamos*. It might be noted that as the "willingness" of the bride was formal and not necessarily actual, so also was the "unwillingness" of the victim of rape/abduction. In the context of a traditional society such as classical Athens, abduction may have functioned as an alternative to a parentally and socially approved marriage. See the abduction observed by Polemo (*de Physiognomonia Liber* 69) and discussed by J. Winkler, *The Constraints of Desire* (New York and London: Routledge & Kegan Paul, 1990), 71–72.

50. Harrison, *Law of Athens*, 1:1.

51. D. Konstan, "Between Courtesan and Wife," *Phoenix* 41 (1987): 122–39, esp. 127.

52. Sealey, "Lawful Concubinage," 132.

53. Cf. Vernant, "Le mariage," 65–66. *Kouridiē alochos* (*Iliad* 1.114, 19.298) apparently meant something like "virgin bride" and so was usually used of what we would call a man's wife in distinction to a prostitute or concubine (cf. Herodotus 6.138). The husband was called by extension *kouridios posis* (*Iliad* 5.514).

54. *Trachiniai* 406, 428. See the translation of Michael Jameson, *Sophocles II* (Chicago: University of Chicago Press, 1959).

55. Redfield, "The Greek Wedding," 188. On "panic" marriage Redfield cites P. Borgeaud, *Recherches sur le dieu Pan* (Rome: Institut Suisse de Rome, 1979), 115–35. On *hieros gamos* see Burkert, *Greek Religion*, 108–9. Redfield claims (188) that "civil marriage" is a *hieros gamos* on the basis of, it seems, two occurrences of the term in

Plato (*Republic* 5.458e and *Laws* 8.841b). But Plato's views on marriage do not reflect ordinary usage on this point: he was trying to change ordinary marital practices in his ideal cities and to create a system in which all marriages would in fact be arranged and carried out in official ritual settings.

56. This is made specific in the marriage contract from Hellenistic Egypt (*P. Tebtunis* I:104) in which the husband, Philiskos, agrees not to "bring home for himself another wife (*gunē*) in addition to Apollonia nor to maintain a female concubine nor a little boyfriend nor to beget children by another woman while Apollonia is alive"; trans. with discussion by Sarah B. Pomeroy in *Women in Hellenistic Egypt* (New York: Schocken Books, 1984; paperback reprint, Wayne State University Press, 1990), 87–98). In this contract between two "Persians of the Epigone" (a "pseudo-ethnic" according to Pomeroy, 87) nothing is taken for granted. Although marriage contracts were a long-established Egyptian tradition—see the discussion of K. Hopkins, "Brother-Sister Marriage in Ancient Egypt," *Comparative Studies in History and Society* 22 (1980): 303–54—I think these particular "moral requirements" can be taken as reflecting traditional Greek norms now in need of specific enunciation at a time when traditional means of enforcing those norms, that is, family and community pressure, were lacking.

The Athenian law cited by Diogenes Laertius (2.26) allowing an Athenian man to marry one Athenian woman and have children by another (γαμεῖν μὲν ἀστὴν μιάν, παιδοποιεῖσθαι δὲ καὶ ἐξ ἑτέρας) does not in any way disprove the statement that the Athenians understood marriage to be a "singular" arrangement. First, the law (if genuine) was apparently an emergency measure prompted by the manpower losses of the Peloponnesian War, and second, the law does not actually legalize "bigamy." (See my brief discussion in *Pericles' Citizenship Law of 451/0* [New York: 1981], 142–43.) The law makes a significant distinction between *gamein* and *paidopoiein*, terms which usually went together to describe the married state, implying that in the straitened circumstances of the last years of the war an Athenian could produce legitimate (and thus citizen) children with an Athenian woman other than his wife. For discussion of the notion that the Athenians recognized something called "lawful concubinage" see my forthcoming article "Those Athenian Bastards," and below, note 61.

57. On the asymmetry of the marital relationship note Aristotle's discussion of friendship between husband and wife (above, note 32). On the different significance of marriage for husband and wife compare J. du Boulay's comment, *Portrait of a Greek Mountain Village* (Oxford: Clarendon Press, 1974), 121: "Thus, socially as well as symbolically, a man is the vital validating factor of a woman's life, whereas for a man a woman is merely the necessary condition to the creation of a particular situation. For a man, the married state is important—it may be said that it is as important for a man as for a woman—but it is not important in the same way."

58. See note 53. Attic writers, however, apparently preferred other ways of

denoting a wife. *Alochos* is used primarily by the dramatists (especially Euripides), sometimes with such qualifying adjectives as *suzeuxos* or *philē* (Euripides *Alcestis* 166, 599); Aristophanes (*Frogs* 1050, Aeschylus is speaking) refers to *gennaias alochous*.

59. See the law cited in note 2; and below.

60. For a discussion of the status of bastards in Athens see my "Those Athenian Bastards."

61. I have discussed the problem of the "citizenship" of Athenian women in "Hai Attikai: The Other Athenians," *Helios* 13 (1986): 49–67. Whether or not we choose to call them citizens, Athenian women were clearly part of the privileged "insider" community of the Athenian polis. When Sealey argues ("Lawful Concubinage," 117) that "many Athenians were very poor" and so gave their daughters as concubines without dowries rather than by *enguē* with a dowry, he misrepresents the significance of the dowry and of the relationship between the dowry and the *enguē*. The dowry was the daughter's share of her family estate and contribution to the new joint conjugal estate created by her marriage and inherited by the children of that marriage. If her family had nothing, she could bring nothing; but we should not suppose that dowries were given only by the rich. And finally, if a man gave his daughter as a concubine to another Athenian, he would have thereby jeopardized the citizen status of her children and his own grandchildren. Citizenship may arguably have been of slight importance to some at the lower edges of Athenian society, but nonetheless it was not a privilege to be dispensed with casually.

62. See note 2 above and related discussion in text.

63. Cf. Harrison, *Law of Athens*, 1:2: "there is some doubt as to how much weight should be put on this passage." He does not, however, enlarge upon the source of this doubt. A preliminary survey of the orators' use of *sunoikein* seems to indicate that Apollodorus is right on the mark in his "definition."

64. On the character of Xenophon's advice see Sheila Murnaghan, "How a Woman Can Be More Like a Man: The Dialogue between Ischomachus and His Wife in Xenophon's Oeconomicus," *Helios* 15 (1988): 9–18. Certainly, ignoring childbirth and child-rearing will contribute to making the woman "more like a man."

65. Treggiari, "Concubinae," 61.

66. Cf. Robert Garland's prefatory comments on the sources for the study and interpretation of Greek attitudes towards death, in *The Greek Way of Death* (Ithaca: Cornell University Press, 1985), x–xi.

67. E.g., in Demosthenes 39, 40, "Against Boiotos," or Isaeus 3, "On the Estate of Pyrrhos."

68. *Digest* 23.2. For discussion of the later history of this and other Roman definitions of marriage in medieval (Roman and canon) law see C. Donahue, "The

Case of the Man Who Fell into the Tiber: The Roman Law of Marriage at the Time of the Glossators," *American Journal of Legal History* 22 (1978): 1–53.

69. On this point see L. Foxhall, "Household, Gender and Property."

70. The use of the marriage bed (*eunē* or *lechos*) to represent marriage itself is common poetic usage; the metaphor is particularly powerful in *Odyssey* 23 (181–204), where the marriage bed of Odysseus and Penelope is essential to their happy reunion—if not quite the way envisioned by Vernant ("Marriage," 66), who changes the order of events at the end of the *Odyssey*.

71. I am aware that many take a different view of Apollo's arguments in the *Oresteia* (particularly in regard to his comments on the "true parent," 558–60) and see the whole trilogy as essentially misogynistic, following the influential article of F. Zeitlin, "The Dynamics of Misogyny: Myth and Mythmaking in the *Oresteia*," *Arethusa* 11 (1978): 149–84. Because a note is not the place to argue this point, I shall simply say that I do not think "misogyny" is a useful term to use, unless with great care, in general reference to either Aeschylus or classical Athens.

ANN ELLIS HANSON

Continuity and Change:

Three Case Studies in Hippocratic

Gynecological Therapy and Theory

The women of the Hippocratic Corpus appear with their menfolk in treatises concerned with diseases of mankind.[1] The gynecology of the Corpus, however, is women's own, devoted exclusively to the treatment of women in their womanly conditions. The Hippocratic doctors not only broadened the traditions of Greek medical writing so as to include female reproductive organs and their pathology within its perimeter,[2] but they also established gynecology as a separate and special endeavor within Greek medical literature.[3] The medical writers explored such female afflictions as sterility, superfetation, dystocia, female flux, and uterine displacements, together with their treatments. The four largest of the gynecological treatises of the Corpus are of particular concern here: *Diseases of Women 1, Diseases of Women 2, Barren Women*, and *Nature of Women*.[4] Of these four treatises, *Nature of Women* was never mentioned by title during antiquity, but *Diseases of Women 1* and *2* and *Barren Women* were mentioned by title and in such a manner as to suggest that their author was assumed to be the great Hippocrates, the Father of Medicine.[5] At the same time, some gynecological material which appeared in the Corpus was also assigned to others than Hippocrates even in antiquity.

The Greek medical writer and doctor Soranus, who practiced at Rome toward the end of the first century A.D., offers an example of ancient habits in assigning a name to the medical writer, or writers, responsible for gynecological material in the Corpus. When Soranus criticized the therapy of suspending a female patient suffering from uterine prolapse upside down on a ladder (*Gyn.* 4.36.7 = *CMG* IV, 149.9–15),[6] he attributed "ladder therapy" to Euryphon, a physician born perhaps as early as 500 B.C.[7] The procedure was prescribed for uterine prolapse in *Diseases of Women* 2, *Nature of Women*, and *Barren Women*.[8] From a modern perspective, however, the presence of "ladder therapy" in three gynecological treatises ultimately proves nothing about the name of the author, or authors, of the three "Hippocratic" treatises, and Soranus' testimony offers no more than the fact that he, Soranus, associated Euryphon with "ladder therapy."[9] When Soranus turned to discuss the prescription of abortive drugs, however, he cited as by Hippocrates both the Hippocratic Oath, which seemed to forbid all abortions with its "I shall not give a woman a destructive pessary," and *Nature of the Child* 13, which described an abortion accomplished not by drugs, but by a woman being advised by the medical writer to jump up and down and to touch her buttocks with her heels at each leap (*Gyn.* 1.60 = *CMG* IV, 45.5–10).

On the one hand, Soranus was following the general tendency of antiquity to attribute-early Greek medical writings to the Father of Medicine, but on the other, he was also consciously strengthening his own argument about the proper use of abortives through the invocation of the name of Hippocrates on a topic that was certainly debated in Soranus' own day. Soranus emphasized that the abortion supervised by the author of *Nature of the Child* (13) made use of leapings, not abortive pessaries, and he tried to draw a distinction between *ekbolia*, or expulsive maneuvers, and *phthoria*, or abortive drugs.[10] By attributing both treatises to "Hippocrates, the Father of Medicine," Soranus could thus gloss over the apparent contradiction between the two "Hippocratic" statements about abortion and could summon the prestige of "the great Hippocrates" in support of his own position: namely, that while it was the task of medicine to guard and preserve human life, he, Soranus, could on occasion recommend therapeutic abortion with the aid of drugs, when continuation of a pregnancy endangered the mother's life.[11]

The gynecological treatises occupied a firm position within the Hippocratic Corpus that circulated in Graeco-Roman antiquity. The specific attribution of gynecological material to Hippocrates at times meant no more than that the medical writings in question were considered early and probably contemporary with Hippocrates' lifetime. On other occasions, however, attribution of gynecological materials to Hippocrates made special appeal to his position as Father of Medicine, through the desire either to demonstrate the breadth of the founder's medical competence,[12] or to manipulate Hippocrates' authority in medical matters to come to the support of a particular stance.

Hippocrates and the Hippocratic Gynecology

Questioning Hippocrates' authorship of the gynecological works began tentatively with Renaissance editors and gained momentum from the eighteenth to the twentieth centuries.[13] The case against the gynecological treatises as writings worthy of the great Hippocrates proceeded along the following lines. First, it emphasized the apparent contradiction between the Hippocratic Oath, which seemed to prohibit abortions, and the many gynecological therapies that offered abortive advice and the several descriptions of an aborted fetus, related without censure. A mid-nineteenth-century translator of Hippocrates into English concluded that "all modern authorities of any note" were certain that Hippocrates was not responsible for the gynecology of the Corpus, and hence he chose not to include gynecological treatises in his translation.[14] Second, critics of Hippocratic attribution disdained the diffuse and repetitive style of the gynecological treatises, which resembled notebooks of detailed observations for morbid female conditions and their treatments, often repeating the same or very similar material within a single treatise and from treatise to treatise. Third, the gynecological treatises were also faulted for lacking the unified argumentation that characterized *Airs, Waters, Places,* or *Epidemics* 1 and 3—treatises which earlier scholars often considered worthy of Hippocrates. Moreover, along with other therapeutic treatises, the gynecology was identified with a medical school on Cnidus, viewed as a doctrinal and attitudinal rival to the school of Hippocrates on Cos and its "rational" approach to medicine.[15] With the negative judgment on authorship came the assignment of a relatively late date for the gynecology of the Corpus to the mid-fourth century B.C., close to but earlier than Aristotle, who seemed familiar with and often critical of opinions voiced in the Corpus.[16] The gynecology's richness was thus undervalued, and the prevailing advice offered to medical students in late antiquity urged them to "read the gynecological treatises last of all in the Corpus, since they dealt with feces, urine, and the like."[17] The consequences of this scholarship, which put a premium on Hippocratic authenticity, had profound effects on the degree

of serious attention paid to the gynecology of the Corpus and its therapies, essentially consigning them to oblivion.

Yet all of these criteria were inadequate for an intelligent understanding
of the gynecology of the Corpus in its own right.[18] The stylistic criteria
failed to account, for example, for the fact that the major gynecological
treatises were each shaped according to the same principles, with narrative sections, which combined observation and treatment, capped by
collections of appropriate therapies.[19] The doctrinal criteria which associated therapeutic treatises in general, including the gynecology, with a
medical school at Cnidus have been discredited for the entire Corpus.
Apportioning Hippocratic treatises between rival medical schools now
appears to have been a futile exercise in scholarly ingenuity and an invalid
model for the fifth century B.C., the time at which most treatises of the
Corpus were composed.[20] The doctrinal explanations were also inadequate in their own right, in that they failed to account for the fact that
when nongynecological writers of the Corpus discussed women's diseases, their assumptions about the functioning of the female body were
essentially the same as those of the gynecological writers. Earlier scholars
had assigned the gynecology to Cnidus and *Epidemics* 1 and 3 to Cos, but
the two collections seem to share similar notions about the anatomy and
physiology of the female body.[21] Finally, a date in the mid-fourth century
B.C. for the bulk of the major gynecological works of the Corpus was
unsatisfactory. Although Aristotelian reflections of Hippocratic gynecology suggested a *terminus ante quem* in the later decades of the fourth
century B.C., the presence of a therapy named for the fourth-century
doctor Philistion of Locri did not confirm a mid-fourth-century date as a
terminus post quem. Rather, it merely suggested that recipes were being
inserted into a living text, still used by medical professionals during and
after the lifetime of Philistion.[22]

Scholars currently working on the Corpus seldom pose the Hippocratic
question in so naive a fashion, and the importance of the individual
treatises for the picture they offer of the human body has been established
independently of the question of authorship.[23] Even so, the tendency to
"read the gynecological treatises last of all in the Corpus" has continued
to the extent that exploitation of the Hippocratic gynecology is only now
gathering impetus.[24] Modern editions of the Greek texts are an important
facet of this new interest, and scholars in France and Germany have
devoted close philological attention to the gynecological treatises.[25] Of

particular interest here is the work of Hermann Grensemann, who has identified compositional layers within the gynecology.[26] Differences in style of presentation, in use of technical terms, and in preference for a therapeutic orientation or a physiological one, distinguish Grensemann's five gynecological "viewpoints," which he labeled "A1," "A2," "B," "C," and "D," to indicate a chronological progression extending from the middle decades of the fifth century B.C. down into the middle decades of the fourth century.[27]

Grensemann's stratification is overprecise, both in its assignment of dates to the strata and in its attempts to attach authors' names and school affiliations (Cos or Cnidus) to specific viewpoints. Further, the notion that one or another of the viewpoints, now spread across the catalogues which are the major gynecological treatises of our Corpus, once circulated in other, more integrated forms recalls arguments of early the Homeric analysts, long ago replaced by more accurate models for how oral epics were composed. What an early Greek medical writer did when he went about the business of composing a gynecological treatise and what he thought his choice of genre imposed upon him has not yet been demonstrated. That the compositional model permitted repetition of material and recipes already incorporated into a written treatise seems assured by the writer of *Barren Women*, whose first sentence shows that he was aware of other, gynecological treatises and who incorporated in *Barren Women* material also found in our *Diseases of Women* 1 and 2 and in our *Nature of Women*.[28] That the compositional model also required lists of familiar therapies to cap narrative text seems assured by the presence of recipe collections at the ends of the major gynecological treatises in our Corpus.

Yet when stripped of bewildering complexities, Grensemann's compositional strata seem to me not only defensible, but useful—certainly for their separative value within what are, in our present Corpus, discrete treatises and perhaps also for the implied chronology of the strata. That is, viewpoint "A" in both its aspects is found largely in *Nature of Women* and *Diseases of Women* 2, for the two treatises share much common material; "A" probably represents the earliest stratum.[29] Viewpoint "B" is less distinct, but viewpoint "C" dominates in *Diseases of Women* 1, and its author self-consciously cross-references his *Diseases of Women* in his other compositions: *Nature of the Child* and *Diseases* 4.[30] "Viewpoint D" dominates in *Barren Women*, and that treatise was composed after other gynecological writings were in place. In what follows I employ Grensemann's stratification, as the strata may serve as an independent guide for identifying chronological developments in medical reasoning about gynecological problems; but I do so without commitment to the more cumbersome and intricate aspects of Grensemann's arguments.

It has often been assumed that the gynecological therapies, especially the recipes which appear primitive or naive, provide a glimpse of pre-Hippocratic gynecological practices and early Greek "home remedies," handed down in oral tradition before achieving written form in the Corpus.[31] Evidence offered in support of such an assumption has included similarities with earlier Egyptian and Babylonian therapies, with Homeric therapeutics, and with folk practices in present-day Greece.[32] Aline Rousselle has described a pre-Hippocratic and oral medical tradition, visible behind the gynecology of the Corpus, but she sees that oral tradition as being preserved solely by women and knowledge of it as restricted to women's circles.[33] G. E. R. Lloyd has more appropriately emphasized the ongoing dialogue between folk medical traditions and the professional physicians of Greece and Rome, as well as the interaction between female patient and male doctor in the gynecology of the Corpus, thus underscoring the processes whereby medical information belonging to the society at large came to play a role in doctors' writings.[34] I too have gathered evidence for a continuous tradition of medical lore and home remedies in Greek (and subsequently Roman) society, which developed independently of Hippocratic and later medical systems yet was also available to medical writers.[35] There was, I believe, considerable overlap between the gynecology of Graeco-Roman medical writers and the societal traditions and experiences familiar to anyone who cared to think on gynecological topics, and there was, as well, free circulation of ideas and recipes back and forth between the two traditions.

The Hippocratic writer of Grensemann's earliest stratum referred to recipes for gynecological ailments as "women's things," *ta gynaikeia*,[36] because such recipes were of concern to women, both as patients and as practitioners who shared the woman patient's experience. The medical writers of the Corpus, however, were men and spoke with male voices.[37] Nonetheless they too collected *ta gynaikeia* and reacted in various ways to these therapies for women's ailments. In what follows I try to establish the gynecological therapies of the Corpus as an important repository for information about the dialogue between medical traditions of Greek society and the Corpus, arguing that Hippocratic therapies, themselves an encapsulation of earlier folk medical theory and practice, in their turn affected the "specially medical reasoning" the Hippocratic gynecology employed.[38] I examine three sets of therapies: a clyster or uterine infusion; odor therapies for uterine dislocations; and therapies for dystocia, or difficult birth. The first example demonstrates specific ties to a tradition of home remedies and permits us to glimpse the medical writer's attempts to distance himself from practices he attributes to women. The second example shows an increased sophistication in Hippocratic thinking about odor therapies, as gynecological writers not only juxtaposed to such therapies others which presupposed a more mechanical model for the behavior of female organs but also enunciated with apparently increasing clarity mechanical causes for uterine displacement. The third example reveals folk medical theory and its therapies as determining and directing subsequent Hippocratic theory and practice along a misguided path, for the recipes and therapies of the folk tradition betray an ignorance of uterine contractions in childbirth that the medical writers not only shared but elaborated upon in their theories about birth.[39] In all three examples inherited gynecological therapy interpenetrated with and affected the development of subsequent Hippocratic theory and practice.

The ability to explain how the human body functioned and what were the causes of disease vindicated the Hippocratic doctors' right to intervene in the sicknesses of their patients in order to cure, or at least to alleviate distress. The pathology for women's bodies which Hippocratic writers were developing supplied new and more rationalized contexts for therapies already in use, and Hippocratic anatomy and physiology tried to explain why female bodies suffered from the diseases which inherited therapies aimed to cure. The specially medical reasoning of Hippocratics adopted earlier Greek medical practice and theory for women's bodies, systematizing and elaborating what it had borrowed in order to claim for doctors a role in the treatment of diseases of women.

A Clyster to Relieve Pain from Harsh Pessaries

The position of a therapy within the written treatises of the Corpus and its relation to Hippocratic practice were not static. The manipulation of a simple clyster, or uterine infusion, not only illustrates the adaptability of a therapy once it entered the Corpus but also points to an oral tradition as source for the therapy.

In one of Grensemann's later chronological strata, a passage from *Dis-*

eases of Women 1 ("C"), the medical writer notes that women's use of strong pessaries was one cause of inflammation and lesions in the womb:

> Suppose that after an abortion[40] a woman receives a serious lesion, or that she causes ulcerations in her uterus with harsh pessaries (such as women produce in treating themselves and others), and her fetus is destroyed, and the woman herself is not cleansed, but her uterus becomes very inflamed and closes, such that it is not able to release the lochial flows, unless they came out at first together with the child: if the woman is treated right away, she will be healthy, although barren. (*Morb. mul.* 1.67 = 8:140.14–19)[41]

The active ingredients of purging and/or abortive pessaries often included strong substances, such as cantharid beetles,[42] which could produce harmful side effects.[43] A therapy for discomfort caused by pessaries, the condition decried in this passage from *Diseases of Women* 1, is given twice in close succession among the collection of recipes at the close of *Diseases of Women* 2. At that point the recipes correspond to chapters in *Diseases of Women* 2 which deal with inflammation of the uterus and which belong to Grensemann's earliest chronological stratum, "A1":[44]

> If excessive pain takes hold of a woman purged by pessaries: a saucer of myrrh, an equal amount of incense, black cumin, cyperus, seseli, anise, linseed (*linou*),[45] netopon, honey, resin, goose grease, white vinegar, Egyptian myrrh, equal parts of each; grind in two cotyls[46] of sweet wine, and administer with warm clysters. (*Morb. mul.* 2.209 = 8:404.1–5)

> . . . Or a saucer of myrrh, an equal amount of incense, an equal amount of black cumin and cyperus, seseli, anise, celery seed (*selinou sperma*),[47] netopon, honey, resin, goose grease, white vinegar, Egyptian myrrh: dilute equal parts of each of these in sweet wine, and administer with warm clysters. (*Morb. mul.* 2.209 = 8:404.9–13)

The therapy is likewise included in nearly identical form in the collection of recipes which closes *Diseases of Women* 1, the treatise dominated by viewpoint "C," and at the point in its collection of recipes that corresponds to the criticism by "C" of women's misuse of harsh pessaries quoted above.[48] The same therapy recurs in a fourth locus in the recipes at the end of *Nature of Women* ("A2").[49] In *Diseases of Women* 1 the therapy appears under the heading "clysters for lesions of long duration," and in

Nature of Women under the heading "if the mouth of the womb is ulcer-ated." In these headings from Grensemann's later strata the therapy is no longer disease-specific but has been generalized into an omnibus therapy for troublesome sores in the uterus. In Grensemann's earliest stratum in *Diseases of Women* 2 ("A1"), however, it is bounded in both its appearances by an introductory heading to the specific pain that came as after-effect from acrid pessaries—the condition the medical writer in *Diseases of Women* 1 ("C") decries as originating in women's misguided medical practices.

In his criticism of women's use of harsh pessaries the medical writer of viewpoint "C" explicitly and self-consciously distances himself from "home remedies" and from women who, he claims, produced lesions in their wombs or, by their doctoring, produced lesions in the wombs of other women. In separating himself from female practitioners he consid-ers outside his Hippocratic tradition, this medical writer not only gives voice to Hippocratic professionalism, which saw itself as different from previous medical traditions, but also draws attention to women's unskill-ful and unlettered habits.

The tale of the clyster, told according to the the the chronological implica-tions of Grensemann's chronology, thus might go as follows. The thera-peutic clyster originated as a "home remedy," an analgesic for specific pain, and in this form it entered the armory of doctors' medicaments as complement to "A1." Grensemann's later viewpoints ("A2" and "C") re-tained the clyster because the therapy was a useful one, yet generalized its prescription to a wider variety of uterine applications. The clyster contin-ued in use as a panacea and held on to a place within Hippocratic medica-ments, but no longer as a disease-specific remedy. The elasticity and tenacity of the clyster are as worthy of note, as is its manipulation by women and subsequently by Hippocratic practitioners.[50]

Odor Therapies for Uterine Displacements

One of the longest-lived gynecological therapies was the application of odors to the vagina and to the nose. These applications appeared fre-quently not only in the Hippocratic Corpus as medicaments for uterine displacement,[51] but they lived on in gynecological therapies of the writers of the Roman period.[52] The conviction that odor therapy was useful in uterine displacement depended in origin upon the notion that the uterus was a sentient being, able to recoil from fetid smells and be attracted by pleasant ones, such as Timaeus of Locri described in the Platonic treatise named after him. According to Timaeus, the gods created the desire for sexual intercourse by making the organs of generation, both male penis and female uterus, animated creatures in their own right. The penis was rebellious and, like an animal, disobedient to reason; when maddened with lust, it sought to dominate. The uterus in woman was an animal within her body, desirous of procreating children, and when unused, it wandered through her body at will, obstructing respiration and causing pain and sickness (Pl. *Ti.* 91a6–d6). Uterine prolapse, especially after difficult birthing among multiparous barnyard animals such as the pig, provided visible examples of the uterus' capacity to move downward, to descend into the vagina, and even to issue out from it.[53] At the same time, the uterus had no place of its own inside the female body, because the male body had no space set aside for one. Therefore in popular imagination the uterus lacked the rooting and the fixed position which held an undisciplined penis to its place.[54]

The gynecology of the Corpus was concerned both with the uterus's ability to rise within the body and with uterine prolapse downward into the vagina. The topic was treated exhaustively in thirty-one consecutive chapters in *Diseases of Women* 2, proceeding in a "head to heel," or *a capite ad calcem*, arrangement.[55] Uterine displacements were also treated in individual chapters in *Nature of Women, Diseases of Women* 1, *Barren Women,* and *Places in Man.*[56] In contrast to Timaeus, Hippocratic writers of all gynecological strata juxtaposed to the odor therapies other therapies which presupposed a more mechanical theory for uterine displacements, and writers of later strata, especially "C," enunciate with greater clarity mechanical causes for uterine movement. Overexertion, chills and sneezing, malnutrition, and abstinence from sex produced temperature imbalance and dryness in the unstable womb, causing it to displace. The empty and belabored uterus was attracted toward opposite climatic environments and sought them where it could—within the body, or outside it. It was set in motion by mechanical motives to seek the restoration of its former equilibrium:

> Every excuse is sufficient to dislodge the uterus, if it is in bad condition—from a chill of feet or loins, from dancing, winnowing grain, chopping wood, running up and down steep inclines, and from other things. (*Morb. mul.* 2.138 ("B") = 8:310.23–312.2)

Whenever a postpartum woman lifts a burden greater than her custom, or winnows grain, or chops wood, or runs, or does other things
like this, her uterus is likely to fall out. Sometimes it happens because
of a sneeze, for a sneeze is forceful, especially if she sneezes with
force and takes hold of her nose. (*Morb. mul.* 2.153 ("uncertain, but
not A") = 8:328.1–12)

[Displacement] happens more frequently to barren women, especially after hard work. When a woman works hard and her uterus
heats up and sweats, her uterine mouth turns out through the vagina, since it was in a wetter, more slippery, and hotter place than
previously. When this happens, the womb rushes toward the cold
and its turned mouth moves toward the outside. (*Morb. mul.* 2.145
("C") = 8:320.2–7)

If suffocation comes on suddenly, it happens especially to those who
do not have sexual relations with men and to older women, rather
than to younger ones, for their wombs are more empty. It especially
happens because of the following: whenever she happens to be
empty and works harder than is her custom, her uterus is heated[57]
from the toil and it turns, because it is empty and light. Women, in
fact, have empty space so that the womb can turn, whenever the
belly is empty. . . . Wombs, in fact, go upward toward moisture,
whenever they are dried out by more hard work than usual. The liver,
as you know, is moist. When the womb heads for the liver, it produces choking (suffocation) all of a sudden, as it stops the breathing
which is around the belly. (*Morb. mul.* 1.7 ("C") = 8:32.1–12)

Hippocratic descriptions of uterine movement do not necessarily presuppose the Timaean notion of the uterus as an animal of independent
movements, and Timaeus' description may be idiosyncratic, old-fashioned, and easy to refute.[58] Nevertheless, application of sweet odors at
the vagina and fetid odors to the nose in order to draw the uterus downward, and of fetid odors at the vagina and sweet to the nose to draw it
upward, in Hippocratic medicaments vividly recalls the organ's sentient
capacities.[59] In the only discussion of suffocation in a pregnant woman,
surely an uncommon phenomenon, as the baby normally would ballast
the uterus in place, it is the fetus, not the uterus, which is said to go in
search of the moisture (*Morb. mul.* 1.32 ("C") = 8:76).[60] When Soranus
criticized his predecessors, who in his opinion had damaged inflamed

female parts by administering ill-smelling substances, he made explicit the connection between the Timaean picture and odor therapy: "The uterus does not creep forth like a wild animal from its lair, taking delight in fragrant smells and fleeing fetid ones" (*Gyn.* 3.29 = CMG IV, 113.4–5).[61] Further, throughout the Hippocratic gynecology the women afflicted with uterine displacement are most often those who abstained from sexual relations, or for whom sexual intercourse was fruitless: older virgins, widows too young in their widowhood, the barren, the sterile, the menopausal.[62] Intercourse and pregnancy not only prevented uterine displacement, through the moisture of sperm and the ballasting provided by a baby, but frequently served as cure.[63]

The odor therapies of the Hippocratic gynecology were not, however, prescribed in isolation. Rather, as noted above, they appear in the treatises in combination with other medicaments more in keeping with the mechanical etiologies for uterine displacement which Hippocratics endorsed.[64] Baths and a wide variety of uterine infusions and clysters, all designed to restore proper temperature and proper degree of humidity, often precede prescription of odors, whether uterine dislocation is upward or downward.[65] Probes and the doctor's hand or finger rectified the uterus' position or that of its mouth; binders tied the uterus off from moist organs or humid places, such as the liver or flank.[66] Induced vomiting corrected extreme prolapse by drawing a woman's uterus upward, as also did elevating the end of her bed, succussion on a ladder, and restriction of her movements.[67]

Prolapse down the vagina was visible or, at the least, palpable by Hippocratic doctors and their assistants. Attraction toward moist, inner organs, however, was deduced from pain and/or malfunctioning in or near the attracting organ, as that organ's environment was now overcrowded by the upward thrust of the uterus and by the subsequent bending and blocking that occurred in the passageways and in the empty spaces between the uterus and other organs once the dislocation had taken place. That is, the womb's ascent in the direction of the head brought pain to the vessels in the woman's nose and under her eyes; she became comatose and foamed at the mouth.[68] Dislocation toward the legs and feet caused the woman's big toes to be drawn under her toenails and brought pain to her legs and thighs.[69] Dislocation toward the bladder caused strangury, toward the anus brought the desire to defecate, in addition to pain in or near the affected part.[70] Suffocation, or choking off of breath, often accompanied uterine movements inside the body, because the aberrant uterus had come to occupy spaces for breath in the central cavity, pushing against the diaphragm, blocking passageways, and squeezing upper, more sensitive organs.[71] Suffocation resulted in symptoms such as aphasia, weakness and fainting, chills, and signs associated with seizures, such as foaming at the mouth, grinding the teeth, or rolling the eyes.[72]

It has been suggested that the Hippocratic imagination saw uterine suffocation as caused by the uterus's actual arrival at a woman's upper organs, passing through her diaphragm by means of a capacious, central tube which connected nose and mouth to vagina, "from lower mouth to upper mouth."[73] Hippocratics did imagine a central tube, extending from nose and mouth, by way of the throat, stomach, and intestines to the anus, but this channel was common to male and female bodies alike.[74] Bodies of both sexes received breath and nourishment by means of this alimentary and breathing tube. Residues were usually purged downward through the tube, although drugs could facilitate purging in either an upward or downward direction, whichever was the more advantageous in a particular sickness.[75] One Hippocratic writer says that the tube has four paths of exit from the body—mouth, nostrils, rectum, and urethra, showing that his scheme was based on the male body; other writers added additional points of exit to the list, such as skin, blood vessels, eyes, and ears.[76]

As a group, however, Hippocratics apparently distinguished urethra from vagina, although Aristotle apparently did not.[77] For them, the bladder emptied into the urethra; the extra female organ, the uterus, emptied downward into the vagina, its own special path of exit for menses, lochial blood, and babies. The uterus was also connected in an upward direction by special passageways which carried milk to and fro between uterus and breasts. These channels, which lay dormant in the prepubertal girl, were opened up and forged by the forceful circulation of blood and other fluids first in menstruation and later in childbirth.[78] Nevertheless, the uterus was also believed to be connected to the central alimentary and breathing tube that was common to males and females, so that in a woman the uterus could also spew excess menstrual blood in an upward direction, as did the stomach in both sexes. Hence menses sometimes departed the woman's body from her nose in epistaxis.[79] Menstruation began the process of opening up the young girl's body. Pregnancies and births completed it, by breaking down the young girl's resistant body, by widening her passageways, and by making her compact flesh soft and spongy. Each successive pregnancy increased the amount of open space in the woman's body for free movement and evacuation of excess fluids or for their storage. Each pregnancy broke down her flesh, so that it was ever more spongy and better able to manage a mature female's surplus fluidity.

Birth prognoses which predicted a woman's ability to conceive from the fact that smells moved from her vagina to her nose or mouth do not prove that Hippocratics imagined the uterus as arriving at the organs above the diaphragm by means of the central alimentary and breathing tube.[80] These fecundity tests did presuppose that odors moved along inner passageways: first up the vagina to the uterus and then upward to the mouth and nose via the interconnecting channels which joined the uterus to the central tube. The tests predicted whether or not a menstruating woman could become pregnant, and the failure of an odor applied at the vagina to arrive at nose or mouth meant that the smell did not complete the first leg of its journey. The odors never reached the uterus in the first place, for they were stopped by the same impediment which would prevent male seed from reaching the womb for the conception of a child. Thus therapies for sterility often concentrated on straightening the passageway from vagina to cervix; or on redirecting the vagina into the uterine mouth, when it deviated and did not empty into the uterus; or on softening and opening the uterine mouth, whenever it had hardened and closed; or on removing vaginal and cervical impediments which prevented seed from reaching the womb.[81]

Ultimately neither the movement of odors from vagina to mouth nor the movement of breath and liquids up and down the many interconnecting passageways of the female body, or up and down the central tube common to male and female bodies, can be taken to mean that Hippocratics envisioned a passageway along which the uterus could move into the upper regions of the body and above the diaphragm. Although the uterus, when dry, was believed to move toward and touch moist organs in the lower body, there is no evidence, so far as I am aware, that Hippocratics thought that the uterus actually arrived at and made contact with the wet places and the moist organs above the diaphragm. In fact the collocation in *Nature of Women* 48 and 49 of uterine movements toward the head and toward the legs and feet suggests that the Hippocratic imagination did not expect the uterus to arrive at either extremity. The introduction to a therapy for suffocation in *Diseases of Women* 2 is more explicit:

If the uterus seems to sit *under the diaphragm* (*hypo tas phrenas*), the woman suddenly becomes speechless; her hypochondria [soft, upper abdominal areas] are hard, and she experiences suffocation; she grinds her teeth and, when called, does not respond. You should fumigate her under her nose, burning some wool and adding to the fire some asphalt, castoreum, sulphur, and pitch. Rub her groin and the interior of her thighs with very sweet-smelling unguent; or have her drink black starfish from the sea and cabbage, mixed together in sweet wine. (*Morb. mul.* 2.201 = 8:384.12–18)

Uterine movements to new places produced overcrowding. When the uterus moved upward toward the already crowded center of the body, it applied pressure on sensitive, cognitive organs. From this new position directly below the diaphragm it blocked passageways and obstructed breathing. Doctors were aware that the symptoms produced by uterine suffocation resembled those in Herakles' disease—epilepsy and other seizures.[82] The uterus as irrational animal was already being separated from Hippocratic theory in all strata of the gynecology, as the omnipresent mechanical therapies suggest, and this separation may have begun even before odor therapy entered the Hippocratic armory of medicaments. In any case, it was with increasing sophistication that Hippocratics eschewed the notion of an auto-directed uterus, because it was less amenable to medical intervention than their mechanical explanations for uterine movements. The same medical environment which produced physiological explanations for seizures and for epilepsy, such as they appear in the Hippocratic *Sacred Disease*, fostered an analogous approach to uterine displacement and to the suffocation which might accompany the displacement.[83] Hippocratic doctors were inserting themselves into areas of health care previously reserved for practitioners other than doctors, and they now claimed the right to treat the sudden seizures of madness and of uterine suffocation.

Therapies for Dystocia

In this final example, inherited therapy not only affected Hippocratic theory but also determined the direction it followed. The therapies which the Hippocratic Corpus employed in cases of dystocia, difficult birth, reinforced Greek society's ignorance of uterine contractions by clinging to the image of an active baby and a passive uterus during childbirth, and they fostered in Hippocratic doctors a continued insensitivity to the peristaltic-type muscular movements of the uterus that expel the child in childbirth.[84] These same therapies encouraged Hippocratics to extend the analogy between the uterus and a jar, positioned in women upside down, in both their anatomy and their physiology.[85]

The Hippocratic writer of *Nature of the Child* ("C") described the birth process in some detail. Birth took place because the baby broke the membranes which surrounded it in a restlessness and frustration that sprang from hunger, as the fetus grew to birth size and no longer received nourishment adequate to its needs from its mother. The baby battered its way out from the mother's uterus and thus came into the world. If this was her first child, the blows also distended her hip bones, making subsequent births easier for her.

When it is time for the mother to give birth, what happens is that the child by the spasmodic movements of its hands and feet breaks one of the internal membranes. . . . For nothing has any strength to hold it once the membranes fail, and when the membranes have been carried away, the womb itself cannot hold the child back. . . . Once the child is on its way, it forces a wide passage for itself through the womb, since the womb is soft. . . . My assertion then is that what brings on birth is a failure in food supply. . . . My evidence for this is as follows: Consider the way in which a chicken develops. . . . When the supply of nutriment from the egg gives out, then not having enough to live on, it looks for more and moves about violently in the shell, and ruptures the membranes. When the hen notices the violent motion of the chick, she pecks at the shell and hatches it. . . . It is the same with the child. . . . Once the membranes are ruptured, if the infant's momentum is in the direction of the head, the birth is easy for the mother. . . . In childbirth it is the women who are having their first child who suffer the most, because they have had no experience of the pain; apart from the general discomfort of the body, they suffer most in the loins and the hips, because these become distended. Those who have more experience of bearing children suffer less; much less, if they have had a large number of children. (*De nat. pueri* 30 ("C") = 7:530–38)[86]

The uterus was conspicuous for its attractive properties. The Hippo-cratic treatise *Ancient Medicine* compared the uterus to a cupping jar, because the womb drew in blood, the residual product of nourishment, from the stomach into itself (*Vet. med.* 22 = 1:626.14–628.5).[87] The mature woman expended the blood which had collected in her uterus as menses; in pregnancy she used it to nourish her fetus; in lactation after pregnancy it became milk and was transported to her breasts by interconnecting passages.[88] The uterus also drew into itself male seed, which mixed with the woman's seed to congeal into a fetus in pregnancy; the gynecological treatises frequently refer to the initiation of pregnancy as "taking up the seed and retaining it."[89] In sum, the uterus imagined by Hippocratics was in the habit of getting, not giving.

Galen's description of the uterus, written more than five hundred years later, is couched in terms of the organ's ability both to retain and to expel. Galen, however, had dissected gravid animals himself and was aware that the uterus was active, the baby passive, in the birth process:

For when everything connected with a pregnancy proceeds properly, the expulsive faculty remains dormant as though it did not exist. But if anything goes wrong either with the chorion or any of the other membranes or with the fetus itself, and completion of the pregnancy seems unlikely, then the uterus no longer awaits the nine months, but the retentive faculty ceases and allows the previously inoperative faculty to come into action. . . . Thus it is the work of the retentive faculty to make the uterus contract upon the fetus at every point, so that, as might be expected, when the midwives palpate it, the os [mouth] is found to be closed, while the pregnant women them-selves, during the first days—and particularly on that day on which conception takes place—experience a sensation as if the uterus were moving and contracting upon itself. (*Nat. fac.* 3.3 = 2:148.15–150.1)[90]

This awareness of the uterus's active role in birth perhaps stemmed from dissections of the uterus by Herophilus in the early decades of the third century B.C. and his identification of the layers of muscle tissue which composed the organ.[91] Later medical writers, such as Soranus, Rufus of Ephesus, and Galen, relied on Herophilus for their knowledge of uterine anatomy.[92]

The pangs of childbirth and the anguish of the woman in travail were mentioned not infrequently in Greek literature prior to and contemporary with the Corpus, although the source of the mother's pains was not, so far as I am aware, specified. The most explicit expression of the notion that a parturient's pains were due to blows from her rambunctious infant as it forced its way out from the maternal womb is met in a transferral to the animal kingdom. The fate of the lioness is a commonplace in Greek literature, preserved in similar form by Herodotus and Aesop:

> The lioness, who happens to be the strongest and boldest of animals, bears only once in her life a single cub. She expels her uterus, in fact, together with her cub during the birth. This is the reason: when the cub first begins to move in its mother, because it has claws much sharper than those of any other creature, it tears the uterus, and as it grows, it scratches and tears all the more. Thus when its birth is near seldom is any of the uterus left intact. (Hdt. 3.108)

Aesop's version centers on the response of the lioness when she was reproached by a fox because she only bore a single cub. "Yes," she said proudly, "but I bear a lion."[93] Aristotle claimed that "the story told about the lioness losing her uterus in parturition is pure fable and was made up to account for the scarcity of the animal."[94] In his criticism, however, Aristotle neither attacked the concept of the uterus as passive in birth, implicit in the fable (awareness of a uterus active in birth may have come only in the early decades of the third century B.C., as suggested above), nor did he attribute the story to particular individuals, such as Herodotus or Aesop. The latter omission suggests that Aristotle knew many who not only believed the fable through lack of experience with lions but also found the story reasonable, because it corresponded to their view of the birth process in man.[95]

The notion that the human baby, like the lion cub, had to force its way out of the uterus and into postnatal life dominated the thought of the medical writer of *Nature of the Child* as he wrote about childbirth. His belief not only supplied him with the analogy between the baby in birth and the chicken hatching from its egg, but it also gave him an image for visualizing the complications of breech delivery, wherein "the woman's suffering is similar to having someone throw a fruit pit into a small-mouthed jar, not suitably formed for extracting the pit when it lies sideways" (*Morb. mul.* 1.33 ("C") = 8:78.4–7).[96] Further, this was the writer, mentioned above, who described uterine dislocation in a pregnant woman such that it was the fetus itself, not the uterus, which was said to move in search of moisture at the liver or in the hypochondria (*Morb. mul.* 1.32 = 8:76).[97] This physiology for birth in "C" does not, however, stand alone in the

Corpus. The embryological treatise *Eight Months' Child* also credits the fetus with initiating its own birth by breaking the membranes which had surrounded it, thereby compelling the birth to take place.[98] Indeed, the therapies for dystocia throughout the Corpus likewise presuppose an active baby and a passive uterus, which suggests that ignorance of uterine contractions in birth was widespread.

When the baby did not proceed along its path as expected, Hippocratic doctors first induced a forceful sneeze. The parturient was told to hold her nose and lips tightly closed to maximize the effect of the sneeze, as forceful sneezing was thought to shake the uterus.[99] Grensemann has assigned the section on dystocia in *Diseases of Women* 1 to viewpoint "B," and it begins in this manner:

> All babies which cannot be delivered in the course of a miscarriage are as follows: sometimes the baby is too large in its entirety, or in its parts, or sometimes it is too small, but lies in transverse position and is without strength; even so, if the baby is proceeding as it should, administer the drugs I will mention and bathe the mother first with much warm water. Now if the baby wants to go out and is in proper position, but it does not go along easily, administer a sternutative, and have her sneeze, while taking hold of her nostrils and holding her mouth shut tight, so that the sneeze may have maximum effect. (*Morb. mul.* 1.68 = 8:142.13–20)

If this milder shaking for the uterus did not enable the baby to get out, succussion, or shaking, was next prescribed in order to speed the baby on its way. Succussion on a ladder was also treatment for straightening humped backs. The Hippocratic writer of *Joints* claimed that the procedure was ineffective in many instances and was employed by practitioners who wished to draw a crowd of curious onlookers. Although he considered it a very old-fashioned practice, he also expressed his admiration for the man who first invented succussion, and he prescribed it himself for humps high up on the back, provided it was carried out according to his own specifications (*De Articulis* 42–44 = 4:182–88). The passage on dystocia from *Diseases of Women* 1, quoted just above, continues with a prescription for succussion:

> You should also employ succussions and carry out the shaking as follows. Take a high, strong bed; put a covering on it and have the

woman lie supine upon it. Fasten her down to the bed at chest, armpits, and hands with a length of cloth, or a wide strip of leather. . . .
When you are ready, prepare a bundle of soft twigs, or something
like that, of a size which, when the bed is thrown toward the ground,
will not permit the legs at the head end of the bed to touch the
ground. Tell the woman to hang on to the bed with her hands. Hold
the bed high at the head end, so that it slants down toward the foot
end, taking care that the woman will not slip forward. As these
things are being carried out and the bed is raised, from behind push
the twigs underneath, keeping the bed as straight as possible so that
the legs [at the foot end] will touch[100] the ground when the bed is
thrown, and will bounce off the twigs. Have a man raise the bed at
each leg, on this side and on that, so that the bed will fall straight,
smoothly, and evenly, and so that there is no jerking. Have the
shaking coincide as much as possible with the pain. If she is delivered, then stop, but if not, shake her from time to time, and swing
her as she is carried on her bed. (*Morb. mul.* 1.68 ("B") = 8:142.20–
144.16)

Other methods Hippocratics used for shaking the parturient in dystocia
advised tying the woman to a ladder which was raised and then dropped;
still others shook the parturient while she was held either under her
armpits, or by her hands and feet.[101] The story of Simos' wife, who was
shaken during childbirth, was narrated in *Epidemics* 5 and again in *Epidemics* 7, perhaps likewise suggesting that succussion as a medical procedure
for dystocia was widely practiced.[102]

When shaking the uterus failed to dislodge a recalcitrant fetus, the
medical writer of the passages on dystocia in *Diseases of Women* 1 resorted
to more drastic measures. If presentation was faulty and legs or shoulders
appeared first, the baby was thrust back into the cavity of the womb and
manipulated so that it turned head downward in natural position.[103] If
these maneuvers failed to accomplish the birth, the doctor then turned to
relieving the mother of her burden. The procedure entailed the death of
the child, because in order to release the mother from her burden, the
baby was crushed and dismembered. Other means, however, had failed,
and the child was now considered too weak to make its own way into this
world and survive. Attention focused instead on saving the life of the
mother.

Every fetus which is dead and has either a leg or a hand sticking out is best treated as follows: if possible, thrust it back inside and turn it head first; if this is impossible and it is swollen, dismember it in the following way. Cut off the head with your knife, crush it with your compressor (so that it won't get in your way), draw out the bones with your bone-extractor, and thrusting with your hook along the collar bone so that it will hold, draw it along, not forcibly, but a little at a time, relaxing your grip and again straining. When you have drawn it along, but it is on its shoulders, cut off both hands at the joints with the shoulders. . . . If it can move, draw the rest out easily; but if it does not obey, split the fetus' chest open all the way to the throat. Take care not to cut in the region of its belly and strip bare some bone, for belly and intestine and feces go out; and if some of these do fall out, the case is already a more troublesome one. Then compress its sides and draw its shoulder blades together, and the rest of the fetus will travel out easily, unless it has already swollen in its abdomen. . . . If the hand or the leg of the dead fetus has fallen out, it is best to thrust both back in, if at all possible, and to straighten the fetus' position. If you cannot do this, cut off whatever is outside, as high up as possible; grope for the rest, push that back in, and turn the fetus' head first. When you are about to turn the baby or to dismember it, you should trim your fingernails. The knife you use for cutting should be more curved than straight, and you should cover up its tip with your forefinger as you grope and lead the baby on its path, for fear lest you touch the uterus. (*Morb. mul.* 1.70 ("B") = 8:146–48)[104]

According to Celsus, a Roman writer of the first century A.D., the operation to excise a dead fetus was a difficult one, requiring extreme caution, and it brought great risk to all (*Med.* 7.29).[105] Several generations later Soranus expressed his disapproval of sternutatives and succussion in delivering a retained afterbirth,[106] although he too felt that in spite of the difficulties involved, surgical dismemberment of the child might be called for as a means of saving the mother's life.[107] At the same time, he also warned that excision was a dangerous procedure, likely to involve "accompanying fevers; sympathetic nervous conditions, and sometimes even excessive inflammation; and should gangrene appear, one must have very few hopes."[108] Special surgical instruments designed to aid the doctor in his task of removing the fetus are mentioned by writers from throughout antiquity. Some instruments were for extinguishing life, others were for compressing the fetal body or for hooking it and dismembering it for removal.[109]

Modern obstetrical techniques have so lowered maternal and infant deaths during birth that comparison with the Hippocratic techniques is profitable principally for underscoring how closely linked therapy and theory are. Confidence in the ability of the uterus to contract and to expel determines modern discussions of dystocia, and current gynecological textbooks repeatedly caution against premature interference by the doctor, even when labor seems to turn difficult. Induction of labor is said to be risky; forceps delivery may cause serious permanent injury, if improperly performed; cesarean section entails the hazards of major surgery for both mother and child.[110] "Interfere as little and as late as possible" is the modern refrain. In addition, excision of a dead fetus appears in modern accounts as a remedy for uterine rupture that has resulted in extrauterine fetal growth, or for other advanced ectopic pregnancies.[111] In most circumstances the uterus absorbs or expels an aborted fetus,[112] and modern clinical practice advocates removal primarily in cases where the ectopic or extrauterine fetal tissue impedes those natural processes. The prominence given to surgical dismemberment and excision of the dead or dying fetus in Hippocratic treatises, however, meshes with Hippocratic notions of how and why birth was accomplished. To Hippocratics the uterus was passive in the birth process, and thus there was no incentive to wait until it expelled its burden. Rather, in dystocia Hippocratics intervened to remove the dead or dying child in an attempt to save the mother, that adult life which was also at risk in the birth process.

The therapies for dystocia mentioned in the Corpus progress from sneezing, a mild form of shaking for the uterus, to succussion, a far more violent shaking, and then to excision. These gynecological therapies were borrowed by Hippocratics from folk practices, as the tale of the lion cub implies. Once the therapies were incorporated within the Hippocratic milieu, they not only determined Hippocratic theories about birth, as enunciated by the Hippocratic writer of viewpoint "C," but sternutatives, succussion, and excision served as the Hippocratic procedures for dystocia, as reported by viewpoint "B" and mentioned elsewhere in the Corpus. The therapies reinforced the mistaken notion that the uterus was passive in birth and lacked expulsive properties, and they fostered the notion that the baby was the active party, essentially responsible for birthing itself.[113] The baby that could not march energetically into the arms of mother and waiting birth attendants was obviously less desirable.

The anatomy, physiology, and sociology of gestation and prenatal development in the Corpus, and likewise in the pre-Socratics, complemented therapies whose aim was to assist a passive uterus in the course of difficult birth. The male fetus was usually pictured as quicker to articulate its parts and earlier to move in the uterus with greater force. Pregnancy with a male was less taxing on the mother, and her health might actually improve if she carried a boy.[114] Because the mother was healthier, the uterine environment was also healthier for the male fetus, so that it came to birth stronger and better able to stride into this world.[115] Until an actual baby appeared, those attending a birth assumed that a fetus less able to effect its own egress must be either a female, weaker by nature, or an effeminate male of deficient strength. In either case its death from succussion or dismemberment and excision was not so great a loss to family and society, as the baby was considered less strong and was otherwise less desirable.[116]

The story of the active lion cub, more vigorous than other animals in forcing its way from the passive womb of the mother, thus belonged to the same intellectual world as the Hippocratic therapies of sternutatives, succussion, and excision for dystocia—a society which did not recognize uterine contractions as responsible for the delivery of the unborn. This course of therapy for difficult childbirth was inherited by Hippocratics from home remedies, and it maintained its position in the Corpus without apparent theoretical or practical modification.[117] The notion survived its transition from folk remedy to Hippocratic remedy, and it not only interpenetrated with and determined subsequent Hippocratic theory for birthing but also encouraged medical writers to cling to the analogy between the uterus and the jar in their explanations of conception. The vitality of the notion underscored the grip that such a view of the birth process held on the minds of parturients, medical attendants, and Hippocratic theorists alike.

In the first of the case studies addressed in this essay, the gynecology of the Hippocratic Corpus attempted to break away from the amateurism of inherited home remedies; in the second, the gynecology of the Corpus fostered more mechanical therapeutic and theoretical approaches to uterine displacements so as to make a place for doctors' interventions in uterine suffocation. In the third case study, however, Hippocratic gynecology accepted folk traditions about birthing and elaborated them with scientific seriousness. The dialogue between Hippocratic therapy and theory and the home remedies of Greek society, *ta gynaikeia*, was complex and various. The Hippocratic effort to equip these remedies for women with a medical sophistication that offered a more coherent female anatomy, physiology, and etiology for female diseases resulted in the evolution of a new medical genre, the gynecological treatise, which interspersed narrative and therapy in a kind of catalogue of morbid conditions that was likely to share material with other, similar gynecological catalogues. When referring to the most important of their writings, the Hippocratics themselves and their contemporaries employed the title "Female Diseases," using both adjective and noun to characterize the writings.[118] In post-Hippocratic times, however, the genre was called simply *Ta gynaikeia* (or, in Latin, *Gynaecia*).[119] "Diseases of Women" is the conventional English translation for both titles, *Gynaikeia nousoi* and *Ta gynaikeia*, but the translation blurs the Hippocratic distinction between the two. *Gynaikeia nousoi* was used as the proper title for a gynecological treatise, but *Ta gynaikeia* was used to indicate the gynecological recipes that formed part of such a treatise. Later centuries preferred to use *Ta gynaikeia* or *Gynaecia*, the Hippocratic term for gynecological recipes, as the title for gynecological treatises. Such a practice underscores the dominant role therapeutic remedies played and continued to play in the gynecology of Graeco-Roman antiquity.

Notes

1. For the male body as norm in the Corpus see, e.g., Paola Manuli, "Donne mascoline, femmine sterili, vergini perpetue" and "Appendice" in *Madre materia: sociologia e biologia della donna greca*, ed. Silvia Campese, Paola Manuli, and Giulia Sissa (Turin: Boringhiari, 1983), 147–92, esp. 155. For treatment of female patients by doctors in treatises of general pathology (*Epidemiae* 1–7), as compared with male patients, see G. E. R. Lloyd, *Science, Folklore and Ideology* (Cambridge: Cambridge University Press, 1983), 62–68.

2. Identifying the audience for which the Hippocratic gynecology was composed is beyond the scope of this essay. Nevertheless, discussion below does show that Hippocratic writers were aware of what their fellows were writing and that in at least one instance a prevailing scientific assumption of the time passed from oral

tradition about the birth process in humans into medical literature via the Corpus. For the audiences of medieval gynecological treatises see Monica Green, "Women's Medical Practice and Care," *Signs* 14 (1989): 434–73, esp. 457–69.

3. The gynecological treatises were grouped together in the earliest Byzantine manuscript of the Corpus, Marcianus Venetus 269 (tenth century); see the list of contents in W. H. S. Jones, *Hippocrates*, Loeb Classical Library (London: Heinemann; Cambridge: Harvard University Press, 1923), 2:lviii; cf. lix for the index in Vaticanus Graecus 276, which antedates this twelfth-century manuscript in which it appears. The sixth-century papyrus codex from the medical school at Antinoopolis in Egypt (*P. Antinoopolis* 3.184) contained at least three gynecological treatises within its covers; see Marie-Hélène Marganne, *Inventaire analytique des papyrus grecs de médecine* (Geneva: Librairie Droz, 1981), 124–25.

4. *Diseases of Women* 1 and 2 are cited below as *Morb. mul.* 1 and 2; *Barren Women* as *De steril.*; *Nature of Women* as *Nat. mul.* Other works in the Hippocratic Corpus are cited similarly by English title and Latin abbreviation. Unless otherwise noted, all references to the Hippocratic Corpus are from the edition of the Greek text by Emile Littré, *Œuvres complètes d'Hippocrate*, 10 vols. (Paris, 1839–61; reprinted Amsterdam: A. M. Hakkert, 1961–62). Line numbers in the Littré edition are cited only when part of a chapter, rather than the entire chapter, is pertinent. Unless otherwise specified, other classical works and modern references are abbreviated according to the systems in *L'année philologique* and the second edition of the *Oxford Classical Dictionary*.

5. For Hellenistic and early Roman examples see, e.g., Hippoc. [*Ep.*] 21 = 9: 392.2–3, a letter claiming to be written by Hippocrates to Democritus that cited *Diseases of Women* as by the writer of the letter, that is, by Hippocrates; the Neronian glossator Erotian included both *Diseases of Women* 1 and 2 and *Barren Women* in his Hippocratic glossary (Erotian 36 = 9.16 Nachmanson).

6. Soranus' *Gynecology* is cited below as Soranus *Gyn.* Unless otherwise noted, all references to Soranus are from the edition of the Greek text by Johannes Ilberg, *Sorani Gynaeciorum libri IV* (Leipzig and Berlin: B. G. Teubner, 1927) = *Corpus medicorum graecorum* (CMG), IV. Line numbers in the Ilberg edition are cited only when part of a chapter, rather than the entire chapter, is pertinent.

7. Hermann Grensemann, *Knidische Medizin*, vol. 1, *Die Testimonien zur ältesten knidischen Lehre und Analysen knidischer Schriften im Corpus Hippocraticum* (Berlin and New York: de Gruyter, 1975), 198–201.

8. *Morb. mul.* 2.144 = 8:318.21–322.2; *Nat. mul.* 5 = 7:318.11–14; *De steril.* 248 = 8:462.3–5. For succussion in the treatment of dystocia, see below; "ladder therapy" is also discussed by Lesley Dean-Jones, "The Cultural Construct of the Female Body in Classical Greek Science," this volume.

9. For an assessment of Soranus' testimony which gives greater prominence to the name of Euryphon see Grensemann, *Knidische Medizin*, 1:43 (= T31), 61, 201–2.

10. The gynecological recipes of the Corpus do not, however, support Sora-

nus' distinction, for only the term *ekbolion* (or *diekbolion*) is employed, never *phthorion*, and though one therapy does advise shaking the parturient (*Morb. mul.* 1.78 = 8:180.14–15; see also below, on therapies for dystocia), the majority of *ekbolia* were drugs, specifically directed against an impaired or dead fetus (e.g., *Morb. mul.* 1.78 = 8:186.4–7, 188.13–14, etc.).

11. Soranus also glossed over the fact that the abortion in *Nature of the Child* was cosmetic, carried out by the medical writer so that a slave-danseuse belonging to his kinswoman "would not loose her value" (*De nat. pueri* 13 = 7:488–90). See also discussion in Paul Burguière, Danielle Gourevitch, and Yves Malinas, *Soranos d'Ephèse: Maladies des femmes* (Paris: Les Belles Lettres, 1988), 1:xcviii–c, 99–100.

12. E.g., the first example in note 5 above. For a general description of ancient habits of talking about Hippocrates see Wesley D. Smith, "Note on Ancient Medical Historiography," *BHM* 63 (1989): 73–109.

13. For a general summary of early scholarship on the Corpus see [Johannes] Gossen, *RE* 16 (1913): cols. 1809–12, s.v. Hippokrates; for the later period see also Wesley D. Smith, *The Hippocratic Tradition* (Ithaca: Cornell University Press, 1979), 13–60.

14. Francis Adams, *The Genuine Works of Hippocrates*, 2 vols. (London: Sydenham Society, 1849), 1:110. Iain M. Lonie, *The Hippocratic Treatises "On Generation," "On the Nature of the Child," "Diseases IV"* (Berlin and New York: de Gruyter, 1981), 165 and n. 301, corrected the mistaken view that Hippocratic gynecology condoned abortion. Despite the presence of abortive remedies among the recipes and neutral references to abortions, the stance of the gynecology was pronatalist: e.g., *Morb. mul.* 1.25 = 8:66.15–68.17.

15. See, e.g., Johannes Ilberg, "Die ärzteschule von Cnidus," *Berichte über die Verhandlungen Sächs. Akademie der Wissenschaften Leipzig*, Phil.-hist. Klasse 76, part 3 (1924): 20–26; or Jacques Jouanna, *Hippocrate: pour une archéologie de l'école de Cnide* (Paris: Les Belles Lettres, 1974).

16. See, e.g., Gossen, *RE* 16 s.v. Hippokrates, col. 1830. See also, e.g., Arist. *Gen. an.* 4.1.765b, where Aristotle criticizes those who believe that the female's abundance of blood proves that she is hotter than the male, as stated in *Morb. mul.* 1.1 = 8:12.20–22. Gossen's date for the gynecology of the Corpus was based on a recipe in *Diseases of Women* 2 labeled a "philistion" after Philistion of Locri, a doctor whose dates are ca. 427–347 B.C. (*Morb. mul.* 2.201 = 8:386.9–11).

17. Stephanus Philosophus *In Hippocratis prognosticum*, praefat. and ad 1.1 = CMG XI.1.2, 32.25–27, 34.8–9 Duffy.

18. An important exception was H. Fasbender, *Entwickelungslehre, Geburtshülfe und Gynäkologie in den Hippokratischen Schriften* (Stuttgart: F. Enke, 1897), still an intelligent analytical survey.

19. In *Diseases of Women* 1 and 2 the recipes at the end are arranged more or less according to the order in which morbid conditions were considered in the narrative (recipes in *Morb. mul.* 1.74–91 = 8:154–220 follow the order of topics in chap-

ters 1.3–73, and in *Morb. mul.* 2.192–212 = 8:370–406, the order of topics in chapters 111–91. In *De steril.* the capping recipes (234–49 = 8:448–462) are thematically appropriate to what precedes, as are the recipes which conclude each of the two sections of narrative in *Nat. mul.* (32–34 = 7:346–375; 50–92 = 7:392–430). See also Helga Trapp, "Die hippokratische Schrift *De natura muliebri*: Ausgabe und textkritischer Kommentar" (Ph.D. dissertation, University of Hamburg, 1967), 31–34.

20. See Wesley D. Smith, "Galen on Coans vs. Cnidians," *BHM* 47 (1973): 569–85; idem, *The Hippocratic Tradition*, 22, 33–34, 142 and n. 68. See also I. M. Lonie, "Cos and Cnidus vs. the Historians I and II," *History of Science* 16 (1978): 42–75, 77–92; A. Thivel, *Cnide et Cos? Essai sur les doctrines médicales dans la collection hippocratique* (Paris: Les Belles Lettres, 1981).

21. See Ann Ellis Hanson, "Diseases of Women in the *Epidemics*," in *Die hippokratischen Epidemien—Theorie, Praxis, Tradition: Verhandlungen des Ve Colloque international hippocratique*, ed. Gerhard Gaader and Rolf Winau, Sudhoffs Archiv, Zeitschrift für Wissenschaftsgeschichte, Beiheft 27 (Stuttgart: Franz Steiner, 1989), 38–51. Similar conclusions are reached by Lesley Ann Jones, "Morbidity and Vitality: The Interpretation of Menstrual Blood in Greek Science" (Ph.D. dissertation, Stanford University, 1987), 116–18, and by Helen King, "The Daughter of Leonides: Reading the Hippocratic Corpus," in *History as Text*, ed. Averil Cameron (Chapel Hill and London: University of North Carolina Press, 1989), 13–32.

22. For the therapy named "philistion" see above, note 16. Alteration of recipes in an ancient medical text is well documented, for example, in the papyri of Galen's pharmaceutical works. See Ann Ellis Hanson, "Papyri of Medical Content," *YCS* 28 (1985): 44–45 and n. 52.

23. See, e.g., G. E. R. Lloyd, "The Hippocratic Question," *CQ*, n.s. 25 (1975): 171–92, and the references cited above, note 20.

24. The increase in the number of dissertations on Hippocratic gynecology may serve as an index: e.g., Trapp, "Die hippokratische Schrift *De natura muliebri*" (1967); Ann Ellis Hanson, "Studies in the Textual Tradition and Transmission of the Gynecological Treatises of the Hippocratic Corpus" (University of Pennsylvania, 1971); Sarah George, "Human Conception and Fetal Growth: A Study in the Development of Greek Thought from the pre-Socratics through Aristotle" (University of Pennsylvania, 1982); Helen King, "From παρθένος to γυνή: The Dynamics of Category" (University College, London, 1985); Monica Green, "The Transmission of Ancient Theories of Female Physiology and Diseases through the Early Middle Ages" (Princeton University, 1985); Nicolas Countouris, "Hippokratische Gynäkologie: die gynäkologischen Texte des Autors B nach den pseudohippokratischen Schriften *De muliebribus* I und II" (University of Hamburg, med. diss., 1985) (not seen); Jones, "Morbidity and Vitality" (1987).

25. E.g., Trapp, "Die hippokratische Schrift *De natura muliebri*"; Hermann Grensemann, ed., *Hippokrates: Über Achtmonatskinder, Über das Siebenmonatskind* (Berlin:

Akademie Press, 1968); Robert Joly, ed., *Hippocrate*, vol. 9, which contains *Eight-Months' Child*, plus the embryological treatise *Generation / Nature of Children* (Paris: Les Belles Lettres, 1970); Cay Lienau, ed., *Hippokrates: Über Nachempfänges, Geburt-shilfe, und Schwangerschaftsleiden* (= *De superfetatione*) (Berlin: Akademie Press, 1973) = *CMG* I.2.2; Hermann Grensemann, *Hippokratische Gynäkologie: die gynäkologischen Texte des Autors C nach den pseudohippokratischen Schriften De muliebribus I, II, und De steril* (Wiesbaden: Franz Steiner, 1982); Countouris, "Hippokratische Gynäkologie: die gynäkologischen Texte des Autors B."

26. Grensemann, *Hippokratische Gynäkologie*; idem, *Knidische Medizin*, vol. 1; idem, *Knidische Medizin*, vol. 2, Hermes Einzelschriften, 51 (Stuttgart: Franz Steiner, 1987). In his most recent discussion, summarized in *Knidische Medizin*, 2:66–72, Grensemann argues that the earliest stratum ("A1") of the gynecology of the Hippocratic Corpus derived from the school on Cos and is the oldest Greek medical prose we possess; "A2" derived from Cnidus and contained material by Euryphon (see above, note 7) and perhaps Herodikos, whereas the later strata ("B," "C," and "D") revealed influence from Hippocrates' Cos.

27. Grensemann divided stratum "A" into "A1" and "A2" only in *Knidische Medizin*, 2:16–63.

28. Opening sentence: "There has already been discussion of the things which women suffer in each malady, but now I shall clarify why women are totally barren and why they do not give birth until they are healed" (*De steril.* 213 = 8:408.1–3). Although Grensemann assigns much of *Barren Women* to "D," he gives the first chapter, 213, to "C," arguing that in this sentence "C" referred back to his own *Diseases of Women*—an example of the complexity of Grensemann's arguments. For material common to *Barren Women* and other Hippocratic gynecological treatises see his *Knidische Medizin*, 1:203.

29. Robert Joly's attempt to show that "C" was prior to "A"—see "Indices léxicaux pour la datation de *Génération-Nature de l'enfant—Maladies IV*," in *Corpus Hippocraticum, Actes du colloque hippocratique de Mons 1975*, ed. Robert Joly (Mons: Université de Mons, 1977), 136–47—has been satisfactorily answered by Grensemann, *Hippokratische Gynäkologie*, 36–37 and n. 36. At the same time, Grensemann accepts Joly's objection that his date for "C," some decades into the fourth century, is too late; Lonie, *The Hippocratic Treatises*, 52–54, likewise accepts Grensemann's stratification but prefers Joly's date for *Nature of the Child* and *Diseases 4*.

30. See, e.g., Lonie, *The Hippocratic Treatises*, 51–53, for references and earlier bibliography; Grensemann, *Knidische Medizin*, 1:103–15, with earlier bibliography in his n. 11.

31. See, e.g., Manuli, "Donne mascoline, femmine sterili, vergini perpetue," 202 and n. 14; Lloyd, *Science, Folklore and Ideology*, 91 and n. 124, 132–33; Robert Joly, *Le niveau de la science hippocratique* (Paris: Les Belles Lettres, 1966), 49–60; and Lesley Dean-Jones, "Cultural Construct of the Female Body," this volume.

32. See E. Iverson, "Papyrus Carlsberg no. viii, with Some Remarks on the Egyptian Origin of Some Popular Birth Prognoses," *Det kgl. Danske Videnskabernes Selskab.*, Historisk-fil. Med. 26, no. 5 (1939); Dietlinde Goltz, *Studien zur altorientalischen und griechischen Heilkunde* (Wiesbaden: Franz Steiner, 1974), 150–65; Grensemann, *Knidische Medizin*, 2:40–41; A. R. Mills, "Peasant Remedies from the Greek Islands," *BHM* 22 (1948): 441–50. Georg Harig has cast doubt on the usefulness of comparing widely differing medical traditions in his review of Goltz in *Deutsche Literaturzeitung* 96 (1975): cols. 654–58. Heinrich von Staden, *Herophilus: The Art of Medicine in Early Alexandria* (Cambridge and New York: Cambridge University Press, 1989), 1–31, judges as minimal the influence of Egyptian medicine upon Greek medicine as it developed in Ptolemaic Alexandria.

33. "Images médicales du corps: observation féminine et idéologie masculine: le corps de la femme d'après les médecins grecs," *Annales ESC* 35 (1980): 1089–1115, esp. 1091–92. For the view that the same gynecological material came from "male practice and theory" see Paola Manuli, "Fisiologia e patologia del femminile negli scritti ippocratici dell'antica ginecologia greca," in *Hippocratica: actes du colloque hippocratique de Paris, 4–9 septembre 1978*, ed. Mirko Grmek (Paris: Editions du CNRS, 1980), 393–408.

34. Lloyd, *Science, Folklore and Ideology*, 62–86 (esp. 76–79), 168–200.

35. Ann Ellis Hanson, "The Medical Writers' Woman," in *Before Sexuality: The Construction of Erotic Experience in the Ancient Greek World*, ed. David M. Halperin, John J. Winkler, and Froma I. Zeitlin (Princeton: Princeton University Press, 1990), 309–38.

36. *Morb. mul.* 1.64 ("A1") = 8:132.23; *Morb. mul.* 2.113 ("A1") = 8:244.4.

37. See also, e.g., Lloyd, *Science, Folklore and Ideology*, 63; Manuli, "Donne mascoline, femmine sterili, vergini perpetue," 154.

38. I treat the "specially medical reasoning" of Hippocratic gynecology in greater detail in "Doctors' Choices: Conception and Gestation in the *Hippocratic Corpus*," in *Helios* (in press).

39. For therapy as determiner in modern psychiatry see B. Pasamanick, S. Dinitz, and M. Lefton, "Psychiatric Orientation and Its Relation to Diagnosis and Treatment in a Mental Hospital," *American Journal of Psychiatry* 116 (July–December 1954): 127–32.

40. Greek expressions for termination of pregnancy, such as *trōsmos* here, do not distinguish between "spontaneous" and "induced" abortion; LSJ⁹ gloss with "miscarriage."

41. The Greek text is from Grensemann, *Hippokratische Gynäkologie*, 138–39, reading in the parentheses *iētreuontai* of manuscripts Θ and V instead of the *iētreuousi* of M and the *recentiores*. The subject matter, the use of pessaries to induce abortion, is most of all a concern of women, and it would seem that the active verb in M and the *recentiores* represents a correction of the morphologically ambiguous

and potentially unrecognized middle, *iētreuontai*. Grensemann, however, translates "wozu die Frauen durch eigene und ärtzlich Behandlung kommen," that is, "to which (ulcerations) women come through their own and through doctors' therapies." His note to the text (171) underscores the fact that he understands these lesions as occasioned as often by medicaments from male physicians as they are by women who self-medicate, for he asks, "Von Selbstbehandlung oder Quacksalberei?"—"By self-medication or quackery?" But this medical writer ("C") is by no means reticent to point out mistakes of of fellow practitioners when they came to treat women patients, and it is his habit elsewhere to give full vent to his criticisms of other physicians (e.g., *Morb. mul.* 1.40 = 8:96–98, or 62 = 8:126). In this passage, then, his concern is with women's unskillful use of abortifacients on themselves and on other women.

42. See John Scarborough, "Nicander's Toxicology II: Spiders, Scorpions, Insects, and Myriapods," *Pharmacy in History* 21 (1979): 73–92; Malcolm Davies and Jeyaraney Kathirithamby, *Greek Insects* (Oxford and New York: Oxford University Press, 1986), 91–94.

43. E.g., the use of cantharid beetles in Hippocratic hemagogic pessaries was sometimes glossed by an explicit reference to their potency. See *Morb. mul.* 1.74 = 8:160.3–7; 1.71 = 8:150.14–18; and perhaps 1.74 = 8:158.3–6, all recipes presumably linked with later strata of the gynecology (probably "C"). In earlier strata the caveat was lacking: e.g., *Morb. mul.* 2.127 ("A2") = 8:274.1–2; 2.157 ("A2") = 8:334.4–5.

44. *Morb. mul.* 2.169–71 = 8:348.6–352.14 (esp. 169 = 8:348.19–20; 171 = 8:352.10).

45. The textually inferior versions read *selinou sperma* in place of *linon* or *linou sperma*. The inferior version of the recipe with the variant "celery seed" may be responsible for the fact that the recipe appears twice in quick succession in *Diseases of Women 2*.

46. Hippocratics estimated the amount of blood lost during menstruation at two cotyls, a magnification of approximately sixteenfold over the norm of modern measuring, and although the volume of the nongravid womb is but two to three ounces, they often prescribe the infusion of two cotyls (= one pint) into a nongravid womb. See Lesley Dean-Jones," Menstrual Bleeding According to the Hippocratics and Aristotle," *TaPhA* 119 (1989): 177–91.

47. For *selinou sperma* see above, note 45, and below, note 48.

48. "Clysters for lesions of long duration: a saucer of myrrh, incense, seseli, anise, celery seed (*selinou sperma*), netopon, resin, honey, goose grease, white vinegar, white Egyptian myrrh; grind smoothly equal parts of each into a container, then with two kotyls of white wine; administer with warm clysters": *Morb. mul.* 1.78 = 8:192.16–21.

49. "Clysters: . . . if the mouth of the womb is ulcerated. . . . A saucer of myrrh, incense, seseli, anise, linseed (*linou sperma*), netopon, resin, honey, goose grease,

white vinegar, the Egyptian [myrrh]; grind equal parts of each of these, dilute in two kotyls of white wine and administer with a warm clyster: *Nat. mul.* 33 = 7:366.20–368.2.

50. In "The Medical Writers' Woman," 320, I argue that had the Phaedra of Euripides' *Hippolytus* taken her malady to a doctor, as the chorus suggests at lines 293–96, instead of to her nurse, his prescription would also likely have included intercourse, or simulation of intercourse, since her wasting illness came upon her during the absence of her husband. Like folk theory, Hippocratic theory accepted the premise that sexual intercourse was necessary for health in postpubertal women.

51. See Dean-Jones, "Cultural Construct of the Female Body," this volume, for the role which a "wandering womb" played in characterizing the female sex in popular and Hippocratic imagination.

52. Celsus *Med.* 4.27; Soranus *Gyn.* 4.38 = *CMG* IV, 151.10–12; Galen *De compositione med.* 9.10 = 13.320.5–8. Unless otherwise noted, all references to Galen are from the edition of the Greek text by C. G. Kühn, *Opera omnia*, 20 vols. (Leipzig, 1821–33; reprinted Hildesheim: G. Olms, 1964). Line numbers in the Kühn edition are cited only when part of a chapter, rather than the entire chapter, is pertinent. Aretaeus 5.10 = *CMG* II, 139.27–141.10, esp. 139.29–30, 140.170–26 Hüde; Oribasius 10.19 = *CMG* VI.1.2, 61.20–62.18 Raeder; Theodore Priscian *Euporiston* 3 (= *Gynaecia*) 6, 229.6–230.3 Rose; Paul Aegineta *Epitomae medicae* 3.71 = *CMG* IX.1, 288.27–289.6 Heiberg.

53. So also King, "From παρθένος to γυνή," n. 158.

54. Male sexual apparatus and male sexual experience offered medical writers a model from which to deduce female experience and a vocabulary with which to name female organs: e.g., emission of female seed in the heat of intercourse (*De gen.* / *De nat. pueri* 4 = 7:474.16–22); or Herophilus' calling ovaries "testicles" (Galen *De sem.* 2.1 = 4:596.4–597.15; for which passage see von Staden, *Herophilus*, T61 and pp. 183–86, 230–34). The habit of thinking about unseen female reproductive organs as analogous to the seen males one was made explicit in Galen *De usu partium* = 14.6–7 = 4:164.1–165.4 and 171.6–13.

55. *Morb. mul.* 2.123–53 = 8:266–330; these chapters included material from Grensemann's "A1," "A2," "B," and "C."

56. *Nat. mul.* and Grensemann's "A2": 3–5 = 7.314–18; 8 = 7.322–24; 14 = 7.332; 25–26 = 7.342. *Nat. mul.* and "A 1": 38 = 7.380–82; 40 = 7.384; 43–44 = 7.386–88; 47–49 = 7.390–92; 54 = 7.392. *Morb. mul.* 1 ("C"): 7 = 8.32; 32 = 8.76. *De steril.* 248 ("A2") = 8.460–62. *Loc. hom.* 47 = 6.344.

57. Reading *thermantheisai* with ms. Θ; so also Grensemann, *Hippokratische Gynäkologie*, 100.

58. See in particular King, "From παρθένος to γυνή," 113–16. Cf. also D. F. Krell, "Female Parts in *Timaeus*," *Arion* 2 (1975): 400–421.

59. For odor therapies see, e.g., *Morb. mul.* 2.128 ("A2") = 8:274.13–20 (upward

dislocation); 2.131 ("A2") = 8:278.19 (downward dislocation); and 2.143 ("A2") = 8:316.9–10 (prolapse). Centuries later a magical charm on a papyrus from Graeco-Roman Egypt addressed the womb, ordering it not to move about the body and not to "gnaw into the heart like a dog," *PGM* VII.260–71 = *Papyri Graecae Magicae: Die Griechischen Zauberpapyri*, 2 vols., 2d ed., ed. Karl Preisendanz et al. (Stuttgart: B. G. Teubner, 1973–74), for a translation of which see Hans Dieter Betz, *The Greek Magical Papyri in Translation* (Chicago and London: University of Chicago Press, 1986), 123–24.

60. See also below, note 97 and surrounding discussion in text.

61. Cf. also *Gyn.* 1 = *CMG* IV, 7.11–13.

62. E.g., *Morb. mul.* 2.127 ("A2") = 8:272.11–15; 2.137 ("B") = 8:310.11–12; for "C," *Morb. mul.* 2.145, quoted in the text just above.

63. E.g., *Morb. mul.* 2.127 ("A2") = 8:274.5; 2.128 ("A2") = 8:276.8; 2.131 ("A2") = 8:280.2; 2.134 ("A2") = 8:304.22; 2.135 ("A2") = 8:308.2–3; 2.139 ("A1") =8:312.20–21; 2.141 ("A1") = 8:314.19–20; 2.146 ("A2") = 8:322.20. For adverse effects of intercourse on uterine prolapse see 2.143 ("A2") = 8:316.12 and 2.149 ("A1") = 8:324.21–326.1; Soranus criticized intercourse as therapy for uterine dislocations, *Gyn.* 3.29 = *CMG* IV, 113.22–24.

64. So also Grensemann, *Knidische Medizin*, 2:40.

65. For bathing see, e.g., *Morb. mul.* 2.123 = 8:266.15; 2.129 = 8:276.16; 2.131 = 8:278.18; 2.133 = 8:286.12–13, 288.5, 292.10, 294.18, 298.5, 300.12–13; 2.134 = 8:302.18; 2.135 = 8:306.7, 306.21; 2.137 = 8:310.2, 310.15; 2.138 = 8:312.9–10; 2.139 = 8:312.19; 2.140 = 8:314.8; 2.141 = 8:314.15; 2.145 = 8:320.14; 2.146 = 8:322.9–10; 2.150 = 8:326.11; 2.153 = 8:153.5. In the few instances where bathing was prohibited, intercourse was usually also forbidden, from fear of accumulation of moisture inside the woman's body in excess, often a concern in maintenance of female health: e.g., *Morb. mul.* 2.143 = 8:11–12; 2.144 = 8:318.13–18; 2.153 = 8:328.14. For uterine "drinks" (*pisai katō*, etc.) see, e.g., *Morb. mul.* 2.124 = 8:268.5; 2.127 = 8:272.21; 2.128 = 8:276.1–3; 2.129 = 8:276.15; 2.131 = 8:278.22; 2.137 = 8:310.3–4. For uterine infusions see, e.g., *Morb. mul.* 2.125 = 8:268.17; 2.127 = 8:274.3; 2.128 = 8:276.7; 2.131 = 8:278.17; 2.134 = 8: 302.19; 2.139 = 8:342.17–18; 2.144 = 8:316.21; 2.145 = 8:320.17; 2.146 = 8: 322.18.

66. For manual manipulation, often followed by application of binders, see, e.g., *Morb. mul.* 2.127 = 8:272.16–17; 2.129 = 8:278.1–3; 2.134 = 8:304.1–3; 2.135 = 8:306.11–12; 2.144 = 8:318.5–8 (see above, note 8); 2.145 = 8:320.15; 2.149 = 8:324.17. For probes see, e.g., *Morb. mul.* 2.133 = 8:288.13–292.10; 2.134 = 8:304.5.

67. For vomiting see, e.g., *Morb. mul.* 2.142 = 8:314.22; 2.143 = 8:316.7; 2.146 =8:322.8–9; 2.149 = 8:324.12; 2.153 = 8:328.13. For elevation and rest, 2.143 = 8:316.8–9; 2.144 = 8:316.22–318.20 (see above, note 8); 2.149 = 8:324.10–12; 2.153 = 8:328.14.

68. *Nat. mul.* 48 = 7:392.9–10; *Morb. mul.* 2.123 = 8:266.11–14. Cf. Grensemann, *Knidische Medizin*, 2:86–87.

69. *Nat. mul.* 49 = 7:392.16–17; *Morb. mul.* 2.150 = 8:326.8–11. Cf. Grensemann, *Knidische Medizin*, 2:87.

70. *Morb. mul.* 2.127 = 8:274.16; cf. also 2.137 = 8:308.16–18.

71. *Morb. mul.* 1.7 = 8:32.10–12 (quoted just above); 1.32 = 8:76.7; 2.124 = 8:268.1; 2.201 = 8:384.12; for the havoc which pressure from misplaced menstural blood wreaks when crowded near the heart and diaphragm see *Virg.* 1 = 8:466.15–468.12.

72. E.g., *Morb. mul.* 1.7 = 8:32.21–24; 1.32 = 8:76.7–10; 2.126 = 8:270.10–12; 2.127 = 8:272.9–11; 2.129 = 8:276.14; 2.131 = 8:278.16; 2.138 = 8:312.7–8; 2.139 = 8:14; 2.151 = 8:326.14.

73. King, "From παρθένος to γυνή," 137–39, although she admits that the "central tube from mouth or nostrils to vagina" was "never anatomically described." This notion that Hippocratics endorsed a traveling tube for the uterus has been accepted by, e.g., Ralph Jackson, *Doctors and Diseases in the Roman Empire* (London: British Museum Publications, 1988), 89, and Dean-Jones, "The Cultural Construct of the Female Body," this volume.

74. See, e.g., formation of the tube in the fetus in *De carnibus* 3.4 = 8:586.14–19.

75. E.g., *Loc. hom.* 33 = 6:324.22–326.1.

76. *De morb.* 4.41 ("C") = 7:562.8–10; *Epidemiae* 2.1.7 = 5:76.17–78.8; 4.46 = 5:188.11–16.

77. See Jones, "Morbidity and Vitality," 88–90, and Dean-Jones, "The Cultural Construct of the Female Body," this volume.

78. On passageways for menstruation see, e.g., *De gen. / De nat. pueri* 2 ("C") = 7:472.17–474.3. For milk, *De nat. pueri* 21 ("C") = 7:512.16–20; *Morb. mul.* 2.133 ("B") = 8:280.17–18. Widening in childbirth, *De nat. pueri* 24.4 ("C") = 7:520.22–522.7; 22.2–5 = 7:514.13–516.17; *Morb. mul.* 1.1 ("C") = 8:10.2–13, 12.6–14.7; 1.2 ("C") = 8:14.8–9, 22.3–4; 1.3 ("C") = 8:24.5–7, 24.13–15; 1.73 ("C") = 8:154.5–8.

79. E.g., *Aphorismi* 5.33 = 4:544.1–2; *Epidemiae* 1.2.8 = 2:648.4–5; 7.123 = 5:468.4–6. For the special significance of these passages see King, "The Daughter of Leonides."

80. For fecundity tests of this nature see, e.g., *Morb. mul.* 1.78 = 8:178.15–17; 2.146 = 8:322.12–14; *Nat. mul.* 96 = 7:412–14; *De steril.* 214 = 8:414.20–416.2; 219 = 8:424.6–13; 230 = 8:440.12–14; *De superfetatione* 25 = 8:488.18–490.2; *Aphorismi* 5.59 = 4:554.

81. E.g., *De steril.* 213 = 8:408.4–16; 217 = 8:418.2–9; 223 = 8:432; 230 = 8:438.10–15.

82. *Morb. mul.* 1.7 = 8:32.23–24 (like "Herakles' disease"); 2.151 = 8:326.17 (like "the sacred disease"); cf. *Morb. mul.* 2.126 = 8:270.6–7 ("as from helebore," a common cure for madness). In early Greek thought the upper abdomen (*phrēn*,

phrenes) was the seat of the emotions and intellectual activity, and in the Homeric epics *phrēn* and *phrenes* are often translated as "heart," "mind," "wits." By the time of the Corpus the head and the brain were also associated with thinking and perceiving, although some treatises, such as *Diseases of Young Girls* (see above, note 71), rely on the earlier assumption that cognition is a function of the midsection of the body. The ambiguity is seen in the Corpus, for example, when medical writers use *phrēn, phrenes* to refer to the midriff, usually translated as "diaphragm," but speak of *phrenitis*, or "inflammation of the *phrenes*," as the "delirium that accompanies a high fever," often equated with "brain fever." Thus in the practice of the translators in *Hippocratic Writings*, ed. G. E. R. Lloyd (London and New York: Penguin, 1987), 86 and 172: "Abcesses and tumours also occur very commonly here [in the hepatic area], as well as beneath the diaphragm (*phrenas*). The extent of the diaphragm (*phrenōn*) is considerable and is opposed to other organs; nevertheless, its more sinewy and stronger nature makes it less liable to pain," *Vet. med.* 22 = 1:634; and "In cases of acute fever or of pneumonia and in brain-fever [*en phrenitisin*] and headache, it is a bad sign and portends death if any of the following things are noted," *Prognos.* 4 = 2:122.

83. For similarities of style and doctrine between "C" and the Hippocratic treatise *Sacred Disease* cf. Lonie, *The Hippocratic Treatises*, 54, 71, 110. See also Dean-Jones, "Cultural Construct of the Female Body," this volume.

84. So also Fasbender, *Entwickelungslehre, Geburtshülfe und Gynäkologie*, 126–28. Fasbender's view was contested by Paul Diepgen, *Die Frauenheilkunde der Alten Welt* (Munich: J. Bergmann, 1937), 165, but the passages Diepgen proffered as evidence for awareness of contractions are considered inconclusive by Lonie, *The Hippocratic Treatises*, 244–46 (commentary to *De nat. pueri* 30). Although he finds Diepgen's evidence indecisive, Lonie argues that midwives must have known about uterine contractions, but he offers no evidence. Lonie was ultimately led to doubt that the medical writer "C" had ever witnessed the birth of a child, where he would have seen the workings of uterine contractions. Rather, as I argue below, that writer's view that the uterus was passive in birth was shared by many contemporaries in the fifth century B.C.

85. Notions of the uterus as upside-down jar have been considered at length in Hanson, "The Medical Writers' Woman," 324–30. The image of the uterus as upside-down jar continued to play a role in conception for Soranus and Galen, who likewise endorsed the notion that a woman's uterus closed at the initiation of a pregnancy: see Ann Ellis Hanson, "The Restructuring of Female Physiology at Rome," in *Actes du IIe colloque international sur les textes medicaux latins antiques, septembre 1986*, ed. Phillipe Mudry (forthcoming).

86. The translation is based on that by Lonie, *The Hippocratic Treatises*, 18–20. Other translations from the Greek given in this essay are my own, except for this passage and that from Galen's *On Natural Faculties*, for which see below, note 90.

87. The image of the cupping jar is retained by Soranus (*Gyn.* 1.9 = *CMG* IV, 7.22–23).

88. See above, note 78 and surrounding discussion in text.

89. E.g., *Morb. mul.* 1.8 ("C") = 8:34.9–10; 1.10 ("B") = 8:40,12–14; 1.11 ("B") =8:46.17–48.1; 1.24 ("C") = 8:62.19–64.1; 2.132 ("B") = 8:280.4–6; 2.146 ("A2") = 8:322.5–6; 2.154 ("A1") = 8:330.3; 2.162 ("A2") 8.338.15; 2.163 ("A1") = 8:342.15; *De steril.* 220 ("D"?, Grensemann, *Knidische Medizin*, 1:203–4) = 8:424.16–21; 222 ("D") = 8:428.15–22.

90. The translation is based on that by Arthur J. Brock, *Galen: On the Natural Faculties,* Loeb Classical Library (London: Heinemann; Cambridge: Harvard University Press, 1916), 231–33. Cf. also Galen *Nat. fac.* 3.12 = 2:183.10–184.14.

91. See Ludwig Edelstein, "The History of Anatomy in Antiquity," in *Ancient Medicine: Selected Papers of Ludwig Edelstein* (Baltimore: The Johns Hopkins University Press, 1967), 247–301 = English translation of "Die Geschichte der Sektion in der Antike," *Quellen und Studien zur Geschichte der Naturwissenschaften und der Medizin* 3 (1932): 50–106. The period of human dissection should probably be limited to the third century B.C.: see Fridolf Kudlien, "Antike Anatomie und menschlicher Leichnam," *Hermes* 97 (1969): 78–94; see also Peter M. Fraser, *Ptolemaic Alexandria,* 3 vols. (Oxford: Oxford University Press, 1972), 2:511 n. 94; von Staden, *Herophilus,* 26–31, 139–53.

92. Soranus *Gyn.* 1.10–13 and 3.3 = *CMG* IV, 8–10, 95.17–18; Galen, *De uteri dissect.* 2–6 = *CMG* V.2.1, 36–44 Nickel. Features of Herophilus' now lost description of the uterus were likely to have included (1) identification of separate parts, (2) a clear statement of the changes which pregnancy and repeated parturition brought to the uterus, (3) mention of the pelvic and spinal bones and their action in birth, (4) measuring of the genital tract and its parts by finger-lengths, analogous to his measuring of the "twelve-finger" duodenum (see, e.g., Rufus *De corporis humani appellationibus* 111 = p. 147 Daremberg and Rouelle; Soranus *Gyn.* 1.18 = *CMG* IV, 12.15–22; Galen *De usu partium* 14.11 = 4:193.6–7; 5.3 = 4:223.5–224.2; *De semine* 2.1 = 4:597.5; *De uteri dissect.* 3 = *CMG* V.2.1, 38.4 Nickel).

93. Aesop 257 Perry; Aesop's *to dia pantos hena tiktein* is less precise than Herodotus' *hapax en tōi biōi tiktei hen.*

94. Arist. *HA* 6.31, 579a; also Ael. *NA* 4.34.

95. For a different interpretation of Aristotle's failure to mention Herodotus see Walter W. How and Joseph Wells, *A Commentary on Herodotus,* 2 vols. (Oxford: Clarendon Press, 1912), 1:291.

96. See also *De gen. / De nat. pueri* 9 ("C") = 7:482.14–19.

97. See above, note 60 and surrounding discussion in text; cf. also *Morb. mul.* 1.40 ("C") = 8:96.9. For similarities between *Morb. mul.* 1.32 and modern clinical descriptions of convulsive eclampsy see Y. Malinas and Danielle Gourevitch, "Cronique anachronique, I: suffocation subite chez la femme enceinte." *Revue*

française de gynécologie et d' obstétrique 77 (1982): 753–55.

98. *De octimestri partu* 1 (5) = 7:436.8–14 (= *CMG* I.2.1, 90.3–9 Grensemann).

99. *Morb. mul.* 2.153 = 8:328.1–5 (quoted above in discussion of uterine displacement); *Aphorismi* 5.49 = 4:550; *Epidemiae* 2.5.25 = 5:132.10–12.

100. Omitting the negative with ms. Θ.

101. *Morb. mul.* 1.78 = 8:180.14–15; *De exectione foetus* 4 = 8:514.14–516.9; cf. also *De superfetatione* 8 = 8:482.1–5.

102. *Epidemiae* 5.103 = 5:258.9–12 = *Epidemiae* 7.49 = 5:418.1–4.

103. *Morb. mul.* 1.69 = 8:146.1–3, 146.13–18.

104. For other Hippocratic procedures see *De exectione foetus* 1 = 8:512–14, in which the doctor is advised to cover the parturient's face before he begins to remove the baby; *De steril.* 249 (= 8:462) urged that fetal skin be left intact during excision as protection for the uterus; *De superfetatione* 5–7 (= *CMG* I.2.2, 74.17–76.6 Lienau) describes manual interventions during surgery.

105. Celsus, an encyclopedist rather than a practicing physician, stressed the fact that the fetus which died during birth required surgical removal, because it could not exit the womb on its own.

106. Soranus *Gyn.* 4.14 = *CMG* IV, 144.21–145.3.

107. Soranus *Gyn.* 4.9 = *CMG* IV, 140.2–11.

108. Soranus *Gyn.* 4.9 = *CMG* IV, 140.6–9. Normal births are not discussed in the Corpus and apparently were usually handled by midwives and female relatives; see, e.g., Sarah B. Pomeroy, *Goddesses, Whores, Wives and Slaves: Women in Classical Antiquity* (New York: Schocken Books, 1975), 84, 168–69. For explicit statements in later writers see, e.g., Soranus *Gyn.* 2.1–6 = *CMG* IV, 50.1–55.10 or Galen *Nat. fac.* 3.3 = 2:151.12–152.12.

There is little unequivocal evidence to show direct male participation in normal childbirth, even in later antiquity. Male midwives (*maioi*) celebrate the adoption of a foundling by an inscription to Eileithyia on Paros in the first century A.D. (*IG* XII.5:199), but the text seems playful in tone. The epitaph of the doctor Evandros, set up in Lambaesis, capital of the Roman province of Numidia in the third century A.D., alludes to children he delivered; see B. Helly and J. Marcillet-Jaubert, *ZPE* 14 (1974): 252–56. A letter of Maximus to Tinarsiegis about birth, on an ostrakon from Egypt in the second century A.D., was an exchange between two women, whatever meaning may be attached to the name "Maximus"; see *O. Florida* 14, in R. S. Bagnall, *The Florida Ostraka: Documents from the Roman Army in Upper Egypt, GRBS* Monograph 7 (Durham, N.C.: Duke University Press, 1976), 51–54, and, on the name Maximus, J. D. Thomas, *CE* 53 (1978): 142–44.

109. "Fetal slaughterer," *embryosphaktēs*: Tertullian *De anima* 25.5. "Compressor," "fetal compressor," *piestron*: *Morb. mul.* 1.70 = 8:146.23; *embryothlastēs*, Galen *Hipp. Lex.* = 19.104.6–7. "Bone extractor," *osteologia*: *De steril.* 249 = 8:462.17. "Fetal hook," *embryoulkos*: Soranus *Gyn.* 4.9–10 = *CMG* IV, 140.2–141.30; Aetius 16.23 = 31.13–33.23 Zervos.

110. See, e.g., R. C. Benson, *Handbook of Obstetrics and Gynecology*, 5th ed. (Los Altos: Lange Medical Publications, 1974), 155–56, 383–89, 423–24.

111. "If intra-abdominal pregnancy occurs and death comes to an advanced fetus, it cannot be absorbed. It may become infected; it may become a mummified, calcified mass or lithopedion; or it may be converted into a grayish, greasy mass called an adipocere" (Benson, *Handbook of Obstetrics and Gynecology*, 236). The incidence of abdominal pregnancy is one in fifteen thousand pregnancies.

112. This was apparently known to some Hippocratic writers: the author of *Fleshes* claimed that an aborted fetus fell out (*epidan de ēdē diaphtharēi, ekpiptei hōsper karx, De carnibus* 19 = 8:610.5–6), and the writer of *Superfetation* pictured the dying fetus as first swelling, and then melting, putrefying, and finally exiting, soft flesh before the bones (*De superfetatione* 9 = 8:482.13–15). *Superfetation* belongs to the later strata of Hippocratic gynecology: Lienau, *Hippokrates: über Nachempfänges*, 37–42, argues that it derived largely from *Barren Women*. The date of *Fleshes* (*De carnibus*) is uncertain, but see Robert Joly, *Hippocrate* (Paris: Les Belles Lettres, 1974), 13:182–83, for a summary of arguments that set *Fleshes* at the end of the fifth century. Lonie, *The Hippocratic Treatises*, 53–54, argues that *Fleshes* 19 was based on *Nature of the Child* 13, but such a view does not necessarily overturn Joly's argument.

Multipurpose pessaries and infusions, said to lead down menses, lochial flows, and the dead or impaired fetus, are frequent among gynecological recipes (e.g., *Morb. mul.* 1.78 = 8:176.8–10, 178.1–12, 182.13–20; 1.84 = 8:208.15–210.4; 1.91 = 8:218.13–15, 220.16–18), but these are hemagogues and early abortives, without bearing on dystocia.

113. A late antique Christian charm for childbearing in a Greek papyrus from Roman Egypt claimed that Christ called the child to come out from the uterus: see *PGM* CXXIIIa.48–50, with a translation in Betz, *The Magical Greek Papyri*, 319.

114. Hanson, "Diseases of Women in the *Epidemics*," 48–49.

115. For the superiority of male over female in pre-Socratic thinking, see George, "Human Conception and Fetal Growth," passim and summary remarks, 264.

116. The superstition that a child born after eight months in the uterus was not viable but that a child of seven months would live, likewise reinforced society's preference for the birth of a strong, male baby and also offered an acceptable explanation for the death of supposedly weaker neonates: see Ann Ellis Hanson, "The Eight Months' Child and the Etiquette of Birth: 'Obsit Omen!' " *BHM* 61 (1987): 589–602, esp. 600–602.

117. The fact that two authors in the Corpus knew that a dead fetus exited the uterus without medical intervention (see above, note 111) by no means brought an end to medical discussion of excision of the fetus (see, e.g., the references cited above, notes 103, 108).

118. *Gynaikeia nosemata*: *Morb. mul.* 1.62 ("C") = 8:126.18; *De nat. pueri* 15 ("C") = 7:496.9–10; *De morb.* 4.57 ("C") = 7:612.21–22; *De steril.* 213 = 8:408.19

("C," according to Grensemann; see above, note 28); *Loc. hom.* 47 = 6:344.3. *Gynaikeiai nosoi: Morb. mul.* 1.1 ("C") = 8:10.1, preceded by a title which looks to the later development (so also Grensemann, *Hippokratische Gynäkologie*, 88, 148); *De gen.* / *De nat. pueri* 4 ("C") = 7:476.16; Eur. *Andr.* 955–56. *Gynaikeia symphora: De affect.* 54 = 6:264.12.

119. *Gynaikeia* or *Gynaecia* served as title for the gynecological writings of, e.g., Diocles Carystius, Soranus and his Latin adapters Caelius Aurelianus and Mustio, and Vindician and his pupil, Theodore Priscian.

LESLEY DEAN-JONES

The Cultural Construct of the

Female Body in Classical Greek Science

In most cultures an individual is ascribed to one sex or another at birth on the evidence of external genitalia, and this categorization is taken to predict his or her physical and mental development and capabilities, which in turn support the differentiation between the sexes in the home, the workplace, religion, the law—even in hairstyles and dress. There is an obvious correlation between genitalia and an individual's role in the propagation of the species, but no culture considers this difference in external genitalia in and of itself sufficient to justify the complete separation of male and female roles in society. Rather, cultures support this division by claiming that there are other, less apparent physical, mental, and emotional traits which naturally differentiate the sexes. The traits that a culture decides are typical of a male or a female form the construct of that sex in that society. These stereotypes are often contradicted by individuals. Taking our own culture as an example, a woman can be more muscular or more aggressive than many men, a man can be smaller and more gentle than many women. However, these challenges to the cultural constructs of male and female are neutralized by claiming that they are exceptions to a natural law.[1] The belief in a natural law of the disjunction of the sexes can find its initial expression in mythology or religion, as in the derivation of Eve from Adam's rib. And although, as a society develops, this mythological expression can appear allegorical at best, the deeply implanted cultural belief that men and women are radically different can condition the interpretation of empirical evidence so that science, in its turn, supports the belief that perceived differences between men and women are a result of biology rather than social conditioning.[2]

In ancient Greece the polarization of sexual roles was far more marked than in our own society, and consequently there was a stronger need to sever the male from the female. This disjunction was expressed in Greek myth by the separate origins of the sexes. In *Works and Days* (60–95) and *Theogony* (570–616) Hesiod portrays man as already existing when woman, a later manufactured product of the gods, was given to him.[3] But after the beginnings of natural philosophy in Ionia in the sixth century B.C., mythology was no longer universally accepted as giving a true explanation of the world; as in our own society, science assumed the task of bolstering the traditional dichotomy between male and female.[4] However, although the Greeks could observe the difference in external genitalia and typical secondary sexual characteristics, they did not dissect the human body and so had only the vaguest understanding of the internal reproductive organs; nor, obviously, could they have any knowledge of genetics or endocrinology. The strict biological polarization of the sexes was thus even more dependent on external sexual characteristics than our own society. But because, as today, many bodies would have been annoyingly recalcitrant in conforming to the culturally determined sexual norm, the archetype of the male or female body could not be substantiated by referring simply to the actual bodies that men and women possessed. The cultural paradigm of masculinity and femininity had to be supported by demonstrating that typical male or female observable characteristics (both genitalia and the less constant differences of body shape and behavior) were evidence of a more perfectly male or female invisible nature (*physis*). Once the cultural archetype was shown to be grounded in nature, a man or woman who deviated from this norm could be viewed as aberrant— lacking in something essentially masculine or feminine—rather than as a challenge to what it was to be male or female, and the traditional polarization of the sexual roles could claim a scientific foundation.

The sexual roles in ancient Greece were complementary; men were thought to be best suited to dealing with matters outside the home, the *polis*, and women with the concerns of the household, the *oikos*. The female role in managing the *oikos* was recognized as important, and a woman could gain satisfaction and respect from performing her tasks well; but she was nevertheless considered inferior and subordinate to her husband.[5] She was barred from the male sphere by her inability to perform certain mental and physical tasks. On the other hand, although a man could not bear or nurse a child, he was not thought incapable of performing female tasks in the same way; the management of a household was considered beneath rather than beyond him.[6] Hesiod's account of the first woman as a gift (albeit malicious) of the gods to men reflects this cultural construct of woman as secondary and subordinate to man. In the same way, scientific theories attempted to justify not only the polarization of the sexes but also the subordination of the female to the male. This essay demonstrates how Greek scientific theories of female anatomy and physiology were conditioned by cultural assumptions of female nature: specifically, how Greek scientists used menstruation, breasts, womb, and lack of body hair to define female physical nature as fundamentally different from and inferior to the physical nature of the male, and how, on occasion, their assumptions led them to misinterpret or overlook data which could have challenged their theories.[7]

Little explicit reference is made to female anatomy or physiology in the majority of Greek literature, but there are two sources which discuss these matters in great detail. The first of these is the gynecology of the Hippocratic Corpus, a collection of theoretical and therapeutical treatises written between the last quarter of the fifth and the middle of the fourth century B.C.[8] The treatises were written by several different authors, and although they are on the whole consistent with each other, there are occasions where differences of opinion are evident (as on the origin of menstrual blood, discussed below). I draw attention to these differences where it is necessary, but for most purposes here I refer to a general "Hippocratic" model of the female, because the Hippocratic theories have a great deal more in common with each other than they do with the second source with which I want to compare them. This second source is the biology of Aristotle (primarily *History of Animals*, *Parts of Animals*, *Generation of Animals*), written around the third quarter of the fourth century B.C. Some of the later Hippocratic authors may have still been writing when Aristotle began to compile his biology, but even if all the gynecological treatises had been completed before Aristotle began his researches, there is no indication that there was any revolution in medical theory during the fourth century. Thus the theory and practice of Hippocratic gynecology was in all probability still flourishing when Aristotle wrote.[9] Therefore, although the Hippocratic gynecological theories were produced slightly earlier than Aristotle's biology, they functioned in the same culture.

The Hippocratic theory is the product of different physicians in different generations concerned, primarily, with pathology. Aristotle, on the

other hand, was a single philosopher of nature, interested more in norma-
tive physiology and in developing a thoroughgoing theory of the female
which could explain the similarities as well as the differences between the
male and the female, between the human and other animals. This is not to
say that the Hippocratics would have come up with the Aristotelian
theory had they attempted to systematize, but it explains in some measure why Aristotle rejected many Hippocratic ideas.[10] Still, although the
Hippocratics and Aristotle constructed different models of the female
body and observed or overlooked different pieces of evidence in support
of their theories, their constructs were similar in that both were shaped by
their cultural assumption that the female body was inherently inferior to
that of the male.

Both the Hippocratics and Aristotle argued that despite the difference
in external genitalia which developed in the fetus, the fundamental differentiation between the sexes which occurred at conception did not
become apparent until puberty.[11] The Hippocratic treatises rarely characterize prepubescent children by sex, and a similar homology underlies
Aristotle's statement that a woman's body is like a boy's.[12] According to
Aristotle, at puberty a man's body changes more drastically than a woman's; until then the two sexes are very similar. Once puberty is passed,
however, the female body is marked as differing in many aspects from the
male. The two most striking observable developments in the female body
at puberty—menstruation and breasts—are explained by both the Hippocratics and Aristotle as the manifestation of the hitherto concealed female
nature which made it difficult for women to perform in the male sphere.

Diseases of Women 1.1 (= 8:2) attributes menstruation to the very nature
of a woman's flesh, which at puberty becomes loose and spongy, causing
her body to soak up excess blood from her stomach (where it has been
converted from the food she has consumed). The author uses an analogy
to explain the difference between female and male flesh. If wool and cloth
of equal weight are stretched above water and left for two days and
nights, at the end of this period the wool will have become much heavier
than the cloth. It soaks up more moisture because it is more porous
(*araia*).[13] So it is with men and women. A woman's spongy, porous flesh is
like wool (*eirion*) and soaks up more moisture from her belly than a man's
from his.

If a man should have any excess moisture in his body after exercise, it is
absorbed by his glands, which are especially constructed for this purpose.

The author of *Glands* 1 (= 8:556) describes their nature as spongy, porous, and plump (*spongōdēs araiai kai piones*), language very similar to that which is used in *Diseases of Women* to describe the female body in general. Later in the same chapter the author likens the texture of glands to *eirion*, wool, and emphasizes how much they differ from the rest of the body in this: "and there is no flesh like it in the rest of the body, nor anything like it at all in the body."[14] In chapter 16 (= 8:572), however, he says: "The nature of glands in women is porous, *just like the rest of the body*."[15] The body of a mature woman was one big gland and therefore similar to that flesh in a male body which functioned only after a man had evacuated or used up most of his excess fluid through vigorous activity. The implication is that a truly feminine woman would be incapable of developing the sort of flesh that would enable her to perform the same tasks as a man, despite the fact that many female slaves worked very strenuously and must have developed leaner and more muscular bodies than some men.

The breasts were regarded as glands, and the difference in the size of male and female breasts was used as another indication of the extent to which a woman's body is looser than a man's. In both sexes they swell at puberty, but the treatise says that breasts become prominent (*diairontai*) only in those who make milk,[16] because man's firm flesh prevents the spongy parts of his body from swelling too far. Even where the bodies of both sexes are constructed to soak up moisture, women soak up more. *Epidemics* 2.6.19 (= 5:136) states that a large vein runs to each breast and that these are the seat of the greatest part of consciousness. From this the author draws the conclusion that if a person is about to be mad, blood collects in the breasts. That women would always be more susceptible to having more blood in their breasts than men, would give a "scientific" basis to the belief that women were always closer to the irrational than men.[17]

Here we see how the biological facts of menstruation and breasts were used to create a biological construct which upheld society's characterization of a woman's body as inherently inferior to that of a man. Underlying the Hippocratic characterization of male and female flesh is a value judgment: firm and compact is good/loose, and spongy is bad. This is clear from the fact that a contributory reason for a man's flesh remaining compact was his more excellent mode of life. He was thought to work much harder than a woman and thereby to use up all his nourishment in building a stronger body. A woman soaks up moisture through inac-

tivity; a man does not, because labor strengthens his body.[18] *Regimen* 1.34
(= 6:512) says that women are colder and moister than men in part
because they use a more frivolous (*rhaithymotereisi*) regimen. *Diseases* 4.45
(= 7:568) states that if a person remains at rest and does no work (which,
to the Greek mind, would be to follow a more typically feminine way of
life), the body of that person contains illness (*kakon*), even if the person is
not immediately aware of it because the body is otherwise so healthy. Less
work, therefore, does not simply result in a different type of body; characterizing the result of idleness as *kakon* shows that the change was looked
upon as a deterioration. This could lead one to ask whether, on this
theory, a woman could change her body type and cease to menstruate if
she led a strenuous life. But although various means are suggested for
reducing the menstruation of women who menstruate too abundantly
(for example, by curtailing food intake, and by bleeding at the breasts),
no Hippocratic author recommends that an overmenstruating woman
should work harder or increase her exercise, and nowhere in the Hippocratic Corpus is there a suggestion that a woman could overcome her
inherently inferior *physis* to the extent that she could cease to menstruate
altogether.[19] In fact, however, if, as now seems to be the case, regularly
monthly periods among women are a phenomenon of better nutrition in
the postindustrial age,[20] it seems likely that women of that time would
have menstruated less than the Hippocratics expected rather than more.
Nevertheless, despite the frequency of menstrual cycles which must have
lasted longer than the canonical month, the Hippocratics assumed that an
absence of menses for longer than a month meant that the blood was
trapped in a woman's body, not that there was no excess blood to be
evacuated.[21]

By the second century A.D., when, perhaps partly as a result of dissection, partly under the influence of Aristotelian theories, male and female
bodies were treated as members of the same species partaking in basically
the same *physis*, Soranus expressed the opinion that excessively active
women did cease to menstruate.[22] It is recognized today that female
athletes, gymnasts, dancers, and others who are strenuously active can
cease to menstruate if the ratio of body fat to total body weight drops
below a certain level, and perhaps Soranus had seen this syndrome. On
the other hand, as the exercise he cites explicitly is singing competitions
and traveling toward the sea, perhaps he had not. He was more probably
simply following his theory through to its logical conclusion: men and

women have the same *physis*; if women lived more like men, their bodies would become more like men's. Because the Hippocratics believed that the difference between men and women was to be explained primarily by biology rather than by their socially allotted ways of life, they did not believe the female could ever assimilate to the male in this way or, thus, could ever expect to live more like a man. The converse, however, seemed quite possible. The description of Scythian men in *Airs, Waters, Places* 20–22 (= 2:72–82) shows that if a man pursues a sedentary lifestyle, his body becomes loose, flabby, and moist (though he does not begin to menstruate) and therefore more like a woman's. The Scythians who developed this condition were able to follow a female life-style (apart from bearing children), because this always lay within the capabilities of every man, though it was usually avoided.

The majority of Hippocratic gynecological treatises implicitly subscribe to the view articulated in *Diseases of Women* 1 that menses are unused nourishment soaked from the stomach into the flesh and drawn from there into the womb. Although it is not the residue of digestion as feces and urine are, menstrual blood is still considered something of a waste product as it can begin to corrupt if trapped in the body too long. However, *On Generation* 2 (= 7:472–74) may indicate an alternative origin of the menses among the Hippocratics.[23] Here the appearance of menstruation is viewed as analogous to the production of semen by the male. In children, it is claimed, the passages of the body are narrow, so that the humors cannot become agitated. As children grow, there is more room for the humors to be roused by movement. This agitation produces a foam, and so semen flows in a boy and menses in a girl. The semen is said specifically to have been drawn from all the humors of the body, not directly from the residue of food, and by implication this holds for the girl's menses too; they are not necessarily a sign of an inferior spongy body type, nor are they a waste product. However, there is a difference in that semen is called forth when the male is aroused sexually—as is female seed: this is not true of menses. The author seems to be aware of the difficulty: in *On the Nature of the Child* 20 (= 7:508) he says that the way is opened in young girls for the passage of both menses and seed at the same time, two secretions where the male has only one.[24] In general, throughout the work, the author treats semen and female seed as more alike than semen and menses, and he gives no indication of a process whereby female seed might be derived from menstrual fluid. Elsewhere in the Hippocratic Corpus semen is similarly thought to correspond to female seed, not menses. The author of *On Generation* and *On the Nature of the Child* arrives at the additional equation of semen and menses because they first appear at roughly the same time in young men and women, whereas there is not necessarily any outward sign of female seed in pubescent girls.

Aristotle's theory of menstruation includes elements present in both *Diseases of Women* 1 (unused nourishment resulting from an inferior body type) and *On Generation* (parallel physical developments in male and female, producing semen in the former and menses in the latter).[25] He considered the stomach to be like the earth from which an animal took nourishment after the food had been converted by concoction (a form of heating) into blood.[26] This blood was drawn from the stomach to the diaphragm, where it was infused with *pneuma* from the heart, making it more suitable to nourish a living body.[27] The residue of blood which was not used up in nourishment (of which residue the male had less than the female, because he used more material in maintaining his larger body, producing hair, etc.)[28] was further concocted by the natural heat of the male into semen.[29] The female was unable to perform this final concoction both because she had a greater amount of blood left over (Nature did not allow her to use all her nourishment on her own body, as it was needed to form and nourish the fetus should she become pregnant)[30] and because of her colder nature. The heat in her diaphragm was able to concoct it a little further, but a woman still discharged her seminal residue as blood.[31]

Both semen and menses therefore were presumed to come from the same source, as in *On Generation*, and from the same reasoning, that they appear in adolescent males and females at the same time,[32] but this source was the immediate residue of nourishment, as in *Diseases of Women* 1, not the agitated humors. Males were unable to concoct semen before puberty because they lacked sufficient heat, and in this a boy's physique was thought to be like a woman's and a woman's like a sterile man's, all because of the same inability.[33]

For Aristotle the manifestation at puberty of the male's superior heat was a result not of a superior flesh or life-style, but of the development of his genitals.[34] At *Generation of Animals* 718a11–15 he mentions that a small initial part of the vas deferens contains blood: it is thus the seminal ducts around the testes which perform the last stage of the concoction. He adduces further evidence for this from the feminine appearance of men who have been castrated.[35] After puberty, when the penis is rubbed, *pneuma* rushes down to the seminal ducts directly from the heart and enables them to perform the final concoction of the seminal residue into generative material.[36] It is possible that Aristotle thought the *pneuma* was at work in the womb too; the blood stored there was suitable for procreation, unlike the rest of the blood in the body, and he likens the womb to an oven (764a12–20).

Aristotle believed that the same *pneuma* caused the swelling in both male and female breasts.[37] Room was made for this swelling by the descent of the seminal residue for generative purposes at puberty; the thoracic region became emptier in women in proportion to their greater amount of residue and was therefore more easily inflated.[38]

The models of female physiology developed by the Hippocratics and Aristotle were in large measure attempts to explain menstruation. The relative status of male and female in Greek society meant that although the female body was acknowledged to be necessary and its differences from the male valuable for society as a whole (a woman was most precious to society in her reproductive years, when her body was thought to diverge most widely from the male's), science used menstruation to construct a female body inherently weak and capable of exerting influence on her emotions and intellect, thereby buttressing her subordinate and restricted position in society. For the Hippocratics the weakness of a woman's body (her porous flesh) caused menstruation; for Aristotle menstruation caused her physical weakness.

In the Hippocratic theory, the release of excess matter in menstrual blood once a month prevented a woman's body from becoming diseased. Even if menstrual fluid had no role to play in childbearing, a woman would have had to produce it as it was only thus that she could approach the male ideal of health. For Aristotle, on the other hand, the production of menstrual blood for the sake of generation was what forced women away from the ideal of male health. He attributes a woman's paleness and deficiency of physique to her heavy menstrual flow.[39] Moreover, at *Generation of Animals* 728b10–15 he comments on the abundance of menstrual fluid in women in comparison not only with men's seminal fluid but also with other female animals.[40] Consequently, whereas Aristotle considers the male of almost every species as physically superior to the female, the ascendancy in humans is more marked.

Let us now consider how the "scientific" accounts of the external indicators of the female gender (menses and breasts) were related to theories of the internal organ of the womb.

The position the Hippocratics and Aristotle granted to menstruation in the context of a woman's general health is reflected in their descriptions of the functioning of the womb. As the Hippocratics thought that far from causing her weak bodily state, the menstrual flow was the only process which allowed a woman to maintain any health at all, they theorized that the role the womb played in effecting this discharge was equally as important as the role it played in procreation. Its primary function was to act as a receptacle (*angeion*) for the excess blood before it was discharged from the body.[41] The author of *On Ancient Medicine* 22 (= 1:628) describes the action of the womb as analogous to that of a cupping instrument (a broad, shallow bowl with a narrow mouth); that is, it actively draws the blood to itself from all over the body.[42] The parts of the body which were spongy and porous readily soaked up moisture but did not easily discharge it; if the womb did not actively draw the excess blood to itself, the blood could remain in the flesh of a woman and harden, as did excess moisture in the liver or spleen.[43] The passing of the blood into the womb was easiest in women who had given birth, as the abundant lochial flow was thought to break down the passages in a woman's body so that the scantier normal menstrual flow had no trouble in passing through.[44]

Aristotle, on the other hand, believed that the womb existed in the body as the proper receptacle for the female seminal residue when it had been finally concocted and that the menses flowed into the womb naturally without any force. At *Generation of Animals* 737b28–34 he explicitly contradicts the model of the womb as a cupping instrument in *On Ancient Medicine* 22: "Each of the residues is carried to its proper place without the exertion of any force from the *pneuma* and without compulsion by any other cause of that sort, although some people assert this, alleging that the sexual parts draw the residue like cupping-glasses and that we exert force by means of the *pneuma*, as though it were possible for the seminal residue or for the residue of the liquid or of the solid nourishment to take any other course unless such force were exerted."[45] Because of his teleological principles, Aristotle would deny that any receptacle in the body had to exert any force on its own proper residue; he would also deny that the bladder acted like a cupping instrument. But whereas he believed with the Hippocratics that the only reason for the existence of the bladder was to flush the fluid residue from the body, he did not believe that the womb existed for the sake of flushing the blood from a woman's body. In Aristotle's theory the prime purpose of the womb was to act as a store-house for the female seminal fluid until it was used in conception and reproduction or had reached such a volume that it *had* to be evacuated to prevent the menses from swamping the semen. At this point the womb would open, but until then it performed no mechanical functions of its own in the body—no drawing or sucking of blood into itself.

On the Nature of the Child 15 (= 7:492–94) says that the drawing of the blood from the woman's body into her womb happens all at once each month when she is not pregnant; perhaps this is an attempt to account for some of the symptoms that some women report before menstruation each month, which have been termed "premenstrual syndrome." Once the womb has collected the blood, it discharges it through the vagina—if its mouth is open and it is correctly aligned. The passage may be blocked, particularly in young girls, for whom the best way to remove the impedi-ment is to be married as soon as possible.[46] Lack of sexual intercourse can cause the womb of a woman who has already been deflowered to close over again; hence the impediment seems to be regarded as a constriction of the *stoma*, which could be relaxed and prized apart by the warmth and friction of intercourse.[47] The Hippocratics believed that an imperforate membrane could stretch across the vagina, but they viewed this as an unusual pathological symptom, not as a natural hymen common to all women.[48]

The womb could become misaligned with the vagina by tipping slightly in one direction or the other or by moving to a different position in the body altogether. The concept of "the wandering womb" has its most famous statement in Plato's *Timaeus* (91b–d), where the womb is por-trayed as an animal traveling round the body of a woman seeking satisfac-tion in sexual intercourse and pregnancy. The Hippocratics never describe the womb explicitly as an individual animal wandering at will within the body of a woman.[49] Their explanation of its movements throughout a woman's body is that if it is not anchored in place by pregnancy or kept moist by intercourse, it becomes dry and is attracted to the moister organs of the heart, the liver, the brain, and sometimes to the bladder and the rectum (it is especially easy for it to move if the stomach has emptied itself more than usual and so does not get in the way).[50] Young girls, widows, and other women who are not having regular sexual intercourse are prone to this displacement of the womb.[51] The wombs of older women are lighter, not only because they have their wombs moistened less by sexual intercourse and pregnancy but also because after a certain point they cease to produce menstrual fluid.[52] A womb which was full of menstrual blood or a fetus was not quite as peripatetic as an empty womb.

The womb could prolapse completely and issue from the vulva as a result of intercourse too soon after childbirth or a difficult birth.[53] A prolapsed uterus is recognized as a medical condition today, and it has been suggested that it was this which gave rise to the belief that the womb could wander in other directions. However, the prolapse of the uterus is simply a falling downward of the organ through the vagina; it can, and does, occur in spite of the tendons that usually hold it in place. This could in and of itself have suggested that the female body was possessed of an ambulatory womb and convenient upward and downward thorough-fares. Much more significant is Hanson's remark that as men's bodies held no uterus, the human body had no special place for it to reside, so of course it wandered.[54] However, even this is not sufficient to explain the tenacity of the concept in the Greek imagination.[55] That "rational medi-cine" did not reject such a strange idea out of hand suggests that it fulfilled an important role in characterizing the female sex.

One of the main explanatory values of the wandering womb was to account for the suffocating sensation (*pnix*) some women experienced in the chest and for various other pains dispersed throughout the body. Aline Rousselle has argued that it was women themselves who attributed various subjective physical experiences to the movement of the womb and that male Hippocratic doctors merely adopted their explanation.[56] There is no evidence for a divergent oral tradition among women on this matter, but even if women did "volunteer" such observations, they were put-ting them in a framework which already constructed their bodies as infe-rior and in need of external control. The odor therapies which the Hippo-cratics seem to have taken over from folk medicine presuppose an irratio-nal womb moving about the body at whim.[57] In their explanations of womb movements the Hippocratics were rationalizing the theories, not of women themselves, but of a culture which needed to promote, and yet at the same time wished to maintain control over, women's power of pro-creation.

The wandering womb, while providing a convenient explanation for various illnesses in a woman's body, simultaneously deprived a woman of independent control over her own sexuality.[58] Manuli has demonstrated that even within their rationalization the Hippocratics retain the model of the womb as a separate animal within the woman which, without the intervention of a man (husband or doctor), is in danger of subjugating the woman's own life force (*psychē*) if it does not have its own wants satisfied. Its preferred destinations (heart, liver, brain) were all thought to be possible seats of the *psychē*, and the method the Hippocratics suggest for drawing the womb back to its proper position is to administer foul-smelling substances to the nostrils while the woman is sitting on a bowl filled with sweet perfumes, simultaneously repelling the womb from one end of the body and attracting it to the other.[59] Manuli points out that employing perfumes in attracting the womb parallels the use of incense in invoking a god, an entity with a very definite mind of its own which is not easy for even a man to control.

King, however, asserts that the idea of the womb as an independent animal is not present in the Hippocratic texts and would not suggest itself if we were not reading back from the *Timaeus*. In citing the principles of attraction of the dry to the moist, she says, the Hippocratics give a completely mechanical explanation of the movement of the womb, which does not necessitate attributing to it any desires of its own.[60] This is true so far as the displacement of the womb is concerned, but even so we have to ask why the Hippocratics expended so much effort explicating a traditional belief which seems to us to have such little basis in reality. Just as the treatise *On the Sacred Disease* pours ridicule on traditional explanations of the causes of epilepsy, so it lay within the purview of the gynecological writers to dissent from the common opinion that the womb was mobile, using as evidence the anatomy revealed in female sacrificial animals. As it is, although the Hippocratics may have attempted to deny that the womb had any desires by explaining its movements away from its normal position as a function of the attraction of the dry to the moist, the use of foul- and sweet-smelling substances to draw it back contradicts the idea that their system was totally mechanical. The belief in the efficacy of this therapy derived from some prerational theory of womb movements and depended upon an assumption that the womb enjoyed the sense of smell in some way.[61] The Hippocratics might have denied this had it been put to them in so many words, but that they still prescribed such a treatment is an indication of the strength of the cultural construct of the female body binding their "scientific" theory.

As Aristotle denied that the womb was active in even so minor a role as drawing the blood to itself, he was hardly likely to allow it any capacity for desire or decision making. Moreover, as he did not regard the human female as quite so anomalous in comparison with the female gender of other species or the other gender of the human species, he asserted that the womb was held in place just like the wombs of other animals and like the seminal passages in the male.[62] Nevertheless, even he thought that when the womb was empty it could be pushed upwards and cause a stifling sensation.[63]

Surprisingly, at *History of Animals* 582b22–26 Aristotle explains a prolapsed womb as a result of lack of sexual intercourse: it descends and will not return to its proper position until it has conceived.[64] No rationale is offered for this, and it is hard to imagine a physical explanation that could justify weighing down with a fetus a uterus that was already protruding beyond the vulva. A prolapsed uterus is one of the rare female conditions for which the Hippocratics recommend abstinence from intercourse.[65] Aristotle may have been more rigorously "scientific" in observing anatomical and physiological phenomena, but to some extent (perhaps because he never had to translate his theories into therapy) he was more bound by his cultural assumptions than the Hippocratic doctors.

King has provided a solution to the mystery of how the womb was ever thought to pass through the diaphragm. The nostrils and the vagina of a woman were thought to be connected by one long hollow tube giving the womb free passage from the top to the bottom of the body. Hence a favored method for deciding whether a woman could conceive was to sit her over something strong-smelling (garlic was a standard ingredient for these recipes) and see if it could be smelled through her mouth. If it could, all was well; if not, her tube was blocked and steps had to be taken to unblock it before she could conceive.[66] These steps often included pessaries made from such ingredients as cuttlefish eggs and dung beetles. The model of a tube connecting the mouth to the vagina perhaps explains why the gynecology includes a specific cure for bad breath in women.[67] This involves taking the head of a hare and three mice or rats (two having had all their innards removed apart from their brains and liver), mixing these up with various other ingredients, and smearing them on a woman's gums for a period of days. One would imagine that however rancid a woman's breath was naturally, it would smell sweet in comparison to the cure![68]

Aristotle mentions using pessaries to test if a woman could conceive.[69]

He agrees that if the pessaries cannot be smelled through the mouth, it shows that the passages in the body have closed over. However, the connection he posits between the genital area and the breath is not quite as simplistic as the Hippocratic tube. He believed that the seminal secretion originates in the area of the diaphragm, and just as this passes down to genitalia, any movement set up in that area passes back to the chest, such that it is from here that the scent becomes perceptible on the breath. The seminal discharge could also pass up the body to the eyes, the most "seminal" part of the head;[70] hence another check on whether all the passages in the body were open as they should be was to rub pigments on the eyes and see if they colored the saliva. The Hippocratics also mention this test, but without any indication of how it would indicate a woman's ability to conceive.[71] Unless they too thought that the eyes were full of seminal fluid, demonstrating a sympathy between mouth and eyes would do nothing to prove that the passages to and from the womb were clear.

The Hippocratics frequently refer to the human womb in the plural, and Aristotle explicitly says that it is double.[72] This presents no problem in Aristotle's physiology, but it is a little difficult to reconcile a double womb with *On Ancient Medicine*'s picture of the womb as a broad, shallow cupping instrument. If we do try to conceive of the two models in conjunction, we should picture the body of the receptacle as divided into two longitudinal compartments. The occasional birth of twins probably confirmed this belief. The misapprehension could also have arisen from the observation of other mammalian uteri, particularly that of the pig, which is divided. The Hippocratics showed no hesitation in transferring their knowledge of animal anatomy to the human female where they had no strong cultural counter-assumption of a woman's body to prevent them. When such a counter-assumption did exist, as in the belief that a woman possessed a wandering womb (which ran counter to the observation that other mammalian wombs were held in place by tendons), they did not use animal anatomy to construct a woman's internal space. Ironically their conception of woman led them to assimilate her anatomy to other female animals where it differed (in the double womb) and to differentiate it where it shared a common feature (the tendons holding the womb in place).

From the internal reproductive organs we can now move on to a consideration of one particular part of the external female genitalia: the vagina.

Because they were compiling a pathology rather than a physiology, the

Hippocratics did not describe in detail every part of the female anatomy of which they were aware. They generally refer to the genitalia by the commonplace plural form *ta aidoia* and use the singular *to aidoion* to refer to the vagina when describing treatment for the womb. They explicitly differentiate this from the urethra in *Airs, Waters, Places* 9 (= 2:40–42) and often advise inserting pessaries into the vagina without any directions for steps to avoid obstructing the flow of urine, which again suggests that they viewed the vagina solely as the passage to the womb and completely separate from the urethra.

Although he was interested in physiology per se and particularly in noting the differences between male and female, Aristotle failed to make the distinction between the vagina and the urethra. This was a direct result of one of the founding principles of his biology: that the female is a less perfect representative of the human form than the male. The same principle led him to make other erroneous claims. He states that a man has more sutures in his skull because he has a bigger brain and a bigger brain needs more ventilation.[73] Men and women have the same number of sutures in their skulls, so it may seem as if here Aristotle is citing completely nonexistent evidence as proof of the male's superiority over the female. However, at *History of Animals* 491b3–5 he enumerates the sutures as three in a man and one circular one in a woman. Ogle records, "it is by no means uncommon for the sutures on the vertex to become more or less effaced in pregnant women; so common is it, that the name 'puerperal osteophyte' has been given to the condition by Rokitansky."[74] In this condition the sagittal suture disappears and the lamboid, lateral, and coronal sutures form a circle. Aristotle may have seen or heard of such a skull and, as it was different from a normal skull (perhaps seen most commonly on battlefields and therefore easily identified as male), explained its unusual features by saying it was female, even if he did not know for a fact that it was a woman's skull.

At another point, on the principle that men are naturally superior to women, Aristotle claims that men have more teeth,[75] which he associates with a longer life-span (perhaps because this allows men to masticate more and therefore digest their food better). Here again, we know that men and women have exactly the same number of teeth, at least to start with. Aristotle's statement that other animals have not yet been examined (*epi de allōn ou tetheōrētai pō*) suggests that he considered some sort of survey to have been held on this topic, and it is conceivable that, by sheer coincidence, in all the mouths he examined men had lost fewer teeth than women.[76] In this case Aristotle's presupposition of female inferiority would have led him to a wrong inference from correctly observed empirical phenomena.

Aristotle claims that in most blooded animals and in all Vivipara there are two passages for evacuating fluid and solid residues from the body.[77] The existence of two passages is a sign of the superiority of the Vivipara over the Ovipara and lower animals, as the higher up the *scala naturae* an animal is, the more it is specialized in its parts.[78] That passage through which the fluid residue is voided lies higher up and in front of that for the evacuation of solids. However, the existence of the forward passage is for the sake of generation, a channel for the reproductive fluids of semen and menses. Urine uses this passage as it is a fluid residue and it is reasonable that things that are alike should share the same part. It is easy to understand why Aristotle would think that men had only two passages for voiding residues from the body. But the urethra and the vagina in women are distinct. That he did *not* distinguish the two forward passages in women is shown clearly at *Parts of Animals* 689a6–9: "Nature employs one and the same part for the discharge of the fluid residue and for copulation in all blooded animals (with a few exceptions), male and female alike, and in all Vivipara without exception."[79] In fact, the urethra and vagina in other female mammals do share the same external orifice, but had Aristotle made an even cursory examination of a human female he would have discovered that this was not the case in all Vivipara "without exception." It may be that such intimate examination, even of his own wife, was taboo for a nonmedical investigator, but Aristotle could have asked his wife to make the examination herself. His usually astute readings in contemporary medical literature should also have suggested this anatomical fact to him. Aristotle did not assimilate this knowledge because what would here seem to be a legitimate difference between man and woman, unlike the spurious differences he lists elsewhere, would make a woman superior in some respect by the further specialization of her body to separate her two fluid residues. This is one difference Aristotle simply failed to register because he did not expect it or think of looking for it: it went against one of his most basic tenets.[80]

Finally, I would like to discuss one of the secondary sexual characteristics in the light of the "scientific" theories on the more fundamental issues of gender.

The seemingly most superficial of physical differences between men and women, that men are on the whole hairier, is credited to a man's greater volume and agitation of semen by the author of *On the Nature of the Child* 20 (= 7:506–10). Hair, he claims, needs moisture (primarily semen) to grow, and the reason humans have so much on their heads is because that is where the semen is stored and where the epidermis is most porous. Secondary body hair first makes its appearance at puberty, around the genital area as a direct result of the agitation of semen in the body and of the flesh in this area becoming more porous. Thus women have some semen, but not as much as males, nor does it become agitated in women throughout the whole body, so that the genital area is the only place secondary body hair grows. On the other hand, during intercourse the agitated semen of a man has to pass from his brain through the length of his body. Hair grows on his chin and chest because he is normally facing downward and these project beyond the straight course of the semen and so act as reservoirs which have to be filled up before the semen can continue on its journey.[81] The same theory is used to explain why men become bald and women do not. The semen in the brain, in becoming agitated, heats up the phlegm which burns through the roots of the hair on the head. The theory is consistent within itself and with the observed physical differences between men and women. It is predicated upon the assumption that men derive greater pleasure from intercourse (a view not held universally in the ancient world) and that they normally face downward during the act of intercourse—though the theory can obviously accommodate men with hairy backs too.

Aristotle thought hair grew when moisture was able to seep through the skin and then evaporated, leaving an earthy precipitate behind. Humans diverted a greater amount of their nourishment to producing a greater volume of seminal residue in accordance with their size than did other animals; hence there was not as much nourishment left over to be diverted into hair, nor was human flesh as loose-textured.[82] People had most hair on their heads because the brain was the moistest part of the body and the sutures in the skull would allow the fluid to seep through.[83] Pubic hair grew when the seminal fluids began to be produced, because the flesh was less firm in the genital area.[84] At *Generation of Animals* 782b18, Aristotle states that it is because the brain is fluid and cold that it causes most hair growth.[85] From these considerations the adult man would seem to be the most fluid, cold, and loose-textured member of the human race. However, Aristotle attributes the hairier appearance of the adult male in comparison with other humans to the fact that women, children, and eunuchs are unable to concoct semen, which men can do because of their heat. He does not explain further, but it would seem that he imagines the semen in a man's body coming near the surface at times and being encouraged to evaporate by the man's heat, whereas a woman's unused fluid residue would remain as blood in the interior of her cold body. Men go bald at the front of their heads because this is where semen is stored. Hair begins to drop out after sexual activity begins, because the emission of semen results in a deficiency of hot fluid.[86] One might well ask why women, children, and eunuchs do not begin to go bald much sooner than men, as they are presumably always deficient in hot fluid. Aristotle has difficulty in attaining consistency in his theory of hair growth because adult men produce more but also lose more, and he wants both to be indications of male superiority.

To summarize: The sexual differentia of menstruation, breasts, and womb are all accounted for in Hippocratic theory by the nature of female flesh. They are utilized in procreation, but they are the result of a difference between men and women which does not have sexual generation as its prime purpose. For this purpose men possess a penis and both women and men produce seed; as a man produces more and it becomes more agitated, he produces more hair. Thus in Hippocratic theory there are two fundamental causes for the observable differences in male and female physiology, and it is the differences between male and female flesh rather than those between reproductive fluids which dictate a woman's incapacity to perform in a man's world.[87] Aristotle's theory is more economical in that it ties all differences to a man's naturally greater heat, which allows him to to concoct nourishment to a greater degree for the purposes of sexual reproduction.

Because of this one small difference Aristotle considered women to be less "other" and more like men than the Hippocratics, but he could only maintain this general theory while adhering to the principle of male superiority in every feature at the loss of some consistency (as in hair growth) and the neglect of some observable anatomical realities (as in the distinction of the urethra and the vagina). Because they thought woman was a completely different creature and not simply a substandard man, the Hippocratics did not have to look for a correspondence between all male and female body parts. They felt woman was inferior, of course, but her "otherness" allowed her body to be defined more by its own parameters. However, because they thought a woman was so different, these parameters sometimes spread a little too widely (as in the case of spongy flesh and the wandering womb).

Whether Greek scientists focused their construct of the female body on assimilation to the male or on divergence, however hard they tried to take the empirical evidence into account and to bring rational argument to bear on the "facts," the culture's unwavering belief in female inferiority constrained their theories.

Notes

A few frequently cited texts from the Hippocratic Corpus are abbreviated as follows: *On Generation (Gen.)*; *Diseases of Women (DW)*; *On the Nature of the Child (NC)*; *Nature of Women (NW)*. Parallel references with Hippocratic citations are to *Œuvres complètes d'Hippocrate*, ed. Emile Littré, 10 vols. (Paris, 1839–61; reprinted Amsterdam: A. M. Hakkert, 1961–62). Unless otherwise noted, other abbreviations conform to those used in *L'année philologique* and the second edition of the *Oxford Classical Dictionary*.

1. During the nineteenth century many people still believed intelligence to be an exclusively male attribute. In 1879 the French scholar Le Bon (whose work on crowd psychology is still widely respected) stated, "Without doubt there exist some distinguished women, very superior to the average man, but they are as exceptional as the birth of any monstrosity, as, for example, of a gorilla with two heads." He believed that recent work in craniometry, demonstrating that the average woman had a smaller head and therefore a smaller brain than the average man, proved scientifically that she was also less intelligent. He failed to take into account the fact that the average woman is smaller than the average man overall, and that large men with large heads were not always more intelligent than smaller representatives of the male sex. See Stephen Jay Gould, "Women's Brains," in *The Panda's Thumb: More Reflections in Natural History* (New York: W. W. Norton, 1982), 152–59.

2. Hence the misinterpretation of the data on XYY males which led to the supposed discovery of a gene for aggression on the Y chromosome; see Stephen Jay Gould, *The Mismeasure of Man* (New York: W. W. Norton, 1981), 143–45; Anne Fausto-Sterling, *Myths of Gender* (New York: Basic Books, 1985), 150–53. I do not wish to argue that it has been scientifically proven that all supposed male and female behavioral patterns are socially rather than biologically conditioned, or that there can be no biologically determined differences between men and women

apart from their reproductive roles. However, I do believe that thus far all attempts at accounting biologically for supposed male-female dichotomies have proved, at best, inconclusive.

3. For a discussion of the mythological separation of the sexes see Jean Pierre Vernant, "Hestia-Hermes: The Religious Expression of Space and Movement in Ancient Greece," in *Myth and Thought among the Greeks* (London: Routledge & Kegan Paul, 1983), 127–75; Nicole Loraux, *Les enfants d'Athéna: idées athéniennes sur la citoyenneté et la division des sexes* (Paris: F. Maspero, 1981), 75–117; Helen King, "From Parthenos to Gyne: The Dynamics of Category" (Ph.D. dissertation, University of London 1985), 15–27.

4. Though it should be clearly understood that "science" has a more assured institutionalized position in our society than it did in the ancient world.

5. This view of woman's position relative to man's is that of elite males, the authors of the overwhelming majority of our sources from ancient Greece. The extent to which women concurred in this opinion is an extremely complex question which will not be discussed in this essay but of which the reader should be aware.

6. Ischomachus in Xenophon's *Oeconomicus* (7.22–30) states that a man is fitted for the outdoors whereas a woman is suited to the interior of the house and, in addition, that it is more honorable for them both to remain in their natural spheres. However, a woman's physical limitations (as described by Ischomachus) play a greater part in restricting her sphere of influence than do a man's. The indoor tasks were allotted to her because she was less capable of physical endurance than a man. The only positive attribute she has over a man is her greater affection for the newborn. It might seem as if Xenophon wishes to argue that her fearfulness makes her a better protector of the household stores than a man, but all he actually says is that this is not a disadvantage (*ou kakion esti*). The male's greater amount of courage would not disqualify him from protecting the stores. In fact, Ischomachus is so well informed on how to run a household that it is he who undertakes the training of his own wife in these matters. Various scholars have noted how improbable this was; the girl would normally have received such instruction from her mother before she married. See Sheila Murnaghan, "How a Woman Can Be More Like a Man: The Dialogue between Ischomachus and His Wife in Xenophon's *Oeconomicus*," *Helios* 15 (1988): 9–22, for an explanation of the strategy of the dialogue. Nevertheless Xenophon, although male, believed he knew how to run a well-ordered household and did not think it unsuitable to portray his hero Ischomachus as displaying the same knowledge. It was simply unseemly that men should actually engage in such activities, not impossible.

7. I do not consider this to have been a conscious manipulation or falsification of data to maintain the status quo; rather, the theories were the result of a good-faith effort by intelligent men to explain what they considered to be the facts of the

world. I suspect that the vast majority of Greek women, raised under the same cultural conditioning, concurred in these beliefs, though they may have drawn somewhat different implications from them. Ann Ellis Hanson, "Continuity and Change: Three Case Studies in Hippocratic Gynecological Therapy and Theory," this volume, demonstrates how cultural preconceptions caused ancient physicians to overlook the role of uterine contractions and to assert that it was healthier for a woman to be pregnant with a boy than with a girl.

8. See Hanson, "Continuity and Change," for a fuller description of the composition of the Hippocratic gynecological treatises.

9. Aristotle takes issue with theories that are espoused in those treatises; e.g., the theory of pangenesis as described in *Gen.* 8 = 7:480–82 is crticized in *GA* 712b12–24a14.

10. The significance of Hippocratic clinical practice and Aristotelian teleology is addressed more fully in Lesley Ann Jones, "Morbidity and Vitality: The Interpretation of Menstrual Blood in Greek Science" (Ph.D. dissertation, Stanford University, 1987).

11. *Gen.* 2 = 7:472–74. At *GA* 737b11 Aristotle says that conception is not complete until the fetus is differentiated as either male or female. *GA* 716a27–31 locates this differentiation in the specifically male and female parts rather than in the body as a whole. *GA* 765a35–766b10 says that male and female each have their own instrument (*organon*), which Nature gives to each simultaneously with its secretions and abilities. These secretions and abilities are related to their instruments in the same way as the ability to see is related to the eye. An animal cannot see without an eye, and an "eye" that cannot see is an eye in name only. Obviously, newborn boys and girls, although differentiated in genitalia, do not have generative abilities and secretions. They possess both the tools and their powers potentially. The receptacles and residues are not fully developed until puberty (*GA* 728b22–32).

12. *GA* 728a17.

13. Ann Ellis Hanson, "The Medical Writer's Woman," in *Before Sexuality*, ed. David Halperin, John Winkler, and Froma Zeitlin (Princeton: Princeton University Press, 1990), 309–38, has detailed how fleeces were used in this way to locate underground water sources in Mother Earth.

14. The Greek reads: *kai estin oute sarkia ikela tōi allōi sōmati, oute, allo ti omoin tōi sōmati.* Unless otherwise stated, translations throughout this essay are my own.

15. The Greek reads: *tēisi men gynaixin araiē te hē physis kata tōn adenōn, hōsper to allo sōma.* Where Littré simply suppresses a *kai* that appears in the manuscripts before *kata*, Robert Joly, *Hippocrate* (Paris: Les Belles Lettres, 1978), 13:121, adopts Zwinger's emendation to *karta*. This could be interpreted as an even stronger statement, that a woman's glands were very porous, even more porous than a man's glands, just as the rest of her body was more porous than a man's body.

16. It is perhaps surprising that in *Prorrhetic* 2 = 9:54, when listing factors which predict good childbearing capacity, the Hippocratics give a positive endorsement to large breasts, for as Jeffrey Henderson remarks in *The Maculate Muse* (New Haven: Yale University Press, 1975), 148–49, "firmness and thus youthfulness is the usual attribute" desired of breasts in a *parthenos*. The Hippocratics, on this occasion, did not ratify the culture's ideal female body type (for a lover at least) as the most fertile. It may be relevant that the gradual movement away from assimilation of the proportions of female statues to male—documented by Eleanor Guralnick, "Proportions of Korai," *AJA* 85 (1981): 269–80—began in Ionia, the geographical origin of Hippocratic medicine. However, even the more feminine shapes of the Classical period retained small breasts, and Soranus at *Gyn.* 2.84 advises swaddling an infant girl tightly around the chest, but letting the bandages loose around the buttocks, as this is a more becoming shape.

17. See Ruth Padel, "Women: Model for Possession by Greek Daemons," in *Images of Women in Antiquity*, ed. Averil Cameron and Amélie Kuhrt (Detroit: Wayne State University Press, 1983), 3–19.

18. *DW* 1.1 = 8:14, *dia tēn argiēn*; *Glands* 16 = 8:572, *ho ponos kratynei autou to sōma*. Hesiod (*Theog.* 592–99) and Semonides (*On Women*; only the bee-woman actually works) also characterize the typical female life-style as slothful.

19. Curtailing food intake, bleeding at the breasts: *DW* 1.5 = 8:28; *Aphorisms* 5.50 = 4:550. *DW* 1.11 = 8:44 advises a woman who is too moist because of phlegm (not menses) to exercise (*gymnazesthai*) frequently.

20. Cf. Doreen Asso, *The Real Menstrual Cycle* (Chichester: John Wiley & Sons, 1983), 17, 90, 148.

21. For a more detailed discussion of this issue cf. Lesley Dean-Jones, "Menstrual Bleeding according to the Hippocratics and Aristotle," *TAPhA* 119 (1989): 179–94.

22. *Gyn.* 1.22–23.

23. There is an excellent translation and commentary on the whole treatise in *The Hippocratic Treatises "On Generation," "On the Nature of the Child," "Diseases IV,"* ed. Iain M. Lonie, Ars Medica 2, no. 7 (Berlin and New York: de Gruyter, 1981). *Gen.* segues into *NC* to form a continuous treatise.

24. The lack of interest in explaining this doubling, which had no therapeutical repercussions for the Hippocratics, shows how pragmatic even their theoretical treatises were.

25. For a more detailed discussion of Aristotle's theories of male and female in the context of his whole philosophy cf. Jones, "Morbidity," 187–216; Maryanne Cline Horowitz, "Aristotle and Woman," *JHB* 9 (1976): 183–213; Johannes Morsink, "Was Aristotle's Biology Sexist?" *JHB* 12 (1979): 83–112. Briefly, Aristotle believed that the two sexes existed in the higher animals for the sake of separating the two necessary elements of reproduction (he believed specialization of parts increased

corresponding to an animal's higher place on the *scala naturae*). The two elements are form (the male contribution) and matter (the female). Form is superior to matter insofar as it makes a thing the sort of thing it is. The female is a "stunted" male because although she possesses the form herself, she is unable to pass it on to her offspring.

26. *PA* 650a3–b19.

27. See A. L. Peck, "The Connate Pneuma: An Essential Factor in Aristotle's Solution to the Problem of Reproduction and Sensation," in *Science, Medicine and History: Essays in Honour of Charles Singer*, ed. E. A. Underwood (London: Oxford University Press, 1953), 111–21.

28. *GA* 727a16–19.

29. *GA* 725a11–22. As evidence of its origin as blood Aristotle remarks that the loss of semen is just as exhausting as the loss of healthy blood (*GA* 726b3–13).

30. *GA* 730b2–4.

31. *GA* 726b31–727a1. The hot-cold issue continued to be debated throughout antiquity. The Hippocratic gynecologists tended to view women as hot, Aristotle and the author of *Regimen* 1 as cold. Plutarch has a discussion on the topic in *Mor. Quaest. conviv.* 3.4; cf. King, "Parthenos," 131–33. Whether women were considered hotter or colder than men, it was always they rather than the men who were considered *too* hot or *too* cold.

32. *GA* 727a5–7.

33. *GA* 728a17.

34. *GA* 728b18–31.

35. *GA* 716b10–12.

36. *HA* 510a13–29; *GA* 717b23–718a15.

37. *GA* 728b27–31.

38. *GA* 776b19–22.

39. *GA* 727a22–25.

40. Here Aristotle appears to be confusing the menstrual discharge of primates with the estrus discharge of all other mammals.

41. Cf. Hanson, "Continuity and Change."

42. The gynecological treatises do not describe the womb explicitly as drawing the blood to itself. The most commonly used verb of the blood's movement to the womb is "flow," *chōreō*. However, the author of *NC* 15 = 7:494 says that in a pregnant woman the blood flows (*chōreei*) into her womb on a daily basis because the seed in the womb draws (*helkei*) the blood from her body. The frequent use of the verb *chōreō*, therefore, does not necessarily preclude the idea that the womb exerted a drawing force on the menstrual blood in the body. However, as has been mentioned, the treatises in the Hippocratic Corpus were written by a variety of authors who did not necessarily share the same theories. The theory put forward by *On Ancient Medicine* here is denominated a general "Hippocratic" theory for the purposes of contrast with Aristotle's theory.

43. *Affections* 30 = 6:228; *Internal Affections* 30–34 = 7:244–52.

44. *DW* 1.1 = 8:10.

45. Translated by A. L. Peck, *Aristotle: Generation of Animals*, Loeb Classical Library (Cambridge: Harvard University Press, 1942; reprinted 1979), 179.

46. *Diseases of Young Girls* = 8:468–70.

47. *DW* 1.2 = 8:16.

48. *DW* 1.20 = 8:58–60. At *GA* 773a15–29 Aristotle mentions a pathological condition in which the *os uteri* grows together and has to be surgically separated. His coalescing of the vagina and the urethra (see below) would have prevented him from positing an imperforate membrane across the passage itself. See Giulia Sissa, "Une virginité sans hymen: le corps féminin en Grèce ancienne," *Annales ESC* 39 (1984): 1131–32. Hanson, "Medical Writer's Woman," argues against this this interpretation.

49. But see Paula Manuli, "Fisiologia e patologia del femminile negli scritti Ippocratici dell'antica ginecologia greca," in *Hippocratica, actes du colloque hippocratique de Paris (4–9 septembre 1978)*, ed. M. D. Grmek (Paris: Editions du CNRS, 1980), 393–408, and "Donne mascoline, femmine sterili, vergini perpetua: la ginecologia greca tra Ippocrate e Sorano," in *Madre Materia*, ed. Silvia Campese, Paola Manuli, and Giulia Sissa (Torino: Boringhieri, 1983), 149–204. For more details of uterine displacement see Hanson, "Continuity and Change."

50. *DW* 2.124 = 8:266–68 (heart); 2.127 = 8:272–74 (liver); 2.123 = 8:266 (brain); 2.137 = 8:308–10 (bladder and rectum); 1.2, 1.7 = 8:14, 32 (empty stomach). However, as Hanson, "Continuity and Change," points out, mechanical reasons could also cause displacement, and sometimes the womb could move because it became too wet.

51. *DW* 1.7 = 8:32.

52. *DW* 2.137 = 8:310.

53. *NW* 4, 5 = 7:316, 318. These chapters suggest as treatment for this condition that a woman be strapped upside down on a ladder, bounced up and down a few times, and left overnight. Succussion on a ladder was also practiced on male patients in *Joints* 42 (= 4:182–84; cf. Hanson, "Continuity and Change"), but this does not seem so bizarre nowadays, when people buy special boots for hanging upside down to cure backache. Indeed the effects of gravity probably brought about some short-term relief for a prolapse, and many women may have sanctioned the treatment. It is also possible that many women claimed to be cured to avoid any similar solicitous intervention in their welfare.

54. Hanson, "Continuity and Change."

55. After the dissection of human bodies at Alexandria in the third and second centuries B.C., Greek physicians had a much clearer idea of female reproductive organs and knew that they were held in place by tendons and connected to other organs in the abdomen. Even so, in the second century A.D. Soranus (*Gyn.* 1.8), Galen (*Diss. Ut.* 4), and Aretaeus (6.10) described the uterus as being very loosely

moored and capable of causing severe discomfort by displacement in all directions.

56. "Observation féminine et idéologie masculine: le corps de la femme d'après les médecins grecs," *Annales ESC* 35 (1980): 1089–1115; *Porneia: de la maîtrise du corps à la privation sensorielle, IIe–IVe siècles de l'ère chrétienne* (Paris: Presses Universitaires de France, 1983).

57. On odor therapies see below, and Hanson, "Continuity and Change."

58. See Bennet Simon, *Mind and Madness in Ancient Greece* (Ithaca: Cornell University Press, 1978), 238–68.

59. *NW* 3, 14 = 7:314, 332. Cf. Manuli, "Fisiologia e patologia" and "Donne mascoline."

60. King, "Parthenos," 115. But see now her "Once upon a Text: The Hippocratic Origins of Hysteria," in *Hysteria in Western Civilization*, ed. G. S. Rousseau and R. Porter (Berkeley and Los Angeles: University of California Press, forthcoming).

61. Soranus (*Gyn.* 3.29) denies that this treatment has any efficacy, but he indicates that some of his contemporaries were still using it on the theory that "the uterus fleeing the first-mentioned [evil] odors, but pursuing the last-mentioned [fragrant], might move from the upper to the lower parts"; trans. Oswei Temkin, *Soranus' Gynecology* (Baltimore: The Johns Hopkins University Press, 1956), 152.

62. *GA* 720a12–14.

63. *GA* 719a21–22.

64. This echoes the description of the wandering womb in the *Timaeus*, where it issues forth looking for sexual fulfillment if a woman does not have intercourse.

65. See Hanson, "Continuity and Change."

66. *DW* 2.146 = 8:322; *NW* 96 = 7:412–14; *Aphorisms* 5.59 = 4:554. See King, "Once upon a Text."

67. *DW* 2.185 = 8:366.

68. There is no specific cure for halitosis in a male in the Hippocratic Corpus, but the *Philogelos* (a collection of jokes put together in the second century A.D. but containing some jokes dating from much earlier) has a section of twelve jokes on smelly-mouths (*ozostomoi*), in one of which (235) the patient complains to his doctor that his uvula (*staphylē*) has "gone down" (*katebē*). The doctor recoils from his examination and says, "No, your anus has come up." This suggests a connection between mouth and anus in men paralleling that between mouth and vagina in women.

69. *GA* 747a7–23. He does not identify the passage in which they should be inserted, merely that the smell should penetrate "from below upward" (*katōthen anō*).

70. Thus if a person overindulged in sexual intercourse, the first part of his body to show it would be the eyes, which become hollow and sunken. Note that Aristotle is concerned with the movement of seminal fluids around the body, not with the movement of organs.

71. *NW* 99 = 7:416.

72. *GA* 716b32–33.

73. *PA* 653a27–29; 653b1–3.

74. William Ogle, ed., *Aristotle: On the Parts of Animals* (London: K. Paul, Trench & Co., 1882), 168.

75. *HA* 501b20–24.

76. It may not have been so much a coincidence if men had a consistently superior diet and women had lost more teeth due to calcium deficiency in pregnancy. This would also account for Aristotle's observation that women were more knock-kneed than men (*HA* 538b10). In addition Aristotle may have beem comparing young wives whose wisdom teeth had not yet come through with older husbands whose had.

77. *GA* 719b29–34, 720a7–10; *PA* 689a4–17; *HA* 493a24–b6, 497a24–35.

78. *PA* 656a2–7. On the biological continuum see Stephen R. Clark, *Aristotle's Man* (Oxford: Clarendon Press, 1975), 28–47, esp. 44–45.

79. Translated by A. L. Peck, *Aristotle: Parts of Animals*, Loeb Classical Library (Cambridge: Harvard University Press, 1937; reprinted 1983), 383. At *HA* 493b4–6 Peck translates, "there is an 'urethra' outside the womb; it serves as a passage for the semen of the male. In both sexes the urethra serves as an outlet for the fluid residue"; *Aristotle: History of Animals*, Loeb Classical Library (Cambridge: Harvard University Press, 1965; reprinted 1979), 51. He encloses the word urethra in inverted commas presumably to indicate that Aristotle does not mean to use the word in its proper sense here. The only evidence for this interpretation is our own knowledge that the urethra does not lie directly outside the womb.

80. Had he noticed it, of course, it would not have caused him to reevaluate his opinion of the inferiority of the female. His theory would have developed to accommodate this apparent anomaly.

81. Cf. Pseudo-Aristotle *Prob.* 10.24, 10.53.

82. *GA* 728b19–23.

83. *PA* 658b2–6.

84. *GA* 728b26–27.

85. And at *GA* 783a23–27 he says that sea urchins produce long spines because they are too cold to concoct nourishment and have to use up the residue.

86. *GA* 783b18–784a12.

87. The Hippocratic theories viewed the male and female contributions to conception as more nearly equal than Aristotle did; thus they could not hang male-female differences from this hook.

CLAUDE MOSSÉ

Translated by Sarah B. Pomeroy

Women in the Spartan Revolutions

of the Third Century B.C.

In the third century B.C., Sparta, the city which all Greeks envied because of its stability and excellent constitution, underwent a period of revolution which ended with the victory of the Romans and of the Achaean League over the tyrant Nabis in 193 B.C. and the assassination of Nabis the following year.[1] The Spartan revolutions are known to us essentially through three sources: Plutarch's *Lives of Agis and Cleomenes* (which are based on a work of Phylarchus); fragments of Polybius concerning Cleomenes and Nabis; and, on Nabis, chapter 34 of Livy, which is drawn from Polybius. That Phylarchus was an admirer of the Spartan revolution is clear from Plutarch's text; in contrast, the Achaean Polybius and the Roman Livy are hostile to it. I do not intend to review all the problems concerning the different attempts at revolution but shall confine myself to merely recounting the principal stages and characteristics.

What we customarily call the Spartan revolution began toward the middle of the third century B.C. It was initiated by the young King Agis IV, of the Eurypontid dynasty. To revive the supposed ancient Spartan egalitarianism, the only means of allowing the city to regain its bygone power, Agis proposed an abolition of debts and a new distribution of land. In order to put into effect this last measure, which would permit the apportionment of *klēroi* ("lots") to forty-five hundred Spartiates and to fifteen thousand *perioikoi* ("free inhabitants"), everyone would be required to contribute his or her own private property. Opposed by his colleague, Leonidas, and by the people with wealth, Agis found support only among the poor as well as among certain rich men, including his uncle Agesilaus, who had incurred debts.

According to Plutarch (*Agis* 13.2), Agesilaus urged the young king to proclaim the abolition of debts immediately but to delay the new distribution of land. Various troubles arose. Leonidas, who had been banished from the city and replaced by his son-in-law Cleombrotus, returned from his exile in Tegea and saw to it that Agis was condemned to death. The first attempt had thus failed. But the revolutionary program was revived several years later by Cleomenes, the son of Leonidas. Cleomenes had been married by his father to Agiatis, the widow of Agis. When he became king, he decided to resume the efforts of his predecessor, convinced that only a significant reform of the distribution of property would allow Sparta to regain its past grandeur. But warned by the execution of Agis, Cleomenes did not hesitate to resort to force to eliminate the ephors, the five magistrates, elected every year, who were guardians of the constitution. He proclaimed the abolition of debts and the joint possession of land before the new distribution. The defeat did not come this time from within Sparta. Afraid to see the Spartan revolution expand through all the Peloponnese following the military victories of Cleomenes, Aratus of Sicyon, the commander of the Achaean League, appealed to the Macedonians. Cleomenes was defeated at Sellasia and was forced to flee to Egypt, and the Macedonian king, Antigonus Doson, reestablished the ancient constitution at Sparta.

But troubles did not cease in the following years until Nabis seized power in 207 B.C. Nabis was, it seems, of royal blood, of a branch of the Eurypontids. But because he was the sole king of a city which since its origins had been ruled by two kings, he seemed to his contemporaries a tyrant rather than a legitimate king. Nabis in his turn revived the projects of Agis and Cleomenes and attempted to reestablish equality by means of a new distribution of land. But in order to be assured of support, he intended to crown this measure with one even more revolutionary: the enfranchisement of a large number of slaves, a term employed by Livy, but which doubtless referred to the dependent population in Sparta who were known as "helots." Nabis ruled Sparta until his assassination in 192 B.C., shortly after he was defeated by Philopoemen, the commander of the Achaean League.[2]

The Spartan revolutions have a special character. Although they were initiated by kings, they were inspired, or claim to have been inspired, by ancient tradition. The reforms to which the classical period attributed the originality of Spartan institutions were credited to the archaic lawgiver Lycurgus. These included the austere way of life, a military education strictly controlled by the city, avoidance of profit-making pursuits and of using money, and a new distribution of land. This last problem is the most controversial.[3] The evidence derives from Plutarch's *Life of Lycurgus* (8.3–6): the legendary Spartan lawgiver persuaded his fellow citizens to make one parcel of all the *chōra* ("territory") and to divide it again into nine thousand *klēroi* given to the Spartiates. Land seized in Laconia was divided into thirty thousand lots and given to the *perioikoi*.[4] These *klēroi* were equal and supplied the same quantity of barley, fruit, and vegetables. It is clear that such a reform would require perpetual control of the city in order to keep the number constant.

A few modern historians have attempted to understand the functioning of such a system and have suggested that land was redistributed periodically.[5] But many doubts about the real equality of lots and the extent to which land was publicly controlled remain.[6] It appears that the notion of an equal redistribution of lots by Lycurgus did not actually appear before the end of the classical period. No one before Polybius (6.45), who wrote at the end of the second century B.C., gives information about the subject. Xenophon, a good observer of Lacedaemonian life, does not give any information about land tenure in classical Sparta. Plato (*Laws* 3.684d) and Isocrates (*Archidamos* 20) mention an egalitarian distribution of land when the Dorians subdued the Peloponnese but do not connect the distribution to a Lycurgan reform. It is thus likely that Polybius echoes the propaganda of the third-century reformers who invoked Lycurgus to lend authority to their innovative distribution of land.

The tradition detected in Polybius also informs Plutarch's *Life of Lycurgus*. But what was the origin of the tradition? It has been suggested that Ephorus was the first writer who ascribed to Lycurgus the idea of an equal redistribution of land and that he took this idea from a pamphlet written by the exiled king Pausanias at the beginning of the fourth century B.C.[7] May we conclude that land in Sparta—as in the rest of Greece—was in private possession? To answer this question it is necessary to refer to Aristotle (*Pol.* 2.6.1270a15–16), who insists on the uniqueness of the system of land tenure in Sparta and on the responsibility of the lawgiver who permitted land to be given as gifts and bequests.[8] If Aristotle had Lycurgus in mind, as was recently suggested,[9] we must conclude that all the land in Sparta was in private possession. But if, as I think, the anonymous lawgiver was the same Epitadeus referred to by Plutarch (*Agis* 5.3) who introduced a law permitting a man to give his estate (*oikos*) and lot (*klēros*) to anyone he wished, it is necessary to offer another hypothesis. I suggest that it is necessary to distinguish between the inherited patrimony (*oikos*) and the *klēros*: only the latter was under the control of the city and linked with military service and participation in common meals.[10] The free disposition of the patrimony played a large part in the exclusion of the poorest from the civic community and promoted the concentration of land which, along with love of wealth, Plato implies was a relatively recent phenomenon (*Rep.* 8.547c–d; cf. Xenophon *Lac. Pol.* 14.1–3).[11]

The description of Spartan land tenure by Aristotle (*Pol.* 2.6.1270a15–30) contains another point essential for the present investigation. Aristotle connected the concentration of land with the special status of women. The status of Spartan women is a subject as controversial as the subject of Spartan land tenure. James Redfield and Paul Cartledge have restated the issues.[12] I shall limit my remarks to three topics: education of girls, marriage, and ownership of property by women.

Education of Girls

Here, we are on firmest ground. The literary testimony is confirmed by archaeology. The Spartan girl was given physical education, and her nakedness was the subject of an Athenian joke: Aristophanes' *Lysistrata* (80–81) refers to Lampito's ability to throttle a bull. Nevertheless the girls' training differed from the boys', not only because it was milder but because it did not involve a communal life such as the one described by Xenophon in the *Lacedaemonion Politeia* (2.7–9, 3.1–5). The girls participated in common dances and choirs, but they lived at home with their mothers, as in other Greek cities. Xenophon (*Lac. Pol.* 1.3) contrasts the Spartan girls with the girls in other cities. The latter are enclosed in their houses and live like craftsmen. The Spartan girls spend part of their lives outside the walls of their homes, and their training has a purpose: procreation of vigorous sons. But this training is only for the *parthenoi* (unmarried girls). After marriage, Spartan wives cease to train their bodies.

Plutarch (*Lyc.* 14) gives more information about the training of girls but cites the same purpose: procreation. Nevertheless he adds that this *paideia* (training) permits the girls to obtain *aretē* and *philotimia* (virtue and honor), the two main virtues of Spartan men. Here the influence of Plato's views in *Republic* 5.451e–452c is evident: the wives of the guardians will have the same training as the male guardians. In the *Laws* 7.806a, however, Plato criticizes the education of Spartan girls, and his criticisms corroborate my earlier comment: the training concerns only the unmarried girls (the word in Plato is *korai*); the Spartan wives (*gynaikes*) spend their lives managing their households (*therapeia* and *tamieia*) and tending their children (*paidotrophia*).

Marriage

Xenophon (*Lac. Pol.* 1.6) and Plutarch (*Lyc.* 15.4) report that girls were married in Sparta at their *acmē* (prime), and modern commentators think that *acmē* was around eighteen years.[13] The Spartan custom was quite different from that which prevailed at Athens. Athenian girls married as soon as they attained puberty, around fourteen. The reason given for the Spartan custom by the two Greek writers is that eighteen is a healthier age for conception. Both insist also on the relative rarity of sexual intercourse between husbands and wives.[14] This continence has, they say, a double purpose: to preserve fecundity by storing it, and to keep desire potent. But Plutarch adds some details which depict intercourse between husband and wife as a sort of secret play: the husband stole home at night to have intercourse with his wife but lived with his companions the rest of the time, outside his home. However, Xenophon says nothing about this secret play or about the communal sleeping arrangements for men. He reports that after the common meal every man returned to his own home. I am inclined to prefer Xenophon's testimony to Plutarch's.

The same problem of the reliability of the ancient sources arises in regard to the wedding ritual described by Plutarch (*Lyc.* 15.4–5). Xenophon ignores the subject. The ritual consisted of two parts: the seizure of the bride (*harpagē*) and transvestism. (The girl was dressed in man's clothing and her hair was cut.) These two customs have been often discussed by modern commentators,[15] who explain them as a survival of primitive practices surrounding the transition between childhood and maturity, and as "rites d'initiation."[16] Barton Lee Kunstler considers various interpretations of these practices.[17] I doubt that they were common in classical times. No one before Plutarch gives information about them. But it is impossible to come to a definite conclusion.

In the same chapter of his *Life of Lycurgus* (15.6–7) Plutarch describes another marriage practice mentioned also by Xenophon (*Lac. Pol.* 1.7–8). It is interesting to compare the two texts. Two situations are described. An old man married to a young woman can introduce into his home a younger man to impregnate his wife. This situation is described just after the discussion of the optimum age for marriage. I presume that the purpose of this practice was to give heirs to a man who could not procreate. Another situation is that a man who does not want to *synoikein* with a woman (that is, a man who does not want marriage) can borrow another man's wife and have children by her. Xenophon commends this second practice: he says that women like to have two *oikoi* and that men, in this way, create for their sons brothers who will not be heirs of the patrimony, as the only heirs are the legitimate sons.[18]

Plutarch's comment is quite different. He suggests that Lycurgus believed that children were not their fathers' property but were common property of the state. On this subject Xenophon (*Lac. Pol.* 6.1) gives quite a different opinion: every father can exercise authority over the children of others, but children belong to their father's *oikos*.

Plutarch's remark (*Lyc.* 15.17) that adultery did not exist in Sparta is also dubious. Again we find the Platonic pattern behind the so-called Lycurgean constitution. In the city described in *Republic* 5.457c–d children are possessed in common, as indeed are wives. Adultery does not exist. It is interesting to find in Plutarch (*Lyc.* 15.5) the same analogies with dogs and horses that appear in Plato.[19]

Is it possible to discover the real situation? I am inclined to suppose that the arrangements reported by Xenophon were only emergency arrangements, perhaps to stop the manpower shortage at the end of the Peloponnesian War.[20] But even if these arrangements did not have this purpose, they show that in Sparta the relationship of children's legitimacy to their citizenship was not so strict as it was in Athens. As MacDowell remarks, we must not forget that in the two situations described by Xenophon the husband's authorization was required. Intercourse without such authorization was as culpable as adultery.[21]

Unfortunately we have no documentation for Sparta comparable to the Athenian private orations. And the only adultery we know of in Sparta concerns members of the royal families. For these reasons I adopt Mac-Dowell's conclusions: "The rule about *moicheia* (adultery) observed in the early period, but not later, must have been that a man might not have sexual intercourse with another man's wife unless the husband gave permission, nor with an unmarried woman unless, being unmarried him-self, he carried her off to keep her in his own house, which would consti-tute marriage."[22]

Ownership of Property by Women

I am convinced that the testimony about common ownership of land and of women is utopian. Nevertheless I think that we can accept the testi-mony given by Aristotle (*Pol.* 2.6.1270a23–29) about women's property. Regarding the role of women, Aristotle gives two reasons to explain the inequality of land tenure: the large number of *epiklēroi* (heiresses of a patrimony when there were no male heirs) and the size of dowries. The first reason is based on the fact that *epiklēroi* were free to marry outside the paternal lineage and yet could keep a part of the patrimony, as they could in Crete according to the laws of Gortyn (7.35–52, 8.8–12). Perhaps they even inherited all of their fathers' land (as did Agiatis, who inherited the wealth of her father, Gylippos; Plut. *Cleom.* 1.2). The number of *epiklēroi* was also related to the well-known *oliganthrōpia* (scarcity of men).

The second reason given by Aristotle is more problematic. According to tradition, Lycurgus forbade dowries, so that they would not serve as a motivation for marriage. This moralizing tradition doubtless is based on the notion of the "Spartan mirage" rather than on reality. We should be reminded of the philosophical discussions about dowries in the fourth century. In Plato's *Laws* (5.742c) dowries are forbidden. Phaleas of Chalce-don proposed that dowries be used to equalize fortunes: the poor would receive them without giving any in turn, and the rich would give them without receiving any.[23] We find here another example of Platonic influ-ence on Plutarch's testimony. I think that the real explanation is the same as that proposed for the *epiklēros.* As in Gortyn, the Spartan woman, even when she had brothers, inherited a part of her father's patrimony. (In Gortyn this part was half the portion of the son.) And this inheritance could be taken as a dowry.

The two reasons given by Aristotle lead to the same conclusion: women in Sparta could possess land. From this conclusion we can deduce that land tenure was not tied exclusively to military service and that it is necessary, as I said above, to distinguish between *klēroi* and privately owned land. In any case Aristotle draws attention to the point which explains the special role of women in the Spartan revolutions of the third century B.C.

Aristotle also points to another aspect of the status of Spartan women: their political influence. He asks what difference it makes if the women rule, or if the men who rule are ruled by women (*Pol.* 2.6.1269b32–34). Aristotle's question draws attention to a point important for our purpose: the women who were to have an influential role in the revolutions of the third century were not ordinary women. They were the mothers, daughters, and wives of kings. First of all, the young king Agis was forced to convince his mother, Agesistrata, of the value of his projects, for she exercised authority in the city, where she was often involved in public matters (Plut. *Agis* 6.7). Helped by her own mother, Archidamia, and other women in the family, Agesistrata endeavored to convince her friends and other Spartan women of the value of her son's policy. According to Aristotle (*Pol.* 2.6.1269b25, 32–34), the Spartan men obeyed their wives and allowed them to become active in public matters to a greater extent than the men themselves were involved in domestic affairs.

The same situation was repeated under Cleomenes. His father, Leonidas, had arranged a marriage between him and the widow of Agis, Agiatis, who had inherited a large fortune. Agiatis came to exercise a considerable influence over her young husband: "Cleomenes became passionately fond of her as soon as he married her, and sympathized with her devotion to the memory of Agis, so that he would often ask her about the career of Agis, and listen attentively as she told of the plans and projects of her late husband" (Plut. *Cleom.* 1.3). Thus the son of the most stubborn adversary of Agis, under the influence of a woman, revived the projects of Agis. Further, he associated his own mother, Cratesicleia, the widow of Leonidas, in his politics. After he won his mother over, "she furnished resources to him generously, because she shared his ambitions. It is even said that although she had had no intention of remarrying, for the sake of her son she took a husband who was first among the citizens in reputation and power" (*Cleom.* 6.2).

We might suppose that Plutarch emphasized the role of women in the initiation of the revolution in order to illustrate Aristotle's remarks on women's political influence. But Polybius (13.7) also reports an anecdote about Nabis which indicates that this same influence was exercised by the tyrant's wife, Apega. In order to subdue recalcitrant Spartans, Nabis had constructed an image of a woman, richly dressed, in the likeness of his wife: but this device was actually an infernal machine. Any unfortunate man intending to petition the queen would find himself attacked by the machine and compelled to accept the tyrant's demands.

Because these women were queens or mothers of queens, we can attempt to compare them with contemporary Hellenistic queens, of whom Sarah B. Pomeroy has written that they were "instrumental in the social, political, and cultural changes that transformed the Classical era into the Hellenistic."[24] Although at first glance the double Spartan monarchy had little in common with the Hellenistic kingdoms, we should nevertheless attempt a comparison. An early third century B.C. inscription of Delphi awards proxeny "to the king Areus and the queen Chilonis."[25] This double citation brings to mind similar inscriptions honoring the Ptolemaic rulers, with whom Areus enjoyed a close relationship in other respects as well.

However, I think we should not lose sight of the specifically Spartan qualities, in particular the character traits which Plutarch imputes to the women. Their behavior was essentially virile and heroic, as would necessarily be the case with women who had received an education so admired by the other Greeks. After the death of Agis, his mother, Agesistrata, agreed to share the fate of her son as much as she had shared his ideas, and "as she rose to present her neck to the noose, said: 'My only wish is that this may be good for Sparta' " (Plut. *Agis* 20.7). Cratesicleia displayed the same heroic attitude. Ptolemy Euergetes had promised help to Cleomenes in his struggle against the Macedonians but demanded the Spartan king's mother and children as hostages. Cleomenes hesitated to reveal this demand to his mother. Finally, when he decided to tell her about it, Cratesicleia burst into laughter and told her son to carry out Ptolemy's request without delay. Here again Plutarch ascribes significant words to the old queen: "send me where you think my body will be of most use to Sparta," and much later, "let us be quiet as we depart, so that no one may see us weeping or doing anything unworthy of Sparta" (*Cleom.* 22.6–7).

Two other women displayed the same grandeur of spirit in adverse circumstances. The first, Chilonis, was the daughter of Leonidas, the foe of Agis. When Leonidas was forced to go into exile and was supplanted by his son-in-law Cleombrotus, Chilonis chose her father against her husband and followed him into exile. But when Leonidas returned and prepared to take vengeance against his son-in-law, she went away with Cleombrotus. Plutarch ascribes to this young woman speeches of a high

moral tone and concludes that "if Cleombrotus had not been totally cor-
rupted by vainglory, he would have considered that exile with such a
woman was a greater blessing to him than the kingdom" (*Agis* 23.3). The
second of the Spartan heroines is the wife of Panteus, who had followed
Cleomenes to Egypt. This woman, "sturdy and tall," like Lampito in
Aristophanes, died "heroically," worthy of the fame of Spartan women
(*Cleom.* 38.5–12).

We cannot consider all these anecdotes as "history"; however, they
constitute traditions which contribute to the idealized portrait of Spartan
women. Moreover, it is interesting to find them in the description of the
revolutions of the third century. They attest, in effect, that these women
who played an active role in the political upheavals were first of all Spartans. Their heroism and their noble spirit were an integral part of themselves and were totally compatible with the influence which they exercised over their sons or their husbands. In this sense the picture which
Plutarch gives of them is distinct from the one painted by Aristotle. Far
from living a life "of total license and luxury," the heroines of Plutarch are
worthy of their native city. If they exercised power over men, it was for the
greatest benefit of the city. And "the love of riches" did not stop the best
of them from fostering a radical revolution of which they would be the
first victims.

As we have seen, the aim of the Spartan revolutions was to put an end
to the unequal distribution of wealth which was the major cause of the
city's decline. But in contrast to other violent revolutions which erupted in
the Greek world with the slogans "abolition of debts and distribution of
land,"[26] the Spartan revolutions were initiated by kings, rather than by a
popular uprising. Furthermore, they illustrate, in a way, the recommen-
dations of fourth-century theoreticians who urged that in order to avoid
the danger of uprisings and civil strife, the rich of their own free will
should put their wealth at the disposal of everyone. As Plato wrote in the
Laws (5.736d–e): "to produce the change there must already exist some
men who themselves possess considerable land and have many people in
their debt, and who are kind enough to wish to give a share of these
things to those who are most needy, partly by remitting their debts, and
partly by distributions of land, making a kind of rule of moderation, and
considering that poverty consists not in a decrease of wealth but in an
increase of greed." In part the revolutionary kings, with their egalitarian
dreams, endeavored to put this program into effect. The kings' goal

clearly assumed the compliance of the rich who possessed the majority of the land, and especially of the women.

Among these wealthy women, two groups were diametrically opposed. The first was comprised of women of the royal families who were to turn over their considerable fortunes to the community, of their own free will. Agesistrata and Archidamia, whom Plutarch described as "the wealthiest among the Spartans" (*Agis* 4.2), and who therefore had a large number "of retainers, friends, and debtors," supported Agis' program and contributed their wealth to the common stock (*Agis* 7.7, 9.5–6). In the same way, Agiatis, who, as I have already mentioned, was a wealthy *epiklēros*, and Cratesicleia, widow of Leonidas and mother of Cleomenes, made contributions to help the king accomplish his goals (Plut. *Cleom.* 1.2, 6.2). But there were other women, as well, who did not belong to the two royal families and who were not involved in reform movements. In contrast to the queen they saw themselves in the first ranks of those who were threatened, and they played a decisive role in the failure of the revolutions. According to Plutarch, these were the women who were afraid to be deprived not only of the luxury to which they were accustomed but even more, perhaps, of the honor and influence which they enjoyed as a result of their wealth. They urged Leonidas to oppose the reforms of Agis, an opposition which brought about the death of the young king (*Agis* 7.5–7).

Thus women's economic power, noted by Aristotle, appears as one of the essential features of the Spartan revolutions, inasmuch as it permitted women to play an active role in politics if they belonged to the royal family, or to arouse opposition which brought about the defeat of the attempts at reform. Because they owned the majority of the land, the women held the fate of the city in their hands.

This economic importance of women manifested itself in another way in the course of the final revolutionary attempt of the third century, that of Nabis. I have already discussed the different kinds of sources which inform us about this episode in Spartan history. In contrast to the moralizing and idealizing description of Plutarch is the dry passage of Polybius: "[Nabis] exiled the citizens who were distinguished for their wealth and illustrious ancestry, and he gave their property and wives to his foremost supporters or to his mercenaries" (13.6, 16.13). Livy, who used fragments of Polybius which are no longer extant, makes it clear that Nabis wanted to reestablish the ancient Spartan equality and to increase the number of citizens eligible to serve in the army. Thus he essentially revived (although with different methods) the political program of Agis and Cleomenes (Livy 34.32.18).

The union of the wives and daughters of the proscribed with the tyrant's mercenaries or enfranchised slaves was not an exceptional measure. There was a Greek tradition associating servile revolutions with female power. We find it in the stories concerning the foundation of Locri Epizephyrii in southern Italy, in the story of the Partheniai who founded Tarentum, and also in the more historical events which unfolded at Cumae after the inauguration of the tyranny of Aristodemus, as well as at Argos after the defeat at Sepeia.[27] In the case of Nabis, we can ask whether the connection between servile revolutions and women is applicable. All that I have said about the fortunes of Spartan women leads me to think that the union imposed by the tyrant had another purpose: gaining access to land by means of marriage to those who owned it. We must also note that neither Polybius nor Livy mentions that the Spartan women opposed the tyrant's demands. What is more, the death of Nabis was not followed by a return of exiles, as if the Spartan women had continued to exercise over their new husbands as much power as they had had over their former husbands: their husbands had been their slaves.[28]

But this reference to the tradition associating slavery with the rule of women leads me to ask a final question. Can we not explain the importance which the ancient sources accord to women in the Spartan revolutions by the traditions which associate women with the inversion of civic values and which portray them as inimical to the social order? To such a question, I think, we must give a careful response which takes into account the historical conditions of the period (that is, the social crisis), the unique position of women, especially of queens in the Hellenistic world, the original character of Spartan society, and the particular place of women within that society. We must also not neglect the fact that we know these revolutions only through literary sources which inherited an old tradition in which a woman held a definite place, simultaneously as mistress of the *oikos* and in that role as an agent of stability, but also, in opposition, as a person who retained considerable powers which associated her with all that was subversive of the social order.[29]

Notes

This essay is a new version of two papers first delivered in the National Endowment for the Humanities seminar on the family in classical and Hellenistic Greece directed by Sarah B. Pomeroy and at the Seventh Berkshire Conference on the History of Women (Wellesley, June 1987). Translations of classical texts were adapted from Loeb Library versions.

1. The bibliography on Sparta is large and cannot be reviewed here. I have limited myself to drawing attention to the following: for the epoch of the revolutions of the third century see especially P. Oliva, *Sparta and Her Social Problems* (Prague: Academia, 1971), 201–98, and the articles of A. Fuks collected in *Social Conflicts in Ancient Greece* (Jerusalem: The Magness Press, 1984), 230–59. Unless otherwise indicated, abbreviations are the standard ones from *L'année philologique* and the second edition of the *Oxford Classical Dictionary*.

2. On Nabis see my *La tyrannie dans la Grèce antique* (Paris: Presses Universitaires de France, 1969), 170–92.

3. On this problem see most recently S. Hodkinson, "Land Tenure and Inheritance in Classical Sparta," *CQ* 36 (1986): 378–406. After reviewing various hypotheses of modern scholars, Hodkinson concludes that the supposed equal land distribution was a later invention. In reality, Sparta, like other Greek cities, had a system of private property with partible inheritance and the right of bequest. The only unique feature of the Spartan system concerned the rights accorded to women. Although I disagree with several of Hodkinson's points (see below, note 9), I nevertheless support his conclusions, especially insofar as they relate to the importance of private property and the property rights of women.

4. Plutarch attributes the property system of Lycurgus to the early history of Sparta, preceding the conquest of Messenia. It is thus a question of the partitioning of Laconia. In reality, I think that if the city preserved the memory of a partitioning of property, this partitioning must have been of the land conquered after the Second Messenian War. See my "Sparte archaïque," *PP* 28 (1973): 7–20.

5. Inter alia, see H. Michell, *Sparta* (Cambridge: Cambridge University Press, 1964), 205–9; A. H. M. Jones, *Sparta* (Oxford: Blackwell, 1968), 40–47; W. G. Forrest, *A History of Sparta, 950–192 B.C.* (London: Hutchinson University Library, 1968), 135–41; and Oliva, *Sparta and Her Social Problems*, 36–38.

6. See Hodkinson, "Land Tenure and Inheritance," 380–83.

7. Cf. Hodkinson, "Land Tenure and Inheritance," 381–82, and Jones, *Sparta*, 41.

8. *Pol.* 2.6.1270a16–18: "Some of them have come to possess excessively large fortunes, and some extremely little; therefore the land has fallen into few hands."

9. Hodkinson, "Land Tenure and Inheritance," 390–91, develops this point. He bases his argument on the fact that in two other passages in the *Politics* in connection with the lack of control over the women, the "legislator" is anonymous, yet in

another elsewhere (2.6.1269b19–22, 1270b6–8) Lycurgus is named. It is, however, doubtful that Aristotle could have made Lycurgus responsible for the unequal division of land, although tradition made him the founder of Spartan equality. One might suppose that, as at Athens, the possibility of bequests in favor of someone who did not belong to the *anchisteia*, the group formed by the rightful claimants—though appearing quite late—permitted the alienation of land. On the law of bequest attributed to Solon see Louis Gernet, "La loi de Solon sur le testament," *Droit et société dans la Grèce ancienne* (Paris: Sirey, 1955), 121–50.

10. On the origin of the double system see my "Sparte archaïque."

11. Plato does not name Sparta. But since he describes the decline of the timocratic city, one must think of the decline of Sparta, the city where the citizens scorned manual labor and profitable professions, and, trained for war, became increasingly greedy for wealth which they kept hidden from all and "dispensed for women." Xenophon remarks clearly: "I understand that formerly they were afraid to be found possessing gold, but now they take pride in collecting it."

12. James Redfield, "The Women of Sparta," *CJ* 73 (1977–78): 146–61. Redfield begins by remarking that "the Spartan women were like men," adding "like men elsewhere in Greece, and therefore unlike the men of Sparta." He demonstrates that the Spartiates had politicized their society as much as possible and had expelled women from this society. But by this very act they had left the entire private sphere in the hands of women.

Paul Cartledge, "Spartan Wives: Liberation or Licence?" *CQ* 31 (1981): 84–109. Cartledge relates the conditions of Spartan women to the unique nature of the city but also draws attention, rightly, to the customs of the Greek world in general. As other Greek women, the Spartan woman was a "minor." The role of women in the revolutions of the third century demonstrates this: only the queens and the women belonging to influential families could have any political influence.

On Spartan women, in addition to Redfield and Cartledge, see J. Christien, "Quelques réflexions à propos de l'image de la femme spartiate dans Aristophane," *Mélanges R. Mandrou* (Paris: Presses Universitaires de France, 1985), 143–57; and Barton Lee Kunstler, "Women and the Development of the Spartan Polis: A Study of Sex Roles in Classical Antiquity" (Ph.D. dissertation, Boston University, 1983). In a recent paper, "Family Dynamics and Female Power in Ancient Sparta," in *Rescuing Creusa: New Methodological Approaches to Women in Antiquity*, ed. Marilyn B. Skinner, *Helios* n.s. 13, no. 2 (Texas Tech University Press, 1987), 31–48, Kunstler reexamines the question of Spartan women and, accepting Plutarch's testimonies, concludes, against Cartledge, that "it is not exaggeration to speak of the 'power' of Spartan women" (42).

13. See Sarah B. Pomeroy, *Goddesses, Whores, Wives, and Slaves: Women in Classical Antiquity* (New York: Schocken, 1975), 42–64, and Cartledge, "Spartan Wives," 94–95: "Girls normally married at the age when their brothers became fully adult

warriors, probably at twenty." See also D. MacDowell, *Spartan Law* (Edinburgh: Scottish Academic Press, 1986), 73.

14. *Lac. Pol.* 1.5, "it would be shameful for a Spartan to be seen entering or leaving his wife's bedroom"; and *Lyc.* 15.8–10, "this obstacle to seeing one another resulted in continence and temperance."

15. Pomeroy, *Goddesses, Whores, Wives, and Slaves*, 38; Cartledge, "Spartan Wives," 101–2; and Kunstler, "Women and the Development of the Spartan Polis," 435–37. The secret aspects of the Spartan wedding ceremonial contrast with the wedding ritual in Athens. See the paper by Cynthia B. Patterson, "Athenian Marriage," in this volume; Patterson insists upon the public character of the ceremony.

16. On marriage as a rite of initiation see especially P. Vidal-Naquet, "Le cru, l'enfant grec et le cuit," in *Le chasseur noir* (Paris: Maspero, 1981), 205–6.

17. Kunstler, "Women and the Development of the Spartan Polis," 436–37.

18. Although Xenophon discusses the dispositions of Lycurgus without distinguishing the sex of the babies, in the following paragraph (1.9) he refers to giving brothers to legitimate children. Xenophon, an Athenian, does not take account of the particular character of the rules of succession at Sparta and can understand only the usefulness of having sons. This supports my proposal below that a disposition attributed to "Lycurgus" probably took place during the Peloponnesian War to ameliorate the poverty of men.

19. Plato (5.451d), to justify his proposal that the educational system of the guardians also be imposed on their women, compares female dogs who hunt and keep guard as the males do, although the females in addition look after the young. Plutarch uses this comparison in a different context, where it concerns choosing the best males. But it is clear that, as in numerous passages in the *Life of Lycurgus*, Plutarch connects the reforms attributed to the Spartan legislator with the program developed by Plato in the *Republic*.

20. See now T. J. Figueira, "Population Patterns in Late Archaic and Classical Sparta," *TAPhA* 116 (1986): 165–213. Figueira concludes that the decline in population began with the earthquake of 465 B.C. (181–82) but was accelerated after the defeat of Pylos (193).

21. MacDowell, *Spartan Law*, 85–86.

22. MacDowell, *Spartan Law*, 87.

23. Aristotle *Pol.* 2.6.1266b2–5.

24. Pomeroy, *Women in Hellenistic Egypt* (New York: Schocken, 1984; paperback, Detroit: Wayne State University Press, 1990), 3.

25. *SIG* III:430.

26. On the problem of the abolition of debts and the distribution of land see David Asheri, *Distribuzione di terre nell'antica Grecia*, an entire issue of *Memorie dell'Accademia di Torino*, ser. 4, no. 10 (1966), and "Leggi greche sul problema dei debiti," *SCO* 18 (1969): 5–117. See also Andrew Linttot, *Violence, Civil Strife, and*

Revolution in the Classical City (Baltimore: The Johns Hopkins University Press, 1981), and Fuks, *Social Conflicts*.

27. On these traditions see P. Vidal-Naquet, "Esclavage et gynécocratie dans la tradition, le mythe et l'utopie," in *Le chasseur noir* (Paris: Maspero, 1981), 267–88, originally published in *Recherches sur les structures sociales dans l'antiquité classique*, ed. C. Nicolet (Paris: CNRS, 1970).

28. On this point see André Aymard, *Les premiers rapports de Rome et de la Confédération Achaienne* (Bordeaux: Féret et fils, 1938), 241–42, and my *La tyrannie dans la Grèce antique*.

29. Compare the character of Praxagora in Aristoph. *Eccl.*, who is both guardian of tradition (214–31) and initiator of a radical redistribution of property (590–94).

ELIZABETH CARNEY

"What's in a Name?":

The Emergence of a Title for Royal

Women in the Hellenistic Period

During most of the first half of the fourth century B.C. the kingdom of the Macedonians seemed irretrievably mired in a morass of political troubles, largely centered on the royal family itself. Kings died young, leaving disputed successions and troubled regencies in their wake; assassination plots generated within the royal family and/or the aristocracy were the stuff of gossip and sometimes truth; both barbarian tribes to the north and the Greek city-states to the south attempted, often with considerable success, to capitalize on these internal difficulties to their own advantage.[1] The women of the Argead house (the Macedonian royal family) during this troubled period are largely ciphers; usually we know little more than their names and the names of the men they married (indeed, even in less troubled periods, the situation is little different).[2] The only exception to this generalization is Eurydice, wife of Amyntas III, and even about Eurydice much of what little is known is of dubious authenticity.[3]

Then, when it must have seemed that this Macedonian mess would never be cleaned up, in 359 B.C. the greatest Macedonian ruler yet, Philip II, came to power and, with remarkable rapidity, dealt with the internal problems of Macedonia. By 338 Philip had transformed once chronically divided Macedonia into the dominant power in the Greek peninsula.[4] In 336, shortly before he planned to lead a joint Graeco-Macedonian expedition against the great Persian empire, Philip was assassinated.[5] Philip was polygamous, as in all probability were Macedonian kings before him,[6] but toward the end of his reign his dealings with two of his wives, Olympias, mother of his heir Alexander III, or the Great, and Cleopatra, the last of his royal brides, became notorious and may well have led to his assassination.[7]

On Philip's death his son Alexander became king, and so it was Alexander who led the planned expedition to the Persian empire and great military glory. Alexander left Macedonia in 334 and never returned. During this unprecedentedly long absence of the reigning monarch, the king's mother, Olympias, and his full sister, Cleopatra, became prominent in Macedonia and in his mother's homeland of Epirus, although what each woman was doing and what her official role was during this period remains controversial.[8] Certainly Alexander's failure to marry until late in his reign, and then the fact that his brides were all eastern, tended to give greater predominance to his close female relatives.

When Alexander died, male Argeads were in scarce supply: there was only a mentally deficient half-brother, and Alexander's wife Roxane was pregnant with a son, later known as Alexander (IV). After considerable strife a Macedonian noble was chosen as regent for these two joint kings, and the rest of Alexander's generals moved to seize parts of the empire he had conquered. Female members of the royal family were more plentiful in this period than males: Olympias, Alexander's full sister Cleopatra, two half-sisters, and a niece (soon married to his half-brother) survived him. Ultimately all of these women were murdered, but several served, at least temporarily, to legitimize claims of various males, and several more tried to capitalize on the scarcity of royal males to seize various kinds of power for themselves.[9]

Finally, near the end of the century, in 306/305, first Antigonus and his son Demetrius Poliorcetes took the royal title and diadem, and soon the surviving Macedonian generals followed (Diod. 20.53.2–4; Plut. *Dem.* 18.1–2), although the balance of power among the various Hellenistic monarchies did not more or less stabilize until about 280. As Alexander's Successors moved in the direction of becoming kings, the women connected to them (wives, daughters, sisters, some of them relatives of Philip and Alexander) often were used in various ways (such as marriage alliance) to legitimize power that was not hereditary and that as yet lacked a firm foundation. Once the political situation had stabilized and the Hellenistic monarchies and dynasties had been established, in some cases the importance of royal women, which had increased so significantly in the later fourth century, tended to diminish (this is true of the Antigonids); but in other cases it either endured or, for the Ptolemies and in some degree for the Seleucids, increased over time.[10]

This is the historical background for the emergence of a title for royal women of Macedonian blood. I would hesitate to apply the English word *queen* to these women because of its distressing inexactitude. The wife of a living king, a female sovereign, a widowed royal wife acting as regent, and a dowager might all have that term applied to them. Moreover, in actual usage *queen* strongly implies an official and unique status (this last doubtless the result of the now fairly long monogamous tradition in the West). It is difficult to prevent this muddy baggage of meaning in English usage from being carried along when we look at female members of royal Macedonian families. Certainly, as Macedonian kings were polygamous and no evidence suggests an official chief wife, there is no reason to call any royal consort (or for that matter, any other female member of the royal family) "queen" until, minimally, after the death of Alexander.

So much for English, but what about Greek? My distinguished predecessor in the study of royal Macedonian women, Grace Macurdy, believed that by the time of Alexander's mother, Olympias, and quite possibly earlier, *basilissa* (a term she and others wrongly believed to be of Macedonian origin) had become a title.[11] *Basilissa* began to supplant earlier formations like *anassa* and *basileia* and *basilis* in the course of the fourth century.[12] It was formed by adding a feminine suffix roughly equivalent to *-ess* in English *princess* to the root of the word for king, *basileus*.[13] Although initially applied to royal consorts, it was soon, at least in some Hellenistic dynasties, applied to the kings' daughters as well and would later be used by royal women acting as regents or even as sovereigns.[14]

Macurdy was mistaken, both about the existence of the title and about the assumption behind it, that in some sense there was an institution of queenship (minimally as chief wife) in Olympias' day. The question of when *basilissa* began to be used as a title is significant for several reasons: what it may tell us about the role and status of royal Macedonian women; how it changed in the late fourth and early third centuries; and what it may tell us about changes in the nature of Macedonian monarchy in the same period.

Two major factors, as well as several minor ones, suggest that *basilissa* did not develop as a title for royal women until at least the period after the death of Alexander and in all likelihood until some time no sooner than 306/305. First, in the tiny number of inscriptions prior to 323 which involve royal Macedonian women, the women appear with merely their personal names. Eurydice, mother of Philip II, used a patronymic[15] but no title. Olympias, for whom there is a bit more evidence and of whom it might be said that she would certainly have employed a title had one been available to her, appears merely as Olympias in inscriptions[16] and is referred to not by title but rather by personal name in contemporary writers (Hyp. *Eux.* 19, 20, 24, 25). It could be claimed that these inscriptions date to the period of widowhood for both Eurydice and Olympias, but in several cases their relative date is unclear, and in any event we do not necessarily know that, if the title *basilissa* had existed, it would have been given up upon the death of the husband.[17] Significantly, the fact that Olympias and her daughter Cleopatra, wife/widow of Alexander of Molossos, both appear without titles on a list of grain recipients from Cyrene (*SEG* IX:2), has been taken to mean that they were both functioning as heads of state (this on the basis of parallel male usage).[18]

Second, there is nearly universal agreement that Macedonian kings did not themselves use titles until the transitional reign of Alexander. Philip and his predecessors appear on treaties and other inscriptions simply with personal name and patronymic;[19] although others, largely Greeks, might refer to one of them as a *basileus*, they themselves did not choose to use the title.[20] Alexander began to use the title, on some occasions. His innovation may have related to his claims to be legitimate successor to the Achaemenids, who were referred to in Greek by their title (and the definite article).[21] Although Alexander's immediate heirs, Philip Arrhidaeus (his half-brother) and Alexander IV (his posthumous son), probably took the title *basileus* on at least some occasions,[22] the real change came, as we have seen, in the period of the Successors, in 306/305 and shortly thereafter. According to Diodorus (20.53.2–4), after a great victory at Salamis, Antigonus and his son Demetrius took the title *basileus* as well as the diadem. Diodorus says that their defeated opponent Ptolemy soon did the same and that Seleucus, Lysimachus, and Cassander followed. Plutarch's account of the occasion is slightly differrent (Plut. *Dem.* 18.1–2).[23] It would be astonishing if the wives of Macedonian kings prior to Alexander used titles when their husbands did not.

In addition to these two persuasive reasons for doubting the existence of a female title prior to 323, I would suggest some other, more tenuous factors which also tend to invalidate Macurdy's argument. As mentioned earlier, no real evidence exists to justify the assumption that there was any sort of queenship in Macedonia prior to Alexander's death. Not only would the practice of polygamy and the absence of any official chief wife suggest this, but the way royal Macedonian women appear in the surviving evidence would also tend to deny such an assumption.[24] Moreover, the political habits of the Macedonians would also make the use of a female title unlikely; little was defined and apparently nothing was written down. The Macedonians seem to have functioned on the basis of a very roughly observed tradition and on the basis of current political demands.[25] In such a political ("constitutional" would certainly be the wrong word) milieu, the use of a title by a royal wife would seem incongruous, legalistic, and anachronistic.

Certainly the evidence Macurdy brings forward for her view does nothing to controvert the arguments I have given. Macurdy's primary evidence is a pair of passages in Athenaeus (13.586c = *FGrH* 115 F254a; 13.595a–e = *FGrH* 115 F254b), both at least partially attributed to the testimony of the historian Theopompus and one (13.595c) also referring to the comic playwright Philemon.[26] In the first passage Athenaeus cites Theopompus for a story about a *hetaira* of Harpalus (Alexander's undependable treasurer) named Glycera.[27] According to the story, the people of Tarsus did *proskynēsis* to her and addressed her as a *basilissa*, and she and Harpalus both wore crowns. Even if we put aside questions about the authenticity of this story, it clearly tells us absolutely nothing about Macedonian court practice—the *proskynēsis* reference alone makes this impossible[28]—although it may tell us something about Persian court practice. The second passage, also largely attributed to Theopompus and also largely dealing with Glycera, repeats similar information and adds that Glycera was honored by gifts more suited to Alexander's mother or wife (Athen. 13.595c). Note that the reference to the royal Macedonian women has nothing to do with titles or crowns, but rather with apparently splendid gifts. The fourth-century comic writer Philemon is also quoted in this passage of Athenaeus (13.595c); the quotation seems to imply that another of Harpalus' courtesans, Pythionice, was addressed as *basilissa* of Babylon, as Harpalus was addressed as *basileus*. Again, we learn nothing of Macedonian court practice from this passage, even if it is accurate. Both passages, however, are intriguing for other reasons: one cannot help but wonder if the model for the use of a royal title and other royal trappings by later Macedonian women is ultimately Persian, or at least Near Eastern.[29]

Although it seems certain that there is no firm evidence for a female royal Macedonian title prior to the death of Alexander, there does exist a body of information dealing with a phenomenon which may amount to a quasi title. Both the general question whether royal Macedonian women sometimes changed their names (and if so, for what reasons) and the more specific problem whether "Eurydice" had a tendency to become a dynastic name for royal wives of the Argeads have recently become the subject of scholarly controversy.[30] That controversy is relevant to discussion here because of the possibility of a connection between the practice of changing the names of royal women and the emergence of *basilissa* as a title.

Despite the arguments of Heckel and Prestianni-Giallombardo in support of an elaboration of Macurdy's idea, it is difficult to believe that "Eurydice" was tending to become a throne and/or dynastic name, whether for royal Macedonian wives in general or for those of Illyrian origin in particular. In addition to Badian's persuasive arguments,[31] I would note that the whole idea of a formalized female throne name does not suit what we know about Macedonian monarchy at this stage in its development, when very few royal trappings—titles, ceremonies, whatever—as yet existed.

On the other hand Badian underestimates the amount of name-changing that went on among royal Macedonian women. He grants, as does virtually everyone, the validity of the information that Adea changed her name to Eurydice on the occasion of her marriage, just as her husband changed his from Philip to Arrhidaeus at the time he became king.[32] Having granted one case, it becomes difficult to argue that all others are dissimilar, especially when one knows that Philip Arrhidaeus and his wife were under particular pressure to be traditional; indeed they owed their positions to the army's somewhat less than pragmatic adherence to tradition.[33]

In reference to a passage in Plutarch (*Moral.* 401a–b) which says that Olympias had four names, Pomeroy has suggested that some of these names may have been epithets or nicknames rather than replacements for original names.[34] At least one earlier example of name changing exists: the wife of the tyrant Periander (Diog. Laert. 1.94).[35] Moreover, despite Badian's assertion to the contrary,[36] there does seem to be a connection between the practice of changing the name of a royal wife and the tendency to name female members of the royal family for political or propaganda purposes (for example, the names of Philip II's daughters Thessalonice and Europe); indeed, if Olympias' name was not hers from birth, then the two customs would appear to overlap.[37]

In the case of both name changing of wives and commemorative names for daughters, the effect was to give these royal women semipublic status; it would seem the opposite of Athenian attitudes about female names.[38] In both situations the woman's name was also a reflection of the actions or status of her male relatives.[39] If a name given at birth or newly received upon marriage had a title-like function—the royal woman in question had a peculiarly public name—then it would seem no accident that the practice of female name changing seems to have come to an end about the time *basilissa* first appeared as a title.[40] I would not go so far as to say that one practice replaced the other (there is simply not enough evidence for name changing to make it possible to think that it was regular practice), but probably one overshadowed the other. Another possible interpretation of this apparent shift is that no real change in fact occurred, but rather the early obscurity of Macedonian royal women—and thus even their names[41]—yielded to greater publicity which involved knowledge that individuals had both personal names and epithets (for example, Philadelphus); but it is more likely that the quasi titles disappeared with the quasi queens (most obviously Olympias and Adea-Eurydice).

Although the changing of royal women's names upon marriage and the naming of daughters after their fathers' accomplishments are customs which seem to date back to the Archaic period and appear part of the traditions of the Greek world, another sort of public role for royal women involving their names—naming cities after them—apparently occurred for the first time not long after 316. Shortly after Cassander married Philip II's daughter Thessalonice (Diod. 19.52.1–2, 61.2; Just. 14.6.13), he founded Cassandreia (Diod. 19.52.1–5) and the still-surviving city of Thessaloniki (Dion. Hal. 1.49.4; Strab. 7, F21, 24). Although a Persian king may have named a city after a royal woman, Thessalonice appears to be the first example in the Graeco-Macedonian world.[42] Naming cities after royal women became, of course, very common in the Hellenistic period, but the function of this royal habit changed over the course of time. Later Hellenistic commemorations of royal women by city names would seem to have been part of the general tendency to elevate the dynasty by elevating all its members, much as in the case of the deification of royal women, whereas Cassander's motivation was likely to have been more specific. Thessalonice was vital to his claim to legitimate rule of the homeland of Macedonia; what better way to demonstrate his right to reign than by city-founding, in itself a kingly act, not only naming a new foundation after himself as Philip and Alexander had done, but also naming a foundation after Philip's daughter and Alexander's sister, his tie to legitimacy?[43] Thus Cassander's need to establish his rule, yet not offend against Macedonian tradition, may have led to an innovation which was soon imitated by others.

Logically one would expect the title *basilissa* to appear after or at the same time that men began to take the title, that is, in 306/305. Because only literary evidence dealing with Alexander's wives and with Adea-Eurydice survives, the earliest evidence from documents confirming the use of *basilissa* as a title refers to the wives of the Successors mentioned in Diodorus' and Plutarch's accounts of the taking of the male title. Obviously either one of Alexander's wives or Adea-Eurydice might have used the title in documents which no longer survive, but for reasons I shall discuss below I think it unlikely. The earliest usage of the title appears in an inscription referring to Phila, wife of Demetrius Poliorcetes (one of the first two males to take a title). The inscription has been dated to shortly after 306.[44] Apamea, wife of Seleucus, is given the title *basilissa* in an inscription dated to late 300, and Berenice, wife of Ptolemy, appears as *basilissa* ca. 299 in *OGI* 14. In all probability the wives of some of the Successors assumed the title at the same time the men did or only shortly thereafter, and the use of the title rapidly became the rule.[45]

Now that the period shortly after 306 has been established as the historical context for the assumption of the title *basilissa* by the wives of the Successors (and soon by some of their daughters),[46] it is possible to consider the significance of this assumption. Let us look first at what the change meant for Macedonian monarchy in general. Discussions of why Macedonian kings so long avoided the use of a title and then began to move to its use in Alexander's reign and later are helpful. Generally it has been thought that Macedonian kings did not originally take a title because of Greek public opinion: in the fifth and early fourth centuries monarchy seemed an outmoded institution, perpetuated largely by barbarians. Macedonian monarchs, and other semihellenized kings in the northern regions, chose not to emphasize a role which made them seem backward and old-fashioned. Then, in Philip and Alexander's reigns, not only did monarchy become dominant once more, but Alexander's claim to be legitimate heir to the Archaemenids required a different approach, and the situation began to change. Finally, the Successors sought ways to legitimize the power they had seized, and taking the title and diadem and other royal trappings were devices meant to give credibility to their power (as well as, possibly, to recognize the fragmentation of Alexander's empire).[47]

Another reason why earlier Macedonian monarchs avoided a title was that there was no need for one. In some ways the absence of a title was more impressive: they reigned because they were Argeads, and all they needed was their Argead personal names and a patronymic. Conversely, the Successors, all non-Argeads, could make no such claim.[48] Thus the appearance of *basilissa* as a title was part and parcel of a series of legitimizing devices and acts: the taking of the male title; royal cults and ultimately deification; eponymous city-founding; diadems; diadems for women and the appearance of women on coins;[49] and finally, the use of royal women via marriage alliances as legitimizing devices.

The appearance of the title *basilissa* had, naturally, more significance for royal women than a title had for their fathers or husbands. Whereas kingship in Macedonia had existed long before Macedonian kings chose to use a title, "queenship" in Macedonia did not, it seems to me, exist much before the appearance of the title *basilissa*. Pomeroy is certainly right to point out that Hellenistic queens were not public officials,[50] but they were public figures, in a way that their early fourth-century predecessors had not been.

As I have suggested above and argued at length elsewhere,[51] several factors acted to make royal Macedonian women from the reign of Philip on into Hellenistic times more prominent than they had been before. During the reigns of Philip and Alexander there were drastic changes in the nature of Macedonian monarchy; the previous troubles which had acted as a check on the powers of the Macedonian monarchy had in good part been dealt with, and as the monarchy grew more powerful and separate from the rest of Macedonian society, so did all its members, male and female. Deification and divine sonship affected royal women, if at first only indirectly. Conceptualization of power, at least monarchical power, had always been in some degree familial, but now the isolation of the royal family increased the tendency.

Moreover, the practical political situation from 334 until the end of the century acted to expand the importance of Macedonian royal women: Alexander's uniquely long absence, followed by an extended period in which the only competent Argeads were female, inevitably inflated the significance of women of the blood of Alexander and Philip. This significance should not, however, be exaggerated. Women such as Thessalonice and Cleopatra were primarily potential vehicles of legitimization, and in the end it proved more useful for the Successors to eliminate them in order to prevent their rivals from manipulating them than to use them themselves.[52] Women of unusual ambition, drive, and ability like Olympias, Cynnane, and her daughter Adea-Eurydice were able to gain power unprecedented for royal women, but they were not able to retain it, primarily because they lacked the comparatively secure military base of the male Successors. And even Olympias and Adea-Eurydice operated largely through traditional female royal roles involving connections to sons or husbands or both.

Adea-Eurydice may be the pivotal figure in the development of Macedonian "queenship." I say this not so much because her husband's permanent incapacity gave her an unusual power base, but rather because, unlike earlier Macedonian royal brides, she was married to the king because she was royal: that is why the Macedonian troops forced the marriage—because she was the most Argead of anyone then alive. It was her royalness, not any political alliance, that enabled the troops to force the marriage (Arrian *FGrH* F9.22–23). And with Adea-Eurydice there is the clearest evidence, as we have seen, that her name change was a change from personal name to (sloppy though it is, I can think of no better term) a throne name (*FGrH* 156 F1.19). Similarly, it was Olympias' relationship to Philip and Alexander, her *axiōma* as Diodorus calls it, that brought her victory against Adea-Eurydice and nearly preserved her life despite Cassander's ultimate victory (Diod. 19.11.1, 51.4–5).

That the Successors gave the title *basilissa* to their wives and later to their daughters did not necessarily mean that the power of royal women in the Hellenistic period continued to grow. With the end or at least a stabilization of the conflicts which had brought royal women new prominence and power and with the successful institutionalization of the new dynasties, some of the old limitations on royal women's political activities reappeared, particularly in Macedonia. Of the three major dynasties, only Ptolemaic queens frequently asserted political power; indeed their power grew.[53] On the other hand, the new public role for royal women signaled by their assumption of the title *basilissa* did create a base which a woman like Arsinoë Philadelphus could use in the initial stages of her remarkable career.[54] Being a *basilissa* did not in itself convey any specific power, but it did offer a potential which might be realized by royal women bold enough to try.

Notes

This essay was originally presented as a paper at a 1985 National Endowment for the Humanities seminar on women in antiquity, directed by Mary Lefkowitz. I would like to thank her for her suggestions and assistance. I would also like to thank our editor, Sarah B. Pomeroy, for her helpful comments.

Unless otherwise indicated, abbreviations are the standard ones from *L'année philologique* and the second edition of the *Oxford Classical Dictionary*. Inscriptions are cited according to the abbreviations in the 1968 printing of Liddell, Scott, and Jones's *Greek Lexicon*.

1. For a narrative of these events see N. G. L. Hammond, in N. G. L. Hammond and G. T. Griffith, *A History of Macedonia* (Oxford: Oxford University Press, 1979), 167–200.

2. See Hammond, in Hammond and Griffith, *Macedonia*, 154. See also G. H. Macurdy, *Hellenistic Queens* (Baltimore: The Johns Hopkins University Press, 1927), 1–8, 13–17, and "Queen Eurydice and the Evidence for Woman-Power in Early Macedonia," *AJP* 48 (1927): 201–7.

3. On Eurydice see Macurdy, *Queens*, 17–22, and "Eurydice," 102–14. See also A. Oikonomedes, "A New Inscription from Vergina and Eurydice Mother of Philip II," *AncW* 7 (1983): 52–54; W. S. Greenwalt, "Amyntas II and the Political Stability of Argead Macedonia," *AncW* 18 (1988): 41–44.

4. On the reign of Philip II see Griffith, in Hammond and Griffith, *Macedonia*, 203–674; J. R. Ellis, *Philip II and Macedonian Imperialism* (London: Thames & Hudson, 1976); G. Cawkwell, *Philip of Macedon* (London: Faber & Faber, 1978).

5. On the murder of Philip see Griffith, in Hammond and Griffith, *Macedonia*, 675–98; E. Badian, "The Death of Philip II," *Phoenix* 17 (1963): 244–50; J. R. Fears, "Pausanias, the Assassin of Philip II," *Athenaeum* 53 (1975): 111–35; J. R. Ellis, "The Assassination of Philip II," in *Ancient Macedonian Studies in Honor of Charles F. Edson*, ed. H. J. Dell and E. N. Borza (Thessalonike: Institute for Balkan Studies, 1981), 99–137.

6. Satyrus as given in Athen. 13.557b–d. See especially A. M. Prestianni-Giallombardo, "Diritto matrimoniale, ereditario e dinastico nella Macedonia de Filippo II," *RSA* 6–7 (1976–77): 81–118; A. Tronson, "Satyrus the Peripatetic and the Marriages of Philip II," *JHS* 104 (1984): 116–26. P. Green, "The Royal Tombs at Vergina: A Historical Analysis," in *Philip II, Alexander the Great and the Macedonian Heritage*, ed. W. L. Adams and E. N. Borza (Washington, D.C.: University Press of

America, 1982), 138, recently tried to reassert the older view that Philip and earlier kings were not polygamous; for persuasive arguments against this view see Ellis, *Philip*, 62, 213–14, 254 n. 96, and "Assassination," 114–15; Tronson, "Satyrus," 116–26; and now W. S. Greenwalt, "Polygamy and the Succession in Argead Macedonia," *Arethusa* 22 (1989): 19–45.

7. Plut. *Alex.* 9.3–5. In addition to the works cited above in note 5 see discussion of the possible role of Olympias in the murder of Philip in W. Heckel, "Philip and Olympias (337/6 B.C.)," in *Classical Contributions: Studies in Honour of M. F. McGregor*, ed. G. S. Shrimpton and D. J. McCargar (Locust Valley, N.Y.: Augustin, 1981), 51–57; E. D. Carney, "Olympias," *AncSoc* 18 (1987): 43–48.

8. N. G. L. Hammond, "Some Passages in Arrian Concerning Alexander," *CQ* 30 (1980): 471–76, and "Some Macedonian Offices c. 336–309 B.C.," *JHS* 105 (1985): 158–59, argues for an official and legally defined role for Olympias in this period; but against this see Carney, "Olympias," 49–53.

9. On the activities of these royal women see Macurdy, *Queens*, 22–55, and, more recently, W. Heckel, "Kynnane the Illyrian," *RSA* 13–14 (1983–84): 193–200; also E. D. Carney, "The Career of Adea-Eurydice," *Historia* 36 (1987): 496–502, and "The Sisters of Alexander the Great: Royal Relicts," *Historia* 37 (1988): 385–404.

10. On the marriage alliances see J. Seibert, *Historische Beiträge zu den dynastischen Verbindungen in hellenistischer Zeit*, *Historia* Einzelschriften, no. 10 (Wiesbaden: Steiner, 1967). See also G. M. Cohen, "The Marriage of Lysimachus and Nicaea," *Historia* 22 (1973): 354–56, and "The Diadochoi and the New Monarchies," *Athenaeum* 52 (1974): 177–79. The career of Phila, daughter of Antipater, is a good example; see, most recently, C. Wehrli, "Phila, fille d'Antipater et épouse de Démétrius, roi des Macédoniens," *Historia* 13 (1964): 140–46. On Antigonid women after Phila see Macurdy, *Queens*, 69–76.

11. Macurdy, *Queens*, 8, and "*Basilinna* and *Basilissa*," passim. See O. Hoffman, *Die Makedonen, ihre Sprache und ihr Völkstum* (Göttingen: 1906), 159; W. Koch, "Die erster Ptolemäerinnen nach irhren Münzen" *ZfN* 34 (1923): 74 n. 2; G. H. Macurdy, "*Basilinna* and *Basilissa*, the Alleged Title of 'Queen Archon' in Athens," *AJP* 49 (1928): 281. All argue for the Macedonian origin of the term; but cf. the persuasive argument of C. D. Buck, "Is the Suffix of *Basilissa*, etc., of Macedonian Origin?" *CP* 9 (1914): 370–73. Obviously my argument here offers further confirmation of Buck's thesis by demonstrating the relatively late date at which Macedonians began to use the word. *Basilissa* first appears in Greek literature at about the same time in Xenophon and the comic writer Alcaeus. In Xen. *Oec.* 9.15, Ischomachus says that his wife must treat her household *hōsper basilissan*, awarding praise and punishment. One wonders what *basilissa* Xenophon, writing about the middle of the fourth century, might have had in mind—a Persian one, perhaps. On the Alcaeus passage see J. M. Edmonds, *The Fragments of Attic Comedy* (Leiden: Brill, 1957), 1:886. Even Macurdy, "*Basilinna* and *Basilissa*," 279, concedes that Greek writers often say "the wife of the king" where one might expect "queen."

12. Buck, "Suffix of *Basilissa*," 372–73; Macurdy, "*Basilinna* and *Basilissa*," 278–80.

13. Buck, "Suffix of *Basilissa*," 270.

14. See H. W. Ritter, *Diadem und Königsherrschaft* (Munich: Beck, 1965), 116, for evidence that both the Ptolemaic and the Seleucid dynasties gave the title to kings' daughters—against the assertion of E. Bikerman, *Institutions des Séleucides*, Syria, Service des antiquités, Bibliothèque archéologique et historique, 26 (Paris, 1938), 27, who excludes Seleucids from the practice. Koch, "Ptolemäerinnen," 79 n. 3, notes that even the heir apparent did not take the title *basileus*, doubtless because the male title conveyed very real power whereas the female title conveyed no specific powers. W. Kahrstedt, "Frauen auf antiken Münzen," *Klio* 10 (1910): 269— followed by Koch, "Ptolemäerinnen," 77–78, and Macurdy, *Queens*, 8—believes that *basilissa* meant "female king" when it appeared on coins of women functioning as regents. This seems not quite the point: *basilissa* was applied to virtually all sorts of royal women and did not mean or refer to a particular office (in this respect its usage is even broader than our English *queen*).

15. Oikonomedes, "Eurydice," 62–64; L. Robert, "3249 Vergina-Aigai," *REG* 97 (1984): 450–51. Oikonomedes also discusses Plut. *Moral.* 14c, which has usually been taken to be a copy of a now lost inscription.

16. In *SIG*³ 252N 5–7. Olympias makes dedications at Delphi ca. 331/330. *SEG* IX:2 shows Olympias receiving grain from Cyrene. There is also a tomb inscription—see C. Edson, "The Tomb of Olympias," *Hesperia* 18 (1949): 84—which A. Oikonomedes, "The Epigram on the Tomb of Olympias at Pydna," *AncW* 5 (1982): 9–16, argues was actually inscribed on the tomb of Olympias itself, rather than an associated, later monument. If my thesis here is correct, the absence of *basilissa* from the inscription would tend to confirm Oikonomedes's view.

17. Oikonomedes, "Eurydice," 64, seems to assume that the title would have been given up on widowhood. In any case, although the Olympias inscriptions all clearly date from the period after the death of Philip, the new Eurydice inscription suggests no particular date, and the passage from Plutarch (*Moral.* 14c) would imply that Eurydice might not yet be a widow.

18. P. Charneux, "Liste argienne de Théarodoques," *BCH* 90 (1966): 178; Hammond, "Passages in Arrian," 474.

19. See references in R. M. Errington, "Macedonian 'Royal Style' and Its Historical Significance," *JHS* 94 (1974): 20; A. Aymard, "Le protocole royal grec et son évolution," *REA* 50 (1948): 232–63, and "BASILEUS MAKEDONON," *RIDA* 4 (1950): 61–97.

20. See below on why Macedonian monarchs preferred not to use a title.

21. See recent discussion and references in L. Mooren, "The Nature of Hellenistic Monarchy," in *Egypt and the Hellenistic World*, ed. E. van' t. Dack, P. Van Dessel, and W. Van Gucht (Leuven: Katholieke Universiteit, 1983), 214 n. 34, for a useful discussion of the problems of dating Alexander's initiation of the usage, as well as

for a collection of references. In any event Alexander was not, apparently, consistent once he did begin. Recently N. G. L. Hammond, "The King and the Land in the Macedonian Kingdom," *CQ* 38 (1988): 382–84, 390, has argued that two inscriptions (see his references, 382) show Alexander using the title *basileus* early in his reign, prior to his departure for Asia. Hammond's arguments for the early date of these two inscriptions are not particularly convincing, but even if granted, they would merely signify that Alexander used the title, at least occasionally, early in his reign.

22. For an inscription found at Samothrace, dating to their reign, in which they take the title, see J. McCredie, "Samothrace; Supplementary Investigations 1968–1977," *Hesperia* 48 (1979): 8.

23. Actually Ptolemy probably took the title slightly later, when he had also had a major victory; see A. E. Samuel, *Ptolemaic Chronology* (Munich: Beck, 1962), 4–11. Plutarch's assertion that Cassander did not take the title is interesting, suggesting as it does continuation of Argead practice by the rule of Macedonia. See below, note 43.

24. See Carney, "Olympias," 39 n. 11.

25. This characterization of the nature of Macedonian monarchy is best supported by R. Lock, "The Macedonian Army Assembly in the Time of Alexander the Great," *CQ* 72 (1977): 91–107; R. M. Errington, "The Nature of the Macedonian State under the Monarchy," *Chiron* 8 (1978): 77–133; A. E. Samuel, "Philip and Alexander as Kings: Macedonian Monarchy and Merovingian Parallels," *AHR* 93 (1988): 1270–86. For a recent reassertion of a more constitutional view of Macedonian monarchy see Mooren, "Nature of Hellenistic Monarchy," as well as a series of articles by N. G. L. Hammond: "Passages," 471–76; "Macedonian Offices," 158–59; and "King and Land," 389.

26. The fourth-century B.C. historian Theopompus of Chios survives only in fragments. Opinion differs as to his dependability, particularly in relationship to his portrait of Philip II. See, for example, I. A. F. Bruce, "Theopompus and Classical Greek Historiography," *H&T* 9 (1970): 86–109. A great number of the surviving fragments involve various kinds of moralizing about the bad effects of luxury and self-indulgence; obviously this fragment suits this general picture, but its theme need not mean that its contents are untrue.

Philemon was a fourth-century B.C. comic poet who became an Athenian citizen. J. M. Edmonds, *The Fragments of Attic Comedy* (Leiden: Brill, 1961), 3A:12–13, discusses this fragment from the play *The Babylonians* (the title probably refers to Harpalus himself). Edmonds dates the play to ca. 326, primarily because the courtesan Pythionice was sent to Babylon in 327 and died sometime in 326.

27. On the enigmatic figure of Harpalus see H. Berve, *Das Alexanderreich* (Munich: C. H. Beck, 1926), 2:75–80; E. Badian, "Harpalus," *JHS* 81 (1961): 16–43; W. Heckel, "The Flight of Harpalus and Tauriskos," *CP* 72 (1977): 133–35; E. D. Car-

ney, "The First Flight of Harpalus, Again," *CJ* 77 (1981): 9–12; S. Jaschinski, *Alexander und Griechenland unter dem Eindruck der Flucht des Harpalos* (Ph.D. dissertation, Bonn, 1981); I. Worthington, "The First Flight of Harpalus Reconsidered," *G&R* 31 (1984): 161–69; and now B. Kingsley, "Harpalos in the Megarid (333–331 B.C.) and the Grain Shipments from Cyrene," *ZPE* 66 (1986): 165–80.

28. Alexander's attempt to impose the Persian ceremony of *proskynēsis* on his Macedonian courtiers met with notorious failure. On this well-known episode see discussion and reference in J. R. Hamilton, *Plutarch, Alexander: A Commentary* (Oxford: Oxford University Press, 1969), 150–53.

29. On both the difficulty of knowing much about Persian royal women and the often mistaken ideas about Persian royal women found in Greek writers see H. Sancisi-Weerdenburg, "Exit Atossa: Images of Women in Greek Historiography," in *Images of Women in Antiquity*, ed. A. Cameron and A. Kuhrt (Detroit: Wayne State University Press, 1984), 20–34. However, much as in the case of the mistaken significance of *proskynēsis*, Greeks may have misunderstood the role of Persian royal women, and yet that mistaken image may have functioned as a sort of model. See note 42 below.

30. W. Heckel, "Kleopatra or Eurydike," *Phoenix* 32 (1978): 155–58, "Polyxena, the Mother of Alexander the Great," *Chiron* 11 (1981): 79–86, and "Adea-Eurydike," *Glotta* 61 (1983): 40–42; A. M. Prestianni-Giallombardo, "Eurydike-Kleopatra: nota ad Arr. *Anab.* 3,6,5," *ASNP* 3 (1981): 295–306; E. Badian, "Eurydice," in *Philip II, Alexander the Great and the Macedonian Heritage*, ed. W. L. Adams and E. N. Borza (Washington, D.C.: University Press of America, 1982), 99–110; Sarah B. Pomeroy, *Women in Hellenistic Egypt* (New York: Schocken Books, 1984), 10. See also A. B. Bosworth, *A Historical Commentary on Arrian's History of Alexander* (Oxford: Clarendon Press, 1980), 1:282–83. The argument begins with a remark by Macurdy, *Queens*, 24–25.

31. Badian, "Eurydice."

32. Arrian *FGrH* 156 F1.1, 1.9, 1.23 and Diod. 18.2.4 have not been doubted.

33. On the strange career of Philip-Arrhidaeus see W. S. Greenwalt, "The Search for Arrhidaeus," *AncW* 10 (1984): 69–77.

34. Pomeroy, *Women in Hellenistic Egypt*, 10. Plutarch prefaces his remark about Olympias by the observation that often nicknames concealed real names.

35. Mary Lefkowitz kindly pointed out this passage to me.

36. Badian, "Eurydice," 107.

37. On Olympias' name see Heckel, "Polyxena," 79–86.

38. D. Schaps, "The Woman Least Mentioned: Etiquette and Women's Names," *CQ* 27 (1977): 323–30. The obvious exception to Athenian attitudes on this subject would be Themistocles' naming his daughters to commemorate his ambitions and achievements (Plut. *Them.* 32.2). These rather public names for girls are probably part of the older archaic and aristocratic attitude toward women, an attitude

which, as we have seen, was preserved into the fourth century in the Macedonian royal family. J. K. Davies, *Athenian Propertied Families 600–300 B.C.* (Oxford: 1971), 359–60, notes that there was a brief trend (470–460 B.C.) for Athenian aristocratic families to give male and female children "politically programmatic" names.

39. Pomeroy, *Women in Hellenistic Egypt*, 9, makes this observation about the significant naming of daughters, but it could also apply to wives who changed their names upon marriage or in commemoration of some great event in their husbands' lives. See also M. Golden, "Names and Naming at Athens: Three Studies," *EMC* 30 (1986): 245–69, for a discussion of naming of girls as a means of socializing them. Pomeroy's assertion that "boys, in contrast, were not named for the attributes or ambitions of their male relatives," though generally true, requires qualification: Cimon's admiration of Spartan culture led him to choose a name for at least one of his sons, and possibly two, commemorating this preference. See Plut. *Cim.* 16.1; on the problem of the names of Cimon's sons see Davies, *Athenian Propertied Families*, 306–7; B. M. Lavelle, "Kimon's Thessalian Proxeny," *LCM* 10 (1985): 12–13; Golden, "Names and Naming," 246–47 n. 4.

40. After Adea-Eurydice there is the possible case of Cratesipolis, wife of Alexander son of Polyperchon. Pomeroy, *Women in Hellenistic Egypt*, 10, believes that she took this name upon the conquest of Sicyon. Heckel, "Polyxena," 85 n. 34, makes a similar argument. G. H. Macurdy, "The Political Activities and the Name of Cratesipolis," *AJP* 50 (1929): 273–78, takes the view that the name was hers long before the victory. If so, then with Cratesipolis and with Olympias' last nickname, Stratonice, the practice had already begun to change: significant names might commemorate unusual accomplishments of the women themselves.

41. Badian, "Eurydice," 103, rightly emphasizes the factor of obscurity in attempting to solve the problem of female name change.

42. Strabo (17.70c) claims that Cambyses named Meroë in Egypt after a sister or wife who died there; Diodorus (1.33.1) says that the woman in question was Cambyses' mother. Both assertions are fictitious, apparently the result of an anachronistic application of Hellenistic practice to the period of Persian domination. See H. Kees, *RE* 15.1 (1931): col. 1048, s.v. Meroë 3. Amastris, niece of Darius and married first to Craterus, then to Dionysius the tyrant of Heracleia and later still to Lysimachus, synoecized a city which bore her name (see Steph. Byz. "Amastris"). See U. Wilcken, *RE* 1.2 (1894): col. 1705, s.v. Amastris 7, and now S. B. Burstein, *Outpost of Hellenism: The Emergence of Heracleia on the Black Sea*, University of California Publications, Classical Studies Series, no. 14 (Berkeley: University of California, 1974), 83.

Dating the foundation of Thessaloniki is difficult, although it is usually assumed that like Cassandreia it was founded soon after the defeat of Olympias and Thessalonice's marriage to Cassander (316/315). But see E. I. Mikrogiannakes, "To Politistikon Ergon tou Kassandrous," in *Ancient Macedonia* (Thessalonike: Institute for Balkan Studies, 1977), 2:228–29, who rejects such an early date in favor of one around 305, which he assumes to be the date that Cassander took the title (see below, note 43). W. L. Adams, "The Dynamics of Internal Macedonian Politics in the Time of Cassander," in *Ancient Macedonia* (Thessalonike: Institute for Balkan Studies, 1983), 3:24 n. 31, thinks that Thessaloniki was actually founded before Cassandreia, in 315. On the general topic of naming cities after women see E. D. Carney, "Eponymous Women: Royal Women and City Names," *AHB* 2, no. 6 (1988): 134–42.

43. See Adams, "Dynamics of Macedonian Politics," 25–26, for a discussion of the possibility that Diodorus' statement (20.53.2) that Cassander took the royal title at the same (or at least roughly the same) time that the other Successors did is incorrect and that Plutarch (*Dem.* 18.1) and the Heidelberg Epitome (*FGrH* 155 F1.7) are more nearly correct in omitting him from the list of those who used the title. Adams suggests that Cassander, like Antigonus, waited for a great victory and then, as his coins suggest, took the title ca. 301. For a very different view of Cassander's use of the title within Macedonia, one which assumes a much earlier date for Cassander's assumption of the title (largely in connection to *SIG³* 332), see Errington, "Macedonian Royal Style," 23–25. Cassander's usage, like Alexander's, may have been inconsistent.

44. *SIG³* 333, 6–7, dated by the editor to shortly after 306, most probably to the period of the siege of Rhodes (305/304). The document is a Samian decree honoring a certain Demarchus, said to be a guard in *basilissa* Phila's entourage. L. Robert, "Sur une inscription de Delphe," *Hellenika* 2 (1946): 17 nn. 1–2, confirms the original editor's date. In addition Robert suggests that an Ephesian decree honoring a certain Melesippus, also said to be part of the entourage of *basilissa* Phila, dated by its original editor to ca. 300/299, may in fact date to the same period as the Samian decree. Wehrli, "Phila," 140–43, accepts both of Robert's dates.

45. On the Apamea inscription, *Didyma*, 480, see M. Holleaux, "Le décret des Milésiens en l'honneur d'Apamé," *REG* 36 (1923): 5 n. 4, for a discussion of the date. For a discussion of coins from Cyrene giving a Berenice (perhaps Berenice I) the title *basilissa* see Koch, "Ptolemäerinnen," 74–79, and Kahrstedt, "Frauen," 262. See Ritter, *Diadem*, 116 nn. 1–2, for references to other early usages of *basilissa* as a title.

46. See note 14 above and Ritter, *Diadem*, 116 n. 2.

47. On the use of titles and other devices of power see especially A. Aymard, "L'usage du titre royal dans la Gréce classique et hellénistique," *RD* 27 (1949): 579–90, for the major presentation of this thesis. See also references above, note 19, and Griffith, in Hammond and Griffith, *Macedonia*, 388–89. On the fragmentation of the empire see R. M. Errington, review of O. Müller, *Antigonos Monophthalmos und 'Das Jahr der König'*, in *JHS* 95 (1975): 250–51, against Cohen, "Diadochoi," 177, who argues that the meaningful date for the recognition of separation of the empire is not 306 but 301 (his arguments are based on a perceived change in the nature of

attempted marriage alliances). Both events would seem, rather, to be points on the same line of gradual development.

48. I am indebted to William Greenwalt for the observation that Macedonian avoidance of a title is likely to have had stronger internal than external motivation. To put it another way, within Macedonia, there was no need for an Argead to use a title, and outside Macedonia, avoidance of a title conformed to current usage of other northern rulers (see Griffith, in Hammond and Griffith, *Macedonia*, 388 n. 3).

49. There has been much recent controversy on the subject of diadems, disputing their nature, origin, and significance and the date at which Macedonian kings first began to wear them. On these matters see Ritter, *Diadem*, 31–41 and passim, and most recently, W. M. Calder, " 'Golden Diadems' Again," *AJA* 87 (1983): 102–3.

On the subject of royal women and diadems there needs to be much more work, and only some brief remarks can be made here. Although Diodorus (20.53.2) and Plutarch (*Dem.* 18.1) both associate the Successors' assumption of a royal title ca. 306 with an apparently simultaneous wearing of a diadem and although I have argued that royal women began to use a title either at the same time that their husbands did or soon thereafter, one need not necessarily conclude that royal women began to wear a diadem at the same time they took the title. It is possible that they did: Kahrstedt's identification of Berenice I with the Berenice coin giving the title *basilissa* to a Berenice and showing her wearing a diadem ("Frauen," 262) is suggestive, but not conclusive. Ritter, *Diadem*, 114, argues that Berenice's daughter, Arsinoë II, was the first royal wife to wear a diadem. Lack of agreement about the meaning of the diadem further complicates the issue: because taking a title did not mean the same thing for women that it did for men, it is perhaps dangerous to assume that whatever the meaning of the diadem for men (certainly the occasion in 306 connects royal power and the diadem, but that does not mean that that was the only significance of the diadem), the same meaning and thus the same chronology would apply to women. One can only conclude that the use of both titles and diadems on a *regular* basis (by both women and men) was part of the process of the creation of the institutions of Hellenistic monarchy.

On the growing role of royal women in dynastic cult, and particularly on the question whether Arsinoë II had a cult in her lifetime, see Pomeroy, *Women in Hellenistic Egypt*, 28–40. See S. M. Burstein, "Arsinoë Philadelphus: A Revisionist View," in *Philip II, Alexander the Great and the Macedonian Heritage*, ed. W. L. Adams and E. N. Borza (Washington, D.C.: University Press of America, 1982), 197–212, for an alternate view of Arsinoë's position. On the appearance of women on coins see discussion in Kahrstedt, "Frauen," 261 and passim; Koch, "Ptolemäerinnen"; Pomeroy, *Women in Hellenistic Egypt*, 29–30.

50. Pomeroy, *Women in Hellenistic Egypt*, 11.

51. See Carney, "Olympias," and "Adea-Eurydice."

52. Carney, "Sisters of Alexander." Alexander's full sister Cleopatra is the best

example of this phenomenon. Despite the famous passage in Diodorus (20.37.3–6) commemorating her death, which notes that she was courted by virtually all the Successors, the truth is that none of them married her and that she, like her half-sisters, was ultimately murdered. For the limits of Cleopatra's significance see also R. M. Errington, "Alexander in the Hellenistic World," in *Alexandre le Grande: image et réalité*, Entretiens sur l'antiquité classique, no. 22 (Geneva: Fondation Hardt, 1975), 145–52. Errington, however, overstates her unimportance.

53. Pomeroy, *Women in Hellenistic Egypt*, 12–28.

54. Burstein, "Arsinoë," 119 n. 7, 209 n. 55, reviews the evidence for the attestation of Arsinoë as *basilissa* and dates the earliest incidence to the 280s.

MIREILLE CORBIER

Translated by Ann Cremin

Family Behavior of the Roman Aristocracy,

Second Century B.C.–Third Century A.D.

When we speak of "family" or more specifically of the "aristocratic family," we must first define our terms.[1] In a comparative study of the Roman family it is necessary to distinguish between two competing definitions: (1) Latin vocabulary and its underlying concepts (*gens, familia, domus,* and also *nomen, genus, stirps*),[2] and (2) the language and concepts used by historians of medieval and modern families who assimilate or adapt the definitions and the analyses of anthropologists. At the risk of a certain simplification, let us follow Georges Duby and Gérard Delille and, to a lesser extent, Marc Augé and François Héritier and pursue our discussion in two directions.[3]

First, lineage and line (French *lignage* and *lignée*): we will thus recognize within the *gens* and the *familia* the agnatic lineage and the line of the same name, noticing that *familia* is sometimes used in the sense of *gens,* and we will remember the Roman particularity of *patria potestas* exercised by the eldest of the male ascendants.[4] Second, kin and allies (in other terms, consanguines and affines): the word *domus* can encompass not only bilateral kinship—for the Romans, the "cognates" as such, identified to the sixth Roman degree, equivalent to the third canonical degree (cousins born of cousins) or even the seventh—but also some allies or affines (such as parents-in-law, son-in-law, stepson; the *adfines* for Roman people) and even, in Pliny the Younger, the *adfines* of our *adfines*.[5] Of course, *familia* and *domus* have each a whole range of meanings, including the domestic help (slaves in Rome) for the *familia* or the actual lodging for the *domus*; and the usual syntagm *domus ac familia* (of which there are two examples in this essay) is characterized by an elasticity and multiplicity of meanings which are equally remarkable.

It is useful to recall that the "families" of the Roman aristocracy on which we are working are only artifacts (that is, human constructions) of prosopography. Undertaken since antiquity for the Republican period,[6] this work of reconstituting families has recently been taken up again and pursued notably in the context of epigraphical studies. Its difficulty was already clear for the ancients. In the first century A.D., for example, Asconius, the commentator on Cicero, admitted: "I have not been able to identify Piso's mother-in-law, probably because the authors have not transmitted for the houses and the lineages [or, by hendiadys, the families] the names of the women as well as those of the men, except in the case of illustrious women."[7] One cannot overemphasize the gaps in documentation and the imbalance of information to women's detriment.

During the first century of our era, however, a radical change occurs in our sources. From the first century B.C. until the Julio-Claudian era our sources are chiefly literary and often diverse, though the role of epigraphy was even then constantly increasing. But from the Julio-Claudian period through the third century A.D. the sources become mostly epigraphical (epitaphs, honorary inscriptions), and therefore the reconstitution of families is based primarily on onomastics. We are thus using two types of artifacts constituted from different historical sources. In fact, these two artifacts refer, as is well known, to two different social realities. The great names of the last century of the Republic had nearly all died out. New families had appeared, Italian at first, then provincial beginning in the last third of the first century A.D. Our two types of artifacts thus show major differences. The continuing and ramified *gentes*, united among themselves through intermarriages, which Ronald Syme has reconstituted for the reigns of Augustus and the first Julio-Claudians,[8] are no longer to be found, even with different names, after the middle of the first century A.D. Newer genealogies are too frequently limited to a single line, real or reconstituted as such. And they are also truncated most of the time. Faced with some lines which comprise five or six senators, one encounters mainly segments of two or three generations. The change is thus twofold: it is related both to the size of the family tree and to its chronological depth.[9]

Paradoxically, the relatively "short" families of the second century A.D. have the longest names: but the paradox is only apparent. To the custom of the Republic—transmission of the father's name, the *nomen gentilicium*, to which was added a first name and a surname which could become the *cognomen* of a line (a second *cognomen* could also thus differentiate between brothers and be perpetuated throughout the branches constituted by their descendants, as with the Cornelii Scipiones Nasicae)—were eventually added by stages other onomastic customs. Of particular importance was the appearance of *cognomina* created with the maternal name. Thanks to polyonomy (a practice introduced in the first century A.D.) a senator could integrate notably his paternal and maternal ascendants over several generations. For example, the name of Quintus Pompeius Sosius Priscus, consul in 169 A.D., was composed of fourteen *gentilicia*, twenty *cognomina*, and four first names.[10] The onomastic change reflected different family concepts. But we must make sure that such contrasts are not simply the product of the typological shift in historical sources: the differences are necessarily emphasized by inscriptions, which assign a less important role to women than do literary sources, which sometimes (but we must not forget Asconius' restrictions) are more likely to mention alliances forged on the basis of kinship or affinity.

For lineages with many branches, and for new families which had barely surfaced and which, in general, had not had the time to develop branches, the policy of familial continuity might arise, or have arisen, in different terms. For older families with many branches, the continuity of the *gens* could be more easily ensured by collateral branches bearing the same name (for example, the Cornelii Scipiones). Newer families, often deprived of this resource, could on the contrary, in the absence of sons able to carry on the *domus ac familiae perpetuitas*,[11] be more frequently inclined to take over the resources of the female descendancy by adopting nephews or grandsons born to a sister or a daughter.

Historians of the modern family have warned that when one works on genealogies, the mechanisms of exchange spread out over two or three generations are only obvious if one can reconstitute the whole chain of alliance. According to Alain Collomp, if one wants to understand the game of the alliances, one must be able to see all the cards.[12] But Asconius also gave us a warning. Considering the shortages in documentation and the disparity of information relevant to names of men and women,[13] the historian of the Roman family can simultaneously consider all the "horizontal" marriages during a single generation and the "vertical" succession of marriages undertaken over several generations only with difficulty. But as Gérard Delille has pointed out, a study carried out on incomplete genealogical data, or uncertain data, can be subject to very serious mistakes of interpretation.[14] I would be tempted to add, "if one persists in taking the part for the whole."

To uphold such strictures on the quality of documentation might lead historians of antiquity to give up all studies of the family, with the possible exception of the imperial dynasties. But it is possible to discuss "segments" of genealogy if we bear in mind that we are dealing only with segments and emphasize each time the limits of validity of our conclusions and the limits of our ignorance, as well as the field of hypotheses which remains open.

Roman society, in fact, seems to offer some specific answers to a series of problems on which all study of matrimonial strategies appears to place emphasis: (1) matrimonial behavior allowing the survival to adulthood of one or several male heirs, who can guarantee the transmission of the name without producing, due to their number, a division of the patrimony which might be seen as excessive or dangerous; (2) the choice of partners, whether or not in conjunction with specific interests, material (dowry, or expected inheritance), sociopolitical (alliances which could be useful within the prospective of a career), or familial (reinforcement of alliances); and (3) the practices of succession and transmission of property.

Survival of the Lineage

In Rome, as in medieval and early modern Europe, we are faced with a society in which life expectancy is low and in which infant mortality is very high. In order to guarantee the survival of the family through the male line over several generations, or even centuries (which many noble European lineages managed to do), if one makes allowance for an equal number of male and female children born and for the death before adulthood of one child out of two (one out of four in the first year of life), numerous children must be produced in each generation. This is demonstrated by the family trees of medieval and early modern aristocrats.[15] In addition, these family trees are "neatly pruned." In order to avoid the division of property (other than through testamentary practices which we shall discuss below), access to marriage is often limited. Marriage is restricted to one of the brothers, so that the property of the others, who are without legitimate descendants, can revert to their nephew. Such a solution was systematically adopted by the Venetian patricians and was also well known in feudal France. Younger sons often spent their lives in the military without marrying. A great number of sons and daughters entered the Church, with a small dowry. Furthermore, the practice of having the heir marry early tended to compensate for the high mortality of young men (through wars, jousts, and duels).

In Rome, for the historic period under consideration here, celibacy does not seem to have been envisaged for daughters, at least not for first marriages. Where it is attested for men, it was voluntary and not imposed. It is relevant to remember Augustus' famous separation of the *equites* into two groups in the forum, one made up of bachelors, the other of married men and heads of families, to demonstrate that the first group was larger than the second.[16] The state, with Augustus' legislation, took measures to dissuade at least the members of the upper classes from remaining unmarried. What success did Augustus have?

In Rome a lineage policy did not run into any institutional or biological roadblock. Anyone who really so desired could ensure for himself a descendancy both legitimate and numerous. Roman marriage, founded on the consent of both parties (and of their families),[17] could be ended, not only as a result of death of one of the spouses.[18] Divorce was easy, and barrenness was sometimes the justification (for example, with Sulla) if not the real reason for dissolving a marriage. Prohibited marriages were few: those between *tutor* ("guardian") and ward, senator and freedwoman (as a result of Augustan legislation), and, under the early Empire, a provincial governor and a woman in his province (unless it was his native province) throughout his tenure of office.[19] In our chosen period, there was no restriction on marriage between first cousins.[20] After the precedent of Claudius and Agrippina, it was even possible for a paternal uncle to marry a niece. At the turn of the first and second centuries A.D. the list of prohibited marriage partners under the name of incest (ascendant, descendant, collateral, sister or half-sister, and niece, other than the brother's daughter) ran to four affines: mother-in-law (*socrus*) and daughter-in-law (*nurus*), stepmother (*noverca*) and stepdaughter (*privigna*).[21] But a man could marry his ex-wife's sister, or his brother's ex-wife, or the daughter, born of a previous marriage, of his father's wife. So there was virtually no "impossible marriage" in such a context.[22] Finally there was adoption, as a last resort when a man was sterile or when a sterile couple wished to remain married.

On the other hand, in order to control the size of their families the Romans possessed, in addition to contraception (unreliable, but in any case morally acceptable), an efficient method: the exposure of the unwanted newborn children, which in the parents' minds (but not that of jurists) was different from infanticide.[23] (Let us ignore here infanticide itself[24] and the sale of newborn infants, which probably did not affect the upper echelons of society.)

But what do we really know about the demography or the fertility of the elite? We must free ourselves at the outset from moralizing about the barrenness of the Roman aristocracy. That penchant is not, however, confined to modern authors. In ancient texts themselves, edifying anecdotes and topoi on the subject are not to be taken as clear evidence about social realities. Plutarch's jest concerning Romans who married and bred, not in order to beget heirs, but in order to inherit (*Mor.* 493e), can thus be seen in a context of jokes, at least taken as such,[25] linked to Augustan legislation (which restricted inheritance for people without children).

If the elite did resort to exposure of newborn infants,[26] the practice should more especially have involved daughters. Thus the permission granted by Augustus to members of both orders, senatorial and equestrian, to marry young girls not yet nubile, and allowing *equites* to marry freedwomen as well, has been interpreted as a possible sign of an imbalance of the sexes in their class.[27] This imbalance was also noted by Cassius Dio for this period.[28] But it might be foolhardy to try to confirm this imbalance with the respective numbers of masculine and feminine epitaphs, for epigraphic commemoration has of necessity, as is the case in literary texts, granted an unequal importance to the sexes.

Scholars have explained the low level (real or alleged) of natality within aristocratic Roman marriage in various ways. One explanation is the practice of contraception, although moderns sometimes rely too heavily on allegations by ancient authors about women's wish to preserve their beauty intact, as well as on various misogynistic remarks.[29] Another explanation refers to the normal practice of sexuality by men outside marriage[30] and to the long absences of men, although the longest tours of duty in the provinces were partly compensated under the Empire by the possibility of being accompanied by a spouse.[31] Furthermore, concubinage with women of lower social status could act as a means of limiting legitimate progeny. The relatively late age of men at marriage may likewise have had negative demographic effects counterbalanced by the early age at marriage of girls.

It is difficult to know whether the paucity of children who reached adulthood was caused more by the supposedly low level of natality or by high infant mortality. We can see the importance of the latter in Fronto's letter to Marcus Aurelius in A.D. 165: of six children born to him, Fronto has only one daughter surviving. The other five had died at an early age, probably in their first year, for Fronto was already childless before each new birth.[32] In the same way (three centuries earlier), of the frequently mentioned twelve children of Cornelia, mother of the Gracchi, only two sons and one daughter survived.

In Rome, for the ruling classes in the Augustan age and beyond, three living children defined a large family. The Roman elite therefore found itself combining the effects of a high infant mortality with a conception of optimal family size quite close to ours, one which is unfavorable to continuity of lineage over many generations. Numerous remarks by contemporaries show that the Romans were conscious of the danger of breaking up family property.[33] The underlying conviction persisted that family size ought to be related to family resources. Apuleius mentions, to the discredit of his enemy Rufinus, born into the equestrian class, a *domus exhausta et plena liberis*, "an exhausted house full of children."[34] We must not forget that the *domus* is also the family property. For the emperor, however, it was important to have, like Tiberius at the beginning of his principate, a *plena Caesarum domus* rich with potential heirs and not, like Augustus after the death of his grandchildren Caius and Lucius Caesar, a *domus deserta*.[35]

Alliance and Kinship

The choice of a marriage partner represents a central element in all family strategies, insofar as there are choices between different solutions and therefore estimations and comparisons of the respective advantages of each one. During the period under consideration the choice of spouses was subjected neither to any prescription nor to any prohibition (except for the very close relationships described above), nor to any consciously expressed preference. However, at the start of the second century A.D., in his *Roman Questions*, Plutarch examined marriage as an ethnologist with the outlook of a Greek used to close-kin marriages and made two distinct observations. On the one hand, in Roman Question 108, he notes an actual marriage practice outside the family.[36] On the other, in Roman Question 6, he notes an evolution in the sense of a reduction of the ban as time had gone by: previously the Romans did not marry consanguineously; now their sisters and their aunts remain forbidden, but other relatives, including a first cousin (the Roman fourth degree; in Greek *anepsia*, in Latin *consobrina*) are permitted.[37] An evolution was also observed by Tacitus; while speaking of the emperor Claudius' marriage with his niece, he notes that in olden times marriage with a second cousin (*coniugia sobrinarum*) was not practiced.[38]

Concerning the first practice—that Romans did not marry their close kin—Plutarch offers three explanations.[39] The first is precisely the traditionally accepted explanation of group exogamy: the enlargement of kinship. The second consists of the wish to maintain a strict separation between rights ensured by alliance and rights ensured by kinship. The third, which is based on a premise of feminine weakness, suggests the necessity that a wife who is badly treated by her husband to be entitled to help from her family, which would not be the same as that of the husband. Let us note in passing that this last argument is used in the opposite sense by Germaine Tillion, who emphasizes the strong solidarity of the feminine group in cases of conjugal conflict within the framework of the North African family, which is based on preferential marriage with a parallel patrilateral cousin: the wife thus has her aunt, or more precisely the wife of her uncle, as mother-in-law and her first cousins as sisters-in-law.[40]

In a passage which Philippe Moreau has compared to Plutarch's Roman Question 108 by suggesting a common borrowing from Varro, Augustine at the beginning of the fifth century (*City of God* 15.16) confirms the desire to multiply alliances—by preventing only one person from acquiring kinship relationships which could be distributed between two persons—and to enlarge the group of close kin.[41] Augustine also mentions the normal practice of strengthening kinship bonds in past history: "Thus our distant ancestors, to prevent kinship (*propinquitas*) from becoming too remote (*longius abiret*) when it was divided in too numerous descending lines, and to prevent the end of kinship links (*propinquitas*), scrupulously strengthened them by marriage, when it was not too distant and thus, so to speak, gave it a new lease on life at the moment when it was about to die out (*et quodam modo revocare fugientem*). That is why, when the earth was already peopled by men, they preferred to marry not their sisters, nor their half-sisters by the same father or mother, but women from their family all the same. Who could not imagine, however, that, even at that time, it would have been more moral to forbid marriage between cousins?"

Augustine's reasoning is thus twofold. On the one hand he takes up Plutarch's argument of maximum diversification of alliances. On the other he adds to it a perfect definition and justification for systematic strengthening of kinship. But he situates his demonstration less in the perspective of family interests—which are called upon to manage family capital as well as possible by diversifying and renewing investments—than in that of human society. The *caritas* ensured by alliance and kinship guarantees peace and efficiently creates the bases for "social life." Moreover, he was writing at a time when imperial legislation has just started to prohibit marriage between first cousins (the Roman fourth degree) and when, precisely, a certain Christian elite to which Augustine belonged condemned that type of union.[42]

In the eleventh century Peter Damian (*On Degrees of Kinship* 182) would take up the crux of the Augustinian argument, that is to say, the necessity of tightening kinship bonds and their justification by *caritas*.[43] But by that time the scope of forbidden degrees was considerably enlarged, and Peter Damian was among those in the Church who wanted to widen it to the seventh canonical degree.[44] This profoundly modifies the context and the concrete sense one can give to his remark *iam longius abeuntem quasi fugientem revocat*, inspired by Augustine. It also explains why Augustine identifies kinship with *propinquitas*, whereas from Isidore of Seville to Peter Damian, *consanguinitas* prevails, an expression which Augustine himself employs only once in the same chapter, when speaking of *propinqua consanguinitas* applied to the *consobrina*.

Unfortunately any study of alliance and kinship which goes beyond the recent successful studies of the links thus forged (the relationship between son-in-law and father-in-law, the *socer/gener* couple, for example) is made extremely difficult by the imbalance of information which frequently excludes women.[45] This state of affairs has led to privileging certain great families of the Republican era (with the reservations mentioned above) and above all the imperial families—the only ones, in fact, in which we know for (almost) all the members the (nearly) complete network of alliances over several generations. But the behavior of the latter might well turn out to be exceptional rather than usual. For the aims are actually different: there, it is not so much a question of transmitting family property as power itself. It is therefore better to admit that the conclusions they suggest are fine in themselves and to resist the temptation to generalize such factors to the whole of the Roman aristocracy.[46]

Familial endogamy. In support of his thesis on close-kin marriage in Roman society Jack Goody gives pride of place to the marriage between Claudius and Agrippina (paternal uncle and niece) and above all to the matrimonial alliances of the Tetrarchy, which, at the turn of the third and fourth century, show "remarkable" marriages between parallel patrilateral cousins.[47] But the Julio-Claudian or the Antonine family would have shown him the same marriages between first cousins, parallel as well as cross-cousins. The marriages of princesses, only daughters (Julia, daughter of Augustus, or Faustina the Younger, daughter of Antoninus), or close relatives of the sovereign (Livilla, grandniece of Augustus through her mother, Livia's granddaughter through her father, and only niece of Tiberius) obeyed very precise dynastic strategies: to designate a successor, to enhance the prestige of the "legitimate" line, and also to prevent these princesses from giving other potentially rival families children of imperial blood.

Fecundity. Several princely couples created in order to reign or to transmit the succession were singularly prolific: five children for Agrippa and Julia, nine (of whom three died in early infancy) for Germanicus and Agrippina, thirteen or fourteen for Marcus Aurelius and Faustina (of whom five or six outlived their mother).

Access to marriage. We notice, once the constitution of an "imperial family" began, an early marriage age for its girls and, particularly, the marriage of its boys at an earlier age than was customary in this same group of nobles (where it generally took place between age twenty-two and twenty-four).[48] Precocious marriage of the male heir had already been practiced—with the same intentions—by the patrician families of the "Scipios' century."[49] Certainly Marcus Aurelius was twenty-four years old in A.D. 145, at the time of his marriage with Faustina, who was much younger than he, but Antoninus had betrothed him to his daughter six and a half years earlier, while appointing him his successor. Significantly, the first "Porphyrogenetes," his son Commodus, married at the age of sixteen.

Conversely, the affirmation of a dynastic desire seems to have been accompanied by a more regular resort to concubinage after widowhood by several emperors. Among these was Vespasian, who as soon as he acceded to power announced his intention that his sons should succeed him. Antoninus, widowed after preparing his succession, did not take a second empress. As for Marcus Aurelius, who propagated throughout the empire the image of the imperial couple he made with Faustina, even he, sources suggest, once widowed, resisted the advances made by his first fiancée so as not to give his numerous children a stepmother.[50]

Observation of the "other" aristocratic families leads us to more subtle conclusions.[51] One could put forward, in opposition to the family endogamy argued by Jack Goody,[52] a social endogamy that sought spouses in other families in order to enlarge the circle of allies. Family endogamy is observable at certain times between the great families of the end of the Republic:[53] the Julio-Claudian family did not in this instance really innovate, but rather systematized already established practices for the conservation and the transmission of power.[54] Conversely, the well-known examples of the search for a husband for Tullia, daughter of Cicero, or for a wife for Pliny's protégé, Minicius Acilianus, refer to social endogamy.[55] But both of these latter examples concern new senators who sought alliances in the senatorial class and, if possible, in the older nobility to which they wished to become assimilated.

From this perspective both types of endogamy would have been utilized, but at different stages in a family's ascension. This is what is suggested by the study of a certain number of senatorial families in the early Empire, which, as soon as they endured, acquired a history. Those of Italy and Africa are the best known. One notes that a family's ascension only slowly and partially modified its matrimonial horizons.[56] Where a tradition of intermarriage already existed—geographical and social endogamy at the same time—it could be maintained after achieving nobility. Thus, in cities where several senatorial families settled (Leptis Magna, for instance), it comes as no surprise to find them interrelated or to be able to identify "exchanging" families living in nearby towns (Larinum and Histonium in the Picenum), as well as regional networks (in North Africa or in the Transpadane). First-generation senators were often married to daughters of equestrians. This type of alliance, moreover, was not absent in the second generation, even though union between members of the senatorial order (under the early Empire, the *clarissimi*) seems to have become the rule when the family had acceded to the highest ranks. Enlarging the matrimonial horizon thus arrived at a class endogamy, with the possibility of a return to the practice of close kin marriages.

But human life also contains cycles, and successive marriages of a senator did not always necessarily employ the same strategies. Pliny, after an alliance in the senatorial aristocracy of Etruria,[57] which neither his widowhood nor his remarriage strained, turned for his second marriage to Como, from which his family came, and to the equestrian class into which he himself had been born. He married a young orphan whose paternal grandfather jealously guarded Pliny's interests in the region and whose paternal aunt was (perhaps) married to a "friend" of Pliny. All were people who shared the same sense of values and whose lands, at least in Como, were perhaps next to his own—real *adfines*?

Too often hypotheses concerning the renewal of an alliance are based on simple onomastic clues which do not enable us to know precisely the degree and nature of kinship between spouses. Lack of chronological depth, moreover, even when one is fortunate enough to come across a "remarkable" marriage—two brothers with two sisters, for example, in the case of the Arrii and the Antoniae of Circa (Constantine),[58] which seems to go back to an older alliance, as the *cognomen*, Antoninus, formed on the *nomen* Antonius, was already in use by the Arrii—prevents one from accounting for the intervening generations.

Epitaphs disprove the hypothesis of preferential marriage between parallel patrilateral cousins, which could be easily detected because, owing to Roman onomastic customs, in such cases the wife and husband would have an identical name. But although correct,[59] this observation is not sufficient to leave aside the possibility of a marriage with a cross-cousin, or a parallel matrilateral cousin, or even a second cousin (fifth or sixth degree of kinship in Rome) if not a parallel patrilateral one, as these kin do not bear the same name.[60] If on their double sarcophagus in Histonium (modern Vasto) the senator Publius Paquius Scaeva and his wife Flavia had not indicated both their kinship—*consobrinus idemque vir, consobrina eademque uxor*, "he first cousin and husband, she first cousin and wife"— and their very specific genealogy, one could not have imagined that they were closely related in two ways.[61]

The motives which produced these alliances must have very certainly changed over time, notably with the transformation in the political system. Republican careers, with their elections and the constant struggle for power, implied real political alliances, which could be strengthened or weakened, between families or individuals in conflict or temporarily allied. The imperial system implied more subtle behavior, a more discreet network of patronage and friendships which enabled one to gain access to the prince's favor, and yet also perhaps more stability in this same network.

Inheritance Practices

In order to avoid the division of property, different inheritance practices have been employed at different times and in different places: the right of primogeniture, *mayorazgo* (a Spanish form of entail), fideicommissary substitution and perpetuities, choice of an heir. These means allow a family to pass on the whole or the most important part of its property to one of the children, usually the eldest son, to the exclusion of daughters who have been given a dowry and even of the majority of the children already settled. These customs have often inspired novelists: for example, Jane Austen in *Pride and Prejudice*, Federico de Roberto with *I vicere*.

In fact, Roman society practiced equal division of property between all heirs of the same blood and same rank. Whatever their sex, the *divisio* at least was automatic in case of intestate inheritance. But even in the case of testamentary inheritance (the commonest kind in the upper classes), which would have allowed favoring one child over his brothers and sisters, sources show that there was never any systematic exclusion of daughters and that the idea of the right of primogeniture seems to have been foreign to the Roman mentality. Nonetheless it was precisely "Roman law" which in the south of France from Béarn to Provence enabled throughout the whole of the early modern period the practice of "making an heir," of favoring him, of handing down the house by excluding the other children, or at least by severely reducing their share, even in peasant families.[62]

The Roman will, and also the *fideicommissum*, however, did offer all these possibilities. Did the Romans deliberately ignore them? Certainly Roman society, which privileged masculine values, also left room for seniority. Each time an emperor had two sons, the advantage went to the eldest, nominated as successor or associated with the empire before his brother (Titus and Domitian, Caracalla and Geta; but also Nero and Britannicus). In the aristocracy (at least under the Republic) the father's first name normally was transmitted to the eldest son. Jurisconsults in fact discussed the case in which the testator demanded that the farm or the domain be maintained within the family, defined by the use of the same name, or anticipated special bequests for a daughter if she married a relative in the *familia*.[63] They also invoked cases of unequal sharing between male and female heirs.[64] Their answers, however, do not have any particular bearing on the aristocratic families.

Among the elite, socially accepted rules served to counterbalance the freedom of the testator. Disinheriting a child was characterized by a "dissymmetry" between males and females, the former having to be disinherited "by name" in order not to void the will, the latter being disinherited "collectively"—though ignoring this formula did not impinge on the legality of the testament. However, disinheritance seems to have been limited by the public discredit attached to such a practice.

Whenever it was possible, transmission of the inheritance in the direct line was the rule, and bequests were ordained for grandchildren. Cicero, for instance, mentioned Tullia's son in his will.[65] Some indications, however, suggest a tendency to privilege the heads of lineages rather than their sisters, without withholding from the latter their rights to a part of the property of the mother or father. Thus Scipio's generous attitude toward the women in his family, and Marcus Aurelius' toward his sister and nephew, received lengthy praise in ancient sources.[66] In both examples (and independently, for Scipio, of the possible incidence of the Voconian law of 169 B.C., which prevented members of the first class from permitting women to inherit, but not from leaving them up to a quarter of the assets as a bequest),[67] there seems to be some recognition of a particular right of daughters to inherit maternal property. In both cases, however, adoption had changed the channels of transmission: Scipio Aemilianus benefited both as son by blood of Aemilius Paullus and as grandson by adoption of Scipio Africanus, whose wife Aemilia was Paullus' sister. Marcus Aurelius, orphaned by his father and adopted and brought up by his paternal grandfather, Marcus Annius Verus, had moved up one notch in the order of succession.

A relative concentration of patrimonies on the future heads of lineage could have been brought about by a multiplicity of testaments via the ascendants;[68] the hypothesis in any case is worth mentioning. Heir of his grandmother Ummidia Quadratilla (more precisely, coheir; he to two-thirds, his sister to one-third), the senator Ummidius Quadratus, a friend of Pliny the Younger,[69] had in fact lived with this grandmother, whether paternal or maternal we do not know. Thus the biological chance of having known some or all of one's grandparents occurred; the early marriage age of girls increased this possibility in the female line.

The relationship between a woman and her property—in the framework of "free" marriage, which became normal practice and in which the wife remained a member of her original family and thus (except for emancipation) subject to the *patria potestas* of her father until the latter's death—made Roman marriage an original structure.[70] Spouses held no property in common, and the separation was strictly observed. Even gifts between spouses were forbidden, but not testamentary bequests. (In intestacy, husband and wife were called upon to succeed each other only if there were no surviving kin within the sixth degree.) A significant exception should be noted. In the second century A.D. a wife could help her husband attain the census qualification required for a senator or an equestrian.

Nothing was definite at the time of marriage, for in the case of dissolution of the union by divorce or widowhood, the dowry prepared by the bride's father (known as *dos profecticia*) reverted to him if he were still alive, or to the wife herself if through her father's death she had become *sui iuris*. The entire dowry was returned if there were no children of the marriage; only part, if there were children to bring up. Thus recent historiography has tended to estimate that of the two kinds of paternal property which reverted to the daughter, the dowry was less important than the inheritance, proportionally less important than in other societies, in any case.[71] The mother left her children a specific property, the *bona materna*, but only if she had made a will in their favor. Only during the last quarter of the second century A.D. could children inherit from their mother in intestacy. In order to prevent her resources from being left indirectly to her husband upon her death due to his *patria potestas* over their children, the wife could impose on him a condition of emancipating the child (or children) designated by her as her heir (or heirs). The protagonists of a complicated story of this type mentioned in the *Digest*—members of a senatorial family in Sparta—were recently identified.[72]

One form of property transmission that is specific to the Romans was large-scale gift giving and the large-scale bequeathing of legacies to people who were not "relatives" but "friends."[73] This is a sufficiently original element, in any case, to enable us to oppose a "horizontal" and "extra-familial" transfer of property to what we usually imagine to be "vertical" transmission from one generation to the next, in direct line or within one branch to another, inside the kinship.[74]

A whole range of such "gifts" to friends or to their children is illustrated in Pliny's correspondence: constitution of dowries (*dos adventicia* in this case); donation of the equestrian census; contribution to military equipment; buying back of debts; sale of property at an agreed favorable price.

The senator Caius Cestius (who erected the famous tomb in the shape of a pyramid which is still visible in Rome) appointed as "heirs" six important figures, including Agrippa, even though he had a brother.[75] By giving up his share of the inheritance in favor of that brother, Lucius Cestius, Agrippa adopted an attitude close to that of Augustus, who returned to children, when there were any and when they attained adulthood, any property left him by their parents.

The importance of the stakes in extrafamilial bequests on this scale explains the vigorous protests made against the Augustan legislation that limited, for the top property class,[76] the capacity to inherit and to receive legacies when they themselves had no children. (Bachelors could no longer receive anything; married people without children were only entitled to half of what was left them.) Even if these measures did not affect legacies and inheritances within the six degrees of kinship,[77] they completely or partly excluded *caelibes* and *orbi* (men and women with no spouse or child) from the flow of "horizontal" circulation outside relatives. This flow must be deemed important, given the laws aimed at trying to prevent the dispersal of patrimony through legacies, but they never reserved for the heir (or heirs) more than a quarter of the assets in the inheritance. In their turn the emperors learned how to use this social practice to their advantage (inheritances and legacies from private individuals did flow in to increase the imperial patrimony), which the Church was later likewise to use to its benefit.[78] This drain on private resources can be imagined as important at least in the first century of the Empire.

These two concurrent circulations, one "vertical" and the other "horizontal," should be compared to the double conception of family property suggested in a previous study.[79] A distinction between property inherited from one's parents (*bona paterna* and *bona materna*), which one always strives not to alienate and which one passes on to a blood relative, and acquired property (made up of both earnings and unspent revenues from the patrimony and also of legacies and inheritances from "friends"), which can be disposed of more freely, resolves the apparent contradiction between a "market" in houses and villas and also in land, whose sale can be envisaged in a more detached manner,[80] and the extensive evidence for emotional attachment to ancestral estates, to "roots," in other words.[81] In support of this I should also mention a recent hypothesis by Edward Champlin concerning the famous "alimentary table of the Ligures Baebani": one of the explanations offered for the fact that the names of mortgaged lands were rarely derived from those of their owners is that the leading citizens who took part in this imperial alimentary foundation deliberately preferred to mortgage those of their *fundi* which were not ancestral estates.[82]

This dual conception of patrimony underlies a differential circulation of land (property inherited from parents versus acquired property; isolated or peripheral estates versus assembled estates which one had a tendency to "enlarge") and also of remaining property (real property such as land and houses versus transferable securities). Behind Pliny's remark linking his *liberalitas* to his own *frugalitas*[83] one finds the idea that unspent revenues are the best source for generous gestures. As an heir to the family property, a son, it must be recalled, had to leave the *domus* as he received it (*integro statu*).[84] And diminution of patrimony was a serious accusation.[85]

The same difference of attitude toward "personal" (inherited) property and "acquired" property has been noticed, for example, in the office-holders of the Old Regime in France.[86] Whereas no obligation was felt toward acquired property, it was a duty to transmit "personal" property to one's heirs even if they were deemed unworthy. On this last point the *noblesse de robe* was different from the Roman elite, who felt they had the right to disinherit an ungrateful child.

Other matters undoubtedly deserve to be fitted into this framework. I am thinking in particular of genealogical memory, to which I shall return. It would enable me to refine and complete the analysis which I have only begun here.

We have been trying to reach some conclusions about the family behavior characteristic of the Roman upper classes. The first conclusion is that we must avoid supposing that this behavior was always the same. In spite of the apparent continuity of terminology, this behavior underwent continuous modifications in time and space. Politics were partly responsible, as the Principate entailed the weakening and eventual extinction of the great families—except, for a time, that of the Julio-Claudians. This was a fundamental readjustment of the stakes. It led to a struggle for acquisition and then conservation of power by a single family, whose successors had to be provided for or chosen. It also led to the emergence of new aristocratic families from the provinces, who had grown up there and prospered before changing their horizons, their place of residence, and their partners in the game of alliances. The relative continuity built into the past of the *Urbs* of Rome of the famous old *gentes* contrasts with a new kind of double mobility, frequently rapid and brutal as families ascended, then declined or disappeared. This happened both to imperial dynasties and to the families of those provincial *clarissimi* whom we see struggling to survive for more than two or three generations (even if some such families succeeded in lasting longer).

We have attempted to compare the behavior of the Romans with that of other aristocrats who, in other times and in other social contexts, pursued more clearly the same aims: biological reproduction, the transmission and increase of the family property, and the diversification and growth of their symbolic capital. To achieve these objectives the upper level of Roman society seems to have benefited from far greater freedom than its successors, from whom the Church strove to take away two vital cards in the game: divorce and adoption.[87] But the Roman context, in which these two cards were useful and were used, was radically different. The status of the Roman woman and of her property, which she "owned" and which she was even more responsible for transmitting, suggests, better than any other detail, the "exotic" character, at least from a certain point of view, of this difference.

The most surprising feature remains the coexistence of ideals and of practices which were to a high degree mutually contradictory, as if the supreme achievement—one might almost say the highest asceticism—lay in voluntarily *not* using all the resources of "law." The idealization, in epitaphs and literature, of the *univira*, the woman who had gone through life knowing only one man (this went further than simply praising one marriage as the right number) was perfectly compatible with the common practice of multiple marriages. Similarly the perpetuation of the father's family name was an ideal which nevertheless combined with other practices (such as polyonomy) that suggest far-reaching changes and other wishes. Thus Fronto, in a letter of A.D. 164 to his son-in-law, the senator Caius Aufidius Victorinus who was married to Fronto's only surviving child, Gratia, expressed the hope that the gods would increase "our family (*familia nostra*) with children and grandchildren." This was an unusual expression (one would rather have expected *domus*),[88] whereby Fronto recognized that the line of the Aufidii (the children of Victorinus, but Fronto's grandchildren through his daughter) would be his own. Certainly one of these grandchildren, in whom he was pleased to note his own childish tastes, carried his first name, Marcus, and his *cognomen*, Fronto (which the grandson would in turn pass on to his own son, who died young), but not his *nomen*, Cornelius. Thus Fronto apparently did not adopt this grandson. But the genealogical memory of the Aufidii gave Fronto—the best known personality of the "family"—his prestige. Marcus Aufidius Fronto's epitaph, found in Pesaro, the *patria* of the Aufidii, shows this child (or adolescent) to be Fronto's *pronepos* and the *nepos* of Fronto's son-in-law, Victorinus.[89] The *familia nostra* had thus lasted for three generations.

Notes

This is a slightly revised and translated version of my article "Les comportements familiaux de l'aristocratie romaine (IIe siècle av. J.-C.–IIIe siècle ap. J.-C.)" published in *Annales ESC* 42, no. 6 (1987): 1267–85. I warmly thank Martine and David Bell for their help in the preparation of the manuscript.

Abbreviations used in the notes are the standard ones found in *L'année philologique* and the second edition of the *Oxford Classical Dictionary*.

1. Jean-Louis Flandrin, *Familles: parenté, maison, sexualité dans l'ancienne société* (Paris: Seuil, 1984): 10–15 = *Families in Former Times: Kinship, Household and Sexuality* (Cambridge, 1979).

2. Emile Benveniste, *Le vocabulaire des institutions européennes*, vol. 1 (Paris: Minuit, 1969); Gennaro Franciosi, *Clan gentilizio e strutture monogamiche: contributo alla storia della familia romana; corso di diritto romano*, 2 vols. (Naples: Jovene, 1975–76); Philippe Moreau, "La terminologie latine et indoeuropéenne de la parenté et le système de parenté et d'alliance à Rome: questions de méthode," *REL* 56 (1978 [1979]): 41–54; Richard P. Saller, "*Familia, domus* and the Roman Conception of the Family," *Phoenix* 38 (1984): 336–55.

3. Georges Duby, *Le chevalier, la femme et le prêtre: le mariage dans la France féodale* (Paris: Hachette, 1981); Gérard Delille, *Famille et propriété dans le royaume de Naples (XVe–XIXe siècles)* (Rome and Paris: Ecole Française de Rome [fasc. 259]; Ed. de l'EHESS, 1985); Marc Augé, ed., *Les domaines de la parenté* (Paris: Maspero, 1975); Françoise Héritier, *L'exercice de la parenté* (Paris: Gallimard/Le Seuil, 1981).

4. John A. Crook, "*Patria Potestas*," *CQ* 17 (1967): 113–22; Paul Veyne, "La famille et l'amour sous le Haut-Empire romain," *Annales ESC* 33, no. 1 (1978): 35–63; Yan Thomas, "Droit domestique et droit politique à Rome: remarques sur le pécule et les *honores* des fils de famille," *MEFRA* 94 (1982): 528–80, and "A Rome, pères citoyens et cité des pères (IIe siècle avant J.-C.–IIe siècle après J.-C.)," in *Histoire de la famille*, ed. André Burguière, Christiane Klapisch-Zuber, Martine Segalen, and Françoise Zonabend (Paris: Armand Colin, 1986), 1:194–229; William V. Harris, "The Roman Father's Power of Life and Death," in *Studies in Roman Law in Memory of A. Arthur Schiller*, ed. Roger S. Bagnall and William V. Harris (Leiden: E. J. Brill,

1986), 81–95; Richard P. Saller, *"Patria potestas* and the Stereotype of the Roman Family," *Continuity and Change* 1, no. 1 (1986): 7–22.

5. Pliny the Younger *Letters* 10.51. See Saller, *"Familia, domus."*

6. For instance, in the first century B.C. Atticus, an acknowledged specialist of genealogical research, was even consulted on this point by some great families: see Cornelius Nepos *Atticus* 18.3.

7. Asconius *Pis.* 10 Clark: *Socrus Pisonis quae fuerit invenire non potui, videlicet quod auctores rerum non perinde in domibus ac familiis feminarum, nisi illustrium, ac virorum nomina tradiderunt.*

8. Ronald Syme, *The Augustan Aristocracy* (Oxford: Clarendon Press, 1986), genealogical tables after p. 504.

9. Mireille Corbier, "La 'tavola marmorea' de Bolsena et la famille sénatoriale des *Pompeii," MEFRA* 93, no. 2 (1981): 1063–112, and "Les familles clarissimes d'Afrique proconsulaire (Ier–IIIe siècles)," *Tituli* 5 (*Epigrafia a ordine senatorio*) (1982): 2:685–754.

10. *CIL* XIV:3609 = *ILS* 1104.

11. Seneca *On Benefits* 3.33.4.

12. Alain Collomp, *La maison du père: famille et village en Haute-Provence aux XVIIe et XVIIIe siècle* (Paris: Presses Universitaires de France, 1983), 127.

13. One example: for the eight consuls originating in Padua, of which six came from the same two families, we only know the names of two wives. See Ronald Syme, "Eight Consuls from Patavium," *PBSR* 51 (1983): 102–24 = *Roman Papers* (Oxford: Clarendon Press, 1988), 4:371–96.

14. Delille, *Famille et propriété*, 220.

15. A fine example: the Giroies in the tenth and eleventh centuries. See Philippe Ariès and Georges Duby, general eds., *Histoire de la vie privée*, vol. 2, *De l'Europe féodale à la Renaisssance*, by Dominique Barthélémy et al. (Paris: Seuil, 1985), 623. An English translation, *A History of Private Life* (Cambridge: Belknap Press of Harvard University Press, 1987–), is now becoming available.

16. Cassius Dio 56.1–2.

17. Sarah B. Pomeroy, "The Relationship of the Married Woman to Her Blood Relatives in Rome," *Anc. Soc.* 7 (1976): 215–27; Susan Treggiari, *"Digna condicio*: Betrothals in the Roman Upper Class," *Classical Views: Echos du monde classique* 3 (1984): 419–51; Suzanne Dixon, "The Marriage Alliance in the Roman Elite," *Journal of Family History* (1985): 353–78.

18. Michel Humbert, *Le remariage à Rome* (Milan: Giuffré, 1972); Beryl Rawson, "The Roman Family," in Beryl Rawson ed., *The Family in Ancient Rome* (London and Sydney: Croom Helm, 1986), 1–57; Mireille Corbier, "Divorce and Adoption as Roman Familial Strategies (Le divorce et l'adoption 'en plus')," in *Marriage, Divorce and Children in Ancient Rome*, ed. Beryl Rawson (London and New York: Oxford University Press, forthcoming).

19. Jane F. Gardner, *Women in Roman Law and Society* (London and Sydney: Croom Helm, 1986), 32–33.

20. Sergio Roda, "Il matrimonio fra cugini germani nella legislazione tardo imperiale," *SDHI* 45 (1979): 289–309.

21. Philippe Moreau, "Structures de parenté et d'alliance à Larinum d'après le *Pro Cluentio*," in *Les bourgeoisies municipales italiennes aux IIe et Ier siècles avant J.-C.* (Paris: Editions du CNRS; Naples Bibliothèque de l'Institut Français de Naples, 1983): 118.

22. For the term "impossible marriage" see Elizabeth Claverie and Pierre Lamaison, *L'impossible mariage: violence et parenté en Gévaudan aux XVIIe, XVIIIe et XIXe siècles* (Paris: Hachette, 1982).

23. Contraception: Keith Hopkins, "Contraception in the Roman Empire," *CSSH* 8 (1965): 124–51; Emiel Eyben, "Family Planning in Graeco-Roman Antiquity," *Anc. Soc.* 11–12 (1980–81): 5–82; Paul Veyne, *Histoire de la vie privée*, vol. 1, *De l'Empire romain à l'an mil* (Paris: Seuil, 1985), 35–63. Morality: the Stoic philosopher Musonius Rufus was an exception; on that point see Michel Foucault, *Histoire de la sexualité* (Paris: Gallimard, 1984), 3:198. Parents' perceptions: according to John E. Boswell, "*Expositio* and *Oblatio*: The Abandonment of Children and the Ancient and Medieval Family," *American Historical Review* 89 (1984): 10–33, and *The Kindness of Strangers: The Abandonment of Children in Western Europe from Late Antiquity to the Renaissance* (New York: Pantheon Books, 1988), 128–31. Jurists: cf. Paulus *Dig.* 25.3.4.

24. William V. Harris, "The Theoretical Possibility of Extensive Infanticide in the Graeco-Roman World," *CQ* 32 (1982): 114–16.

25. Cf. Juvenal *Satires* 9.87–90.

26. Tradition retained, from the beginning of the Empire, symbolic gestures by Augustus and Claudius, who refused to accept within the family children produced by adulterous relationships.

27. Cassius Dio 56.7.2. See Richard P. Duncan-Jones, "Demographic Change and Economic Progress under the Roman Empire," *Tecnologia e società nel mondo romano (Atti del convegno di Como 27-28-29 settembre 1979)* (Como, 1980), 66.

28. Cassius Dio 54.16.2.

29. See in that sense Susan Treggiari, review of Keith Hopkins, *Death and Renewal* (Cambridge: Cambridge University Press, 1983), in *AJP* (1985): 256–62.

30. Paul Veyne, "La famille et l'amour."

31. Marie-Thérèse Raepsaet-Charlier, "Epouses et familles de magistrats dans les provinces romaines aux deux premiers siècles de l'Empire," *Historia* 31 (1982): 56–69.

32. Mireille Corbier, "Idéologie et pratique de l'héritage (Ier siècle avant J.C.–IIe siècle aprés J.-C.)," *Index* 13 (1985) (Atti del Convegno di Lecce, 19–24 settembre 1983): 648–50.

33. Martial 5.38; Pliny the Younger *Letters* 1.14.9. See Hopkins, *Death and Renewal*, 77–79.

34. Apuleius *Apology* 76.

35. *Plena*: Tacitus *Annals* 4.3. *Deserta*: Seneca *Consolation to Marcia* 15.2.

36. *Moralia* 289d–e. This remark drew Claude Lévi-Strauss's attention: see *Structures élémentaires de la parenté*, 2d ed. (Paris: Editions de la Maison des Sciences de l'Homme, 1967), 15.

37. Plutarch *Moralia* 265d–e.

38. Tacitus *Annals* 12.6.3. See Philippe Moreau, "Plutarque, Augustin, Lévi-Straus: prohibition de l'inceste et mariage préférentiel dans la Rome primitive," *RBPh* 56, no. 1 (1978): 41–54.

39. "Is it because they want, through marriage, to multiply their kinship relationships and acquire numerous kindred, by giving women to other men, and by receiving women from other men?

"Or is it because they fear that conjugal misunderstandings between kindred might attack natural rights and duties?

"Or else, noting the fact that women's weakness means they need much support, they did not want to marry close kin women, so that the wife's parents can help her, if her husband ill-treats her?" (*Roman Questions* 6).

40. Germaine Tillion, *Le harem et les cousins* (Paris: Seuil, 1966), 152–53.

41. Migne, *Patrologia Latina* 41: col. 459: *propter multiplicandas adfinitates, ne habeat duas necessitudines una persona, cum duae possint eas habere, et numerus propinquitatis augeri*. See Philippe Moreau, "Plutarque, Augustin, Lévi-Strauss"; see also Maurizio Bettini, "Il divieto fino al 'sesto grado' incluso nel matrimonio romano," *Athenaeum* 66 (1988): 88–93.

42. Sergio Roda, "Matrimonio fra cugini germani," 296–300.

43. Migne, *Patrologia Latina* 145: cols. 193–94. For partial translations see David Herlihy and Christiane Klapisch-Zuber, *Les Toscans et leurs familles: une étude du catasto florentin de 1427* (Paris: Presses de la Fondation des Sciences Politiques, 1978), 527–28 = *Tuscans and Their Families: A Study of the Florentine Catasto of 1427* (New Haven, 1985), 338–39. The text is frequently quoted after Héritier, *L'exercice de la parenté*, 140–50; thus by Barthélémy in Ariès and Duby, *Histoire de la vie privée*, vol. 2, *De l'Europe féodale à la Renaissance*, 128. Peter Damian took up the argument at least in part through intermediaries such as Isidore of Seville and Burchard of Worms: see J. J. Ryan, *Saint Peter Damiani and His Canonical Sources: A Preliminary Study in the Antecedents of the Gregorian Reform* (Toronto: Pontifical Institute of Mediaeval Studies, 1956), 24–28.

44. Herlihy and Klapisch-Zuber, *Tuscans and Their Families*, 337–42; Jack Goody, *The Development of the Family and Marriage in Europe* (Cambridge: Cambridge University Press, 1983), 136–37.

45. Sarah B. Pomeroy, "The Relationship of the Married Woman"; Judith P.

Hallett, *Fathers and Daughters in Roman Society: Women and the Elite Family* (Princeton: Princeton University Press, 1984); Dixon, "The Marriage Alliance."

46. Mireille Corbier, "Pour une pluralité des approches prosopographiques," *MEFREM* 100, no. 1 (1988): 187–97.

47. Goody, *The Development of the Family*, 50–55.

48. Treggiari, "*Digna condicio*"; Richard P. Saller, "Men's Age at Marriage and Its Consequences in the Roman Family," *CP* 82, no. 1 (1987): 31–34; Ronald Syme, "Marriage Ages for Roman Senators," *Historia* (1987): 319–32.

49. Syme, "Marriage Ages for Senators," 320–21.

50. *Historia Augusta* Marcus 29.10.

51. Corbier, "Pour une pluralité des approches prosopographiques," 195–97.

52. Goody, *The Development of the Family*, 48–59.

53. Yan Thomas, "Mariages endogamiques à Rome: patrimoine, pouvoir et parenté depuis l'époque archaïque," *RHDFE* 58 (1980): 345–82.

54. See Mireille Corbier, "La maison des Césars," in *Le mariage dans un degré rapproché: études comparatives*, ed. Pierre Bonte (Paris: Ed. de l'EHESS, forthcoming).

55. Susan Treggiari, "*Digna conditio*"; Dixon, "The Marriage Alliance."

56. Corbier, "Les familles clarissimes d'Afrique proconsulaire"; Syme, "Eight Consuls from Patavium."

57. As shown by Corbier, "La 'tavola marmorea' de Bolsena," 1102–7.

58. *CIL* VIII:7032 = *ILAlg.* II:616.

59. Richard P. Saller and Brent D. Shaw, "Close-kin Marriage in Roman Society?" *Man* 19 (1984): 432–44.

60. Corbier, "Pour une pluralité des approches prosopographiques," 197.

61. *CIL* IX:2845–2846 = 5244 = *ILS* 915. See Mireille Corbier, *L'"aerarium Saturni" et l'"aerarium militare": administration et prosopographie sénatoriale*, Collection de l'Ecole Française de Rome, 24 (Rome: L'Ecole Française, 1974), 26–27; Marina Torelli, "Una nuova iscrizione di Silla da Larino," *Athenaeum* 61 (1973): 350–51.

62. Claverie and Lamaison, *L'impossible mariage*; Collomp, *La maison du père*.

63. Susan Treggiari, "Sentiment and Property: Some Roman Attitudes," *Theories of Property: From Aristotle to the Present*, ed. A. Parel and T. Flanagan (Waterloo, Ont., 1979), 53–85.

64. Corbier, "Idéologie et pratique de l'héritage," 514.

65. Cicero *Letters to Atticus* 12.18a.2.

66. Polybius 31.26–28; *Historia Augusta* Marcus 4.7, 7.4. On Scipio, often studied, see most recently Suzanne Dixon, "Polybius on Roman Women and Property," *AJP* 106 (1985): 147–70. On Marcus Aurelius see Corbier, "Idéologie et pratique de l'héritage," 514.

67. See John Crook, "Women in Roman Succession," in *The Family in Ancient Rome: New Perspectives*, ed. B. Rawson (London: Croom Helm, 1986), 70–71.

68. Corbier, "Idéologie et pratique de l'héritage," 514.

69. Pliny the Younger *Letters* 7.24.

70. See Crook, "Women in Roman Succession"; Gardner, *Women in Roman Law and Society*, 97–116, 163–203.

71. Richard P. Saller, "Roman Dowry and the Devolution of Property in the Principate," *CQ* 34 (1984): 195–205.

72. Ulpian *Dig.* 36.1.23. See A. Spawforth, "Families at Roman Sparta and Epidaurus: Some Prosopographical Notes," *Bull. of the Amer. School at Athens* 80 (1985): 191–258; Jane F. Gardner, "Another Family and an Inheritance: Claudius Brasidas and His Ex-wife's Will," *Liverpool Classical Monthly* 12, no. 4 (1987): 52–54.

73. I am not speaking here of the rewards which were also traditional to the nanny or the faithful servants (in Rome principally freedmen and freedwomen).

74. Corbier, "Idéologie et pratique de l'héritage," 521–22.

75. *CIL* VI:1374–1375 = *ILS* 917–917a.

76. Cf. on this point Crook, "Women in Roman Succession," 67.

77. Andrew Wallace-Hadrill, "Family and Inheritance in the Augustan Marriage-Laws," *PCPhS* 207 (1981): 58–80.

78. Goody, *The Development of the Family*, 91–102.

79. Corbier, "Idéologie et pratique de l'héritage," 521–22.

80. Pointed out by Elizabeth Rawson, "The Ciceronian Aristocracy and Its Properties," in *Studies in Roman Property*, ed. Moses I. Finley (Cambridge: Cambridge University Press, 1976), 85–102.

81. This has been analyzed by Treggiari in "Sentiment and Property," a study which can support my proposition.

82. Edward Champlin, "Owners and Neighbours at Ligures Baebiani," *Chiron* 11 (1981): 239–64.

83. Pliny the Younger *Letters* 2.4.3.

84. Seneca *Consolation to Marcia* 26.2.

85. Cicero *Pro Milone* 35.95; Asconius *Mil.* 27 Clark.

86. This information was given me by Robert Descimon. See Ralph E. Giesey, "Rules of Inheritance and Strategies of Mobility in Prerevolutionary France," *American Historical Review* 82 (1977): 271–81.

87. Mireille Corbier, "Divorce and Adoption," and "Construire sa parenté à Rome: mariage et divorce, filiation et adoption," in *Rethinking Family History*, ed. David Kertzer and Richard Saller (New Haven: Yale University Press, forthcoming).

88. Saller, "*Familia, domus.*"

89. *CIL* XI:6334 = *ILS* 1129.

DIANA DELIA

Fulvia Reconsidered

Fulvia is perhaps the most memorable of late Republican women, whom J. P. V. D. Balsdon caricatured as possessing "wealth, birth, charm and talent, unfettered by any moral restraint, hungry for animal pleasure or hungry for power—hungry, perhaps, for both."[1] No woman was quite like Fulvia; in rapid succession she married three radical tribunes of the plebs—P. Clodius Pulcher, C. Scribonius Curio, and M. Antony—whose *popularis* and pro-Caesarian activities conferred notoriety in their own day and ever since. The last of these, M. Antony, was not content to administer the Roman East but contended with Octavian Caesar for supremacy at Rome. The extent to which Fulvia influenced or assisted her husbands' careers is vitally significant because she has recently been viewed as an emancipated woman who abandoned the traditional domestic role enjoined on Roman matrons to exercise real political power instead.[2] Earlier, Charles Babcock had also concluded that Fulvia had directed her energy and assets towards furthering her spouses' careers in a manner reminiscent of corporate wives of the 1960s.[3] Clearly there has been a temptation to interpret Fulvia pursuant to personal presuppositions and contemporary social stereotypes which, in the interests of objectivity, perhaps should not be ascribed to the late Republic.[4]

The purpose of this paper is to investigate the extent to which Fulvia exercised power and directed her spouses' careers. Babcock suggested that Fulvia shared with them certain assets such as wealth and family connections. Indeed, in 44 B.C., Cicero described Fulvia as "wealthy" in a passage which implies that her fortune, at least in part, derived from a legacy of her maternal grandfather, Sempronius Tuditanus.[5] Fulvia's spouses, however, were not necessarily in a position freely to dispose of it. When emancipated Roman women married with *manus*, their property merged with that of their husbands; otherwise paternal or agnatal authority ordinarily restricted a matron's ability to transfer assets and to assume contractual obligations. Because her father, M. Fulvius Bambalio, was alive at the time of her marriage to Clodius,[6] Fulvia as yet possessed no property in her own right. If she married Clodius with *manus*, Fulvia would have been emancipated at his death, eligible to share in his estate and assigned a Claudian *tutor* (guardian). Otherwise, marriage without *manus*, which appears to have been widely practiced during the late Republic, would have prolonged Bambalio's paternal authority over Fulvia; in that case the only matrimonial asset which Clodius might have administered was the dowry that remained in his care only for the duration of the marriage.[7] In subsequent marriages, regardless of whether Fulvia remained under paternal authority or guardianship, she would not have been in a position to dispose of her property without supervision. Indeed, Atticus' loan to Fulvia in 43, relieving her of pressing obligations, suggests that she was unable to dispose of her own assets.[8] Moreover, the exchange of gifts between husbands and wives was prohibited under Roman law.[9] Hence it is unlikely that Fulvia's spouses had earmarked her wealth for their own political advancement, and Cicero's reiterated criticisms that all three were spendthrifts should be dismissed as stock or routine.[10] Lavish expenditure was unavoidable by young men who aspired rapidly to pursue the *cursus honorum* at Rome; but this need not imply that Fulvia was married for her money.

In Fulvia was linked the nobility of the Fulvii and Sempronii Tuditani, two old plebeian noble families nonetheless inactive in the politics of the late Republic.[11] Apart from the dubious Pinarius affair, however, the extent to which Fulvia exploited familial connections on behalf of her husbands is unknown.[12] The supposition that she did is based on the modern axiom that "behind every successful man is a woman."[13] In terms of Roman husbands and wives, however, this maxim may not necessarily hold true. Indeed, Judith Hallett has recently argued that elite Roman women tended to exercise influence through the familial network on their brothers and sons rather than on their husbands.[14]

Babcock's suggestion that Fulvia's "career" ought to be defined in terms of the extent to which she advanced the political careers of all three spouses rests on extremely tenuous grounds. It proceeds from the premise that Fulvia's direct influence on the public career of Antony is unquestionable; *ergo* she exercised a similar decisive influence on the careers of earlier husbands.[15] Nevertheless the silence of Cicero in the 50s, when he bitterly attacked Clodius and considered himself to be Curio's mentor, suggests that if indeed Fulvia had been manipulating these spouses, she had employed remarkable discretion. On the contrary, the evidence over-whelmingly demonstrates that the political activity of Fulvia in association with a husband began only after her marriage to Antony, not before, and that Cicero's criticisms of Fulvia with respect to the early years were retrospective and accordingly suspect. Especially striking is the fact that Fulvia is mentioned only once, without rancor, in Cicero's correspon-dence.[16] If she truly figured prominently in the politics of these years, her exclusion from the subject matter of the letters, in which the activities of Caesar, Clodius, Curio, Antony, and Octavian were frequently and can-didly discussed, is inexplicable.

Two examples of Fulvia's alleged political activities during these early years were cited by Babcock. He claimed that her political debut occurred after the murder of Clodius in 52, when she exhibited his wounded body to the mob gathered outside their residence on the Palatine. Later that year she appeared with her mother at the trial of the chief assassin, Milo. Both appearances, however, may have been due more to natural expres-sions of grief and the personal desire to avenge Clodius' murder than to deliberate dramatization and manipulation of her family for political ends.[17] Moreover, the poignant appearance of relatives on behalf of plain-tiffs, defendants, or victims was not at all unusual at Roman trials, as Suzanne Dixon has also observed.[18]

It was only after the death of Caesar, when Octavian and Antony vied for control of Rome, that Fulvia assumed what now can be called a signifi-cant political role. It was then that she shared in the opprobrium leveled at Antony by his deadliest enemies, Cicero and Octavian. This was when Cicero assailed Antony's masculinity in the vitriolic *Philippics*, penned between September 44 and April 43, by alleging that Antony submissively permitted Fulvia to dominate him.[19]

One of Cicero's rhetorical techniques was to slander the female relations of an enemy so as to make him appear utterly vile.[20] For example, in 44 Cicero described Fulvia as *locuples* in a context which suggested that her wealth was both familial as well as illicitly acquired. Earlier he had impli-cated Fulvia in Antony's reinstatement of the Armenian client-king Deio-tarus for a bribe, suggestively adding that in her quarters "many things have been and are sold."[21] When Antony quelled riotous troops at Brundisium by ordering the execution of some of the centurions and

Fulvia witnessed the slaughter, she was charged by Cicero with cruelty.[22] Cicero's criticism of Fulvia was tantamount to guilt by association.

In the *Philippics* Cicero alleged intimate relations between Clodius and Antony. Cicero had despised Clodius nearly as much as he now hated Antony; but it was only in the Second Philippic that Cicero denounced Antony as the inspiration for Clodius' radical tribunate fourteen years earlier and obliquely insinuated that Antony had then attempted some nefarious deed at Clodius' home.[23] Babcock interpreted this as an allusion to an intrigue with Fulvia. Having sketched in the scenario, the orator left it to the imagination of his audience to supply the worst possible conclusion. Cicero's feigned reluctance to tell all is complemented here and elsewhere in the *Philippics* by sarcasm or studied politeness towards Fulvia with equally devastating results. By projecting himself as decorous, Cicero made his character assassination of Antony and Antony's relations appear all the more convincing.[24] As Griffin notes, "Accusations of every kind of wantonness had always been a part of the standard material of Greek oratory and Roman polemic was no less slanderous." Contrary to what he would now have us believe, however, in 52 Cicero had actually claimed that Fulvia was inseparable from Clodius, accompanying him nearly everywhere; this suggests that they had been on excellent terms, not estranged.[25] From late 44 through 43, when his invective was poised against M. Antony, Cicero appears to have been unconcerned about consistency with his prior claims—for example, that in April 44 he had professed his constant affection for Antony and denied ever having held a grudge against Clodius![26] Nor should the criterion of public delivery have any bearing on an assessment of the veracity of allegations in Cicero's orations.[27] Some speeches, such as the *pro Milone*, were never delivered; moreover, Cicero regularly improvised his speeches at the time of delivery and only wrote them down later on.[28]

Fulvia shared in the rancor directed against her spouse in the Second Philippic, a speech which was never publicly read but instead was circulated as a political pamphlet during Antony's absence from Rome in November 44. Penned with deliberate personal malice, its intention was thoroughly to denigrate Antony.[29] As George Kennedy has observed: "what the second Phillipic best illustrates is the unattractive side of ancient oratory: unbridled use of attack on family and personal life as a means of discrediting the character of the opponent and a general willingness to use lies and deceit and sophistry on behalf of a course regarded by the orator as good." Eleanor Huzar has likewise noted that "the age permitted every excessive verbal attack. Slander was so common against a man, his family, and his actions that only by steadily intensifying vituperation could any impact be made."[30] In subsequent Philippics, Cicero revealed his aim: "I will brand him with the truest marks of infamy and will hand him down to the everlasting memory of men."[31] Perhaps the most astute imitator of Cicero would be the young Octavian, who would revive and refashion to his own ends the character assassination of Fulvia first undertaken by Cicero.

Augustan apologetic shifted the blame for the triumviral proscriptions of 43 to Lepidus and Antony while Octavian and members of his family were portrayed as trying to protect as many persons as possible. Thus the sources relate that Octavia interceded to help save the life of T. Vinius and pleaded on behalf of female relatives of the proscribed, whom Fulvia allegedly had snubbed.[32] Like Cicero, Octavian attacked his enemies through their women; thus after the dissolution of the second triumvirate Fulvia acquired a reputation as rapacious and vengeful, allegedly having precipitated the deaths of many during the proscriptions.[33] This portrait of Fulvia took root. More than a century later Appian would relate that a certain Rufus was added to the list of the proscribed and executed merely because he had refused Fulvia's earlier offer to purchase his house.[34] The charge of rapacity, of course, originated with Cicero, who tried to vilify Antony's need for funds to pay his troops and other debts by alleging motivations of personal greed; by extension the same criticisms were leveled against Fulvia.[35]

On the grounds that "the best propaganda is the exaggeration of a known or credible element," Babcock accepted the attribution of these characteristics to Fulvia, even though it is patent that they were calumny, first pronounced by Cicero in the throes of fury, subsequently enhanced by Octavian, and preserved by later authors whose accounts derived from these two.[36] Overlooked, however, is the fact that every alleged exercise of power by Fulvia was characterized in the extant sources as selfish, malevolent, or treacherous; this argues against the soundness of employing Fulvia as a model of female emancipation during the late Republic. Moreover, if she really was so evil, it is odd that none of the sources even hint at her complicity in effecting the death of her most vitriolic enemy, Cicero.[37]

Phyllis Culham maintains that Fulvia's political prominence is demonstrated by the appearance of her likeness on Roman coins minted earlier even than coins that bear the triumvirs' own portraits.[38] To be sure, a

portrait of Victory that appears as an obverse type on certain late Republican coins was first surmised to be the likeness of Fulvia by Babelon.[39]
B. V. Head restored the legend erased from two Phrygian coins bearing
a similar Victory type as [*ΦΟΥΛ*]*ΟΥΙΑΝΩΝ* and [*ΦΟΥΛΟΥΙΑΝΩΝ*],
dating these to ca. 44–40 although he was not at all certain about the
portrait's identification.[40] The Phrygian coins are probably contemporaneous with two quinarii bearing a similar Victory type minted at Lugdunum, a military settlement founded in 43.[41] The Lugdunum issues are
inscribed A(NNO) XL and A(NNO) XLI respectively; these legends must
refer to the age of Antony,[42] whose name and title as *imperator* are inscribed on the reverse of the latter coin. Antony's date of birth per se has
not been preserved in the ancient sources; Appian, however, relates that
Antony was in his fortieth year when Cleopatra joined him at Tarsus
during the summer of 41.[43] Hence he had been born on 14 January 80, and
the Lugdunum issues date to 40 and 39.[44] The Victory type may be
reminiscent of Philippi or, as Crawford has suggested, may anticipate
Antony's Parthian campaign.[45] All of the Victory portraits, however, bear
a striking physical resemblance to the likeness of Octavia on aurei issued
by eastern mints from 39 to 38, commemorating the marriage of Antony
and Octavia late in 40, and the like.[46] Identification of the Victory portrait
as Fulvia was rejected by Van Sallet, Grüber, and Mattingly; it was questioned by Head, and even Babcock admitted uncertainty. Culham nevertheless employs these coins to enhance her characterization of Fulvia as a
powerful woman in whose honor even a remote town in Phrygia changed
its name.[47] Nevertheless, if the portrait may be identified as Octavia,
then the first Victory issues were released only after Fulvia's death in 40,
and the lacunae on the Phrygian coins ought to be restored as [*ΟΚΤΑ*]-
ΟΥΙΑΝΩΝ and [*ΟΚΤΑΟΥΙΑΝΩΝ*]. Eumeneia probably changed its
name and issued these coins in 39 to celebrate the marriage of Antony and
Octavia; Athens similarly issued a commemorative aureus bearing their
portraits the following year.[48] Eumeneia no doubt resumed its original
name and erased the legend after the marriage of Antony and Cleopatra
in 34.[49]

   The influence of Fulvia has been alleged by Suzanne Dixon and Eleanor
Huzar in connection with the betrothal and subsequent marriage of her
daughter, Clodia, to Octavian after the reconciliation of the triumvirs at
Bononia in 43. As Antony had betrothed his daughter by Antonia to
Lepidus' son the previous year, Clodia may actually have been Antony's
only resource of marriageable age.[50] In the absence of suitable blood

relations, marriage relations appear to have sufficed. Thus Octavian would later marry Scribonia, the sister of Sextus Pompey's father-in-law, and Sextus Pompey's daughter would be betrothed to Antony's stepson and Octavian's nephew, Marcellus.[51] There is, however, no evidence that Fulvia engineered the match.

The most compelling arguments in favor of Fulvia's exercise of political power on behalf of a husband concern her role in the Perusine War. After Philippi, Antony set out to administer the East and to raise funds. Fulvia remained in Italy, where Octavian was to confiscate territory in eighteen Italian cities marked down for distribution among the triumvirs' veterans. His program was thwarted by Antony's brother, the consul Lucius Antonius, who feared that the loyalty of Antony's soldiers would be swayed if Octavian rather than Antony's representatives led out the military colonies comprising Antonian veterans.[52]

Ever an opportunist, Lucius actively canvassed, bringing Fulvia and Antony's children before Antony's legions to urge them not to forget Antony, under whom they had served and to whom they owed the victory at Philippi. Moreover, Lucius assumed the cognomen Pietas, which advertised his claim to be defending his brother's interests.[53] The result was to increase the pressure on Octavian to accede to Lucius' demands.

Uncertain whether Antony had instigated these measures and mindful that Antony controlled the East, Octavian deliberately refrained from breaking with his colleague and directed his attack against Lucius and Fulvia instead. He claimed that while he was expediting the terms of the agreement reached with Antony after Philippi, Lucius and Fulvia were prevaricating in pursuit of their own power. Octavian purportedly made overtures toward reconciliation which were refused; thereupon he sent Clodia packing.[54]

When some of the Italians threatened by dispossession traveled to Rome to seek redress, Lucius espoused their cause; he may have been persuaded that this would yield more power than carrying out the land allotments.[55] Meanwhile Octavian found himself in a most awkward situation. In settling the veterans on confiscated land he had alienated the Italians; but if he failed to proceed as planned, he risked compromising his integrity with the army. He decided in favor of the army. Lucius organized the disgruntled Italians and worked to detach soldiers from Octavian. Fulvia had traveled with her children to Praeneste to seek the protection of Lepidus, apparently without success. Earlier she had permitted Lucius to take Antony's children along to be present at the dedication of the last military colony; there, Lucius claimed, Octavian had sent soldiers against him and the children, causing them to flee to Antonian colonies, where Lucius denounced Octavian as treacherous before the soldiers and obtained a bodyguard for the journey home.[56] Dio preserves the hyperbole of the Augustan tradition when he recounts that at Praeneste, Fulvia girded on a sword, gave out the watchword, and even harangued the soldiers, although she relied on the advice of senators and knights to issue orders to the military network still ostensibly under Lucius' command.[57]

Lucius marched on Rome, occupying the city briefly only to withdraw at Octavian's advance. From Rome he marched northward to Perusia, which Octavian invested with a siege, reducing it early the next year (40 B.C.).[58] Although Fulvia had marshaled reinforcements, her husband's generals in the Gallic provinces displayed notable reluctance to raise the blockade.[59] Octavian gave up Perusia as plunder to his troops, but Lucius was pardoned and sent to govern Spain, where he died shortly thereafter. Fulvia fled with the children, meeting Antony at Sicyon, where she became ill and died.[60]

Ronald Syme perceived the impossibility of discovering the whole truth about the Perusine War.[61] Antony's responsibility for the events in Italy cannot be ascertained. Was Lucius defending his brother's interests, or was he rebelling against the limitations which the triumvirate had placed on his own consular *imperium*? In Appian's account, Lucius admits that he exploited Fulvia and made use of Antony's legions in order to overthrow the triumvirate; nevertheless his republican sympathies are suspiciously latent.[62] In any event, Antony cannily refrained from repudiating Lucius' program prior to the fall of Perusia, pending the outcome.

Fulvia's participation in the Perusine War was limited. Initially she opposed Lucius as "stirring up war at an inopportune time," that is, while Antony was abroad. Believing that they were safeguarding Antony's interests, she and Antony's children were nevertheless reconciled with Lucius and exploited by him to arouse support among the legions.[63] Only after Lucius had taken refuge in Perusia, to which Octavian laid siege, did Fulvia take charge, urging Antony's generals to hasten from Gaul in order to raise the siege and collecting military reinforcements intended to relieve Lucius.[64] Nonetheless posterity has awarded Fulvia the lion's share of the blame.

Fulvia's actions were also predicated on maternal grounds. The only ineluctable legacy from Antony to their children was his name; Fulvia was obliged to champion the reputation and authority that this name conveyed in order to preserve their patrimony intact. After Antony had been compelled to quit Italy as a public enemy in 43, his adversaries not only attempted to despoil Fulvia of her possessions but also plotted to murder her children.[65] In 40 Fulvia appeared with Antony's children and mother before the soldiers to implore them not to forget Antony nor their debt to him as victor at Philippi. Later that year Fulvia's decision to flee with her children to Praeneste was likewise prompted by fears for them.[66] Antony's absence from Rome during the years 44 through 40 deprived his family of his paternal authority; responsibility now devolved upon Lucius, whose loyalties were suspect. "Wartime conditions demanded that women go to extremes to preserve the unity of their families," as Mary Lefkowitz has observed.[67]

When later composing his *Memoirs*, Octavian appears to have deliberately shifted the blame for the Perusine War away from Lucius and Antony onto Fulvia.[68] Hence arose the characterization of Fulvia as ill-tempered, headstrong, overbearing, and meddlesome.[69] In view of his own professed republican sympathies Octavian could hardly criticize Lucius' claims to have been championing republican traditions against the arbitrary rule of the triumvirs.[70] Indeed, in light of their mutual desire for reconciliation by late 41 both Octavian and Antony may have found in Fulvia a convenient excuse for an estrangement that had now become an embarrassment.[71]

Although the *Memoirs* of Augustus no longer exist, they survived long enough to influence the accounts of numerous ancient authorities.[72] For example, Octavian's characterization of Fulvia as androgynous was incorporated into Dio's description of Fulvia at Praeneste, armed with a sword, haranguing the soldiers, and issuing commands; this behavior, Dio relates, especially offended Octavian.[73] Moreover, an epigram of Octavian, preserved in Martial (11.20), taunts Fulvia for her jealousy of Antony's Cappadocian mistress Glaphyra and alleges that Fulvia was waging war with Octavian as a substitute for sex.[74] Antony's affair with Glaphyra occurred in spring of 41; that summer Cleopatra met with Antony briefly at Tarsus, and he later wintered with her at Alexandria. The post-Augustan sources appear to have substituted the more notorious liaison with Cleopatra for that with Glaphyra, but they likewise claimed that this induced Fulvia to stir up war as a ruse to provoke the return of her philandering husband.[75] Octavian's poem, however, which only makes sense if composed during the Perusine War, demonstrates that late in 41 tongues were still wagging about Antony's affair with Glaphyra and that Antony's more recent amour with Cleopatra had not yet become common knowledge.[76]

Cicero and Octavian understood that truth is powerless in the face of myth. The creators of myth, however, might control what others believed to be true. By attacking Fulvia as a virago, as early as 40 Octavian portrayed Antony as unmanly but nonethless innocent of a breach of faith. When the rift between the triumvirs finally became irreconcilable, Augustan propaganda stealthily attacked Antony by extolling the virtues of Octavia and exaggerating her peacemaking activities; this further denigrated Antony, who had treated her with contempt.[77] Octavian would pursue a similar character assassination against the Ptolemaic queen Cleopatra, against whom—not Antony—war was declared. Immortalized by Horace as a *fatale monstrum*, Cleopatra would be portrayed as dominating Antony and making even the strategic decisions during the war.[78]

Though it is indeed true that the antagonism which Roman women aroused is a reflection of the political power that their contemporaries *perceived* they wielded,[79] we can not take it for granted that such perceptions were unbiased or accurate. The image of Fulvia preserved in the ancient sources that derived from the writings of Cicero and Augustus had already been manipulated into an antithesis of the ideal Roman matron whose primary obligation was submission in order to promote harmonious domestic life, not conflict. A proper matron's sphere of activities was traditionally limited to the household; why, even that marvel of a woman, Octavia, was reputed to have woven the garments that her brother wore.[80] On occasion virtuous Roman women had become involved in affairs of state, but only for the most unselfish reasons: Veturia may have interceded with her son, Coriolanus, to prevent war with Rome, and Hortensia spoke out on behalf of female relations of the proscribed. In contrast, Fulvia allegedly incited war in pursuit of self-interest and haughtily repulsed Hortensia's group.[81] The nature of Roman politics was such that women might properly exercise political power only vicariously through the male members of their families. Limitations were imposed by traditional ideology on public conduct of proper Roman women; women who strayed beyond these bounds were branded as both degenerate and dangerous. Moreover, the post-Augustan sources were, without exception, males who appear to have been both fascinated and repelled by the androgynous female stereotype. In their characterizations of Fulvia they perpetuated a distortion so grotesque and overwhelming that few traces of the real person have survived. She became a moral exemplum of the worst possible behavior for a Roman matron, just as the portrait of Octavia was deliberately groomed to project the feminine ideals formulated by Roman men.[82]

Notes

The genesis of this paper dates back to 1983, when I had the honor of participating as a guest in a National Endowment for the Humanities institute on women in classical antiquity directed by Sarah B. Pomeroy, assisted by Helene P. Foley and Natalie Boymel Kampen. Their enthusiasm and the opportunity for total immersion in this new and challenging field stimulated me to have another look at Fulvia. I am also indebted to Meyer Reinhold, Phyllis Culham, and the referees for reading and commenting on earlier drafts of this manuscript.

Unless otherwise specified, abbreviations follow those used in *L'année philologique* and the second edition of the *Oxford Classical Dictionary*.

1. J. P. V. D. Balsdon, *Roman Women: Their History and Habits* (New York, 1965), 55.

2. B. Förtsch, *Die politische Rolle der Frau in der römischen Republik* (Stuttgart, 1935), 108; Sarah B. Pomeroy, *Goddesses, Whores, Wives, and Slaves: Women in Classical Antiquity* (New York, 1975), 185, 189; J. Hallett, "Perusinae Glandes and the Changing Image of Augustus," *AJAH* 2 (1977): 151–71, passim; G. Clark, "Roman Women," *G&R* 28 (1981): 209; S. Dixon, "A Family Business: Women's Role in Patronage and Politics at Rome, 80–44 B.C.," *Class. et Med.* 34 (1983): 109; E. G. Huzar, "Mark Antony: Marriages vs. Careers," *CJ* 81 (1986): 102.

3. "The Early Career of Fulvia," *AJP* 86 (1965): 1–32.

4. Note the sober warning of M. Finley: "It would be a bad mistake to read our own emotions and values into the picture." See "The Silent Women of Rome," in *Aspects of Antiquity: Discoveries and Controversies*, 2d ed. (New York, 1977), 132, echoed by M. R. Lefkowitz, "Wives and Husbands," *G&R* 30 (1983): 31.

5. Cicero *Phil.* 3.16; cf. Val. Max. 7.8.1. On this see Babcock, "Fulvia," 4–5, followed by Pomeroy, *Goddesses, Whores, Wives, and Slaves*, 185. The passage in Valerius Maximus is problematic: "Quam certae, quam etiam notae insaniae Tuditanus, utpote qui populo nummos sparserit togamque velut tragicam vestem in foro trahens maximo cum hominum risu conspectus fuerit ac multa his consentanea fecerit. Testamento filium instituit heredem, quod Ti. Longus, sanguine ei proximus, hastae iudicio subvertere frustra conatus est." Babcock would emend *filium*, which occurs in the two principal ninth-century manuscripts of Valerius Maximus, to read *Fulviam*. Instead the reading *filiam*, preserved in the epitome of Julius Paris that appears in the margin of one of these manuscripts, is much to be

preferred, as it assumes that only a single, rather simple, scribal error was made in the course of manuscript transmission. Moreover, it is unlikely that a legacy to a son would have been challenged; this, however, was not the case for inheritance by daughters. Under the Lex Voconia of 169 B.C., Roman citizens in the first census class might not bequeath their estates to women. Ordinarily, this law might be circumvented by the institution of a *fidei commissum* to a trusted friend who would pass the fortune on to its proper beneficiary. On the basis of Julius Paris's reading, it would appear that the fabulously wealthy and senile Sempronius Tuditanus had bequeathed the bulk of his fortune outright to his daughter. The will was contested by an agnate, Ti. (Sempronius) Longus, Tuditanus' closest blood relation. Accordingly, *Phil.* 3.16 implies that Fulvia would inherit from her mother. See J. Crook, *Law and Life of Rome* (Ithaca, 1967), 125–26; A. Watson, *The Law of Succession in the Later Roman Republic* (Oxford, 1971), 29; Pomeroy, *Goddesses, Whores, Wives, and Slaves,* 162; Pomeroy, "The Relationship of the Married Woman to Her Blood Relatives in Rome," *AncSoc* 7 (1976): 224; Clark, "Roman Women," 206; and J. A. Crook, "Women in Roman Succession," in *The Family in Ancient Rome: New Perspectives,* ed. B. Rawson (Ithaca, 1986), 65–66.

6. His survival down to 43 B.C. is implied by Dio 45.47.4.

7. A husband with *manus* controlled all the property that his wife possessed or might inherit: Gellius *NA* 17.6; cf. Clark, "Roman Women," 203. On marriage without *manus* see J. Hallett, *Fathers and Daughters in Roman Society: Women and the Elite Family* (Princeton, 1989), 59 n. 33. On paternal authority see J. Crook, "Patria Potestas," *CQ,* n.s. 17 (1967): 113–22; W. K. Lacey, "Patria Potestas," in *The Family in Ancient Rome: New Perspectives,* ed. B. Rawson (Ithaca, 1986), 121–44. On guardianship see Crook, *Law and Life of Rome,* 113–16; A. Watson, *The Law of Persons in the Later Roman Republic* (Oxford, 1967), 146–50; Watson, *Roman Private Law around 200 B.C.* (Edinburgh, 1971), 40; Pomeroy, "Married Woman," 222, 225; and M. Lightman, "Women: A Mirror of Change in the Years of the Roman Revolution" (Ph.D. dissertation, Rutgers University, 1980), 60–67. On dowries see W. W. Buckland, *A Text-Book of Roman Law from Augustus to Justinian,* 2d ed. (Cambridge, 1932), 108–10; Watson, *Law of Persons,* 57–76, and *Roman Private Law,* 24–27; and Pomeroy, "Married Woman," 221.

8. Nepos 29.5.2–5. Of course it is also possible that Fulvia married Antony with *manus* and that her property, perhaps acquired as a result of parental *donationes inter vivos,* had merged with his; Antony's infamy as a public outlaw would have prevented the appointment of representatives to act on his behalf and would have tied up his property until his return to Rome. On *infamia* see Buckland, *Text-Book of Roman Law,* 92. Nevertheless Cic. *pro Flacc.* 84 implies that *manus* marriages were no longer commonplace.

On the basis of Cic. *ad Fam.* 14.1.5 and 14.2.2, S. Dixon has demonstrated that Terentia's property was distinct from Cicero's and that the latter had no power to control her financial transactions, as one would expect if Terentia had married without *manus*: see "Family Finances: Terentia and Tullia," in *The Family in Ancient Rome: New Perspectives*, ed. B. Rawson (Ithaca, 1986), 102; see also T. Carp, "Two Matrons of the Late Republic," *WS* 8 (1981): 193–95. Insofar as the free disposal of wealth by Roman matrons is concerned, however, Dixon's assertion that Terentia was "apparently unhampered by the restrictions of guardianship in her commercial transactions and proceedings on the assumption that her activities would be routinely authorized" (102; see also Pomeroy, *Goddesses, Whores, Wives, and Slaves*, 151) is an argument based on silence. Cicero's failure to mention Terentia's tutor does not imply that a tutor did not exercise control. Moreover, Dixon (99–100) and Pomeroy (161–63) impute to strong-minded, upper-class Republican matrons the exercise of greater freedom—that is, that guardianship operated as a rubber stamp for them—on the basis of an analogy with Roman women of the Principate. See also Gaius *Inst.* 1.115 (*coemptio fiduciae causa*) and 1.190, which reflect the freedom exercised by women in the second century A.D., and W. W. Buckland, *A Manual of Roman Private Law*, 2d ed. (Cambridge, 1953), 73, 105. The *laudatio Turiae*, however, suggests quite the reverse for the late Republic: the tutor-husband of "Turia" was not only consulted in connection with dowering her female relations but actually imposed his own, generous terms in lieu of Turia's intentions: *CIL* VI:1547 = *ILS* 8393, also *Eloge funèbre d'une matrone romaine*, ed. M. Durry (Paris, 1950).

9. Buckland, *Text-Book of Roman Law*, 92.

10. For a different interpretation see Babcock, "Fulvia," 5, 9, 11. Clodius: *Har. Resp.* 42. Curio: *Phil.* 2.45; see also Vell. 2.48.3–4; Plut. *Ant.* 2; Cic. *ad Fam.* 2.3.1. Antonius: Cic. *Phil.* 2.66, 72–74, 93; cf. 5.12.

11. Pomeroy (*Goddesses, Whores, Wives, and Slaves*, 185) identifies Fulvia's mother as the Catilinarian Sempronia. Against this identification one may argue that Fulvia's mother was not prosecuted for treason and was still alive in 52, when she made an appearance with her daughter at the trial of Milo; moreover, Sempronia appears to have married L. Licinius Murena, who had voted to condemn the Catilinarian conspirators in 63 B.C. Finally, there is the failure of Cicero, *pater patriae*, to denigrate Fulvia for possessing so notorious a mother. On the conspirator see F. Münzer, *RE*, rev. ed., II.4 (1923), col. 1446, s.v. Sempronia no. 103 and Sall. *Cat.* 24–25, 40.5. F. Münzer, *Römische Adelsparteien und Adelsfamilien* (Stuttgart, 1920), 272–73, speculated that the Catilinarian Sempronia was a daughter of C. Sempronius Gracchus; R. Syme, *Sallust* (Berkeley, Los Angeles, and London, 1964), 134–35, suggests that she might have been Fulvia's aunt. See also E. Ciaceri, "La dama Sempronia nella congiura di Catilina," *Atti Accad. Arch. Nap.* 11 (1930): 219–30; A. Pastorino, "La Sempronia nella congiura di Catilina," *Giorn. ital. di filol.* 3 (1950): 358–63; E. S. Gruen, *The Last Generation of the Roman Republic* (Berkeley, 1974), 422. For Fulvia's mother, alive in 52, see *RE* II.4 (as above), s.v. Sempronia no. 102, and Asc. *in Mil.* 35 (Clark). On Murena see T. R. S. Broughton, *Magistrates*

of the Roman Republic [*MRR*] (New York, 1952), 2:172–73, 580–81, and note 12 below.

12. During Cicero's exile Clodius' followers razed Cicero's house on the Palatine, and Clodius appears to have consecrated the site on which he erected a monument to Liberty: *de Domo*, passim. After his recall and return to Rome in September 57, Cicero demanded the restoration of his property on specious grounds: *de Domo* 118, 134, 139. Least elegant of Cicero's speeches, the *de Domo* was long considered spurious on account of its diffuse, repetitive, and uncontrolled prose, replete with contradictions, emotional outbursts, and raging invective. All of the allegations made therein were rhetorical; none was substantiated. Accordingly, it would be extremely hazardous to conclude that Sempronia and Fulvia had actually pressed Pinarius into service for Clodius, although Babcock ("Fulvia," 22) and Culham (see below, n. 38) cited this as an example of Fulvia's early involvement in politics. Nor did Fulvia profit from the destruction of Cicero's home, for Cicero (*de Domo* 62) claimed that Clodius' only motivations were hostility, cruelty, and glory—that is, to construct on this site the largest portico in Rome.

On the identification of Pinarius' sister as Fulvia see L. R. Taylor, "Caesar's Colleagues in the Pontifical College," *AJP* 63 (1942): 396–97 and n. 34, followed by Babcock, "Fulvia," 6–8. According to Taylor, Sempronia had given birth to a son, Pinarius Natta (*MRR* 2:199, 206, 213), in an earlier marriage. Taylor's hypothesis rests on the identification of L. Natta as Murena's son-in-law (Cic. *pro Mur.* 73) and Clodius' wife as Pinarius' sister (*de Domo* 118).

13. W. W. Tarn, " The Triumvirs," *CAH* 10 (1934): 42.

14. Hallett, *Fathers and Daughters*, 8–11. Hence Hallett has argued (31–32) that greater social prestige was accorded to daughters, sisters, and mothers than to wives. To be sure, activity on behalf of brothers characterized matrons under paternal authority whereas filial focus prevailed in marriages with *manus*. Inasmuch as this privately transpired, Hallett argues that it may be "impossible to distinguish clearly between women's actual influence and women's imagined influence in political matters." See, however, S. Treggiari, "The Influence of Roman Women," *CR* 36 (1986): 102–5.

15. Babcock, "Fulvia," 19–20, 25, followed by Culham (see below, note 38). See also F. Münzer, *RE* VII (1910): col. 281, s.v. Fulvia; Förtsch, *Die politische Rolle der Frau*, 108–9; E. Malcovati, *Clodia, Fulvia, Marzia, Terenzia*, Quaderni di studi romani, Donne di Roma antica, 1 (Rome, 1945), 27.

16. *Ad Att.* 14.12.

17. Asc. *in Mil.* 28, 35 (Clark); Babcock, "Fulvia," 21, followed by Culham (see below, n. 38). Babcock nevertheless astutely noted the similarity of Antony's actions in March 44 on the occasion of Caesar's funeral.

18. Dixon, "A Family Business," 101.

19. *Phil.* 6.4, echoed by Plut. *Ant.* 10. See also Tarn, "Triumvirs," 32; E. G. Huzar, *Mark Antony* (Minneapolis, 1978), 70–71. For Plutarch's reliance on Cicero's *Philippics* to demonstrate Antony's susceptibility to the wiles of others see C. B. R.

Pelling, "Plutarch's Method of Work in the Roman Lives," *JHS* 99 (1979): 89–90, and Pelling, "Plutarch's Adaptation of His Source Material," *JHS* 100 (1980): 129.

20. On Cicero's proclivity to mock his enemies through their women see J. Griffin, *Latin Poets and Roman Life* (Chapel Hill, 1985), 43, and Huzar, "Mark Antony: Marriages vs. Careers," 97, concerning Fadia, Antony's first wife.

21. *Phil.* 3.16; cf. *Phil.* 2.95, *ad Att.* 14.12.1, *Phil.* 5.4.11. On Antony's responsibility in connection with the bribe: Cic. *Phil.* 2.93–96; see also Förtsch, *Die politische Rolle der Frau*, 109. On Fulvia's alleged avarice, note the sarcasm of *Phil.* 3.16: "vellem hanc contemptionem pecuniae suis reliquisset." Cicero's main thrust was directed against Antony for selling Deiotarus his realm; hence it is likely that Fulvia had merely carried out her husband's instructions, assisting in his absence.

22. *Phil.* 3.4, 5.22, 13.18; see also Dio 45.13.2, 45.35.3; App. *BC* 3.43.

23. Cic. *Phil.* 2.48; cf. Plut. *Ant.* 2. See F. Münzer, *RE* VII:281 s.v. Fulvia; W. C. A. Ker, ed., Cicero, *Phillipics* (Loeb Classical Library), note to 2.48; Babcock, "Fulvia," 6, 13; Huzar, *Mark Antony*, 26, 37.

24. *Phil.* 2.113, 3.16. Griffin, *Latin Poets and Roman Life*, 38–39. Intimacy between the Caesarians, Antony, and Curio also was attested: Cic. *Phil.* 2.45 and passim; Vell. 2.48.3–4; Plut. *Ant.* 2.

25. Cic. *pro Mil.* 28, 55; not, however, for political reasons. The impact of these passages is that Clodius' attack on Milo was premeditated. Milo behaved as usual; but Clodius allegedly broke with his custom of traveling with Fulvia and a full entourage of male and female prostitutes in order to ambush his unsuspecting victim.

26. *Ad Att.* 14.13b.

27. For a different interpretation see Dixon, "A Familiy Business," 100.

28. On the *pro Milone*: Asc. *in Mil.* 26 (Clark); Dio 40.54.2–3. On improvisation: Cic. *Brut.* 91–92; cf. G. Kennedy, *The Art of Rhetoric in the Roman World, 300 B.C.– A.D. 300* (Princeton, 1972), 192–93. J. Hombert's classic study of the Ciceronian rhetorical corpus, *Les plaidoyers écrits et les plaidoiries réelles de Ciceron* (Paris, 1925), demonstrates that substantial differences existed between the oral presentations and their written counterparts. See also Dio 46.7.2–3.

29. Cic. *ad Att.* 16.11; *ad Fam.* 12.2.1.

30. Kennedy, *Art of Rhetoric in the Roman World*, 271; E. G. Huzar, "The Literary Efforts of Mark Antony," *ANRW* II.30.1 (Berlin, 1982): 654; see also Huzar, *Mark Antony*, 99, 192, 200, 236–37.

31. *Phil.* 13.40.

32. Dio 47.7–8; App. *BC* 4.32–34, 4.44; cf. Suet. *Aug.* 27.

33. Dio 47.8.2, and especially 47.8.5, which suggests that Antony and Fulvia only spared those capable of purchasing their deliverance. R. Syme, *The Roman Revolution* (Oxford, 1939), 191, also holds that the terrible stories of Fulvia's rapacity and blood lust originated in Octavian's *Memoirs*.

34. App. *BC* 4.29.

35. *Phil.* 2.113, 6.4.

36. Criticism of Cicero's calumny is implied by Dio at 46.10.4 and 29.1, which probably derive from the *contra maledicta Antonii* or the *Historiae* of Asinius Pollio. On Pollio see E. Gabba, "Note sulle polemica anti-Ciceroniana di Asinio Pollione," *Riv. stor. ital.* 69 (1957): 317–39. Fundamental is K. Scott, "The Political Propaganda of 44–30 B.C.," *MAAR* 11 (1933): 7–49.

37. Babcock, "Fulvia," 22. On Cicero's death see Plut. *Cic.* 46, *Ant.* 20; Dio 47.3ff., esp. 47.8.3, 47.11.2; App. *BC* 4.19–20. The Augustan tradition blamed Antony for Cicero's execution, generating stories to the effect that Antony took savage delight in viewing the orator's head and, even worse, permitted his wife vulgarly to defile it. Ironically it was Cicero who had denounced Fulvia as being fatal to her husbands and who had sarcastically exhorted her to pay the Romans her third installment, Antony, long overdue: *Phil.* 2.11–12, 5.11.

38. Phyllis Culham, response to an earlier version of this paper delivered at the Seventh Berkshire Conference on the History of Women, Wellesley College, 20 June 1987.

39. E. Babelon, *Monnaies de la République romaine*, 2 vols. (Paris and London, 1885–86), 1:168, no. 32, 2:242, no. 2 = H. R. Grüber, *Coins of the Roman Republic in the British Museum* [*CRRBM*] (London, 1910), 2:40 and 1:4229.

40. B. V. Head, *A Catalog of the Greek Coins of Phrygia* (London: 1906), Eumeneia, nos. 20–21 (plate xxvii.4–5) and p. lxi.

41. Grüber, *CRR*, 2: Gaul, 40, 48 (plate cii.10) = M. H. Crawford, *Roman Republican Coinage* [*RRC*] (Cambridge, 1974), 489, nos. 5–6. See also *CRRBM*, 1:nos. 4215, 4229 (plate lvi.1, 10) = *RRC*, 514.1, 494.40: an aureus and a denarius with similar Victory obverse types minted at Rome. Cf. A. Alföldi, "Die stadtrömischen Münzporträts des Jahres 43 v. Chr.," in *Eikones: Studien zum griechischen und römischen Bildnis* (Bern, 1980), 23–24, whose identification of *CRRBM*, 1:no. 4215 with Servilia and date of 43 B.C. are unconvincing.

42. O. Hirschfeld, *CIL* XIII.1, p. 251.

43. *BC* 5.8: *etē tesserakonta gegonōs*. The figure is used as an approximation in contrast with *meirakiōdōs*, as also noted by E. Gabba, ed., *Appiani bellorum civilium liber quintus* (Florence, 1970) at section 33. Among ancient authors there appears to have been no consensus on Antony's date of birth; see, for example, Plut. *Ant.* 86, which preserves two different figures for Antony's age at the time of his death in August 30 B.C. This confusion demonstrates the effectiveness of the *damnatio memoriae* decreed against Antony, which expunged his name from public records. Antony's birthday was probably 14 January, inasmuch as this day alone appears as DIES VITIOS(A) EX S.C. on the Augustan Fasti Maffeiani (*ILS* 8744). According to Dio (51.19.3) in 30 B.C. the Senate and Roman people declared accursed the day on which Antony had been born.

44. That would leave six years for the birth of Gaius and Lucius Antonius prior to their father's departure for Crete in 74 B.C. Moreover, as a protegé of Caesar, it is

not unlikely that Antony presented himself for the consulate in 45 without having attained the minimum age of forty-two years. On citations of age in the literary evidence see J. M. Carter, "Eighteen Years Old?" *BICS* 14 (1967): 51–57, esp. 52 (his discussion of Plutarch and Appian).

45. *RRC*, 740.

46. *CRRBM*, 2: East, nos. 144–45 (= *RRC*, 533, 3a) and p. 449 (= *RRC*, 527.1). Cf. *CRRBM*, 2: East, nos. 151–71 (plates cxiv–cxv), pp. 510–16; *RRC* 528 (plate lxiii); M. Barfeldt, "Die Münzen der Flottenpräfekten des Marcus Antonius," *Num. Zeit.* 37 (1905): 9–56 and plates i–iii.

47. A. Van Sallet, "Fulvia oder Octavia?" *Zeitschr. f. Numism.* 1 (1884): 167–74; Grüber, *CRRBM*, 1: no. 4229; H. Mattingly, *Roman Coins*, 2d ed. (London, 1960), 72 n. 2; Head, *Coins of Phrygia*, lxi; Babcock, "Fulvia," 12 n. 23; Culham, above, n. 38. Incidentally, it was on the basis of these Victory coins that A. Helbig attempted to sustain his identification of a marble portrait as Fulvia: see "Osservazioni sopra i ritratti di Fulvia e di Ottavia," *MAAL* 1 (1889): 573–90.

48. See above, note 46.

49. Livy *Per.* 131; Sen. *Suas.* 1.6; Plut. *Comp. Demetr. et Ant.* 1, 4; Suet. *Aug.* 69; Eutrop. 7.6.9.

50. Dixon, "A Family Business," 107; Huzar, *Mark Antony*, 117. On the betrothal of Antonia to Lepidus' son: App. *BC* 5.93; Dio 46.52.2. On the marriage of Octavian and Clodia: Plut. *Ant.* 20; Dio 46.56.3–4; Suet. *Aug.* 62. On the involvement of mothers in the marriage of their daughters, consider Terentia: Cic. *ad Fam.* 3.10; see also J. E. Phillips, "Roman Mothers and the Lives of Their Adult Daughters," *Helios* 6 (1978): 78; Carp, "Two Matrons," 196–97; S. Dixon, *The Roman Mother* (Norman, Okla., 1988): 215–20.

In the Augustan period the minimum legal marriageable age for a Roman female was twelve years (approximating menarche); nevertheless first marriages regularly took place between the ages of eleven and seventeen years: see K. Hopkins, "The Age of Roman Girls at Marriage," *Population Studies* 18 (1965): 309–27. Although it is true that many marriages were arranged by Roman *nobiles* to secure or establish political ties (Münzer, *Römische Adelsparteien*, passim; Dixon, "A Family Business," 92), it does not necessarily follow that the wishes or feelings of the women involved were never consulted; for example, see Cic. *ad Att.* 6.6.1, where *mulieres* surely refers to Terentia and Tullia. Marriages were ordinarily arranged by the parents of the couple, and technically a daughter might only refuse her parents' choice on grounds of moral turpitude: Pomeroy, "Married Woman," 220; S. Treggiari, "Consent to Roman Marriage: Some Aspects of Law and Reality," *EMC* 26 (1982): 34–44; B. Rawson, "The Roman Family," in *The Family in Ancient Rome: New Perspectives*, ed. B. Rawson (Ithaca, 1986), 21.

51. App. *BC* 5.53, 5.73; Dio 48.16.3.

52. App. *BC* 5.14.

53. Dio 48.2.4; see also Grüber, *CRRBM*, 2:400–402.

54. Dio 48.5.3–6, 10–12.

55. Dio 48.6.4.

56. App. *BC* 5.20–21, 27.

57. Dio 48.10.

58. The full accounts are Dio 48.10.3–15.1 and App. *BC* 5.21–35. See also Plut. *Ant.* 28; Livy *Per.* 125–26; Vell. 2.74.3; Florus 2.16.2. The classic study remains that of E. Gabba, "The Perusine War and Triumviral Italy," *HSCP* 75 (1971): 139–60.

59. App. *BC* 5.33. See also M. P. Charlesworth, "The Avenging of Caesar," *CAH* 10 (1934): 29; Syme, *Roman Revolution*, 210–11.

60. Dio 48.27.4; App. *BC* 5.59, 5.62; Plut. *Ant.* 30.

61. *Roman Revolution*, 208.

62. App. *BC* 5.54; see also 5.30, 5.39, 5.43, which probably reflect the unfulfilled aspirations of contemporary republican sources. As tribune of the plebs in December 45 or early 44, he carried a bill in the plebeian assembly which gave Caesar the right to name half of the magistrates save consuls in lieu of public election. In mid-44 he served on a special land commission created by Antony to distribute public land among Caesar's veterans and indigent citizens; this measure was no doubt designed to secure the political support of these groups. See *MRR* 2:317, 323, 332–33. On Lucius' career and divided loyalties see J.-M. Roddaz, "Lucius Antonius," *Historia* 37 (1988): 317–46, whose thesis that Augustan propaganda aimed at minimizing Lucius' role in the Perusine War, while exaggerating that of Fulvia, coincides with my own.

63. App. *BC* 5.19. Similarly, in 43 Fulvia, Julia, Antony's son, relatives, and friends had pleaded with influential senators not to declare Antony a public enemy.

64. App. *BC* 5.33.

65. Nep. 25.9. Fulvia became embroiled in litigation and relied on the legal counsel of Cicero's good friend Atticus.

66. App. *BC* 5.14, 5.21.

67. Lefkowitz, "Wives and Husbands," 42. Roman funerary encomia perpetuated the notion that mothering was the universal feminine role (*ILS* 8043, 8493; see also Pomeroy, *Goddesses, Whores, Wives, and Slaves*, 159), and marriage contracts from Roman Egypt regularly included the formula "for the begetting of children": *PSI* VI:730 (first cent. A.D.); *P. Ryl.* IV:612 (early second cent. A.D.); *P. Mich.* VII:434 (early second cent. A.D.); cf. 442 (Karanis, second cent. A.D.). See also T. P. Wiseman, "Lesbia and Her Children," in *Cinna the Poet* (Leicester, 1974), 114, on Catullus 60 and 61.

Hallett, *Fathers and Daughters*, 35–36, 211–61, has argued that elite Roman women were often preoccupied with their roles within the family; see also Clark, "Roman Women," 205. Not only did Roman mothers apply themselves on behalf of their sons, as in the case of Servilia, who was prepared to use her influence with senators to get the grain commission of Brutus rescinded in 44, but also, like Cornelia, they strove all their lives for the realization by their sons of the achievement and status denied themselves by virtue of their sex. On Servilia see Cic. *ad Att.* 15.11.2, 15.12.1. See also T. W. Africa, "The Mask of an Assassin: A Psychohistorical Study of M. Junius Brutus," *J. Interdisc. Hist.* 8 (1978): 599–626. On Cornelia see Plut. *Tib. Gr.* 1, *C. Gr.* 4; App. *BC* 1.20; Pliny *HN* 34.31; *Ins. Ital.* XIII.3:72. In general see Dixon, *The Roman Mother*.

68. The fragments are preserved in *Historicorum romanorum reliquiae*, ed. H. Peter (Leipzig, 1906), 2:54–65, and *Imperatoris Caesaris Augusti operum fragmenta*, 5th ed., by H. Malcovati (Turin, 1969), 84–97. Scholarly studies of the *Memoirs* include F. Blumenthal, "Die Autobiographie des Augustus," *WS* 35 (1913): 113–30, 267–88, 36 (1914): 84–103; T. Vaubel, *Untersuchungen zu Augustuses Politik und Staatsverfassung nach den Autobiographischen Schriften und der seitgenössischen Dichtung* (dissertation, Giessen, 1934); H. Hahn, *Untersuchung zur Autobiographie des Kaiseres Augustus* (dissertation, Leipzig, 1957); Hahn, "Neue Untersuchungen zur Autobiographie des Kaisers Augustus," *NC* 10 (1958–62): 137–48. See also G. Misch, *Geschichte der Autobiographie*, vol. 1, *Das Altertum*, 3d ed. (Frankfurt am Main, 1949).

69. Reflected in Plut. *Ant.* 10, 30; Dio 48.4.1–6, 48.5.3.

70. App. *BC* 5.19, 5.54; see also Syme, *Roman Revolution*, 212; Gabba, "The Perusine War," 148–49; Gabba, *Appiani bellorum civilium liber quintus*, xvii–xxxvi, lix–lxviii.

71. Plut. *Ant.* 30; App. *BC* 5.51, 5.66; see also Dio 58.28.3.

72. For a survey of the ancient source tradition see Huzar, *Mark Antony*, 233–52. To this should be added J. Geiger, "An Overlooked Item of the War of Propaganda between Octavian and Antony," *Historia* 29 (1980): 112–14; Hahn's two studies on the *Memoirs* of Augustus, cited above, note 68; G. Dobesch, "Nikolaus von Damaskus und die Selbstbiographie des Augustus," *Graser Beiträge* 7 (1978): 91–174; B. Scardigli, "Asinius Pollio und Nikolaus von Damaskus," *Historia* 32 (1983): 121–23; G. Delvaux, *Les sources de Plutarque dans les vies parallèles des romains* (dissertation, Université de Bruxelles, 1941); B. Scardigli, *Die Römerbiographien Plutarchs* (Munich, 1979); R. Scuderi, *Commento a Plutarcho "Vita di Antonio"* (Florence, 1984); I. Lana, "Gli scritti di Augusto nelle 'Vita dei Cesari' di Suetonio," *Studi Urbinati* 49 (1975): 437–58; E. Schwartz, *RE* III (1899): cols. 1684–1722, s.v. Cassius Dio; B. Manuwald, *Cassius Dio und Augustus: philologische Untersuchungen zu den Büchern 45–56 des dionischen Gechichtswerkes* (Wiesbaden, 1979); Gabba, *Appiani bellorum civilium liber quintus*; M. Reinhold, *From Republic to Principate: An Historical Commentary on Cassius Dio's Roman History, Books 49–52* (Ithaca, 1988).

73. Dio 48.10.

74. Glaphyra: App. *BC* 5.7; Dio 49.32.3–4; see also G. H. Macurdy, *Vassal-Queens and Some Contemporary Women in the Roman Empire* (Baltimore, 1937), 51–60. On Octavian's composition of epigrams see Suet. *Aug.* 85; *Imperatoris Caesaris Augusti*

operum fragmenta (Malcovati); H. Malcovati, "De Caesaris Augusti poematis," *Athen.* 7 (1919): 52–54; H. Bardon, *Les empereurs et les belles lettres latines d'Auguste à Hadrien* (Paris, 1940), 16–22.

Obscenities scratched on sling bullets shot into Perusia by Octavian's besieging forces suggest sexual assault on Lucius and Fulvia; conversely, sling bullets prepared by Lucius' soldiers imply both sexual attack on and the homosexuality of Octavian (*CIL* XI:6721; cf., however, Suet. *Aug.* 69 for Octavian's sexual proclivities). As Hallett has observed ("Perusinae Glandes," 154–63), the bullets are analogous to Octavian's epigram in that both trivialize the Perusine War by reducing it to a ribald plane; the epigram celebrates Octavian's virility as well.

75. Plut. *Ant.* 24; App. *BC* 5.19; cf. Dio 48.28.3.

76. For a different interpretation see Gabba, *Appiani bellorum civilium liber quintus*, xliii–xlviii and his note at 5.75. Antony's peccadilloes were notorious. From 49 through 45 the actress Valeria Cytheris, whom Cicero cattily dubbed "a second wife," appears to have been Antony's constant companion: *ad Att.* 10.10; *Phil.* 2.58, 2.61–62, 2.77. On the double standard for marital fidelity at Rome see Griffin, *Latin Poets and Roman Life*, 22–24.

77. A special Senate decree had removed the ten-month restriction on remarriage, permitting the recently widowed Octavia to marry Antony late in 40 in order to seal the fragile peace between the triumvirs. The significance of this union, perhaps immortalized in Virgil's Fourth Eclogue, was advertised on coins minted by Antony immediately thereafter: Plut. *Ant.* 30–31; App. *BC* 5.64; for the coins see note 46 above.

Octavia allegedly interceded in 37 to arrange a reconciliation at Tarentum and the exchange of reinforcements by the estranged triumvirs: Plut. *Ant.* 35; App. *BC* 5.93; see also M. W. Singer, "Octavia's Mediation at Tarentum," *CJ* 43 (1947): 172–77. Pomeroy (*Goddesses, Whores, Wives, and Slaves*, 186) reasonably argues that intercession was the only traditionally commendable political activity of Roman women. Octavia, however, appears to have done more than merely bring the parties together: Appian and Plutarch relate that she participated in the actual negotiations, obtaining an additional transfer of twenty ships to Octavian and one thousand soldiers for Antony in preparation for their respective campaigns: Plut. *Ant.* 35; App. *BC* 5.95; cf. Dio 48.54. This pact was sealed by the betrothal of Octavian's infant daughter, Julia, to Antony's son by Fulvia, Antyllus: Suet. *Aug.* 63; Dio 51.15. Notwithstanding Antony's liaison with Cleopatra in the East from 37 to 32, Octavia allegedly furnished reinforcements and supplies to him: Plut. *Ant.* 35–36, 53; Suet. *Aug.* 69; App. *BC* 5.95; Dio 48.54. Although ordered by Octavian to vacate her husband's home, Octavia allegedly refused, remaining to tend to all of Antony's children. In this way her magnanimous behavior sowed even greater dishonor for Antony. In 36, at Antioch, Antony had donated lands under Roman control to Cleopatra and publicly recognized his three children by her. Octavia's trip to Athens the following year may have been intended to force Antony to disclose his aims or, as Plutarch suggests (*Ant.* 53), to provide Octavian with a suitable pretext for hostilities. During the next three years Octavian methodically exploited Antony's desertion of Octavia as he prepared for war. In 32 he seized Anthony's will and had its provisions, which included a second donation to Cleopatra and their children, read in public. That same year Antony divorced Octavia: Plut. *Ant.* 36, 54, 57–58; Suet. *Aug.* 17; Dio 49–50. M. W. Singer, "Octavia Minor, Sister of Augustus: A Historical and Biographical Study" (Ph.D. dissertation, Duke University, 1945), 105–6, argues that the ancient sources exaggerated the role played by Octavia as the virtuous woman scorned and suggests that Octavia was a political pawn of her brother, whom she unwittingly served to far better advantage than Antony.

78. Hor. *Carm.* 1.37.21; see also Prop. 3.11.30, 3.11.39; Verg. *Aen.* 8.685–723; Plut. *Ant.* 10, 60; App. *BC* 5.8; Dio 48.24.1, 48.27.2–3, 49.34.1, 50.15, 50.33. On the propaganda against Cleopatra and the declaration of war see Syme, *Roman Revolution*, 274; J. R. Johnson, "Augustan Propaganda: The Battle of Actium, Mark Antony's Will, the 'Fasti Capitolini Consulares' and Early Imperial Historiography" (Ph.D. dissertation, University of California, Los Angeles, 1976); M. Reinhold, "The Declaration of War against Cleopatra," *CJ* 77 (1982): 97–103; Griffin, *Latin Poets and Roman Life*, 41; I. Becher, *Das Bild der Kleopatra in der griechischen und lateinischen Literatur*, Deutsche Akad. Wiss. Schriften f. Altertumswiss. 51 (Berlin, 1966).

79. Pomeroy, *Goddesses, Whores, Wives and Slaves*, 185.

80. *Concordia*: Plut. *Mor.* 139F–140A, 140E–F, 143E; *CIL* VI:1527 = *ILS* 8393 (Rome, late first cent. B.C.); see also Crook, *Law and Life of Rome*, 99; Lefkowitz, "Wives and Husbands," 42–45. Obedience: Plaut. *Amph.* 839–42; Cato 61.144–46; Catull. 61.144–45; Plut. *Mor.* 141A–B, 142E; *CIL* VI:10230 = *ILS* 8394 (Rome, Augustan period); see also G. Williams, "Some Aspects of Roman Marriage Ceremonies and Ideals," *JRS* 48 (1958): 19–20; T. E. V. Pearce, "The Role of the Wife as *Custos*," *Eranos* 72 (1974): 20–21. Domesticity: *CIL* VI:15346 = *ILS* 8043 = *ROL* IV:18 (Rome, late second cent. B.C.); cf. *ILS* 8394 (Rome, Augustan period; mentioned just above). Octavia: Plut. *Ant.* 31; Suet. *Aug.* 73.

81. Veturia: Livy 2.40; Plut. *Cor.* 33–34. Hortensia: App. *BC* 4.32–34; Val. Max. 8.3.3; Quintil. 1.1.6.

82. Pomeroy (*Goddesses, Whores, Wives, and Slaves*, 185–86) notes the contrast of Fulvia and Octavia; Finley ("Silent Women of Rome," 125) observes that the paragon of virtue was a fiction, an ideal formulated and imposed by Roman males during the Republic and early Empire; cf. Pomeroy, *Goddesses, Whores, Wives, and Slaves*, 149.

NATALIE BOYMEL KAMPEN

Between Public and Private:

Women as Historical Subjects in Roman Art

Goddesses and female personifications in great number and variety appear in Roman historical reliefs among the multitudes of soldiers, emperors, barbarians, and gods; as for mortal women, there are few: empresses, several vestal virgins, female barbarians, and some women in crowd scenes. Historical reliefs adorned public buildings and monuments in most parts of the Roman Empire from the first century B.C. on.[1] They generally have a propaganda function and thus deal with episodes considered to be history in the terms defined by Roman male historians. War, public speeches, administrative acts and sacrificial offerings by emperors, and conduct that demonstrated the leader's virtues were favored subjects. The formal exclusion of Roman women from the military and most government roles may seem to justify their rarity in this genre, but literature, inscriptions of women officeholders and civic patrons, and other artistic genres show that women were involved de facto in politics as well as in all kinds of economic and religious roles that brought them into public places.[2] Further, images of mortal women were both acceptable and common everywhere in the Roman world. Women were recipients of statues made in their honor for public spaces, and they were patrons for funerary monuments, buildings, and public works.[3] The case of Plancia Magna, discussed in this volume by Mary Taliaferro Boatwright, exemplifies the ability of wealthy women to exercise power in public despite the dominant ideology of female incapacity and domesticity.

Three previously unexplored questions emerge from a feminist consideration of historical reliefs. First, why are there so few women on historical reliefs when literary, epigraphic, and visual evidence reveals women as often active public historical subjects? Second, why so few women when there are so many on coins, which are equally burdened with political and propaganda functions? And third, why not a total exclusion of women from the historical reliefs: what do the exceptions tell us about the rules of genre and those of gender?

I shall answer these questions in reverse order, starting with the last one—about the existence and meaning of the exceptional images of women on the historical reliefs. My answers about the rules of genre will also deal with the problem of coin imagery, and my discussion of the rules of gender will suggest an explanation for the rarity of women on the historical reliefs. My primary focus is the imagery of the empress Julia Domna on the Severan Arch at Leptis Magna in Libya, a monument dated to ca. 206–209 and made to commemorate the Severan family's visit in 203 to the birthplace of the emperor Septimius Severus. I begin with a discussion of a number of related earlier monuments, in a typological arrangement, to locate the imagery of Julia Domna in the context of the conventions of female representation in Roman historical art and Roman thinking about gender.

A brief examination of the major types of images of women on historical reliefs will establish the framework for a more lengthy and specific investigation of the use and meaning of the empress in her rare appearances in historical programs. My hypothesis is that women's images were used on public historical reliefs because they were uniquely recognizable signs of the private world. Set into a public context and noticeable precisely because of their rarity, women's images carried special meaning about the ideal and idealized relationship between public and private, and they appeared during three periods in which that relationship was of primary concern to the Roman ruling class: the time of Augustus (and to a lesser extent that of his heirs, the Julio-Claudians), of the Antonine emperors, and of Septimius Severus. Women's images in these periods helped to define the nature of the Roman social and political universe.

The first category of representation includes Roman and provincial women who appear in the audience at public events. My examples come from two important monuments in Rome: women of the provinces can be seen on the Column of Trajan of about 110 A.D.,[4] and a Roman woman appears in one of the panel reliefs of Marcus Aurelius in Rome, dated around 176.[5] On the Column of Trajan we see the emperor traveling through the provinces on his way to battle the Dacians along the Danube. He enters a prosperous town, and there assembled townspeople and pacified frontier folk join him at a sacrifice (fig. 1). Behind the apparent documentary realism of the column stands a political message of which the women in the audience are a part; they represent the whole community of people who live in a civilized environment, testimony to the benefits of Roman rule for every man, woman, and child. And all are present because they mean Everyone. Just as the barbarian family could be a sign for a community in defeat (see below), so here the presence of women and children signifies the whole and implies a happy future as well as the benefits of *romanitas* to both public and private realms.

The appearance of a woman on the *liberalitas* panel of Marcus Aurelius reused on the Arch of Constantine can be interpreted in the same way (fig. 2). The panel shows Marcus Aurelius distributing money to the Romans and symbolizes his generous concern for the people.[6] The few figures below his platform include two men with children and a woman dressed as a respectable matron, all there to represent the community as a whole and the imperial benevolence in relation to public and to private worlds. Marcus Aurelius' generosity helps to guarantee a peaceful and prosperous future for the Romans, a future of which the woman and the children are symbols and guarantors. Again, it is worth noting that women appear in public settings on these reliefs but signify the ramifications of the actions of emperor and state on the private realm. In turn, the well-being of the private world of the family guarantees the health of the public world of which it is the foundation. Ultimately the private roles of women are to be understood as political and thus public in their consequences.

A second category of women on historical reliefs is the vestal virgins. They appear on a number of monuments as part of state sacrifices at which their attendance was mandatory.[7] They may also have been used in several instances (including a base in Sorrento and a relief in Palermo) to commemorate the emperor Augustus' dedication of a statue and altar to Vesta on the Palatine in 12 B.C.[8] There the vestals appear in connection with a specific event and honor not only the cult they serve but the emperor whose generosity and piety have benefited them.

Banqueting vestals appear on a first-century A.D. relief (fig. 3) erected in Rome probably to honor the deceased empress Livia.[9] The connection between Livia and the vestals during her lifetime was close; in fact the Senate voted her the honors traditionally reserved only for the priestesses, among whom she was even permitted to sit at public events.[10] As

Figure 1. Rome, Column of Trajan, detail: provincial town with native populace,
ca. A.D. 110. Deutsches Archäologisches Institut, InstNeg. 31.375.

protector of the family and the state, Vesta was an ideal model and association for the empress, whose posthumous monument reinforced the
connection of public and private realms through the appearance of the
vestal virgins. The recurrent use of coin legends of Vesta for reigning
empresses into the third century attests the strength of these associations
throughout Roman imperial history.[11]

The last two categories I consider here are also, relatively speaking, the
most common. Representations of empresses and female barbarians on
historical reliefs carry many of the messages alluded to above, of women
other than vestals as symbolic of reproductive sexuality, the family, and
the happiness and prosperity of community and the future. In turning to
empresses and female barbarians, I also turn attention to the program of
the arch at Leptis Magna made for the family of Septimius Severus, who

Figure 2. Rome, Arch of Constantine, detail: *liberalitas* of Marcus Aurelius, ca. A.D. 176. Fototeca Unione, Rome, no. 28746.1988.

Figure 3. Rome, Museo Conservatori: banqueting vestals, ca. A.D. 50. DAI
InstNeg. 36.201.

ruled from 193 to 211 A.D. Because political events have prevented me
from seeing the monument except in photographs, I have avoided commenting on the style and technique of carving the reliefs. In the course of
discussing the arch, I do consider earlier and contemporary monuments
as they represent both imperial and barbarian women and illuminate the
generic and iconographic traditions and gender assumptions on which
the arch's imagery is based.

As noted earlier, the arch was decorated sometime after the imperial
family's visit to Leptis, the emperor's birthplace, in 203, and it is an
extraordinary monument not least because of the unusual presence of the

empress Julia Domna. Although she appears regularly in public statuary and on coins and medallions[12] and enjoyed enormous public importance in the Severan period, she is represented only a few times in historical reliefs.

The empress was regarded as striking, clever, and exotic, but the written sources of the period are relatively poor, and we know only pieces of her biography.[13] Coming from Syria, Julia Domna married Septimius Severus in 186 and became empress when he overcame the other contenders for the throne after the death of the emperor Pertinax in 193. She bore two sons, Caracalla and Geta, and lived to see Geta murdered by his brother a year after Septimius Severus' death in 211. In addition to being famed for her intellect, attested in a book of the Second Sophistic which has a chapter on the philosophical circle of which she was patron, the empress seems to have been tremendously influential.[14] According to the contemporary third-century historian Dio Cassius, she went with her husband and son on their campaigns, may have served as official head of the bureaus of petitions and briefs, *a libellis* and *ab epistulis*, and may even have attended the Senate.[15] Honored by some ancient writers as loyal and long-suffering, vilified by others in the usual Roman clichés as an adulteress and traitor to her husband's interests and regularly accused of angling for public power, Julia Domna died in 218, a year after Caracalla.[16]

The Severan arch, a quadrifrons or four-arched block that no longer stands, had four large panels of relief on the attic.[17] Below, on the outer façades, were depicted barbarian captives, garlands, mythological reliefs, and flying victories; on the inner faces of the piers were eleven panels of historical and mythological imagery. The reliefs are now displayed in the Museum of the Red Castle in Tripoli, Libya, and will someday be published in monographic form. The most recent study has used style and iconography to date the reliefs convincingly between 206 and 209.[18]

The four large panels on the attic measure about 21 feet wide by 5½ to 6 feet high; they were meant to be seen from a distance and to contribute to a general impression of grandeur and triumph. Julia Domna plays an important part in at least two and perhaps three of the reliefs. She is involved in the sacrifice (fig. 4), watches her husband and sons express their royal accord (fig. 8), and may in addition greet the three men in one of the scenes of triumphal entrance (figs. 12a, 12b).

At the sacrifice (fig. 4) only the empress is easy to recognize; the faces of some of the men are damaged, and the center of the panel is lost. Sol-

Figure 4. Tripoli, Red Fort: relief from the Severan Arch of Leptis Magna showing sacrifice of Severan family, A.D. 206–209. Negatives courtesy V. M. Strocka.

diers, civilians, attendants, and sacrificial oxen look in from the sides of the scene toward the now-missing central altar. To the left of the altar stands an unidentified man in a breastplate; to the right is Julia Domna. The middle probably showed the emperor and his sons at the altar; this is likely both because of the content of the scene as a whole and because it follows the centralized and symmetrical composition present in almost all the other reliefs of the arch.

The sacrifice scene differs from most of the sacrifices on Roman public monuments because of the presence of the empress. The best-known precedent for this image comes from the Ara Pacis Augustae of 13–9 B.C. (fig. 5), which shows Augustus, the first emperor, in a religious procession with women and children of the court.[19] An article by Diana Kleiner on these family reliefs has shown that the striking and unusual presence of women and children along with male members of the court and the Senate is meant to signal ideal sexual and familial responsibility.[20] In the wake of the Augustan marriage and adultery laws enacted a few years earlier, upper-class Romans were expected to follow the putative lead of the court by marrying and bearing legitimate children rather than avoiding their responsibilities and following paths of pleasure and decadence. The Ara Pacis used family imagery to reinforce that message as well as to emphasize the great family of potential heirs to the throne, heirs who were insurance against the resumption of civil strife.

Historical reliefs made under later emperors generally adhere to the imagery of sacrifices by men without female family members present. The only post-Augustan exception to the rule, other than the ones in the Severan period, may come from the Parthian victory monument of the emperor Lucius Verus from Ephesus in Asia Minor.[21] Dated to the 170s, these reliefs have tentatively been restored by the Antiquities Museum in Vienna as decoration for a monumental altar.[22] The friezes include scenes of divinities, place personifications, victory or apotheosis scenes, a great battle, and a family ceremony. In the last of these, fragmentary evidence appears for the presence of women and children in association with a sacrifice (fig. 6) and with the adoption by Hadrian of Antoninus Pius, who in turn adopts Marcus Aurelius and Lucius Verus (fig. 7).[23] The adoption attempted to create a dynasty out of several generations where there were no blood heirs. It is impossible to identify any of the women here, so fragmentary or idealized are their features, but the parallels with the Leptis arch and the Ara Pacis are clear.[24] Not only are imperial women

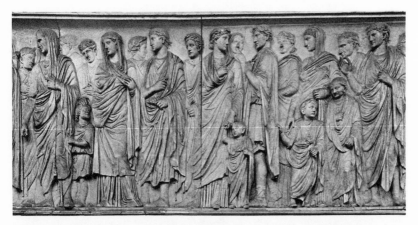

Figure 5. Rome, Ara Pacis Augustae: detail of frieze with imperial family, 13–9
B.C. Fototeca Unione, Rome, no. 3247F.1957.

part of a scene with a sacrifice, but they also appear in conjunction with
the fictional ceremony that creates the dynasty. The imperial women at
Ephesus and on the Ara Pacis, as on the Leptis arch, function as a sign
for a specifically family-oriented program; in it, private and state realms
blend for political purposes.

The empress appears on the Leptis Arch in a second large panel dominated by a handshake (fig. 8). In the center of the relief, among male
citizens and soldiers distributed to the left and right respectively, Septimius Severus clasps the right hand of his older son, Caracalla; Geta stands
between them, and the clasped hands draw attention to him as he turns
slightly toward his father. Watching the *dextrarum iunctio*, the clasping of
right hands, are a military officer, some togate men, personifications of
military virtue, and, at the left, the damaged figure of the empress.[25]

Like the adoption scene on the Parthian monument at Ephesus (fig. 7),
which invents a historical moment that never existed, the Leptis handshake scene probably does not refer to one specific ceremony but to a
symbolic or stereotypic act comparable to the sacrifice just discussed.[26]
That act is the *concordia augustorum*, the harmonious agreement of imperial family members that can be seen on coins with this legend.[27] The
civilian group at the left plays against the military at the right to continue
the notion of concord through the harmony of the imperial family; this all
takes place under the approving eyes of the statuary deities and personifi-

Figure 6. Vienna, Antikensammlung, Kunsthistorisches Museum: relief AS I 882, from the Parthian Monument from Ephesus, women and children, ca. A.D. 169–176. Kunsthistorisches Museum, Antikensammlung, Vienna III.14.237.

Figure 7. Vienna, Antikensammlung, Kunsthistorisches Museum: relief AS I 864, from the Parthian Monument from Ephesus, adoption, ca. A.D. 169–176. Kunsthistorisches Museum, Antikensammlung, Vienna III.18.008.

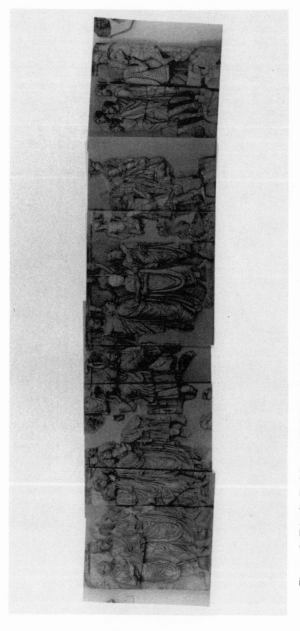

Figure 8. Tripoli, Red Fort: relief from the Severan Arch of Leptis Magna showing imperial concord, A.D. 206–209. Negatives courtesy V. M. Strocka.

cations who locate the scene at Leptis Magna. When family, military, and citizens all agree, the result is, predictably, a world at peace.

Julia Domna's presence in the concord scene makes use of a complex set of models. Emperors shaking hands with their male kin, with gods, or with personifications of places and virtues are found often on coins but are rarer in sculpture.[28] On funerary reliefs from all parts of the empire, women clasp the hands of their husbands (fig. 9); these reliefs document the affection between the couples, whose relationship is made clear by their use of a gesture associated with the wedding ceremony.[29] The two elements, one made for the state, the other for private citizens, eventually come together in the art of the Antonine dynasty in the second and third quarters of the second century. Because of their interest in family relationships, Antoninus Pius and his adopted successors, Lucius Verus and Marcus Aurelius, brought the family *dextrarum iunctio* to new prominence. Their goals were to reestablish traditional values and customs and to legitimize a family created through adoptions and cemented by the marriage of a daughter, Faustina the Younger, with an adopted son, Marcus Aurelius. Coins showed the imperial couple clasping hands under the legend *concordia* (fig. 10), imperially instituted ceremonies for newlyweds made use of the gesture at a sacrifice to the concord of the imperial couple, and eventually even the biographical sarcophagi of the wealthy at Rome, made in the later Antonine and early Severan period (fig. 11), incorporated concord as a virtue demonstrated by a marriage scene.[30] The conflation of the *dextrarum iunctio* by male rulers with the marital gesture of family concord resulted in the odd and unprecedented group at Leptis Magna. Julia Domna watches her husband and sons demonstrate their accord, and thus the peace attendant on a legitimate succession, and she becomes the sign that this act is both familial and dynastic, personal and political.

The last two attic panels of the Leptis arch, which were once almost identical, show a procession with the emperor and his sons in a triumphal chariot. With them are soldiers and male citizens as well as a group of barbarian prisoners. Among the walking and standing male captives we can see a woman with a small child on a litter (figs. 12a, 12b). In front, a boy is being dragged along. In this pathetic and visually arresting group the boy resists, while the infant trying to attract its mother's attention cannot rouse her from her misery. The panels take over standard motifs from triumphal art and develop and emotionalize them to new effect. I

Figure 9. Copenhagen, Ny Carlsberg Glyptotek: funerary relief of Turpilia from Aquileia, ca. A.D. 50. Ny Carlsberg Glyptotek Inv. no. 800.

Figure 10. London, British Museum: coin of Faustina I with obverse portrait and reverse *detrarum iunctio*, ca. A.D. 145. Courtesy the Trustees of the British Museum.

Figure 11. Florence, Uffizi: biographical sarcophagus, ca. A.D. 150. Alinari/Art Resource PIN 1308.

will return to the theme of the female barbarian captive; she is important not only for her relationship to the empress here at Leptis but also because she is the most common mortal woman on historical relief sculpture, and her meaning in relation to imperial and gender ideology needs discussion.[31]

Nowhere in the well-preserved panel of triumphal entrance (fig. 12a) can Julia Domna be seen, but in the more fragmentary version (fig. 12b) she appears in a puzzling way. Two main sections of the latter are preserved: the first has the group of prisoners, and the second some soldiers, part of the chariot, and the upper part of a woman with or before a palm branch. The hairstyle and facial features are Julia Domna's, but her loca-

Figure 12a. Tripoli, Red Fort: relief from the Severan Arch of Leptis Magna showing triumphal entry of men of the imperial family, A.D. 206–209. Negatives courtesy V. M. Strocka.

Figure 12b. Tripoli, Red Fort: relief from the Severan Arch of Leptis Magna showing triumphal entry of men of the imperial family, A.D. 206–209. Negatives courtesy V. M. Strocka.

tion in front of the horses is peculiar; no precedents exist, as far as I know, for an empress associated with these elements of military victory.

The proposed restoration of Julia Domna near the female prisoner does, however, have some parallels that suggest intent, rather than just restorers' liberties. Comparing the relief with the Grand Camée de France (fig. 13), a court gemstone of the second quarter of the first century A.D., reveals similar relationships.[32] Members of the imperial family, including Livia, mother of Tiberius and widow of Augustus, appear in a register above defeated barbarian families. Both pieces show that the future is based on the survival or defeat, not just of the individual, but of the family. The barbarian woman with babe in arms signals the depth of defeat suffered by her society, just as Livia, beneath her divine spouse and next to her ruling son, is the crucial link in the chain of enduring dynastic power.

The increased interest, in the art of the second century, in this motif of the pathetic conquered barbarian family, as exemplified in its occurrence on the Column of Marcus Aurelius in Rome and on biographical sarcophagi of the same period, demonstrates similar concerns.[33] Not only is there a new sense of urgency to representations that show the totality of Roman conquest, the obliteration of the threat even into the next generations, but the recurrent lack of legitimate male heirs and legitimate claims to the throne in the dynastic history of Antonine and Severan Rome would certainly have encouraged the use of an extended family iconography, signaled by the presence of the women and children, in Roman propaganda art.

The panels on the inner faces of the arches, smaller than the attic reliefs, 4 by 6½ feet, are very badly damaged and hard to read, but among them are two which may have shown Julia Domna. More than half the panels contain images of gods and personifications: Apollo with Diana, Mars with Venus Genetrix, and the Capitoline Triad with Tyche. In this last group the figures of Jupiter and Juno are now faceless, but both wear the hairstyles of the imperial couple (fig. 14). Such association of royal figures with divinities is hardly uncommon for the Romans or for Hellenistic rulers before them; the tradition can be seen from a relief of the second quarter of the first century A.D. in Ravenna (fig. 15). Augustus there is usually identified as Jupiter and his companion, Venus Genetrix, as Livia.[34] The emperor and empress are more than mirrors of divine individuals; they have taken the form of the divine family as well.

Figure 13. Paris, Bibliothèque Nationale: Grand Camée de France, first half of first century A.D. Bibliothèque Nationale C200324.

The only other place where Julia Domna might have appeared among the small interior panels is in a family sacrifice (fig. 16). Missing a large chunk in the center, the relief shows the emperor and at least one of his sons and, to his right, a headless man and the lower part of a woman, all accompanied by personifications and statues of gods connected with

Figure 14. Tripoli, Red Fort: relief from the Severan Arch of Leptis Magna showing Capitoline Triad and Tyche. DAI InstNeg. 61.1713.

Figure 15. Ravenna, Museo Nazionale Archeologico: relief with divinized members of Augustan court, second quarter of the first century A.D.
DAI InstNeg. 35.821.

Leptis Magna and the royal house. Whether one can safely identify the woman as Julia Domna is still unclear, but the emperor and empress with their sons in a centralized and symmetrical composition would fit with the organization of the panels elsewhere on the arch. And as has already been noted, the motif of the family at a sacrifice, although hardly common, has models in Roman public and private art from the Ara Pacis to the Arch of the Argentarii in Rome.

The Leptis arch offers Julia Domna in several panels where women would not ordinarily be seen but for which there are imperial models. The small interior panels may show the empress as Juno and may put her into the small sacrifice group. The large panels of the attic place her in a sacrifice, a scene of concord, and perhaps also in one of the two trium-

Figure 16. Tripoli, Red Fort: relief from the Severan Arch of Leptis Magna showing a sacrifice. DAI InstNeg. 61.1711.

phant entry scenes. The program of the arch centers on the reconciliation of public and private worlds, on harmonious relationships among family members, among dynastic past, present and future, and among the various parts of the Roman universe. Julia Domna's presence is essential to the explication of this program, more essential than respecting the dominant traditions that usually excluded imperial women from historical relief sculpture.

Julia Domna's position as link, as creator of harmony, begins with her roles as wife and mother in the hypothetically harmonious family. She signifies family in the concord and sacrifice scenes as well as in the Capitoline Triad panel. Her coins, showing her as Venus Genetrix, Juno Regina, and Vesta Mater and presenting her with her sons, as well as her familial role on the Arch of the Argentarii in Rome, all fit this mold.[35]

As wife and mother the empress also served as a link to the imperial past, especially in her consciously evoked association with Augustus' wife Livia and with the preceding generations of Antonine women. Septimius Severus' self-adoption into the Antonine dynasty in 195 was symptomatic of his desire to legitimize his reign and that of his heirs.[36] As a usurper he needed as many connections with the past as possible; emulating the imperial adoptions of the Antonines in the second century, he gave himself and Caracalla Antonine names, appropriated the Antonine private treasury, and made himself the posthumous heir to Marcus Aurelius. Julia Domna's function in this scheme has not been recognized, but I think she evoked for viewers the memory of Faustina the Elder, wife of Antoninus Pius, and of Faustina the Younger, their daughter and the wife of their heir, Marcus Aurelius.

The iconography of the Arch of the Argentarii and the Leptis arch, with their emphasis on family *concordia*, may well be drawn from such Antonine sources as coins with imperial couples or the column base of Antoninus Pius in Rome (fig. 17).[37] Made about 161, the front of the column base shows the apotheosis of Antoninus Pius and Faustina, the latter by then dead almost twenty years; on the sides two scenes of funeral games, almost exactly the same, seem to indicate that the patrons of the base, the adopted sons Lucius Verus and Marcus Aurelius, each honored their parents.[38] The analogy with the two scenes of triumphant entrance on the Leptis arch may indicate a comparable attempt to stress symmetrical filial piety and family unity as well as a connection with the Antonines. Similarly, the Parthian monument at Ephesus, with its family group and em-

Figure 17. Rome, Vatican Museums: column base of Antoninus Pius, detail of apotheosis, ca. A.D. 161. Vatican Museums XXVI.24.98.

phasis on dynastic continuity, military victory, and imperialism, blends the same issues and demonstrates their wide diffusion in this period. Such Antonine monuments, like the contemporary biographical sarco-phagi, may be seen as models for the iconography of the Severan family. They make the connection between Julia Domna, wife and mother, and Antonine wives and mothers and thus connect the Severan family more closely with its chosen past.

In the Severan arch at Leptis, Julia Domna is the link among elements from the present and the past. As mother of her sons she is, perhaps most importantly, the link with the future. Her reproductive success guaran-tees the future of the Severan dynasty, and her coin legends, *Fortuna Felix* and *Fortuna Saeculi*, express in words the messages of the Leptis arch.

The messages about family and reproduction would have been rein-forced still further if Julia Domna had appeared in the entrance procession of the Leptis arch, but the state of preservation and conservation of the arch (as noted above) makes that uncertain. Near both the chariot and the barbarians, she would have reminded the viewer that the Roman family stood in permanent and happy contrast to the miserable conquered barbarians. The mother of the ruling family, Julia Domna was to see a future with power, peace, and an enduring dynasty, whereas the barbarian mother watched her future dragged along in bondage.

Thus Julia Domna played a central role in the program of the Leptis arch; she was a sign of harmony and continuity. Her presence defines for us and for the Romans the family nature of the arch and separates it from military triumphal monuments. She explains the nature of the monument and its propaganda scheme by virtue not only of her various roles in the reliefs but as well by the mere fact of her presence. Despite being the most public woman of her time, Julia Domna represents reproduction and family, the private roles identified with women. She is a symbol for private values that nonetheless reverberate in the public realm and so could be appropriated by the public sector for political purposes.

A similar appropriation can be detected both in the other historical reliefs I have discussed and in imperial coins. Although the images of royal women are common on coins, there is seldom an instance where the coin legends and the iconography diverge from the dominant ideological patterns that associate women with the private world; they stand for the continuity of the dynasty, the health of the empire, and the virtues of reproductive and familial life. No thorough study of gender iconography has been done for Roman coins, but it is clear even from superficial study that the coins use women to express the programmatic concerns of the state and the emperor.[39] The imperial women on coins appear as identifiable individuals and as members of a dynasty, and by virtue of their legends and attributes they also stand for abstract political and social concepts necessary to the regime. Whether their greater frequency on coins than historical reliefs has to do with genre or format conventions or with possible distinctions between the emblematic and the narrative is unclear; that they were essential on coins as surrogates for the ruler, the dynasty, and the empire as a whole seems clear. In expressing especially those values of the Roman state that were traditionally embodied in the cultural construct of Woman—fecundity, prosperity, continuity—the female members of the Roman imperial family could become symbols for Woman as well as for particular political issues even as they remained within the bounds of a conservative gender ideology.

Conservatism is the key concept to emerge from this discussion of the representation of women on Roman historical reliefs. As a propagandistic form that presents idealizing narratives of power and kinship, historical relief uses both conservative politics and a conservative visual iconography. When women appear at all in this public framework, gender symbolism, rooted in associative traditionalism, places them firmly in the private realm of family and reproduction.

With a few exceptions such as the female barbarians, most of the women on historical reliefs appeared in times when the regime was most uncertain about issues of reproduction, legitimacy, and dynastic succession. The desire to revitalize traditional sexual and family conduct in times of social change had as its deeper goal the strengthening of family, class, and community relationships, and women became both instruments and symbols for this goal. Augustus and his heirs expressed their concern for the growth of the aristocracy and for their own dynastic succession by the iconography of Livia and the vestals, protectors of family and state. Under the Antonines, whose adoptive dynasty required the fiction of blood kinship and the reinforcement of affectionate marriages, the imperial women, contrasted with barbarians and modeled on Livia, again functioned as crucial elements on historical reliefs. And finally, under Septimius Severus, in a time of social and military instability, Julia Domna came to be used in a similar way. That Septimius Severus was the first emperor to permit soldiers in the all-important Roman army to marry and thus to aid romanization and produce legitimate sons for the reproduction of the military and security of the empire adds a new dimension to the iconography.[40] Now marital and familial concord and reproduction became necessary underpinnings of an imperialism verging on crisis. Unlike the Augustan use of historical relief as part of the program designed to give new moral and reproductive vitality to the Roman family, the Severans used the iconography of the empress as part of a program to create new Roman families and thus to safeguard the future of the empire.

The family stands as the traditional Roman social unit, the basis as well as the symbol of political, economic, and imperial relations. Woman, as the sign of family, had to be represented in public art as domestic and privatized; yet implicit in that representation is her centrality to the well-being of the state. The ambivalence revealed not only in the attitudes of Roman male writers toward women but as well in the conflicting evidence is in large measure due to that deeper and often unacknowledged uneasiness about women who are both marginal and privatized and central and public. Historical relief, in what it shows and what it leaves out, mystifies gender relationships and at the same time expresses the ambivalent Roman attitude toward women.

Notes

My thanks, as ever, to John Dunnigan and Sharon Strom for discussing this material with me, to the members of audiences to whom versions of this essay were presented over the past few years, and especially to Elizabeth Bartman for obtaining photographs and to V. M. Strocka for graciously lending me his negatives for the friezes at Leptis Magna. New photos of the restored reliefs could not be obtained in time for the publication of this volume.

1. "Historical relief" is a modern term coined for sculpture that presents identifiable people as the actors in specific or typical happenings connected with public governance, cult, and the military. Historical reliefs usually appeared on public buildings, altars, and triumphal monuments such as the Column of Trajan and the Arch of Titus in Rome. Bibliography on the historical relief can be found in Gerhard Koeppel, "Official State Reliefs of the City of Rome in the Imperial Age: A Bibliography," in *Aufstieg und Niedergang der römischen Welt (ANRW)*, edited by Hildegard Temporini and Wolfgang Haase (Berlin and New York: Walter de Gruyter, 1982), II.12.1, 480–81. For recent work see Tonio Hölscher, "Beobachtungen zu römischen historischen Denkmälern," *Archäologischer Anzeiger* (1979): 337–48, (1984) 2:283–94; Hölscher, "Die Geschichtsauffassung in der römischen Repräsentationskunst," *Jahrbuch des Deutschen Archäologischen Instituts* 95 (1980): 265–321; and several publications by Gerhard Koeppel: "The Grand Pictorial Tradition of Roman Historical Representation during the Early Empire," *ANRW* II.12.1 (1982): 507–35; "Die historischen Reliefs der römischen Kaiserzeit I: stadtrömische Denkmäler unbekannter Bauzugehörigkeit aus augusteischer und julisch-claudischer Zeit," *Bonner Jahrbücher* 183 (1983): 61–144; "Die historischen Reliefs der römischen Kaiserzeit I: stadtrömische Denkmäler unbekannter Bauzugehörigkeit aus flavischer Zeit," 184 (1984): 1–65; "Die historischen Reliefs der römischen Kaiserzeit I: stadtrömische Denkmäler unbekannter Bauzugehörigkeit aus trajanischer Zeit," 185 (1985): 143–213; and "Die historischen Reliefs der römischen Kaiserzeit I: stadtrömische Denkmäler unbekannter Bauzugehörigkeit aus hadrianischer bis konstantinischer Zeit," 186 (1986): 1–90; as well as my own forthcoming study of provincial historical reliefs.

2. See, for example, Ramsey MacMullen, "Women in Public in the Roman Empire," *Historia* 29 (1980): 208–18.

3. On women honored by statues see MacMullen, "Women in Public," and Götz

Lahusen, *Untersuchungen zur Ehrenstatue in Rom: literarische und epigraphische Zeugnisse*, Archeologica 35 (Rome: Giorgio Bretschneider Editore, 1983), for empresses, e.g., 36 (Livia); 39 n. 277 (Iulia Titi); 22, (Sabina); 36 (Faustina I); for nonroyals, e.g., 39 n. 277 (Paterna Nomia). On women as patrons for public monuments see Joseph C. Rockwell, *Private Baustiftungen für die Stadtgemeinde auf Inschriften der Kaiserzeit im Westen des römischen Reiches* (Jena: Universitäts-Buchdruckerei von G. Neuenhahn, 1909), 86–88.

4. The locus classicus for the Column of Trajan is Karl Lehmann-Hartleben, *Die Trajanssäule* (Berlin and Leipzig: Walter de Gruyter, 1926), and more recently Werner Gauer, *Untersuchungen zur Trajanssäule*, vol. 1 (Berlin: Gebruder Mann Verlag, 1977). I am currently preparing a paper about the women on Trajan's Column, a topic not much noted despite a number of interesting representations of women in public settings.

5. For the Column of Marcus Aurelius see Giovanni Becatti, "Colonna di Marco Aurelio," *Enciclopedia dell'arte antica classica ed orientale* 2 (1959): 760–63. For representations of women see, for example, Giovanni Becatti, *La Colonna di Marco Aurelio* (Milan: Domus Editore, 1957), figs. 13–14, 31, 43–45, 56, 61–66. It is interesting that the few scenes in which Roman soldiers brutalize barbarian women and children occur here and on the Gemma Augustea; the former are unsurprising given the often-remarked brutality of the soldiers toward the enemy on the column, but the occurrence of the hair-pulling motif on the Gemma has not been satisfactorily explained.

6. It has recently been suggested by Elizabeth Angelicoussis, "The Panel Reliefs of Marcus Aurelius," *Mitteilungen des Deutschen Archäologischen Instituts, Römische Abteilung (RömMitt)* 91.1 (1984): 141–205, that the emperor appeared with his now-removed son Commodus, whose figure was replaced after his *damnatio memoriae* in 193–194. The iconographic strength of this combination of father and son in the context of the historical *liberalitas* of 177 and the presence of a woman and children in the relief supports that suggestion, confirmed as well by Maria Laura Cafiero in *Rilievi storici Capitolini*, ed. Eugenio LaRocca (Rome: De Luca Editore, 1986), 43–44.

7. No major study of the artistic representations of the vestal virgins exists, although important work has been done on individual monuments. See, for example, Inez Scott Ryberg, *Rites of the State Religion in Roman Art*, an entire issue of *Memoirs of the American Academy in Rome* 22 (1955), 59–75. A superb study of the vestals is Mary Beard, "The Sexual Status of Vestal Virgins," *Journal of Roman Studies* 70 (1980): 12–29.

8. For the Sorrento base and the Palermo relief see Nicola DeGrassi, "La dimora di Augusto sul Palatino e la base di Sorrento," *Atti della Pontificia Accademia Romana di Archeologia, Rendiconti* 39 (1966–67): 77–116.

9. The banqueting vestals have recently appeared in Koeppel, "Die historischen Reliefs . . . augusteischer und julisch-claudischer Zeit," 114–16, with bibliography.

10. For Livia and the vestals see especially Marleen Boudreau Flory, "Sic

Exempla Parantur: Livia's Shrine to Concordia and the Porticus Liviae," *Historia* 33.3 (1983): 309–30, and a paper by Elizabeth Bartman, "Portraits of Livia," presented to American Philological Association Women's Caucus, 1979.

11. For coins with vestal imagery associated with imperial women see, for example, Harold Mattingly, *Coins of the Roman Empire in the British Museum* (London: Trustees of the British Museum, 1923–50), 2:247, no. 144, pl. 47.17 (Julia Titi); 3:106–7, nos. 525–28, pls. 18.12–14 (Plotina); 3:537, no. 1882, pl. 99.2 (Sabina); 4:408, nos. 175–76, pl. 56.15 (Faustina II); 5.1:28, no. 57, pl. 6.17 (Julia Domna). The association seems to appear on coins from the later first century A.D. through the first half of the third century.

12. For some of the many representations of Julia Domna in sculpture see Rendel Schlüter, "Die Bildnisse der Kaiserin Julia Domna" (Ph.D. dissertation, Münster, 1977), which I have not seen, as well as the examples in Klaus Fittschen and Paul Zanker, *Katalog der römischen Porträts in den Capitolinischen Museen und den anderen kommunalen Sammlungen der Stadt Rom*, vol. 3.1-2, *Kaiserinnen- und Prinzessinnenbildnisse/Frauenporträts* (Mainz: Philipp von Zabern, 1983), 27–30 and pls. 38–40 with literature; on the coins and medallions see Mattingly, *Coins of the Roman Empire*, vol. 5.1, passim.

13. For the biographical information about Julia Domna, see *Historia Augusta* Severus 3.9, 21.6–8; Dio Cassius 75.3.1, 76.15.6, 76.16.5, 78.2, 78.6.2, 78.10.2, 78.10.4, 78.18.2–3, 79.23–24; Herodian 4.3.8–9.

14. On the philosophical interests of the empress see Dio 76.7 and 78.18.3. For her political influence see Dio 78.18.2–3, 79.23.2–4.

15. See Dio 79.4.2–3.

16. For conflicting assessments of Julia Domna see *Historia Augusta* Severus 18.8; *Historia Augusta* Antoninus Carcalla 10.1–4; Dio 79.24; Herodian 4.3.8–9.

17. For the arch see Renato Bartoccini, "L'arco quadrifronte dei Severi a Lepcis (Leptis Magna)," *Africa Italiana* 4.1 (1931): 32–152, and Volker Michael Strocka, "Beobachtungen an den Attikareliefs des severischen Quadrifrons von Lepcis Magna," *Antiquités africaines* 6 (1972): 147–72.

18. For the date see Strocka, "Beobachtungen an den Attikareliefs," 169–70.

19. On the Ara Pacis see Erika Simon, *Ara Pacis Augustae* (Tübingen: Verlag Ernst Wasmuth, 1967).

20. Diana E. E. Kleiner, "The Great Friezes of the Ara Pacis Augustae," *Mélanges de l'Ecole Française de Rome, Antiquité* 90 (1978): 753–85.

21. For the Parthian monument, currently awaiting definitive publication by Wolfgang Oberleitner, see Oberleitner et al., *Funde aus Ephesos und Samothrake: Katalog der Antikensammlung, Kunsthistorisches Museum, Wien* (Vienna: Verlag Karl Ueberreuter, 1978): 2:66–94.

22. For the reconstruction see the museum catalogue: Oberleitner et al., *Funde*.

23. For the proposed reconstruction of this part of the frieze see Oberleitner et al., *Funde*, fig. 50.

24. Proposed identifications of some of the female figures include Sabina (Oberleitner et al., *Funde*, 80) or Faustina the Elder (*Funde*, 81). I find insufficient evidence to justify any of these identifications.

25. Strocka, "Beobachtungen an den Attikareliefs," 157–60.

26. Strocka, "Beobachtungen an den Attikareliefs," 147–48, who also notes the probable lack of connection between specific historical events and the overall program of the attic reliefs.

27. For *concordia* coins with agreement between royal brothers see, for example, Mattingly, *Coins of the Roman Empire*, 4:409, nos. 186–87, pl. 56.18 (Marcus Aurelius and Lucius Verus), or 5.1:391, no. 178, pl. 57.2 (Caracalla and Geta).

28. Coins: for example, Mattingly, *Coins of the Roman Empire*, 1:381, no. 67, pl. 62.17 (Vitellius with Roma and the label *Pax Augusti*), or 4:732, no. 237, pl. 96.17 (Commodus with Genius Senatus and the label *Pietati Senatus*). *Concordia* in sculpture as well as coins: Richard Brilliant, *Gesture and Rank in Roman Art* (New Haven: Connecticut Academy of Sciences, 1963), 78–79, 88, 92, 98–99, 108–9, 134, 137–38.

29. For the marital *dextrarum iunctio* see Louis Reekmans, "La dextrarum iunctio dans l'iconographie romaine et paléochrétienne," *Bulletin de l'Institut Historique Belge de Rome* 31 (1957): 23–95, as well as Glenys Davies, "The Significance of the Handshake Motif in Classical Funerary Art," *American Journal of Archaeology* 89.4 (October 1985): 637–39. An important recent addition to the examples of the motif in monumental sculpture is the relief of Claudius clasping the hand of Agrippina from the Sebasteion at Aphrodisias: see R. R. R. Smith, "The Imperial Reliefs from the Sebasteion at Aphrodisias," *Journal of Roman Studies* 77 (1987): 88–138, esp. 106–10, catalogue no. 3, pl. VIII.

30. For the Antonine *concordia* of the imperial couple see Gerhart Rodenwaldt, "Über den Stilwandel in der antoninischen Kunst," *Abhandlungen der Preussischen Akademie der Wissenschaften, Philosophisch-historische Klasse* 3 (1935): 14. On the use of marital imagery in biographical sarcophagi see more recently Natalie Boymel Kampen, "Biographical Narration and Roman Funerary Art," *American Journal of Archaeology* 85.1 (1981): 47–58, esp. 51–53, and Davies, "Handshake Motif," 638–39.

31. For the iconography of barbarians see Annalina Calò Levi, *Barbarians on Roman Imperial Coins and Sculpture*, Numismatic Notes and Monographs 123 (New York: American Numismatic Society, 1952). See also, more recently, Yves-Albert Dauge, *Le barbare*, Collection Latomus 176 (Brussels: Latomus, 1981). No work has addressed the gender or family issues in the representation of barbarians.

32. For the Grand Camée de France, see Hans Jucker, "Der grosse Pariser Kameo: eine Huldigung an Agrippina, Claudius und Nero," *Jahrbuch des Deutschen Archäologischen Instituts* 91 (1976): 211–50, with earlier literature. More recent restoration information for the arch reliefs is currently unavailable to me.

33. For barbarian women on the Column of Marcus Aurelius see Becatti, *La Colonna di Marco Aurelio*. For the biographical sarcophagi see note 30 above.

34. For the attributions of the Ravenna relief see, most recently, John Pollini, "Gnaeus Domitius Ahenobarbus and the Ravenna Relief," *RömMitt* 88.1 (1981): 117–40, as well as, among others, Donata Baraldi Sandri, "Problemi del rilievo di Augusto conservato nel Museo Nazionale di Ravenna," *Felix Ravenna*, ser. 4, fasc. 5–6 (1973): 11–52.

35. For the maternal iconography of the coins of Julia Domna see Mattingly, *Coins of the Roman Empire*, e.g., 5.1:27, no. 46, pl. 6.11 (Fecunditas reverse); 5.1:28, no. 55, pl. 6.16 (Venus Genetrix reverse); 5.1:157, no. 3, pl. 27.1 (reverse with busts of Geta and Caracalla and label *Aeternitas Imperii*); 5.1:164, no. 56, pl. 28.8 (reverse with Julia Domna sacrificing and label *Matri Castrorum*); 5.1:203, no. 255, pl. 33.6 (obverse with Septimius Severus, reverse bust of Julia Domna between Caracalla and Geta and label *Felicitas Saeculi*); 5.1:432, no. 11, pl. 67.12 (reverse with Julia Domna and label *Mat. Augg. Mat. Sen. M. Patr.*). On the Arch of the Argentarii see Massimo Pallottino, *L'Arco degli Argentari* (Rome: Danesi Editore, 1946).

36. For Septimius Severus' fictive relationship to the Antonines see Dio Cassius 76.7.4; *Historia Augusta* Severus 10.3–6, 12.2–4; Herodian 2.14.3.

37. Lise Vogel, *The Column of Antoninus Pius* (Cambridge: Harvard University Press, 1973).

38. Vogel, *The Column of Antoninus Pius*, 66–67.

39. For an example of this process see Walter Trillmich, *Familienpropaganda der Kaiser Caligula und Claudius: Agrippina Major und Antonia Augusta auf Münzen* (Berlin: Walter de Gruyter, 1978). For the connection between erection of official portraits of Julia Domna and dynastic events, for example, nominations of Caracalla and Geta, see Jane Fejfer, "The Portraits of the Severan Empress Julia Domna: A New Approach," *Analecta Romana Instituti Danici* 14 (1985): 131, 133–34.

40. Herodian 3.8.5.

MARY TALIAFERRO BOATWRIGHT

Plancia Magna of Perge:

Women's Roles and Status in Roman Asia Minor

This essay examines Plancia Magna, an eminent woman of the city of Perge in Roman Pamphylia (in modern southwest Turkey), to illuminate both her life and the contemporary mores and institutions impinging on elite women's roles and status in Roman Asia Minor. Complementing Kampen's essay in this volume, which centers on the official representation of an imperial woman, my object is to show the range of possibilities and restrictions affecting the lives of elite provincial women. Plancia Magna has been chosen as a case study. Despite more abundant documentation for her[1] than for other nonimperial women, she shares one central enigma of her life with most of her peers in the Roman world: her financial status. Like other provincial women known to us, Plancia Magna was commemorated because of her magnificent largesse and social and political standing. Yet such largesse and standing are at odds with the gender ideology of the time, which relegated women to the private sphere and roles of dependence on men. This ideology lay behind the laws and customs restricting women's rights to inherit and to dispose of property, making all the more puzzling the munificence of Plancia Magna and other Roman benefactresses. The benefactions and position of Plancia Magna of Perge thus bring to prominence the larger question of women in public life in the Roman world, to be discussed at the end of this essay.

Like so many Roman women, Plancia Magna is known solely from documentary evidence: inscriptions inform us of her official positions in Perge, her family, and her wealth and benefactions. Two similarly inscribed statue bases are dedicated to her respectively by Perge's council and assembly (*boulē* and *dēmos*) and by Perge's (council of) elders (*geraioi*).[2] On these Plancia Magna is identified as the daughter of M. Plancius Varus and as "daughter of the city." She is also identified as *demiourgos* (the annual eponymous magistrate of the city, whose name was used for dating purposes); the priestess of Artemis (Pergaia), the most important deity of Perge; the first and only priestess of the Mother of the Gods, for life; and pious and loving of her city. A fragmentary unpublished inscription from Plancia Magna's tomb similarly gives her patronymic and calls her "daughter of the city."[3] Two unpublished inscriptions mentioned in a report of 1974 add the information that Plancia Magna was a high priestess of the imperial cult.[4] Apparently erected for the installation or donation of something, another lacunose inscription on a fragmentary architrave from Perge commemorates Plancia Magna, the "daughter of the city," together with Coccaeia Ti . . . , a *demiourgos* and gymnasiarch (or director of the gymnasium, the physical and intellectual school for young men and producer of gymnastic festivals).[5] And as yet unedited inscriptions, only recently disclosed, witness that Plancia Magna was the wife of C. Iulius Cornutus Tertullus and the mother of C. Iulius Plancius Varus Cornutus.[6]

A different set of inscriptions establishes that Plancia Magna was responsible for one of Perge's most impressive public buildings during the Empire, its main southern city gate.[7] At the beginning of the second century C.E. a complete renovation was undertaken on this Hellenistic city gate and its two round towers. The exterior, southern entrance was narrowed by the addition of rectangular piers between the towers, focusing attention on what was immediately inside.[8] Here the walls of an interior oval courtyard, originally higher than the 11 meters still standing, were decorated internally by two levels of seven niches, making a total of twenty-eight niches.[9] They and the walls were revetted with marble, and in front of them a new marble two-storied Corinthian columnar façade created the impression of a *scaenae frons* (the elaborate façade of a Roman stage building).[10] The courtyard was visually closed toward the city by a new monumental triple arch. What the arch replaced, if anything, is unknown.[11]

The whole constituted an opulent entry into the city, made programmatic by the choice of statues for the niches and arch. The statue bases establish Plancia Magna as the donor of the renovation. The lower niches of the courtyard held greater-than-life-sized statues of the gods, including the Dioscuri, Aphrodite, and five other Olympian deities.[12] In the upper niches bases inscribed in Greek once carried statues of the city's mythological founders and more historical benefactors, equally called "city-founders" (*ktistai*, sing. *ktistēs*).[13] The bases held statues of, among others, Mopsos the Delphian, son of Apollo; Kalchas the Argive, son of Thestor; and Rixos the Athenian, son of Lykos, identified in turn as the son of Pandeion.[14] Also in the upper tier of niches stood the statues of M. Plancius Varus and C. Plancius Varus, with the inscriptions "City-founder, M. Plancius Varus, the Pergaean, father of Plancia Magna," and "City-founder, C. Plancius Varus, the Pergaean, brother of Plancia Magna."[15] The inclusion of these two and their unusual identification by means of Plancia, rather than the traditional identification of Plancia Magna and C. Plancius Varus by their father, indicate that Plancia Magna played an important role in the embellishment of the courtyard. This is supported by evidence from the nearby arch.

The arch, probably two-storied originally, rises from the paved courtyard on four steps, and the steps, its platform, and the arch itself were made of costly imported marble and the local limestone.[16] Numerous ornamental columnar and pilastered tabernacles and niches decorated the piers. In front of the middle piers were columns on freestanding pedestals, an unusual arrangement, but one that is paralleled in the contemporary Arch of Hadrian in neighboring Attaleia.[17] Both primary faces of Perge's arch reportedly once carried honorary inscriptions on the upper levels, one in Latin and the other in Greek, although neither has been published. These proclaimed that Plancia Magna dedicated the arch to her city[18] and complement inscribed statue bases found near the arch. On the bases simple yet elegantly carved bilingual inscriptions commemorate Plancia Magna's dedication of statues to Diana Pergensis and to the tutelary spirit (in Greek, *tychē*; Latin, *genius*) of the city, as well as to members of the imperial house: Divus Nerva, Divus Traianus, Hadrian, Plotina, Diva Marciana (Trajan's sister and the mother of Matidia), Diva Matidia (Marciana's daughter, Sabina's mother, and the mother-in-law of Hadrian), and Sabina Augusta. In the Greek part of the inscriptions Plancia Magna is identified only by her name; in the Latin, she has the simple patronymic M. f.[19] Hadrian's statue base is dated to 121 by the number of his years with tribunician power listed on it, and the nomenclature of Plotina and Matidia indicates a date from 119 to 122.[20]

We should assume a date early in the Hadrianic period for this comprehensive and expensive renovation of Perge's southern gate. The installation is not unique in the second century C.E. in impressively combining architecture and sculpture. In his monograph on the nymphaeum of Herodes Atticus in Olympia (149–53 C.E.) R. Bol cites other second-century examples of opulent architectural installations by private individuals that display in a *scaenae frons* schema or by some similar means deities, the imperial house, and the family of the donor, including female members. In addition to the nymphaeum of Herodes Atticus and Plancia Magna's gate, Bol's list includes the Antonine renovation of the main gate of Side, about 50 kilometers east of Perge; the Library of Celsus in Ephesus and the "Marmorsaal" of the Baths of the Vedii there; and dedications in the Temple of Apollo at Bulla Regia.[21] The widespread phenomenon of public benefactions (or evergetism) throughout the Roman world, to be discussed below, and the concentration of wealth in the hands of the municipal landowning elite help explain such costly donations, and there must have been many other examples whose components have now been dispersed through spoliation.

It is hard to discern which elements of the lavish and programmatic installations that do remain are conventional and which unusual, but some aspects of Plancia Magna's gate seem especially memorable. One is that her renovated gateway as a whole, with its juxtaposition of Perge's Olympian gods, civic tutelary deities, city-founders, family members, and imperial personages, epitomizes the Greek cities in Pamphylia and other provinces of Asia Minor, which were tenacious of their Greek heritage, proud of their local cults and traditions, boastful of their notables, and loyal to the imperial house. Another is that the triple arch displays more statues of female members of the imperial house than it does of males. Although the second century witnessed a rise in the number of women prominent in the imperial house and therefore in official and private manifestations of loyalty to them,[22] the predominance of females on Plancia Magna's arch is noteworthy in that Plancia Magna was herself a woman.

This last point, the gender of Plancia Magna, has not been sufficiently remarked in discussions of her donation, although it raises important questions. One concerns the resources and motives of Plancia Magna. In turn this relates to an apparent contradiction: this entrance to Perge, so emblematic of the political and social hierarchy of the time, is due to a person who, as a woman, came from a marginalized segment of Roman society.

The means and the background for Plancia Magna's largesse are inseparable from her family and connections. Plancia Magna was from one of the most notable and wealthy families of the Greek cities of Roman Asia Minor in the first and second centuries C.E., the Plancii.[23] The Plancii apparently came as traders to Perge on the southwest Anatolian coast from Latium (in central Italy) at the end of the Republic. They were effective enough for a descendant, M. Plancius Varus, to rise successfully in Rome's imperial service from the 60s to the end of the first century C.E., reaching praetorian rank and the positions of legate and governor in Achaea, Asia, and Bithynia.[24] We now know that this man's daughter, Plancia Magna, married the even more successful Pergaean C. Iulius P. f. Hor. Cornutus Tertullus. Iulius Cornutus Tertullus' ancestry is peregrine (non-Roman) rather than Italian, to judge from his *nomen* Iulius, but his family was prominent in Perge by the Neronian period at the latest, when members apparently donated a gymnasium in Nero's honor.[25] Iulius Cornutus Tertullus, born probably in 43 or 44, was only slightly younger than M. Plancius Varus, but he was more eminent, reaching a suffect consulship for part of the year 100 with Pliny the Younger as his colleague. His official positions continued until 117, in Italy, Aquitania, Bithynia, and Africa.[26] Both Plancius and Iulius Cornutus Tertullus possessed lands and splendid connections far afield of Perge: some inscriptions reveal their presence in Tavium in eastern Galatia and in Apollonia in southern Galatia and suggest that they had marriage alliances with the royal family of Galatia and Pergamum.[27]

The two families prospered through Plancia Magna's generation. M. Plancius Varus' grandson C. Iulius Plancius Varus Cornutus, who we now know was the son of Plancia Magna and C. Iulius Cornutus Tertullus, is honored at Perge as patron, benefactor, and victor in all the contests of the "Varian games," which seem to have been eight-yearly games established by M. Plancius Varus.[28] Closer to Rome, Iulius Plancius Varus Cornutus dedicated a monument in Tusculum to C. Iulius Cornutus Tertullus (*CIL* XIV:2925, 2925a = *ILS* 1024), now identifiable as his father. Either Iulius Plancius Varus Cornutus or Plancia's brother C. Plancius Varus rose to become a governor of Cilicia and consul under Hadrian.[29] In the next generation, the last documented in positions of authority, a Varus of Perge gained fame for his rhetoric, and a possible relative, a Celsus Plancianus, was consul suffectus (a consul for only part of the year) in 166 C.E.[30] The Cornuti drop from the historical record more quickly than the Plancii. Their last known possible representative in imperial service is Plancius

Varus Cornutus, though in Perge a C. Iulius Cornutus Bryoninus was a priest of the imperial cult as well as the producer and judge (*agōnothetēs*) at an unknown date of Perge's games for the imperial cult.[31]

In background and behavior the Plancii and Cornuti exemplify the elite of Roman Asia Minor. One family arrived probably as traders from Italy toward the end of the Republic, to make its fortune in the province then called Lycia-Pamphylia in southern Asia Minor; the other, originally indigenous and peregrine in Roman law, took advantage of the new political situation, were made Roman citizens, and similarly achieved prominence during the same span in the provincial city and in imperial service. By the late first century the wealth of the Plancii and the Cornuti was based in land and they could boast high connections, thus bolstering their prestige and financial means for political careers. These families, like their peers in Pamphylia and the rest of the Roman world, manifested their riches and eminence in the phenomenon known as evergetism.

Evergetism is a close nexus of power, wealth, and status, whose importance in Hellenistic Greek and Roman civilization has been explored by P. Veyne and others. In this social, economic, and political phenomenon the wealthy citizens of a city or region donated time, expertise, and money to a community, on the occasion of holding a magistracy or priesthood, fulfilling a liturgy (a compulsory and expensive public service), or simply spontaneously. In return their political and social eminence was reinforced and vociferously celebrated.[32] For example, as proconsul of Bithynia in the early Flavian period Plancia Magna's father, M. Plancius Varus, dedicated a city gate of Nicaea to both the imperial house and Nicaea and was publicly called the patron of that city.[33] Earlier, the dedication of a gymnasium at Perge to Nero by a husband and wife of the Cornuti family was commemorated publicly by at least four inscriptions.[34]

Plancia Magna's ostentatious largesse at first seems conventional enough against the background of evergetism sketched above. Yet it is remarkable both in her singularity in her benefaction to her city and in her status as a woman: women were traditionally excluded from power, particularly when acting apart from men. This traditional relegation of women to the domestic sphere makes all the more striking Plancia Magna's magistracy as *demiourgos*: her name, as that of the eponymous magistrate of the city, would be used to date all public documents for the year of her magistracy.

The inscriptions attesting Plancia Magna as donor of the gateway and arch make it clear that she was spending her own money, and in her own name. Her father and brother are identified unusually by their relationship with her. Her husband and her son do not appear at all on the remains of the monument, and this apparent silence concerning the Cornuti suggests that Plancia Magna had no connections with that family when she donated the gateway between 119 and 122. When published, the newly disclosed inscriptions establishing Plancia Magna as the wife and mother, respectively, of C. Iulius Cornutus Tertullus and C. Iulius Plancius Varus Cornutus may establish some connection of the two to Plancia Magna's gate. More importantly, such publication may clear up the details of her relationship with these two individuals and enlarge our understanding of her financial status and independence. Nevertheless, until then some speculation about the date of Plancia's marriage to C. Iulius Cornutus Tertullus is in order, on the basis of the few known dates in the second-century history of the two families and on the apparent absence of Plancia Magna's husband and son from her gate.

The probable existence of a Plancius Varus as consul and governor of Cilicia during Hadrian's reign means that either her brother, the city-founder of her courtyard, or her son, the victor of the Varian games who also dedicated a monument in Tusculum to his father, C. Iulius Cornutus Tertullus, was in his twenties to his forties during that period. If the consular Plancius Varus was her brother, both he and Plancia Magna could have been born around the end of the first century, at the conclusion of M. Plancius Varus' career. Plancia Magna thus would have been in her late teens at the time of her donation, marrying only subsequently the much older Iulius Cornutus after his retirement from public life. The age differential here is rather startling: at their marriage after 122 her husband would have been around eighty years old, she around twenty.

If the consular Plancius Varus was Plancia Magna's son, however, her husband, Iulius Cornutus, would probably have been in his sixties at the most when they wed ca. 100–110, a slightly more acceptable figure.[35] This, however, leaves unexplained the absence of her husband and, more particularly, of her son from her courtyard.[36] Even if her husband were dead by 119–122, her son, Iulius Plancius Cornutus Tertullus, would have been either embarked, or just about to embark, on his political career, and one would expect mention of him in his mother's spectacular public benefaction. His ties to the maternal branch of his family seem to have been salient when he won the Varian games established by his grandfather.[37]

In any case the absence of her husband and son from the courtyard, and the spare but unusual way in which her relationships to her brother and father are cited, emphasize Plancia Magna's initiative and individuality in her benefaction to her city. At the moment we cannot explain her generosity as designed to help the male members of her family into positions of power.[38] Her donation seems more personally expedient, and the other inscriptions attesting her reflect the glory and power she acquired for herself in Perge. But her liberality and her public positions must be set in their legal and societal context.

Plancia Magna was a Roman citizen, subject to the Roman laws regulating Roman women's rights to inherit, to receive legacies and gifts, and to dispose of property. These laws are somewhat convoluted but show a slight lessening of restrictions during the imperial period. The Voconian law of 169 B.C.E. had forbidden instituting as heirs women of the highest census class, an elite group to which Plancia Magna belonged. Yet the law may have ceased to be applicable once the census itself became obsolete in Italy in the Flavian period; it also regulated only cases where wills were made, and not intestacy.[39] Augustan legislation limited the ability of the unmarried and childless to receive under a will but did not apply to bequests from relatives.[40] Gifts between husbands and wives were severely limited under the law, but widows and widowers could apparently inherit from a deceased spouse, with widows under the restrictions of the Voconian law.[41] Given the gate's silence regarding the Cornuti, Plancia Magna's wealth appears to have come primarily from her father, probably by bequest, less likely as dowry, which normally passed to the husband at least for "safekeeping."[42] Plancia Magna seems to have received from her father almost as much, if not as much, as did her brother, who presumably needed the wealth for the traditional male political career.[43]

M. Plancius Varus's evenhandedness with his daughter and son may have gone further, for Plancia Magna's apparent autonomy suggests that he emancipated her, establishing her as *sui iuris*, theoretically mistress of her own fate and not under the tutelage or power of a male guardian. The legal position of Roman women in Plancia Magna's time, especially prominent women, is ambiguous.[44] By law and tradition, even if a Roman woman were emancipated, she was to have a *tutor* (guardian) for important property transactions. Yet this principle had been breached by Augustan legislation establishing the *ius liberorum* (right of children), whereby freeborn women with three legitimate children, and freed-

women with four, were exempted from guardianship. Subsequent legislation, including some in Hadrian's reign, further weakened the principle
of guardianship.[45] Just after Plancia's lifetime the jurisconsult Gaius revealed the legal ambivalence concerning guardianship of women. Although he states that former generations wished women, even of the age
of maturity, to be in guardianship because of the "innate weakness of
their sex," he later allows that there is no longer any really cogent reason
for the practice (*Inst.* 1.144, 1.190). Gaius implies elsewhere that most
guardians could be compelled to give their consent even to women's
actions that might diminish the property.[46] The scattered evidence from
the Greek East during this period indicates that in general Greek women
were legally required to have a *kyrios* (guardian), but it gives no real
information as to their relationship with these guardians,[47] which probably varied considerably in different regions.

We should conclude that Plancia Magna controlled her own wealth. But
we must ask the related questions of how normal it was for a woman to act
in the public sphere and to spend her money there, and why a woman
might choose to do so. Plancia Magna's position as *demiourgos*, annual
eponymous magistrate of her city, and her accumulation of Perge's most
important priesthoods, ranging from the civic cult to the imperial one, far
surpass the traditional roles of Greek women as priestesses.[48] Her public
visibility appears anomalous in light of legal and literary evidence, both
Roman and Greek. Focusing on notions of women's innate weakness, in
the early third century c.e. the jurisconsult Paulus reported that women
did not hold civil offices and could not give testimony (*Dig.* 5.1.12.2).
Ulpianus similarly holds that "the modesty befitting women's sex" caused
women to be banned from bringing suit on behalf of others, from involving themselves in others' cases, and from undertaking the functions of
men (*Dig.* 3.1.1.5, cf. 50.17.2).[49] In the Greek East, the prevalent images
were provided by the famous relegation of Athenian women to the domestic sphere, except for sacral functions, and by their lack of control over
property.[50] At the end of the first and the beginning of the second centuries c.e. the domestic roles of women had been reformulated and emphasized anew by Stoic philosophers and other intellectuals who, although
valorizing women as conscious participants in harmonious marriages,
focused almost exclusively on women within a familial, domestic context.[51] The veiling of some women in the imperial Greek East and in North
Africa corresponds to the legal, literary, and philosophical preoccupation

among the elite with the virtuous, modest wife, the pious and silent woman whose main task was to care for her husband and children.[52]

Contradicting the picture provided by the literary evidence, however, are hundreds of inscriptions and coins from Hellenistic and Roman Greece and Asia Minor that attest women such as Plancia Magna, unnoticed in the literary sources. These women were priestesses, gymnasiarchs, theatrical game producers, and the like, as well as magistrates, although the last group is attested only in the Roman imperial period. Many of the inscriptions record women's benefactions, such as those of Plancia Magna: some benefactresses are identified as liturgy payers or officeholders, others not. This epigraphic and numismatic evidence, at such odds with the legal and literary documentation advocating silent and submissive women, to my knowledge has not been studied as a whole since the late nineteenth and early twentieth centuries.[53] Since then additional inscriptions and coins have surfaced, raising the total above the count at that time of more than 160.[54] The plethora of this type of inscription demonstrates that Plancia Magna is not an isolated instance of a powerful and generous woman: there were many others, especially from the first through third centuries of our era. Perhaps a half of these benefactresses, priestesses, and female officeholders are commemorated alone, without mention of any male relative or guardian.[55] These publicly visible women belie the stated attitudes and "norms" of the time.

Various interpretations of women's public visibility have been offered, of political, economic, and social natures. One school is exemplified by P. Paris, the pioneer in this field who published his monograph in 1891.[56] Arguing in part from Athenian precedent, Paris could not conceive of women actually exercising civil power or participating, even as producers, in gymnastic or theatrical festivals. He points to the instances of women and their husbands in related magistracies as evidence that women held at most priestly power and that they were most often dependent on men even when they did ostensibly hold power.[57] Paris combines his view of women as incompetent and unfit for public business with a theory that political life in the Greek East under Roman rule degenerated, from power politics to the simple display of wealth and the trappings of power in festivals and games, and to elections of strictly local magistrates, priests, and priestesses.[58] Paris holds as symptomatic of this decline cities' admission of women to positions of apparent public authority. Since magistracies, priesthoods, and liturgies entailed vast expenditures by their holders for the city, the cities turned to women as potential donors. As women exercised no real power, their appointment to various positions was a painless way for cities to gain money and glitter.[59]

Paris's basic theses, the incapacity of women for positions of civil authority and the political decay of the Greek East, have often been repeated.[60] Yet his specific arguments and analysis of the inscriptions were rebutted almost immediately by O. Braunstein, who in 1911 undertook a more rigorous, but equally subjective, study.[61] Braunstein disallowed Paris's examples from outside Asia Minor and focused on women's secular positions: liturgies and magistracies. Contending that all of the known women in such positions in the Greek East come from Lycia and Pamphylia, southwest Asia Minor (Plancia Magna's region), he explained the phenomenon by the survival here of *Mutterrecht*, matriarchy, from the pre-Greek period.[62] Nevertheless he too stressed that the majority of women's positions were priestly or only nominal.[63] Since his day, however, J. J. Bachofen's theory of *Mutterrecht* has lost much of its sway;[64] furthermore, as mentioned above, other examples of women as civic officials and benefactors have come to light elsewhere in Asia Minor and Greece.

Equally to be discounted are the explanations that the appearance of women in public is a sign of the economic and/or political decay of the Greek East. On the contrary, most of the inscriptions fall precisely in the period when the cities of Asia Minor were most thriving and prosperous, in the first through third centuries of our era.[65] Other scholars link the phenomenon of women in the public sphere in the Greek world, especially the Greek East, to the increased economic and legal power that Greek women had from the Hellenistic period on.[66] This is certainly valid. Yet we must note that recent work indicates that there was not a gradual "empowerment" of these women: rather, the size of the fortunes controlled here by women, and by men, grew dramatically.[67] Analogously, although elite Roman women in the imperial period do seem to have had a certain degree of autonomy in personal and financial matters, many of these freedoms had already been conferred upon them early in Roman history.[68]

What was different now, in both East and West, was the willingness of elite women to play a public role, and the public reception of these roles.[69] Without new evidence we can never know if the female magistrates personally administered their civic duties, giving orders to others who would almost certainly be men. Yet at least as important as such routine administration is the obvious influence these women, and priestesses, benefactresses, and female liturgy payers, commanded simply by being in positions of public respect.[70]

The shift of at least some women from the private sphere to the public one is not simple to explain, as many different factors play a part. Many explanations admittedly do not clarify the enigmatic restriction to the Greek East of women as civil magistrates and liturgy holders,[71] to which we shall turn at the end of this discussion. Yet the following interpretations, some old and some new, do allow us to make sense of the public visibility of women in the Roman empire, so clear in the epigraphic and numismatic evidence and yet so much at odds with the picture presented by the literature.

Two scholars have recently offered insightful analysis, though neither addresses specifically the peculiar situation in the Greek East. R. Van Bremen ties the public visibility of women to growing wealth and the increasing sway of evergetism in the late Hellenistic and Roman periods.[72] Her sophisticated thesis accounts for the apparent contradiction of the documentary evidence with the literature idealizing women's domesticity, for she stresses that the epigraphic language of public benefactions and gratitude often expresses familial attitudes for both men and women. Just as Plancia Magna is called "daughter of the city," munificent men are termed "father of the city" or "son of the city": the phenomenon of evergetism blurred the traditional distinctions between public and private.[73] This conflation of public and private, so obvious when women are made prominent in traditional male spheres, is illustrated also in Kampen's essay in the present volume. W. Eck has recently added another interpretation of the public roles of senatorial Roman women in cities throughout the Roman empire: less needed in Rome than their husbands, fathers, or brothers, these women undertook public roles in their municipalities and provided strong links for the senators to the cities from which they originally came.[74]

Other factors can be discerned in women's choosing public roles. I propose that one must be the example of the women of the imperial court, who were particularly prominent and autonomous in the Julio-Claudian, Antonine, and Severan periods.[75] Imperial women often traveled with the emperors: we know, for instance, that Trajan's wife, Plotina, and his niece Matidia the Elder were with him when he died in 117 in Cilicia.[76] The imperial women could be and were approached directly for favors and influence with their consorts, as Livia was by the Samians and, allegedly, Plotina by the Alexandrian Jews in Plancia Magna's lifetime.[77] Seemingly paradoxically, however, they had a much more conventional public image. They were shown as Pudicitia and other traditional female virtues associated with harmonious families, as Kampen notes for Julia Domna's numismatic representations, or as Ceres and other goddesses strongly associated with women. In her essay Kampen underscores the use of the empresses "to express the programmatic concerns of the state and the emperor," reinforcing the traditional gender ideology.

The influence exerted by imperial women on the phenomenon of women's public visibility was thus ambivalent, justifying both political power and a retiring persona.[78] The political power wielded by imperial women furnished a model to elite women for behavior and aspirations, much as their "exemplary" iconography was to be mimicked.[79] Plancia Magna's gate, depicting more female than male members of the imperial house, may signify the importance of the imperial women for women's assuming public roles.

Even more accessible to elite municipal women were the Roman women who accompanied their husbands and relatives on provincial tasks. M.-T. Raepsaet-Charlier has established that this must have been a fairly common occurrence, and she notes that wives, daughters, and other relatives of Roman governors and legates are found equally in all the provinces.[80] Her epigraphic evidence shows that these "governors' ladies" gave donations and were publicly honored.[81] They were quite obviously in the public sphere, and despite denunciations by Roman moralists of their "influence peddling" and susceptibility to flattery, actual incidents of malfeasance are documented only rarely.[82] Thus elite women in Italy and the provinces could see, at political functions and more informal gatherings, highly placed Roman women who were respected in their public roles. In the competitive society of the imperial elite, this must have encouraged emulation, a point brought out by A. J. Marshall.[83]

A related explanation may be true for the more singular phenomenon of female magistrates and liturgy payers in Roman Asia Minor. This must be tied to the fierce and famous intercity rivalry in the region. Literary sources such as Pliny the Younger, Dio Chrysostom, and Aelius Aristides attest to the intense civic emulation in first- through third-century Asia Minor, as do the splendid ruins of the cities themselves and their inscriptions and coins.[84]

It is more than coincidental, or simply due to the hold of regional architecture and workshops, that one of the closest architectural parallels for Plancia Magna's gate comes from her neighboring city Attaleia. The Attaleian gate is dated by its mutilated inscription to after 129.[85] A distinguished woman of Attaleia, Iulia Sancta, refurbished with her own funds at least one of the towers flanking the gate, and she is known to have dedicated a statue to Domitia Paulina, Hadrian's sister.[86] It looks as though Iulia Sancta followed her neighbor Plancia's example on a slightly less lavish scale. Likewise evincing the competitiveness of neighboring cities in the Greek East, the main Hellenistic city gate of Side was refurbished in the Antonine period as an opulent entry court quite similar to that of Plancia Magna in Perge, only some 50 kilometers to the east.[87]

Similarly, the election of a noble and wealthy woman to be eponymous magistrate or some other civic official in one city could provide a model for a neighboring city. In nearby Sillyum, roughly from Plancia Magna's day, a Greek Menodora was priestess of all the gods; of Demeter; of the ancestral gods of her city, perpetually; and chief priestess of the imperial cult. She also was gymnasiarch, *demiourgos*, and *dekaprōtos* (a financial magistrate).[88] The appearance of women in positions of civil authority, once admitted, would be imitated in this close-knit and wealthy area. It may be that there was some characteristic of Pamphylia and Asia Minor that encouraged women to assume this traditionally "masculine" role, as Braunstein postulated. Although such a trait has not yet been discovered, recognition of the restriction to the Greek East of female magistrates and liturgy payers reminds us of the strength of regionalism in the Roman empire, one element apparent in the program of Plancia Magna's gateway. More important for this discussion, the gathered evidence lets us appreciate the activities and choices of a woman such as Plancia Magna, albeit providing little insight into her personal motives.

It is clear that the vast subject of women in the public sphere throughout the Roman world deserves more intensive study. The compilation of case studies, like this one of Plancia Magna, will provide data for analysis, and the discussion above may help us discern the questions we can profitably ask. We should examine Plancia Magna and her peers not simply in male frameworks such as family politics and prosopography, for these women were individuals in their own right. We may never be able to restore to them a voice, as men, not women, created the literature, philosophy, law, art and architecture, and material artifacts now remaining from the Roman period. But an increasing body of epigraphic, numismatic, and archaeological evidence does enable us to see elite women's lives in more detail, and the contradictions these lives pose to the hegemonic paradigm. Plancia Magna and a significant number of other elite women crossed over into traditionally male roles, public ones, and achieved status and prominence equal to that of many men.

Notes

A version of this paper was read in February 1989 for the North Carolina Society of the Archaeological Institute of America (Chapel Hill), and I thank the audience for many interesting and pertinent suggestions. Thanks are also due to K. J. Rigsby and an anonymous reviewer for many comments that improved the paper.

1. Many of Plancia Magna's positions and benefactions are referred to by M.-T. Raepsaet-Charlier, *Prosopographie des femmes de l'ordre sénatorial (Ier–IIer siècles)* (Louvain: Peeters, 1987), no. 609, pp. 494–95; H. Halfmann, *Die Senatoren aus dem östlichen Teil des Imperium Romanum* (Göttingen: Vandenhoeck & Ruprecht, 1979), no. 31, pp. 128–29; and, briefly, W. Eck, *RE*, suppl. 14 (1974): col. 386, s.v. Plancia Magna. The inscriptions of Perge, including most of the inscriptions mentioning Plancia Magna, have just been surveyed by R. Merkelbach and S. Şahin, "Die publizierten Inschriften von Perge," *Epigraphica Anatolica* 11 (1988): 97–170 (cited below as M&S). Other bibliography is mentioned below. Plancia Magna has also received mention in works on women, as in R. Van Bremen, "Women and Wealth," in *Images of Women in Antiquity*, ed. A. Cameron and A. Kuhrt (Detroit: Wayne State University Press, 1983), 235. Unless specially indicated, abbreviations used below are the standard ones found in *L'année philologique* and the second edition of the *Oxford Classical Dictionary*.

2. M&S no. 36, pp. 122–23 = *AE* (1958): no. 78 = *AE* (1965): no. 209; M&S no. 37, p. 123, correcting *BSA* 17 (1910–11): no. 31, pp. 245–46; cf. C. P. Jones, "The Plancii of Perge and Diana Planciana," *HSCP* 80 (1976): 233. For the honorary appellation "daughter of the city" see L. Robert, in *Laodicée du Lycos: le Nymphée; campagnes 1961–63* (Quebec and Paris: Presses de l'Université Laval, 1969), 317–27.

3. A. M. Mansel, "Bericht über Ausgrabungen und Untersuchungen in Pamphylien in den Jahren 1946–1955," *Arch. Anz.* 71 (1956): 120 n. 87 (not in M&S).

4. J. Inan, "Neue Porträtstatuen aus Perge," in *Mélanges Mansel* (Ankara: Türk Tarih Hurumu Basimevi, 1974), 2:648–49 (not in M&S), commenting on a statue of Plancia Magna (illustrated). The two inscriptions naming Plancia Magna as high priestess of the imperial cult were found in excavations of 1968–69 in the area south of Plancia Magna's gate, helping to identify as Plancia Magna the statue found there that has a stylistic date in the Hadrianic period (it closely resembles a

statue of Sabina found earlier in Perge) and a priestly diadem adorned with four imperial busts (marking the wearer as a priestess of the imperial cult).

5. M&S no. 35, p. 122 = *IGR* III:794. The edition by Merkelbach and Şahin puts *demiourgos kai gymnasiarchos* in apposition to Plancia Magna rather than to Coccaeia Ti . . . , as had earlier editions. This is an unlikely restoration of the fragments, however, as Plancia's supposed gymnasiarchy occurs on no other of her honorary inscriptions.

6. Her marriage to Cornutus Tertullus is mentioned in the commentary on M&S no. 18, p. 114; her parentage of Plancius Varus Cornutus at M&S nos. 28 and 57, pp. 120 and 133; see also M&S no. 29, p. 120. Unfortunately these brief notices give no particulars such as dates, so that (for example) we have as yet no way of knowing if she was a widow at the time of her donations to Perge. Some link between the Plancii and Cornuti has long been presumed, most commonly that M. Plancius Varus, Plancia Magna's father, was the adoptive son of C. Iulius Cornutus Tertullus: see, for example, *CIL* XIV:2925, note ad loc.; S. Jameson, "Cornutus Tertullus and the Plancii of Perge," *JRS* 55 (1965): 54; S. Mitchell, "The Plancii in Asia Minor," *JRS* 64 (1974): 27.

7. Mansel, "Bericht," 99–120. The major excavation was in the 1950s, with subsequent work resulting in (among other finds) the statue of Plancia Magna mentioned in note 4 above. See S. Jameson, *RE* suppl. 14 (1974): cols. 375–83, s.v. Perge.

8. Mansel, "Bericht," 104: after the addition of the piers, which were not bonded with the towers, the entrance measured 5.5 meters wide, 3.7 meters deep.

9. Mansel, "Bericht," 104–5, gives the dimensions of the courtyard as 20.35 meters deep, 17.80 meters in exterior width.

10. In what J. B. Ward-Perkins calls the "marble style": see his *Roman Imperial Architecture* (New York: Penguin Books, 1981), 300–302. Mansel, "Bericht," 105–6, describes the courtyard in detail.

11. Mansel, "Bericht," 111–17: overall dimensions, 20 meters long, 9.10 meters wide; middle fornix 3.40 meters wide, side ones 2.50. Marble cassetts decorated the vaults.

12. Hermes, Apollo, Pan, and Heracles, and an unidentified young male deity: Mansel, "Bericht," 106–9, ills. 56–59. No statue bases were found for these statues.

13. For the meanings of *ktistēs*, an honorary appellation bestowed on eminent individuals for having brought to a city imperial favor or other far-reaching benefits, see L. Robert, *Hellenica* 4 (Paris: Librairie d'Amérique et d'Orient, 1948), 116.

14. Others identified by their bases are the Lapith Leonteus, son of Koronos; Machaon the Thessalian, son of Asklepios; Minyas, from Orchomenos, son of Ialmenos son of Ares; Labos the Delphian, son of Dae[. . .]: Mansel, "Bericht," 109; M&S nos. 24–27, pp. 117–19. Many more heroes are commemorated here than Herodotus and Strabo record as participating in Perge's foundation (Amphilochos,

Kalchas, and Mopsos, Hdt. 7.91; and Strab. 668, citing Herodotus and Callinus). One founder mentioned in both accounts, Amphilochos, is not yet documented in the courtyard. Some of these heroes in Plancia Magna's courtyard, unknown otherwise, had ancient cults in the city: the Rixos inscription mentions a foot of Rixos that seems to have been a reliquary (M&S no. 27a, p. 119; Mansel, "Bericht," 109–10 n. 79).

15. M&S no. 28a–b, pp. 119–20; no. 28b incorrectly gives *adephos* for *adelphos*; cf. *Türk Arkeoloji Dergisi* 6 (1956), pl. VI, fig. 20; Jameson, "Tertullus and the Plancii," 56.

16. Marble revetted the exterior: Mansel, "Bericht," 112. Pamphylia began to import marble in quantity only after Trajan's reign; see Ward-Perkins, *Roman Imperial Architecture*, 299–300.

17. Mansel, "Bericht," 112: on the front sides there was a high pluteum with *aediculae*, and half-round and rectangular niches decorated the short sides. For the gate at Attaleia see note 85 below.

18. Mansel, "Bericht," 117–18: the inscriptions were in bronze letters within *tabulae ansatae*. Mansel points out the rarity of Plancia Magna's dedication of the arch to her city rather than to an emperor. Merkelbach and Şahin do not mention the inscriptions.

19. M&S nos. 29–34, pp. 120–22 (with earlier references): Diana Pergensis/ Artemis Pergaia, Genius civitatis/Tyche poleos, Divus Traianus, Diva Marciana, Diva Matidia, Sabina Augusta. Merkelbach and Şahin mention in their commentary to no. 34 (p. 122, with earlier references) unedited statue bases to (?Divus) Augustus, Divus Nerva, Plotina Augusta, and Hadrianus Augustus. I have encountered no other reference to the purported inscription to (?Divus) Augustus. Unfortunately the bases cannot be matched with fragmentary cuirassed and draped statues also found in the general proximity: see H. J. Kruse, *Römische weibliche Gewandstatuen des 2. Jhs. n. Chr.* (Göttingen: Bönecke Druck, 1975), 281–83.

20. Although it had been assumed from Sabina's epithet "Augusta" that Sabina's statue was erected not before 128, when she received that title officially (e.g., Jameson, "Tertullus and the Plancii," 56), W. Eck has now established that she was called Augusta earlier, probably after 119, when Matidia died, or perhaps after 123, when Plotina died: see "Hadrian als *pater patriae* und die Verleihung des Augustatitels an Sabina," in *Romanitas-Christianitas*, ed. G. Wirth et al. (Berlin and New York: W. de Gruyter, 1982), 226–28. Since "Diva"/"Thea" is absent as an epithet for Plotina, her statue must predate her death and apotheosis in 123.

21. R. Bol, *Das Statuenprogramm des Herodes-Atticus-Nymphäums* (Berlin: W. de Gruyter, 1984), 83–95, 108; for the date of Herodes Atticus' nymphaeum, 98–100.

22. See, for example, the numerous dedications to Plotina, Marciana, Matidia the Elder, and other imperial women, even including (Aelia) Domitia Paulina (Hadrian's sister), at Lyttos, Crete (*IGR* I:992–99, 1004). In Lyttos, however, as in

almost all other such installations, the dedications are made publicly, and representations of imperial men outnumber those of imperial women. See T. Pékary, *Das römische Kaiserbildnis in Staat, Kult und Gesellschaft, dargestellt anhand der Schriftquellen* (Berlin: Mann Verlag, 1985), 90–96, 101–5. I treat the topic of the imperial women of the early second century in an article forthcoming in *AJP* 112, no. 3 (1991).

23. For the Plancii see esp. Jones, "Plancii of Perge," 231–37; Jameson, "Tertullus and the Plancii," 54–58.

24. Halfmann, *Senatoren*, no. 8, pp. 104–5; add C. P. Jones, *Gnomon* 45 (1973): 691, and Mitchell, "Plancii," 27–29; *AE* (1971): no. 463; W. Eck, *RE* suppl. 14 (1974): cols. 385–86, s.v. M. Plancius Varus; idem, "Jahres- und Provinzialfasten der senatorischen Statthalter von 69/70 bis 138/139, II," *Chiron* 13 (1983): 202 n. 571, clarifying more controversial points of his career. For the background of traders (*negotiatores*) in the eastern Mediterranean see B. Levick, *Roman Colonies in Southern Asia Minor* (Oxford: Clarendon Press, 1967), 56–58.

25. Jameson, "Tertullus and the Plancii," 54 n. 4. For the gymnasium see below and note 34.

26. Jameson, "Tertullus and the Plancii," 54; M. Corbier, *L'"aerarium Saturni" et l'"aerarium militare"* (Rome: Ecole Française de Rome, 1974), no. 31, pp. 119–31; Halfmann, *Senatoren*, no. 22, p. 117, with earlier bibliography.

27. Mitchell, "Plancii," 27–39, esp. 31–38, with some other possible landholdings elsewhere in Asia Minor, perhaps as early as the mid-first century C.E. The connection with the royal family would have been through the Iulii Severi of Galatia.

28. M&S no. 57, pp. 132–33 = *AE* (1965): no. 208; Halfmann, *Senatoren*, no. 31, p. 128. Like most scholars working before the discovery of the new inscription marking C. Iulius Plancius Varus Cornutus as Plancia Magna's son, Halfmann identifies this man with C. Plancius Varus; see *Epigrafia e ordine senatorio* 2 (1982): 608, 642. See also *PIR²* I:470; Jones, "Plancii of Perge," 232–33; and Jameson, "Tertullus and the Plancii," 56.

29. For the governorship of Cilicia by a Plancius Varus see R. Syme, "Legates of Cilicia under Trajan," *Historia* 18 (1969): 365–66, referring to *Ephemeris epigraphica* IX:473, no. 900 = *Insc. It.* IV.1:132a–c; he and others infer a consular Plancius from the Hadrianic *senatus consultum Plancianum* (*Dig.* 25.3.3.1). C. Plancius Varus is unequivocally attested only by M&S no. 28b, pp. 119–120 = *AE* (1965): no. 212 = *SEG* XXXIV:1305B, the inscription from Plancia Magna's courtyard discussed above. See also W. Eck, *RE*, suppl. 14 (1974): col. 386, s.v. C. Plancius Varus; Halfmann, *Senatoren*, no. 31, p. 128.

30. The sophist Varus flourished in Perge in the mid-second century C.E.: Philostr. *VS* 2.6; see G. W. Bowersock, *Greek Sophists in the Roman Empire* (Oxford: Clarendon, 1969), 22 n. 5, 84. For (———) Celsus Plancianus, consul (suffectus)

with C. Avidius Cassius and perhaps a member of the Plancii family, see G. Alföldy, *Konsulat und Senatorenstand unter den Antoninen* (Bonn: Habelt, 1977), 181–82.

31. For Bryoninus see *IGR* III:798 = M&S no. 49, p. 128, with new supplements of Bryoninus instead of Bryonianus, and imperial games instead of Varian games. In light of the new information concerning Plancia Magna's marriage, Iulia Tertulla, who married L. Iulius Marinus Caecilius Simplex (cos. suff. 101), is more likely to have been the sister of Cornutus Tertullus than his daughter. See Corbier, *Aerarium Saturni*, 129; Halfmann, *Senatoren*, nos. 22 and 23, pp. 117–18; Jameson, "Tertullus and the Plancii," 54 n. 5; Jones, "Plancii of Perge," 233. A mid-third-century Roman equestrian from Ancyra, Tertullus Varus, whose children and grandchildren entered the Senate, is probably also connected with the two families: see Mitchell, "Plancii," 36.

32. P. Veyne, *Le pain et le cirque* (Paris: Editions du Seuil, 1976), who does not specifically investigate the question of women in this context. For that topic see Van Bremen, "Women and Wealth," 223–42. For evergetism in the Hellenistic period in Asia Minor and Greece see P. Gauthier, *Les cités grecques et leurs bienfaiteurs (IVe-Ier siècle avant J.-C): contribution à l'histoire des institutions* (Paris and Athens: Diffusion de Boccard and Ecole Française d'Athènes, 1985). More briefly for Roman evergetism: P. Garnsey and R. Saller, *The Roman Empire: Economy, Society and Culture* (Berkeley and Los Angeles: University of California Press, 1987), 33–34, 38, 101–2, 198.

33. S. Şahin, *Katalog der antiken Inschriften des Museums von Iznik (Nikaia)*, vol. 1, Inschriften griechischer Städte aus Kleinasien, 9 (Bonn: Habelt, 1979), nos. 25–28, 51–52; another inscription from Nicaea mentioning M. Plancius Varus is to be published by E. Bowie (see Mitchell, "Plancii," 28 n. 5).

34. The children of C. Iulius Cornutus and his unidentified wife may also have been cited as donors on the now fragmentary inscriptions: M&S nos. 18–21, pp. 113–15 = *IGR* III:792, *CIL* III:6734, *IGR* III:789. C. Iulius P. f. Hor. Cornutus Tertullus, the future husband of Plancia Magna, was probably the adopted son of this C. Iulius Cornutus (Corbier, *Aerarium Saturni*, 129; Jameson, "Tertullus and the Plancii," 54).

35. R. P. Saller, "Men's Age at Marriage and Its Consequence in the Roman Family," *CP* 82 (1987): 29–30, arguing from epigraphic and comparative evidence, contends plausibly that in the senatorial order men typically made their first marriages before age twenty-five. B. Shaw, "The Age of Roman Girls at Marriage: Some Reconsiderations," *JRS* 77 (1987): 30–46, shows that the typical age of women's first marriage for the population outside Rome and its environs was the late teens or early twenties, although aristocratic women may have been married in their early or mid-teens. See also K. Hopkins, "The Age of Roman Girls at Marriage," *Population Studies* 18 (1965): 326.

36. Sarah B. Pomeroy, "The Relationship of the Married Woman to Her Blood Relatives in Rome," *Ancient Society* 7 (1976): 215–27, investigates the institutions dealing with women's often competing allegiances to kin and marital relatives.

37. The rarity of "athletic consulars," reflecting the traditional scorn of the political elite for such exhibitionism (cf. Jones, "Plancii of Perge," 232 n. 16), may be further reason to suppose that the Hadrianic consular is Plancia Magna's brother, C. Plancius Varus, rather than her athletic son. On the other hand, honorary considerations often played an important role in athletic contests in the Greek East, so that the "victories" of C. Iulius Plancius Varus Cornutus may simply reflect the fact that he was the leading descendant of the founder's family.

38. As one might expect from the literary evidence discussed below, which in general stresses women's total devotion and dedication to men.

39. J. F. Gardner, *Women in Roman Law and Society* (Bloomington and Indianapolis: Indiana University Press, 1986), 170–78, noting the loophole attested by Cicero that persons not registered (deliberately or not) in the census were not liable to the law. See also S. Dixon, "Breaking the Law to Do the Right Thing: The Gradual Erosion of the Voconian Law in Ancient Rome," *Adelaide Law Review* 9 (1985): 519–34.

40. Gardner, *Women in Law*, 178–79.

41. Gardner, *Women in Law*, 68–71 (with evidence of jurists' cautions regarding legacies to widows), 74–75, 170–78.

42. Gardner, *Women in Law*, 97–116.

43. R. P. Saller, "Roman Dowry and the Devolution of Property in the Principate," *CQ*, n.s. 34 (1984): esp. 196–202, and J. A. Crook, "Women in Roman Succession," in *The Family in Ancient Rome: New Perspectives*, ed. B. Rawson (Ithaca: Cornell University Press, 1986), 58–82, discuss the increasing size of fortunes bequeathed or legated to women during the Empire, which reached proportions similar to those left to men.

44. Gardner, *Women in Law*, 19–22.

45. Gardner, *Women in Law*, 14–22, esp. 19–22; S. Dixon, "*Infirmitas sexus*: Womanly Weakness in Roman Law," *Tijdschrift voor Rechtsgeschiedenis* 52 (1984): 343–71; J. A. Crook, "Feminine Inadequacy and the *Senatus Consultum Velleianum*," in *The Family in Ancient Rome: New Perspectives*, ed. B. Rawson (Ithaca: Cornell University Press, 1986), 83–92.

46. Gai. *Inst.* 2.122, cf. 1.190, 3.44; see Gardner, *Women in Law*, 21; Crook, "Feminine Inadequacy," 85. For "womanly weakness," see especially Dixon, "*Infirmitas sexus*," 356–71.

47. Van Bremen, "Women and Wealth," 231–33.

48. For women as priestesses see Sarah B. Pomeroy, *Goddesses, Whores, Wives, and Slaves: Women in Classical Antiquity* (New York: Schocken Books, 1975), 75–77, 125, 214–16, 223; P. Paris, *Quatenus feminae res publicas in Asia minore, Romanis imperantibus, attigerent* (Paris: E. Thorin, 1891), 17, 120–21; R. S. Kraemer, "Women

in the Religions of the Greco-Roman World," *Religious Studies Review* 9 (1983): 131–32. The appearance of women as priestesses is much more frequent in Greek society than in Roman, where, other than vestal virgins, it occurs regularly only in the imperial period. The independence and actual performance of duties of the *archiereiai* of Asia (high priestesses of the imperial cult) have been established by R. A. Kearsley, "Asiarchs, *Archiereis*, and the *Archiereiai* of Asia," *GRBS* 27 (1986): 183–92. But of course this may be only a regional idiosyncracy; we see, for example, that in the mid-third century B.C.E. the priestess of Aglauros at Athens was represented by her son even when she received honors: see G. S. Dontas, "The True Aglaurion," *Hesperia* 52 (1983): 51–55. See also J. Turner, "Hiereiai: Acquisition of Feminine Priesthoods in Ancient Greece" (Ph.D. dissertation, University of California, Santa Barbara, 1983).

49. On these and similar texts see Dixon, "*Infirmitas sexus*," 356–71; Crook, "Feminine Inadequacy," 85–92. A. J. Marshall, "Ladies at Law: The Role of Women in the Roman Civil Courts," in *Studies in Latin Literature and Roman History*, ed. C. Deroux (Brussels: Latomus, 1989), 35–54, reinvestigates the topic of women's relation to the law in Roman society, to conclude persuasively that both men and women expected and accepted women's legal restrictions in bringing suits and appearing in court on behalf of themselves and others, but that women did attend actively to their legal affairs within the prescribed social limits (for example, by presenting *libelli* to authorities).

50. Pomeroy, *Goddesses, Whores, Wives, and Slaves*, 57–119; J. Gould, "Law, Custom and Myth: Aspects of the Social Position of Women in Classical Athens," *JHS* 100 (1980): 38–59. D. M. Schaps, *The Economic Rights of Women in Ancient Greece* (Edinburgh: Edinburgh University Press, 1979), modifies somewhat the conventional economic picture.

51. For example, in Plancia Magna's day Plutarch wrote that "the speech [of a virtuous woman] ought not to be for the public, and she ought to be modest and guarded about saying anything in the hearing of outsiders . . . ," even as he stressed that wives are to be their husbands' active helpmeets throughout life (*Moralia* 138C; 139D, F; 140A, D–F; 141A; 142C–D; 145A). See M. Foucault, *The Care of the Self* (New York: Vintage Books, 1986), 147–85, who treats the evidence from a different perspective than the present one.

52. Van Bremen, "Women and Wealth," 234. Specifically for women's "modest" attire in Perge and the East, which sometimes included veiling from head to toe except the eyes and nose, see Robert, *Hellenica* 5:66–69.

53. The most extensive treatments are those of Paris, *Feminae*, and O. Braunstein, *Die politische Wirksamkeit der griechischen Frau: eine Nachwirkung vorgriechischen Mutterrechtes* (dissertation, Leipzig, 1911). R. MacMullen, "Women in Public in the Roman Empire," *Historia* 29 (1980): 208–18, provides a briefer and more modern treatment.

54. Some of the newly found inscriptions, together with older ones, appear in

the collection of H. W. Pleket, "The Social Position of Women in the Greco-Roman World," in *Epigraphica II: Texts on the Social History of the Greek World* (Leiden: E. J. Brill, 1969), 10–41; see also W. Eck, "Die Präsenz senatorischer Familien in den Städten des Imperium Romanum bis zum späten 3. Jahrhundert," in *Studien zur antiken Sozialgeschichte: Festschrift F. Vittinghoff*, ed. W. Eck, H. Galsterer, and H. Wolff (Cologne and Vienna: Böhlau, 1980), tables I.c.19, 27, 28, 37–39, 51 (pp. 292–94); D. Magie, *Roman Rule in Asia Minor* (Princeton: Princeton University Press, 1950), 1518–19 n. 50. The figures are derived from Braunstein, *Politische Wirksamkeit*, and R. Münsterberg, *Die Beamtennamen auf den griechischen Münzen* (Vienna, 1911–1927; reprinted New York and Hildesheim: G. Olms, 1973), 256.

55. Figures derived from Paris, *Feminae*, 41–77. MacMullen, "Women in Public," 213, notes that although such eminent women are numerous, they still constitute a relatively small proportion (10 to 12 percent) of the municipal and imperial elite known to us. See also below, note 69.

56. Paris, *Feminae*.

57. Paris, *Feminae*, e.g., 30–31, 57–58, 84–86. But Kearsley, "Asiarchs, *Archiereis*, and *Archiereiai*," 183–92, now argues convincingly that at least the female high priestesses of the imperial cult in Asia were independent of their husbands in their positions.

58. Paris, *Feminae*, 121–32.

59. Paris, *Feminae*, 124–29.

60. See A. J. Marshall, "Roman Women and the Provinces," *Ancient Society* 6 (1975): 124–25; V. Chapot, *La province romaine proconsulaire d'Asie* (Paris, 1904; reprinted Rome: "L'Erma" di Bretschneider, 1967), 158–63; Magie, *Roman Rule in Asia Minor*, 649–50, 1507 n. 34, 1518–19 n. 50. For emphasis on the "political decline" of the Greek East under Roman rule see G. E. M. de Ste Croix, *The Class Struggle in the Ancient Greek World* (Ithaca: Cornell University Press, 1981), 518–37.

61. Braunstein, *Politische Wirksamkeit*.

62. Braunstein, *Politische Wirksamkeit*, 64–88.

63. Braunstein, *Politische Wirksamkeit*, 89.

64. For a critique of Bachofen see, for example, S. Pembroke, "Last of the Matriarchs: A Study in the Inscriptions of Lycia," *Journal of the Economic and Social History of the Orient* 8 (1965): 217–47; E. Fee, "The Sexual Politics of Victorian Social Anthropology," *Feminist Studies* 1 (1973): 23–39; J. Bamberger, "The Myth of Matriarchy: Why Men Rule in Primitive Society," in *Women, Culture and Society*, ed. M. Z. Rosaldo and L. Lamphere (Stanford: Stanford University Press, 1974), 263–80.

65. Pointed out by Van Bremen, "Women and Wealth," 223, 226–33.

66. For example, Pomeroy, *Goddesses, Whores, Wives, and Slaves*, 126, crediting this to (unspecified) legal and economic changes. Veyne, *Pain et cirque*, 215–16, remarks only on the wealth of women as important for their elevation as magistrates and priestesses.

67. Van Bremen, "Women and Wealth," 226–33.

68. Gardner, *Women in Law*, esp. 263–65.

69. There were as many benefactresses in the West as in the East: see J. C. Rockwell, *Private Baustiftungen für die Stadtgemeinde auf Inschriften der Kaiserzeit im Westen des römischen Reiches* (dissertation, Jena, 1909), esp. 88. Overall, the donations of women do not differ from those of men: we do not find, for example, that when a woman paid for a public banquet, only women were invited (see also Van Bremen, "Women and Wealth," 227–30). Female donors may have constituted about a tenth of all attested donors in the Greek East, to judge from the figures of B. Laum, *Stiftungen in der griechischen und römischen Antike: ein Beitrag zur antiken Kulturgeschichte* (Leipzig and Berlin: B. G. Teubner, 1914; reprinted Stuttgart: Scientia Verlag, 1964), 23.

70. Cf. Marshall, "Roman Women and the Provinces," 125, and MacMullen, "Women in Public," 215–16, who notes, however, that women are rarely found in roles requiring their speaking in public.

71. There may be an example of a female magistrate from North Africa, if the Messia Castula *duumvira* of CIL VIII:9407 was a woman who held the position of duumvir (thus Marshall, "Roman Women and the Provinces," 125 n. 74), rather than the wife of a duumvir (as G. Wilmanns ad loc., CIL VIII: p. 808).

72. Van Bremen, "Women and Wealth," 223–42.

73. Van Bremen, "Women and Wealth," 233–37.

74. Eck, "Präsenz senatorischer Familien," 312, with lists including known senatorial women functioning as municipal magistrates and priestesses (pp. 286–309).

75. For a somewhat sensationalist discussion of the ancient evidence for the imperial women in these periods see J. P. V. D. Balsdon, *Roman Women: Their History and Habits* (New York: J. Day, 1963; reprinted New York: Barnes & Noble, 1983), 68–130, 140–64.

76. *HA* Hadr. 5.9; cf. H. Temporini, *Die Frauen am Hofe Trajans* (Berlin and New York: W. de Gruyter, 1978), 171.

77. For Livia and the Samians see J. M. Reynolds, *Aphrodisias and Rome* (London: Society for the Promotion of Roman Studies, 1982), document 13, and Dio 54.9.7; for the circumstances of the grant see G. W. Bowersock, *Gnomon* 56 (1984): 52, and M. Toher, *GRBS* 26 (1985): 201–2. For Plotina and the Jews see *P. Oxy.* 1242 = E. M. Smallwood, *Documents Illustrating the Principates of Nerva, Trajan and Hadrian* (Cambridge: Cambridge University Press, 1966), no. 516; with Temporini, *Frauen am Hofe Trajans*, 90–100.

78. The retiring role is particularly marked in the first part of the second century C.E.: see my forthcoming article "The Imperial Women of the Early Second Century," *AJP* 112 (1991). MacMullen apparently downplays the influence of the imperial women on Greek women ("Women in Public," 217–18).

79. For the iconography see, for example, note 4 above.

80. M.-T. Raepsaet-Charlier, "Epouses et familles de magistrats dans les provinces romaines aux deux premiers siècles de l'Empire," *Historia* 31 (1982): 58–59; see also Marshall, "Roman Women and the Provinces," 109–27.

81. Raepsaet-Charlier, "Epouses et familles," 58 and passim.

82. Marshall, "Roman Women and the Provinces," esp. 122–27; Raepsaet-Charlier, "Epouses et familles," 64.

83. Marshall, "Roman Women and the Provinces," 122–23.

84. L. Robert, "La titulature de Nicée et de Nicomédie: la gloire et la haine," *HSCP* 81 (1977): 1–39, provides a good illustration of this rivalry, with evidence from coins, inscriptions, archaeology, and literature.

85. See Mansel, "Bericht," 112–18; Ward-Perkins, *Roman Imperial Architecture*, 485 n. 48.

86. *IGR* III:773. For Iulia Sancta see Halfmann, *Senatoren*, no. 134, p. 200.

87. For the gate at Side see A. Mansel, *Die Ruinen von Side* (Berlin: W. de Gruyter, 1963), 36–37, ills. 20, 22; for its dating to the Antonine age see J. Inan, *Roman Sculpture in Side* (Ankara: Türk Tarih Kurumu Basimevi, 1975), p. 83, nos. 17, 18, 27, 39, 71, 78.

88. For Menodora see, for example, Van Bremen, "Women and Wealth," 223–24; the most pertinent inscriptions are conveniently located in *IGR* III:800–802 and *BCH* 13 (1889): 486–87.

SHAYE J. D. COHEN

Menstruants and the Sacred

in Judaism and Christianity

In numerous cultures menstruants and parturients (women who have just given birth) are distanced from sacred places, actions, or objects and are isolated from society. The women are regarded as impure or "polluted." Menstrual taboos have been a favorite topic of study for anthropologists and, in recent years, for feminists from various disciplines, but much work remains to be done.[1] Two large and important topics that remain virtually unexplored are the histories of menstrual taboos in Judaism and in Christianity. The regulations governing the impurity and purification of the menstruant were, and for many Jews still are, an essential part of Jewish piety, but aside from two recent articles (in Hebrew) by Yedidyah Dinari, I have not found a single historical study of the subject.[2] Menstrual taboos occupy a much smaller place, of course, in Christianity than in Judaism, but they do have a place, especially in eastern Christianity, even if they have not yet attracted scholarly attention.

This essay is an initial attempt to fill the lacuna. A full treatment of the topic would require an analysis of the purity systems of ancient Judaism; the Jewish attitudes towards sex, sexuality, the body, and bodily functions; the place of women in Jewish law and society; the parallels and contrasts between Jewish and non-Jewish practices; and the Christian analogues to all these matters. The topic also demands of its interpreter expertise in legal history, social history, comparative religion, social anthropology, folklore, and a host of other disciplines. Even if I were competent in all these areas, and I am not, I could not cover the entire topic in the space allotted. Instead I restrict my discussion here to legal history. I first present the biblical material on menstrual impurity and then describe how the biblical laws were applied in ancient and medieval Judaism and in ancient Christianity. The focal point is the Jewish and Christian exclusion of women from the sacred because of menstrual impurity.

Biblical Background

Six passages from the Torah are the essential background to the later Jewish and Christian exclusions of women from the sacred.

1. According to Leviticus 12, after delivering a boy a parturient is impure (or "unclean") for seven days: "as at the time of her menstrual infirmity . . . she shall remain in a state of blood purification for thirty-three days: she shall not touch any consecrated thing, nor enter the sanctuary until her period of purification is completed."[3] If the woman delivers a girl, these numbers are doubled (fourteen days of impurity and sixty-six of blood purification). The text does not clarify the relative severity of the impurity of the initial days versus that of the subsequent days of "blood purification." No matter how it is interpreted, however, the text declares that the parturient, at least initially, has the status of a menstruant and is excluded from any contact with the sancta for forty or eighty days.

2. Leviticus 15 describes four categories of impurity caused by sexual discharge, two for men and two for women. The first (known in rabbinic law as the *zāb*, plural *zābîm*) is the man who has an uncontrollable seminal oozing or dripping; he is impure for as long as the oozing continues and for an additional seven days after it stops. After the seven days are over he is purified through bathing and the bringing of an atonement sacrifice. The second category (known in rabbinic law as the *baʿal qeri*) is the man who has an ejaculation in sexual intercourse; both he and his partner must bathe and are impure until nightfall. The third category (known in rabbinic law as the *niddâ*)[4] is the menstruant, who is impure for seven days. The fourth category (known in rabbinic law as the *zābâ*, plural *zābôt*) is the woman who has a discharge ("oozes") outside of, or in addition to, her regular period; she is impure for as long as the discharge continues and for an additional seven days. After the seven days are over she is purified through the bringing of an atonement sacrifice.

A few notes. Of these four the ejaculant is impure for the shortest period (until nightfall); the impurity of the other three lasts a minimum of seven days. All four categories transmit impurity to persons and/or objects which come into contact with them, but the ejaculant does so only to his female partner, whereas the other three do so to persons and objects which they touch or which touch them (the rules are not precisely the same for the three). Pollution caused by male sexual discharge (the *zāb*, the ejaculant, and the female partner) requires bathing for purification, but pollution caused by female sexual discharge does not (neither the menstruant nor the *zābâ* nor the man who has intercourse with the menstruant is said to require bathing, although a person who has contact with objects rendered impure by a menstruant requires bathing in order to be purified).[5] Last, Leviticus 15:31 explains that the purpose of the purification system is to make sure that the Israelites do not defile God's dwelling or tabernacle (*miškān*) that is among them. The focal point of the purity system is the central sanctuary.

3. Leviticus 15:24 legislates that intercourse with a menstruant confers menstrual impurity on the male partner, but elsewhere Leviticus goes further and declares such a union to be sinful: "Do not come near a woman during her period of uncleanness to uncover her nakedness" (Leviticus 18:19) and "If a man lies with a woman in her infirmity [*dāwâ*, the same word as in Leviticus 12:2] and uncovers her nakedness . . . both of them shall be cut off from among their people" (Leviticus 20:18). Leviticus 18 prohibits not only sexual intercourse with a menstruant but also "coming near" to her for sexual intercourse.[6] Intercourse with a menstruant is the only shared element between the "ritual" or physical impurities of Leviticus 11–15 and the "dangerous" or sinful impurities of Leviticus 18.[7]

4. Leviticus 22:4 disqualifies the following priests from eating sacred offerings: a "leper" (see Leviticus 13), a *zāb*, anyone rendered impure through contact with a corpse (see Numbers 19), and an ejaculant. (Leviticus 22:5 adds other kinds of impurity as well.) The impure priest must bathe and wait until nightfall before partaking of the sacred offerings.

5. In a closely related passage, Numbers 5:1–4, God commands Moses to remove from the camp "the leper," the *zāb*, and anyone rendered impure by contact with a corpse. The category *zāb* certainly includes the first and fourth categories of Leviticus 15 (the male and female "oozers"); it probably includes also the third category (the menstruant) and perhaps even the second (the ejaculant; see text no. 4 above, which makes this point explicitly). If this interpretation is correct, Numbers 5:1–4 is a utopian extension of Leviticus 15:31.[8] The perimeter of the "tabernacle," the central sanctuary, is coterminous with the perimeter of the "camp." As a

result those who are impure, including menstruants and ejaculants, must leave the camp because the divine presence fills not only the sanctuary but the entire community. If this law were enforced, the number of Israelites outside the camp would rival the number of those within.

6. Another closely related passage is Deuteronomy 23:10–15. If a warrior on military campaign has a nocturnal emission he must leave the camp, not to return until the following evening after bathing. The same paragraph also prescribes that all urination and defecation must take place outside the camp. Deuteronomy thus associates ejaculation with "dirt," something that Leviticus never does, and mentions nocturnal emission alone of all the sources of sexual impurity recounted by Leviticus. But these differences cannot mask the conceptual similarity of Deuteronomy 23:10–15 to Numbers 5:1–4: the impure person must not defile the camp where both God and the Israelites dwell.

These passages do not single out women as sources of impurity. True, the recurrent source of impurity for a woman, menstruation, has more severe consequences than the recurrent source of impurity for a man, ejaculation, probably because menstruation lasts longer than ejaculation, but there is no sign that a woman, once purified, is somehow less pure than a man or that a woman is to be secluded from contact with the sacred more rigorously than a man.[9] In fact the biblical record as a whole shows much greater concern over the potential desecration of the sacred by an ejaculant than by a menstruant.[10] The later exclusions of women from contact with the sacred derive, at least nominally, from these biblical laws, as I discuss below, but there is no evidence that the intent or immediate effect of these laws was to discriminate against women. Finally, five of the six passages are part of the Torah's purity system, but one of them is not. The prohibition of "drawing near" to a menstruant for sexual purposes (Leviticus 18:19 and 20:18, no. 3 above) is part of a list of prohibited sexual unions and has nothing to do with ritual purity. Even when the purity system would lapse after the destruction of the second temple in 70 C.E., the prohibition of union with a menstruant would remain.

The Status of the Menstruant in Jewish Law

On the basis of these biblical laws the Jews of late antiquity and the Middle Ages devoted enormous intellectual and spiritual energies to the following three sets of questions: (1) What is the precise definition of a menstruant (*niddâ*), and exactly how is she to be distinguished from a *zābâ* (a woman who has a discharge not during her regular cycle)? What is the place of menstrual impurity within the purity system as a whole? (2) Since a menstruant can transmit impurity to persons and objects, what degree of social isolation is required of the menstruant? To what extent must she be removed from her normal routines? Does she pose a danger to others around her? Since a husband is instructed not to "draw near" to his menstruant wife, how far apart must they be? (3) Since the menstruant, like all other sources of impurity, must beware of polluting the sacred, where are the limits of the sacred which a menstruant may not cross? In particular, after the destruction of the temple in 70 C.E. and the gradual demise of the entire purity system a few centuries later, were there *any* sancta at all from which a menstruant was barred? These three questions are inextricably connected to each other, and I treat the first two briefly before turning to the third.

The Definition of the Menstruant and Her Impurity

The precise definition of the menstruant and her impurity is one of the major subjects of the tractate Nidda and other tractates in the sixth division of the Mishna. The Mishna, like scripture, still distinguishes between the menstruant and the *zābâ*, but unlike scripture the Mishna also distinguishes "pure" blood from impure—they differ in color.[11] The Mishna assumes that both a *zābâ* and a parturient must immerse in water in order to be purified (m. Nidda 10:8), but unless I am mistaken the Mishna nowhere states explicitly that a menstruant must also immerse. Neither Josephus nor any other work of the second temple period requires a menstruant to immerse for her purification, and the Mishna's silence on the subject therefore *may* be significant.[12] The Babylonian and Palestinian Talmudim, however, take it for granted that a menstruant must immerse after her seven days of impurity, and that her immersion must take place, like the immersion of all others undergoing purification, in a special pool known as a *miqweh*.[13] The Talmudim also document a radical change in the law. In the course of the third century the distinction between the *zābâ* and the menstruant disappeared:[14]

R. Zera said: The daughters of Israel have accepted this severity upon themselves, that even if they see but one drop of blood the size of a mustard seed they regard themselves as impure[15] and count seven clean days.

According to this remarkable innovation, which in this formulation was initiated by the women themselves, whenever a woman saw a discharge of any kind, no matter how little or how brief, she regarded herself as a *zābâ*: she was impure for as long as the discharge lasted (which in the case of regular menstruation was later defined to mean a minimum of five days) plus seven "white" or clean days. After counting the seven "white" days she was restored to a pure state through immersion in water. For traditional Jewish women this is still the law to this day.

Medieval rabbinic authorities amplified many of the details of these rules and attempted to enforce rabbinic norms on a community which was often interested in following its own traditional if unrabbinic way of doing things. But all the basic definitions were established by the Mishna and the Talmudim.[16]

Social Isolation of the Menstruant

Many societies isolate menstruants to some degree or another; some ban them completely from the populated areas, consigning them to special zones or apartments, while others merely restrict certain actions. The laws of Leviticus provide two justifications for such isolation: first, a menstruant is impure, and, like all other sources of impurity, must be isolated from those who would maintain themselves in a state of purity; and second, a man is commanded not "to draw near" to a menstruant for sexual purposes.

But even with these two justifications there is no clear evidence that any Jewish group in the second temple period isolated the menstruant from society. The Temple Scroll, discovered at Qumran, ruled that women may not dwell in Jerusalem, no matter what their menstrual state, and that all cities in the land of Israel must have areas outside the city walls where menstruants and other impure people would reside until they were purified and able to rejoin society. But this legislation, inspired by Numbers 5:1–4, was utopian. For the nonutopian present, the men of Qumran lived in an exclusively male community far removed from any contact with the pollutions of the world, especially women.[17] Possible evidence for the social isolation of the menstruant in the real world comes from a stray phrase in the Mishna and from the later practices of the Samaritans and the black Jews of Ethiopia, but this evidence is ambiguous and uncertain.[18] For most Jews of the second temple period the locus of God's presence was the temple and the temple mount, and as long as those affected with impurity stayed away from the sacred precincts Jewish society did not care about their impurity. Thus the Gospel story about the woman with a twelve-year discharge, clearly a case of zābâ, does not give any indication that the woman was impure or suffered any degree of isolation as a result of her affliction (Matthew 9:18–26; Mark 5:21–43; Luke 8:40–56).[19]

The purity system lived on in rabbinic circles for several centuries after the destruction of the temple. Because women were food preparers, and because foodstuffs are readily susceptible to impurity in rabbinic law, the impurity of the menstruant must have freed her to some degree from her regular household chores. The rabbinic texts that discuss the separation of a husband from his menstruating wife, however, base the separation not on her impurity but on the prohibition of "drawing near" to her. There is considerable debate whether husband and menstruating wife may eat at the same table or share the same utensils, and whether they may sleep in the same bed, he on his side in his clothes, she on her side in her clothes. The general tenor of these discussions is that there should be total separation between the two, even if the law does not strictly require it. A righteous man will not touch his wife at all during her menstruation, not because of a fear of contracting impurity but because of a fear of sexual arousal.[20]

The contrast between these two reasons for the isolation of the menstruant is evident in *Differences between the Jews of the East and the Jews of the Land of Israel*, a work of uncertain date which seems to describe the conditions of the sixth or seventh century:

> The Jews of the East say that a menstruant may perform all her household chores except for three: filling her husband's cup, preparing her husband's bed, and washing his face, hands, and feet. The Jews of the land of Israel say that she may touch neither any [foodstuff that has come into contact with a] liquid nor the household utensils, and that with reluctance was she permitted to give suck to her child.[21]

The Jews of Babylonia (the Jews of the East) lived outside the Holy Land and were not affected by the rabbinic purity system. For them the social isolation of the menstruant was needed only to prevent sexual intimacy, or the possibility of sexual intimacy, between husband and wife (see b. Ketubot 61a). The Jews of the Land of Israel, however, still enforced at least some aspects of the purity system and therefore did not allow the menstruant any role in food preparation; presumably other women in the house would have taken her place.

Later jurists maintained in all its rigor the prohibition of any physical contact between a husband and his menstruant wife. For example, several jurists wrote that a husband was prohibited from passing any object to his wife hand to hand; the proper procedure was for him to put the object down somewhere and for her to pick it up. The disciples of R. Solomon ben Isaac of Troyes (known as Rashi, 1040–1105) observed the master tossing his keys to his wife during her period.[22] Husband and menstruating wife were allowed to dine together only if some unmistakable marker indicated a separation between them. However, the jurists were divided on the obligation of a menstruant to separate from her household tasks because of her impurity. For a time the severities that had been observed in the Land of Israel spread to Babylonia (tenth and eleventh centuries) and northern France and Germany (twelfth and thirteenth centuries), even though virtually every other aspect of the purity system had disappeared. But the *rhetoric* of impurity was still powerful, as we shall see, and many Jews believed that a menstruant ought not to do things that would have been prohibited had the purity system remained in force. This view did not prevail, however. With the demise of polygamy and the decline of the extended family, a menstruating wife had to perform her household chores because there was no one else to do them for her. Maimonides (1135–1204) could dismiss as foolish and heretical those Jews who prohibited a menstruant from preparing and cooking food.[23]

The passage from *Differences* quoted above reveals yet a third reason for the social isolation of the menstruant: "and with reluctance (*ūbĕdôḥaq*)[24] was she permitted to give suck to her child." The legal basis for prohibiting a menstruant from giving suck to her child probably would have been expressed in the language of purity and impurity, but the most likely source for the prohibition is the danger that the menstruant represents to those around her, especially tender infants and children. Not only is she *impure*, she also is *dangerous*. The source of the danger is not explained, but presumably it is the demonic power or unclean spirit that resides within the menstruant. Only one passage in the Babylonian Talmud warns of the danger that a menstruant poses to those who come near her (b. Pesahim 111a);[25] otherwise, as far as I have been able to determine, rabbinic literature knows nothing of the kind. The rabbis of antiquity believed that a menstruant is impure, transmits impurity to persons and objects, and suffers a "curse,"[26] but they did not regard her as a source of danger or as possessed by a demon or an impure spirit. She is ritually impure, not dangerously polluted.[27] From impurity to pollution is a significant step, and that step seems to be attested in *Differences*.

Another work, perhaps contemporaneous with *Differences*, documents the same step much more clearly. The *Beraita de Nidda* is a work of uncertain date and provenance but appears to be a product of the Land of Israel in the sixth or seventh century.[28] The work focuses on the impurity of the menstruant and on the dangers of that liminal moment when a woman has just purified herself by immersion and is returning home to have sex with her husband. Nowhere does the work explicitly say that a menstruant is possessed by an unclean spirit or by a demon, but some of the recommended restrictions are so severe and extreme, always justified by the rhetoric of impurity, that the work must be doing so implicitly. Several examples: a menstruant must not cut her fingernails, lest her husband or child accidentally step on or touch the clipping and as a result develop boils and die; a priest whose mother, wife, or any other female member of his household is menstruating may not bless the people, lest his blessing become a curse; a sage who partakes of food prepared by a menstruant will forget his learning; a menstruant's spit, breath, and speech cause impurity in others.[29] During the following centuries regulations of this type made their way into some strands of Jewish piety, even if some authorities, notably Maimonides, polemicized against them.[30]

In sum: the belief that a menstruant poses a danger to those around her appears in Jewish sources for the first time in the sixth or seventh century C.E. Its emergence and acceptance then *may* be the result either of outside influence (whether Christian or Islamic) or of new perceptions of the woman within Jewish society.

The Menstruant and the Sacred

The Jerusalem temple was the focal point of the purity system. It was the holiest place in the world and had to be kept free from all impurity. The most sacred place of all was the inner sanctum, the holy of holies, which was surrounded by zones of decreasing sanctity. Only the high priest could enter the inner sanctum, only priests could enter the sacred area, only Jews in a pure state could enter the inner precincts. Gentiles and impure Jews could enter the outer precincts. The rabbinic and the Josephan testimonies do not fully agree on the details of this arrangement; in particular, Josephus says that women, whether impure or not, were prohibited from the inner precincts, but the rabbis make no such claim, at least not explicitly. Both sources agree that impure persons, specifically ejaculants and menstruants, were excluded from all the inner precincts.[31] The Jews of Qumran, as I remarked above, thought that impure people, especially women, should be excluded not just from the temple but also from the city of Jerusalem and the other cities of the Holy Land. They even transferred to their desert encampment the sanctity of the temple. Other sects too transferred to themselves or their social organizations one or another aspect of the temple's sanctity.[32] Pietists purified themselves before engaging in the sacred actions of praying or eating.[33]

Texts of the second temple period do not indicate whether a menstruant was barred from sacred activities outside the temple, but one passage in Josephus implies that she might have been. Genesis 31 tells the story of Jacob's flight from his father-in-law Laban. Before fleeing, Rachel steals her father's idols. When Laban catches up with Jacob, he searches the camp for the stolen objects. Rachel hides them in her saddlebag, sits upon it, and pretends to be so incapacitated by her period that she is unable to stand when her father enters the tent. In his paraphrase of this story Josephus adds that "Laban thought that his daughter would not approach the images while having such an affliction" (Jewish Antiquities 1.19.10 [323]). It is likely that these thoughts of the pagan Laban reflect the piety of Josephus' Jewish contemporaries: a menstruant would be expected not to approach sacred objects.

With the destruction of the temple in 70 C.E. the purity system lost its focal point but, at least for members of the rabbinic estate, persisted nevertheless in the realm of food. Many rabbis continued to treat food on the table as if it were a sacrifice on the altar. In other areas, however, the purity rules lapsed. The sacrificial cult of the temple was replaced by the study of Torah, the liturgical recitation of scriptural verses, and communal and private prayer, but at first the purity requirements of the temple were not transferred to these sacred activities. The Mishna states (m. Berakot 3:4–6) that an ejaculant may not recite aloud the benedictions of the liturgy or of the grace after meals. The Mishna does not give a reason for the prohibition but implies that the problem is not impurity in general but semen or ejaculation in particular. The Mishna nowhere records a parallel prohibition for a leper, a *zāb*, someone affected by corpse impurity (see m. Berakot 3:1–2), a menstruant, or any other impure person. Only the ejaculant and those who come into contact with semen must be purified before performing the liturgy. The point is made clearly by m. Berakot 3:6:

> A *zāb* who saw semen [in his discharge], a menstruant who released semen [that had been deposited within her before the onset of her period], and a woman who [recently] had intercourse and [now] sees her menstrual period—these require immersion [before reciting the liturgy]. But R. Judah says they do not require it.

Although they are impure, the *zāb* and the menstruant may recite the liturgy; however, if they have a discharge of semen, they, like the ejaculant, must be purified before turning to the sacred. The Tosepta correctly concludes (t. Berakot 2:12, p. 8 Lieberman):

> *zābîm*, *zābôt*, menstruants, and parturients are permitted to read the Torah, and to study Mishna, Midrash, laws, and homilies. But the ejaculant is prohibited from all these.[34]

The prohibition of an ejaculant to study Torah, mentioned in the Tosepta but omitted in the Mishna, is ascribed by the Talmudim to Ezra.[35]

Why of all sources of impurity was ejaculation alone singled out? In their discussion of m. Berakot 3:4 the Talmudim suggest that the reason was to limit the frequency of sexual intercourse ("so that sages should not behave like roosters"). If a man after intercourse could not engage in Torah study or prayer, the quintessential acts of rabbinic piety, until he was purified through immersion, he would think twice before turning from Torah to amorous matters. (The Talmudim even have a remarkable story about an adulterous union that was not consummated because the couple could not find a place to immerse afterwards!) This explanation is not wholly satisfactory, because if the purpose of the rule was to control male sexuality, why does a menstruant who emits semen require purification before prayer? But the talmudic explanation correctly emphasizes the fact that the law is primarily interested in men, not women, and in male actions and intentions, not purity and impurity.[36]

However, the Talmudim also suggest that the notion of impurity was not entirely irrelevant. The Babylonian Talmud records the abolition of the requirement of immersion before prayer and Torah study. The requirement was abolished because "the words of Torah are not susceptible to impurity." This principle is repeated frequently throughout the later rabbinic discussions of these rules, but its original setting in the Talmudim is confusing. Even if the words of Torah are not susceptible to impurity, perhaps sages should purify themselves anyway before engaging in Torah study, in order to make sure that they do not imitate barnyard behavior. And if the words of Torah *are* susceptible to impurity, why does the Mishna single out the ejaculant alone? Any menstruant, not only she who emits semen, ought to be required to immerse before reciting prayers and benedictions. These problems have engaged the attention of talmudic commentators from medieval to modern times, but I cannot pursue the question here. In any case both Talmudim clearly state that the words of Torah are not susceptible to impurity, and neither Talmud raises any obstacle before a menstruant who wishes to pray, study Torah, or recite benedictions.[37]

It is surely no coincidence that the earliest Jewish text (post 70 c.e.) to prohibit menstruants from coming into contact with the sacred is the *Beraita de Nidda*, the earliest Jewish text (along with *Differences*) to reflect a fear of the danger posed by menstruants. A menstruant (p. 27) may neither separate the priestly offering (ḥallâ) from bread dough (although b. Bekorot 27a and m. Nidda 10:7 explicitly permit it) nor light the Shabbat candles. According to m. Shabbat 2:6, the three major rituals entrusted to women are the laws of menstruation, ḥallâ, and the lighting of Shabbat candles; according to the *Beraita de Nidda* when a woman is observing the first of these rituals, the laws of menstruation, she is prohibited from performing the other two. Men are prohibited from greeting a menstruant or reciting a benediction in her presence, lest she respond in kind or recite "amen" and thereby desecrate the name of God (pp. 17, 37). No impure person is permitted to enter a "house of prayer, because he thereby is rendering God's sanctuary impure," but this general prohibition is directed specifically at menstruants; in fact they should not even enter a room filled with Hebrew books (p. 26). Like menstruants parturients too may not enter either synagogues or schools (pp. 31–33).[38] These prohibitions apply not only to menstruants but also to those who come into contact with them. Men who have had contact with a menstruant's spittle are prohibited from entering a synagogue until they have been purified (pp. 3, 36); a midwife who has delivered a child has the impurity of a menstruant and may not enter a synagogue or "stand before the sages" without being purified (p. 6).

Most striking here is the changed status not only of the menstruant but also of the sancta. The Mishna and Talmudim seek to distance prayer and Torah study not from impurity but from male lust. In the Mishna and the Talmudim the synagogue has no inherent sanctity; sacred rituals are performed there, but the building has no sanctity at all.[39] It certainly is not a temple; even a leper is permitted to enter.[40] The laws of purity are irrelevant.[41] By the time of the *Beraita de Nidda*, however, the synagogue was becoming a surrogate temple, a development confirmed by archaeology. In the sixth and seventh centuries synagogues were regularly outfitted with an ark, an eternal flame, and representations of temple vessels (notably the menorah) and were designated with temple terminology ("holy place," "house of God," etc.).[42] Thus in the *Beraita de Nidda* menstruants are explicitly prohibited from entering a synagogue and touching holy books and implicitly prohibited from reciting benedictions and reciting the name of God.[43]

The prohibitions enjoined upon the ejaculant by the Mishna and the Talmudim and upon the menstruant by the *Beraita de Nidda* had a remarkable career in subsequent Jewish piety, a career that can be traced here only briefly.[44] Some authorities held that the prohibitions had the force of law, others the force of custom only, still others no force at all. Some texts link the prohibitions for ejaculants with those for menstruants, or at least devote as much attention to the one as to the other, but some treat only the one and not the other. Ambient culture played a role in these developments; Maimonides observed that the Jewish men of Christian countries before engaging in prayer did not wash after ejaculation, whereas the Jews of Islamic countries did. But even in Christian Europe pietistic circles in both medieval and modern times maintained the necessity of purification for men before prayer and Torah study.

At first the rabbis of medieval Babylonia (the *geonîm*) were opposed to the separation of the menstruant from the sancta: "Even if she is forbidden to her husband, she certainly is not exempted from the commandments [of prayer, benedictions, etc.]." But by the tenth century the restrictive view began to triumph; a menstruant was in some quarters still permitted to pray, but the prohibition of entering a synagogue, certainly during the initial days of her period, became widespread.[45] In the emerging communities of the high Middle Ages a curious pattern developed. Sephardic (Spanish and North African) communities did not accept these prohibitions at all; Maimonides and R. Joseph Karo, the two great codifiers of rabbinic law, both of them Sephardim, omit them entirely. But Ashkenazic (north, central, and east European) communities accepted the prohibitions, if not as law then as custom. A work from the school of Rashi (northern France, twelfth century) reports:

> Some women refrain from entering a synagogue and from touching a Hebrew book during their menstrual periods. This is only supererogation (*ḥumra bĕʿalmā*) and they are not obligated to act in this manner. For what is the reason for them to act this way? If it is because they think that the synagogue is like the temple, then even after their immersion why do they enter it? . . . Thus you see that [the synagogue] is not like the temple and they may enter it [even during their periods]. Nevertheless it is a place of purity, and they act well, and may they be blessed.[46]

From the point of view of law there is no reason for menstruants to refrain from entering the synagogue: the purity system has lapsed; all Jews, both men and women, are impure, for they cannot bring an atonement sacrifice at the temple; and, in any case, the synagogue does not have the legal status of the temple. But oblivious to logic and law, Jewish women of medieval France refrained from entering the synagogue during their periods because they had internalized the fear of menstruation first attested by the *Beraita de Nidda*. Even without a legal basis, the custom is endorsed by the rabbi who reports it, and the women are praised for their piety. Similarly, a contemporary or slightly later authority writes that menstruants refrained not only from entering the synagogue but also from praying "in front of" other, nonmenstruating women.[47]

In a gloss on the law code of the Sephardic R. Joseph Karo, the Ashkenazic R. Moses Isserles (both of the sixteenth century) records that custom requires menstruants during the initial days of their periods to refrain from entering a synagogue, praying, mentioning God's name, or touching a Hebrew book.[48] During the subsequent centuries, however, these customs died out in Ashkenaz; only the fear of touching a Torah scroll remained—and for many Jews still remains—part of the piety of Ashkenazic women.[49] But in a peculiar reversal after the sixteenth century these prohibitions became part of Sephardic women's piety; in contempo-

rary Israel many women from "oriental" countries do not attend synagogue or pray during their menstrual periods, even though the Sephardic
chief rabbi has told them that the custom has no basis in law.[50]

Menstrual Impurity in Early Christianity

In his polemic against Christianity the emperor Julian remarks that the
only difference between Judaism and the religion of the Hellenes is the
peculiar Jewish belief in one god: "All the rest we have in a manner (*pōs*) in
common with them—temples, sanctuaries, altars, purifications (*hagneiai*),
and certain precepts. For as to these we differ from one another either not
at all or in trivial matters" (*Against the Galileans* 306B). Whether Judaism
and Greco-Roman paganism really differ only in trivial matters is a question that need not be pursued here. Certainly many of the Greek and
Roman purification rules closely resemble the Jewish. Numerous cults
and temples excluded ejaculants and parturients and prescribed bathing
as the means of effecting purification. But in strong contrast to Judaism,
Greco-Roman paganism did not as a rule regard menstruation as a source
of impurity that had to be distanced from the sacred. Aristotle and Pliny
testify to the dangerous power that resided in menstrual blood and consequently in the menstruant, but the fears aroused by this alleged power did
not cause the menstruant to be regarded as impure. Only a few cults, all of
them non-Greek, excluded menstruants. On this point Judaism and paganism are substantially different.[51]

It was not paganism but Judaism (and/or Leviticus) that taught early
Christianity to regard the menstruant as impure. Christianity in antiquity
saw no need to define precisely the impurity of the menstruant or to
impose any social restraints on her (beyond the prohibition of sexual
intercourse).[52] However, numerous strands in Christianity from ancient
to modern times have isolated the menstruant from the sacred at least to
some extent. Inasmuch as Christianity, almost from its inception, regarded its rituals, institutions, and clergy as the permanent replacements
of the Jerusalem temple, Christianity excluded menstruants from the
church long before Judaism excluded them from the synagogue. The
earliest attested exclusion of women from the sancta in Christianity is
from the mid-third century; in post-70 Judaism it is from the sixth or
seventh. It is probably not coincidental that separate seating for women in

the church is attested several centuries before separate seating in the synagogue.[53] The three oldest Christian references to the separation of menstruants from the sancta come from third-century Rome, Alexandria, and Syria.[54]

The *Apostolic Tradition* of Hippolytus, written in Rome in the early third century, records that if, on the day set for baptism, a female catechumen has her period, she is to be separated from the other catechumens and be baptized on another day.[55] Hippolytus does not explain this requirement (which has no parallel in rabbinic law), but the simplest explanation surely is that a menstruant is impure and therefore ought not to come into contact with the sancta of the church.[56]

The evidence from Alexandria is much more explicit. In a canonical letter Dionysius of Alexandria, a disciple of Origen, writes as follows:

Concerning women in their menstrual separation (*en aphedrō*), whether it is right for them in such a condition to enter the house of God, I think it unnecessary even to inquire. For I think that they, being faithful and pious, would not dare in such a condition either to approach the holy table or to touch the body and blood of Christ. For even the woman who had the twelve-year discharge and was eager for a cure touched not him but only his fringe. It is unobjectionable to pray in any state and to remember the Lord in any condition and to beseech him to obtain aid, but he who is not completely pure in both soul and body shall be prevented from approaching the holy and the holy of holies.[57]

This responsum of Dionysius is followed by two others, the first recommending that married couples abstain from intercourse before prayer, the second discussing pollution caused by nocturnal emission. Dionysius is transferring to Christianity the pollution categories of Leviticus 15. A disciple of Origen ought to have known how to allegorize the law, but here Dionysius is a decided literalist (even if he argues that nocturnal emission pollutes only if one feels guilty). Dionysius states that a menstruant may pray and may mention the name of God, because prayer does not require purity (even if married couples should abstain from sex before prayer), but she may not enter "the house of God," the church, and may not approach the "the holy table," the altar, in order to partake of communion, the sacrifice. In other words she may not approach "the holy and the holy of holies."[58] The transference of temple terminology to the church is unmistakable. Dionysius proves his point from the Gospel story of the woman with a twelve-year discharge (discussed briefly above). Although eager for a cure, she does not dare touch Christ's body, because that would have been a violation of the sancta; instead she touches only the fringe of his garment (*kraspedon*).[59] Consequently menstruants also (Dionysius here conflates *zābâ* with menstruant) ought not to touch the body of Christ, the Eucharist.

The *Didascalia* was written in the mid-third century in Syria. Its final chapter contains a long polemic against the observance of Jewish practices, notably the Sabbath, prohibited foods, and the purity laws. The polemic against the purity laws is directed primarily at the observance of menstrual impurity but also includes impurity caused by ejaculation and by contact with human corpses and impure animals (pp. 238–245, trans. Vööbus). The polemic demonstrates that Christian women in Syria during their menstruation refrained from prayer, the Eucharist, and scriptural study (p. 238). It also reveals the justification of the practice advanced by the women themselves. They argued that during the seven days of their impurity they were emptied of the Holy Spirit that they had received at baptism and therefore ought not to do holy things (p. 239). The *Didascalia* responds by taking their argument to its next step: during the time when they are emptied of the Holy Spirit on account of their impurity, they will be possessed by unclean spirits that cannot be ejected without renewed baptisms—a possibility which for the *Didascalia* is absurd. Therefore let the women realize that once baptized they are always in the possession of the Holy Spirit (pp. 239–42).

On this account then . . . you shall not separate those [women] who have their period. For she also who had the discharge of blood, when she touched the border of our Savior's cloak, was not censured but was even esteemed worthy for the forgiveness of all her sins. And when [your wives have] those issues which are according to nature, take care, as is right, that you cleave to them, for you know that they are your limbs, and love them as yourselves. . . . On this account, a woman when she is in the way of women, and a man when an issue comes forth from him, and a man and his wife when they have conjugal intercourse and rise up one from another—let them assemble without restraint, without bathing, for they are clean. (Pp. 244–245, trans. Vööbus, slightly revised)

As the *Didascalia* proceeds to explain, impurity is caused by sin. Neither contact with a corpse nor any sexual discharge causes impurity. Not only may a menstruant pray, she may also partake of the Eucharist. As proof the *Didascalia* offers the same text advanced by Dionysius, the Gospel story of the woman with a twelve-year discharge, but whereas Dionysius used it to prove that a menstruant may not touch the body of Christ (she touched the *kraspedon*, not the body), the *Didascalia* uses it to prove the opposite. Dionysius ascribes some impurity to conjugal intercourse and to ejaculation, but the *Didascalia* specifically denies it. The *Didascalia's* rejection of the Levitical impurity laws is so radical that it even rejects the requirement that husband and wife separate from each other during her menstruation. I know no parallel to this statement in early Christianity; the Latin translator was so offended by it that he emended it out of existence (where the Syriac has "cleave to them" the Latin reads *nolite convenire illis*, "do not consort with them").[60] The debate between Dionysius and the *Didascalia* reflects two contrasting strands within early Christianity: the implementation of "Old Testament" law within the new dispensation (Dionysius) versus its complete abrogation (*Didascalia*).[61]

Dionysius justifies the exclusion of menstruants from the church by transferring temple ideology to the church. The Christian targets of the polemics of the *Didascalia* justify the exclusion of menstruants from prayer by asserting that they have been voided of the Holy Spirit. The *Beraita de Nidda*, that peculiar rabbinic (?) work discussed above, combines both approaches. Like Dionysius it transfers temple sanctity to the house of prayer and consequently excludes menstruants from it; like the targets of the polemics of the *Didascalia* it prohibits menstruants from prayer and scriptural study, either because it transfers the sanctity of the temple cult to these sacred activities too, or because it regards menstruants as possessed by some impure spirit (as the *Didascalia* argues), or both. But what is more remarkable than the substance of this parallel between Judaism and Christianity is that Dionysius and the *Didascalia* antedate the *Beraita de Nidda* by at least three centuries.

Concluding Reflections

We moderns find the Levitical impurity rules bizarre and incomprehensible, in spite of the interpretations of Mary Douglas and others. But for the ancients, not just of pre-exilic times but well into late antiquity, the text had a powerful hold on the religious mind. Even Christians did not always believe that their faith in Christ freed them from the impurity rules and food taboos of Leviticus.

From the second temple period to the very recent past the liturgy of Judaism has been the exclusive preserve of men. In some quarters the purity rules of Leviticus and their extensions in rabbinic Judaism are blamed for this state of affairs,[62] but this condemnation is simplistic and unfair. There is no sign that the purity system at any point in its development was intended to discriminate against women or to exclude them from the sacred. Men too were subject to sexual impurity, and at least in rabbinic Judaism the separation of an ejaculant from the sancta (prayer and Torah study) is older and more authoritative than the separation of a menstruant from the sancta (prayer and synagogue). In the post-talmudic period menstruants began to be excluded, and to exclude themselves, from synagogues and from contact with other sancta, but that development, although expressed in the language of purity and impurity, is the result of various considerations, notably the transference of temple sanctity to the synagogue and the liturgy, and the emergence of the view that menstruants were not only impure but also dangerous. Women were marginal altogether in the rabbinic Judaism of late antiquity and the Middle Ages, and the rhetoric of impurity only served to strengthen and justify an order which already existed and which, until recently, both men and women accepted.[63]

Notes

I am grateful to my friends Neil Danzig, Lori Lefkovitz, and Rabbi Leonard Gordon for their helpful comments and suggestions.

1. For a classic anthropological study see, for example, James G. Frazer, *The Golden Bough Part II: Taboo and the Perils of the Soul*, 3d ed. (London: Macmillan, 1914), 145–57. For a modern study see *Blood Magic: The Anthropology of Menstruation*, ed. Thomas Buckley and Alma Gottlieb (Berkeley and Los Angeles: University of California Press, 1988). For feminist perspectives see, for example, Janice Delaney et al., *The Curse: A Cultural History of Menstruation* (New York: Dutton, 1976; 2d ed., Urbana: University of Illinois Press, 1988); Emily Martin, *The Woman in the Body: A Cultural Analysis of Reproduction* (Boston: Beacon, 1987); Karen Ericksen Paige and Jeffery M. Paige, *The Politics of Reproductive Ritual* (Berkeley and Los Angeles: University of California Press, 1981); Penelope Shuttle, *The Wise Wound: Eve's Curse and Everywoman* (New York: Marek, 1978).

2. Yedidyah Dinari, "The Customs of Menstrual Impurity: Their Origin and Development," *Tarbiz* 49 (1979–80): 302–24, and "The Violation of the Sacred by the Nidda and the Enactment of Ezra," *Te'uda* 3 (1983): 17–37 (*Te'uda* is the journal of the Chaim Rosenberg School of Jewish Studies of Tel Aviv University). See also Mordechai A. Friedman, "Menstrual Impurity and Sectarianism in the Writings of the Geonim and Moses and Abraham Maimonides," *Maimonidean Studies* 1 (1990) (in Hebrew). For an excellent brief survey of the Jewish laws and practices concerning menstruation see Israel Ta-Shema, "Niddah," *Encyclopedia Judaica* 12 (1971): 1141–48. Judith Baskin, "The Separation of Women in Rabbinic Judaism," in *Women, Religion, and Social Change*, ed. Yvonne Y. Haddad and E. B. Findly (Albany: SUNY Press, 1985), 3–15, might also be useful.

3. All translations of the Hebrew Bible are from the New Jewish Version; New Testament quotations are from the Revised Standard Version; all other translations are mine unless otherwise noted.

4. In the Tanak *niddâ* often means "pollution" (for example, Leviticus 12 and 15), but Ezekiel 18:6, 22:10 (and 36:17?), and Lamentations 1:8 (and 1:17?) anticipate the rabbinic usage.

5. If those who merely touch an object rendered impure by a menstruant require bathing for their purification, surely the menstruant herself requires bathing for her purification. This is the argument of several medieval rabbis who tried to find a scriptural source for the bathing of menstruants. See, for example, Tosapot, b. Yebamot 47b s.v. *bimqôm šehaniddâ tôbelet*; the commentary of Nahmanides on Leviticus 15:11; and R. Isaac ben Moses of Vienna (ca. 1190–ca. 1260), *Or Zaru'a*, part 1, sect. 359, page 48b (ed. Zhitomir, 1862). The argument has some logic, but it is striking that Leviticus does not state the matter explicitly. Even in Numbers 31, which describes the purification of the Israelite warriors and their booty, the Midianite women are not purified either through bathing or any other ritual. According to the priestly legislator, the only woman who is explicitly said to require bathing is the woman who is rendered impure by semen.

6. Contrast Leviticus 18:7–13 and 15–18. Leviticus 18:19 follows the terminology of 18:6; and cf. 18:14.

7. Tikva Frymer-Kensky, "Pollution, Purification, and Purgation in Biblical Israel," in *The Word of the Lord Shall Go Forth: Essays in Honor of David Noel Freedman*, ed. Carol Meyers (Winona Lake, Ind.: Eisenbraun's, 1983), 399–414.

8. Menahem Haran, *Temple and Temple Service in Ancient Israel* (Oxford: Clarendon Press, 1978; reprinted Winona Lake, Ind.: Eisenbraun's, 1985), 11 n. 11.

9. Although my friend Judith Romney Wegner astutely observes that a *zāb* brings his atonement offering "before the Lord" (Leviticus 15:14), whereas the *zābâ* does not (Leviticus 15:29). But the parallel phraseology in Leviticus 15:15 and 30 implies that this difference is not significant.

10. Shaye J. D. Cohen, "Solomon and the Daughter of Pharaoh: Intermarriage,

Conversion, and the Impurity of Women," *Journal of the Ancient Near East Society* 16–17 (1984–85) [*Ancient Studies in Memory of Elias Bickerman* (1987)]: 23–37.

11. m. Nidda 2:6–7. Jerome adds that the rabbis employed both sight and taste to determine whether a bloodstained garment was pure or impure: "The Jews have as the heads of their synagogues certain very learned men who are assigned the disgusting task of determining by taste, if they are unable to discern by the eyes (alone), whether the blood of a virgin or a menstruant is pure or impure" (Epistle *To Algasia* 121.10.19 = *Corpus Scriptorum Ecclesiasticorum Latinorum* 56:48).

12. See Josephus, *Jewish Antiquities* 3.11.3 (261–64). In the mid-second century C.E. Justin knows immersion only for men after ejaculation and intercourse, not for menstruants; see Justin Martyr, *Dialogue with Trypho* 46.2. Similarly, the *Didascalia*, in a passage to be discussed below, seems not to know regular immersion after menstruation.

13. The earliest archaeologically attested *miqwāôt* are at the Hasmonean palace in Jericho (second century B.C.E.), where their primary users would have been the male priests; see Ehud Netzer, "Ancient Ritual Baths (Miqvaot) in Jericho," *Jerusalem Cathedra* 2 (1982): 106–19.

14. b. Nidda 66a; cf. p. Berakot 5:1 8d middle.

15. The Hebrew is *yôšĕbôt*, "they sit," but the meaning is "they seat themselves apart," that is, "they regard themselves as impure." Compare the Septuagint's use of *en aphedrō*, "in a separate seat," to translate *dāwâ* in Leviticus 12:2.

16. The one area in which some medieval rabbis reversed the definition established by their ancient predecessors was the impurity of the parturient. The Mishna and the Talmudim assume that a parturient, past her initial seven or fourteen days of menstrual impurity, could have sex with her husband during the following thirty-three or sixty-six days even in the presence of a discharge. But the medieval rabbis, after intense discussion of the details of this rule, overturned it. A few, dismissed by Maimonides as heretics, argued that sex was forbidden during the entire forty or eighty days, even if there was no discharge at all, whereas most rabbis decided that any discharge should be treated just like regular menstruation.

17. Yigael Yadin, *The Temple Scroll*, 3 vols. (Jerusalem: Israel Exploration Society, 1983; English edition), 1:285–89, 291–93, 304–7. The references in the scroll are 45:7–17, 46:16–18, and 48:14–17. For further discussion see Lawrence H. Schiffman, "Exclusion from the Sanctuary and the City of the Sanctuary in the Temple Scroll," *Hebrew Annual Review* 9 (1985): 301–20.

18. The ambiguous phrase in the Mishna is *bêt hatūm'ôt* or *bêt hatĕmē'ôt* in m. Nidda 7:4. On the black Jews of Ethiopia, the so-called Falashas, see Wolf Leslau, *Falasha Anthology* (New Haven: Yale University, 1951; reprinted 1963), xxii–xxiii, 38, and Emanuela Tresivan-Semi, "The Beta Israel (Falashas): From Purity to Impurity," *The Jewish Journal of Sociology* 27 (1985): 103–14.

19. This important point, among many other important points, is unappreciated

by Marla Selvidge, "Mark 5:25–34 and Leviticus 15:19–20," *Journal of Biblical Literature* 103 (1984): 619–23, or by Ben Witherington, *Women in the Ministry of Jesus* (Cambridge: University, 1984), 71–75.

20. The major talmudic references are t. Shabbat 1:14, pp. 3–4 Lieberman, quoted in b. Shabbat 13a and p. Berakot 1:3 3a; b. Ketubot 61a, cf. p. Berakot 2:6 5b; b. Shabbat 13a–b, cf. Fathers according to Rabbi Nathan, version A, chap. 2, pp. 4b–5a Schechter.

21. *HaḤilūqîm šebên Anŝê Mizrāḥ ūbênê Ereṣ Yisrā'ēl*, ed. Mordechai Margaliot (Jerusalem, 1938), 79 sect. 11; see Margaliot's discussion on pp. 114–18. See also the edition by Benjamin Lewin, *Oṣar Ḥilūp Minhāgîm* (Jerusalem, 1942), 28–34.

22. See Tosapot, b. Ketubot 61a, s.v. *mĕḥalĕpā*, quoting the *Maḥzôr Vitry*, p. 608 Horovitz. However, R. Meir b. Baruch of Rothenburg (known as the Maharam, d. 1293) declared that a husband was not to toss objects to his menstruant wife, because tossing was a form of contact; see *R. Meir b. Baruch of Rothenburg: Responsa, Decisions, and Customs*, ed. Yizhaq Z. Kahana (Jerusalem: Mosad Harav Kook, 1960), 2:96, para. 104 (Hebrew), or Irving A. Agus, *Rabbi Meir of Rothenburg* (1947; reprinted New York: Ktav, 1970), 231, no. 150 (English).

23. See Dinari, "The Customs of Menstrual Impurity." See the Maimonidean passages listed below in note 30. The connection between changes in family structure and changes in menstruation rules requires investigation. I do not know whether women in a polygamous household would have lived in sufficient proximity to each other to cause their periods to coincide.

24. Perhaps the word should be translated "it was only in an emergency," but the usual phrase for such a meaning is *biš'at haddĕḥaq*.

25. Perhaps the passage is inspired by Persian ideas; the term used for menstruant is *distānā*, a word of Persian origin. In b. Shabbat 110a, a woman can ward off an amorous snake by claiming to be a menstruant (again *distānā*).

26. b. Erubin 100b; cf. Fathers according to Rabbi Nathan, version A, 1, p. 2b and version B, 42, p. 59a (much more misogynistic).

27. Even the Gospel story does not impute demonic possession to the woman who was a *zābâ* for twelve years. Several ancient authors mention the use of menstrual blood in the harvesting of asphalt from the Dead Sea, but this too does not imply anything demonic or dangerous; see Menahem Stern, *Greek and Latin Authors on Jews and Judaism*, 3 vols. (Jerusalem: Israel Academy of Sciences and Humanities, 1974–84), 1:147, commentary on no. 45. In many cultures, even in modern times, the milk of a menstruant mother is believed to be spoiled or dangerous; see Carroll Smith-Rosenberg, *Disorderly Conduct: Visions of Gender in Victorian America* (New York: Knopf, 1985), 329 n. 23. But such a belief is not attested in Judaism before *Differences*.

28. The text of *Beraita de Nidda* is edited by Chaim M. Horowitz, *Tosfata Atiqata*, part 5 (Frankfurt, 1890); a new edition is needed. The text has never been trans-

lated. On the *Beraita de Nidda* see the note of S. Lieberman in I. Gruenwald, *Apocalyptic and Merkavah Mysticism* (Leiden: E. J. Brill, 1980), 241–44.

29. *Beraita de Nidda*, pp. 3, 10, 12–13, 16, 18, 25, 36, 37.

30. For these restrictions in a legal context see, for example, the *Seper Roqeah* of R. Eleazar of Worms (1160–1237), sect. 318 (contrast sect. 317, which omits these restrictions), and the *Or Zaru'a* of R. Isaac ben Moses of Vienna, part 1, sect. 360, p. 48d, who explains that the total separation of husband from menstruating wife is justified not by the laws of impurity but by the "danger" that she poses. For these restrictions in a nonlegal context see the commentary of Nahmanides to Genesis 31:35 and Leviticus 12:4 and 18:19. In his *Laws Concerning a Menstruant* (*Hilkôt Niddâ*, ed. Moshe Hershler, Jerusalem, 1976), however, Nahmanides mentions none of the views that he advances in his commentary and none of the severe restrictions that derive from the *Beraita de Nidda*. For Maimonides' polemics see inter alia the *Guide of the Perplexed* 3:47, and *Mishneh Torah*, Book of Holiness, Laws of Forbidden Intercourse 11.

31. Josephus, *Jewish War* 5.5.2 (199) and 5.5.6 (227); *Jewish Antiquities* 15.11.5 (418–19); *Against Apion* 2.8 (103); m. Kelim 1:8–9; Sipre Numbers 1; b. Pesahim 66b–68a. For discussion see Emil Schürer, *History of the Jewish People in the Age of Jesus Christ*, rev. and ed. Geza Vermes et al. (Edinburgh: Clark, 1979), 2:285 n. 58. It is unclear whether the rabbinic texts imply that women were restricted to "the court of women" and prohibited from entering the next precinct, "the court of Israel." See Tosapot on b. Qiddusin 52b, s.v. *wĕkî*.

32. Jacob Neusner, *The Idea of Purity in Ancient Judaism* (Leiden: Brill, 1973); Shaye J. D. Cohen, "The Significance of Yavneh: Pharisees, Rabbis, and the End of Jewish Sectarianism," *Hebrew Union College Annual* 55 (1984): 27–53.

33. Purification before praying and eating: Judith 12:6–9. Purification before prayer: Sibylline Oracles 3:591–93; Letter of Aristeas 305–6 (in his paraphrase of Aristeas, Josephus changes the context from prayer to Torah study; see *Jewish Antiquities* 12.2.13 [106]). Purification before eating: Mark 7:1–23; see the excellent discussion of Roger P. Booth, *Jesus and the Laws of Purity*, Journal for the Study of the New Testament, Supplement Series 13 (Sheffield: JSOT, 1986).

34. The version in p. Berakot 3:4 6c is substantially identical, whereas the version in b. Berakot 22a has been changed to reflect the later view that menstruants are prohibited from reading the Torah. The Bavli omits *zābôt* and parturients, and substitutes "men who have intercourse with menstruants" for "menstruants." Thus the version in the Babylonian Talmud, unlike that of the Tosepta and the Palestinian Talmud, does not explicitly permit menstruants to perform sacred acts. See Lieberman's commentary.

35. b. Baba Qamma 82a; compare p. Yoma 8:1 44d bottom; p. Ta'anit 1:6 64c bottom–64d top; p. Berakot 3:4 6c. The Talmudim also derive the prohibition from the separation of men from women before the revelation of the Torah at Mount

Sinai (Exodus 19:15), a midrash which implies an origin for the prohibition well before Ezra.

36. See b. Berakot 21b–22b and p. Berakot 3:4 6b–6c.

37. In volume 2 of his commentary on the Palestinian Talmud (New York: Jewish Theological Seminary, 1941), Louis Ginzberg devotes nearly a hundred pages (195–276, 318–25) to elucidation (?) of the talmudic discussions of m. Berakot 3:4 and 6 but does not sufficiently realize that the Bavli and Yerushalmi differ on several crucial points.

38. This legal ruling is supported by the remarkable statement that Israelite women in the wilderness never menstruated because of the divine presence in the camp (p. 39).

39. Shaye J. D. Cohen, "The Temple and the Synagogue," in *The Temple in Antiquity*, ed. Truman Madsen (Provo, Utah: Brigham Young University, 1984), 151–74.

40. m. Negaim 13:12 = t. Nega'im 7:11, p. 627 Zuckermandel.

41. Although the laws regulating the proximity of "dirt" to the sancta (m. Berakot 3:5 with the Talmudim ad loc., based on Deuteronomy 23:10–15) certainly are relevant; see Baruch M. Bokser, "Approaching Sacred Space," *Harvard Theological Review* 78 (1985): 279–99. Synagogues in antiquity were sometimes built in proximity to baths or other sources of water, but I am not sure how to interpret this fact. See Roni Reich, "Synagogue and Ritual Bath during the Second Temple and the Period of the Mishna and Talmud," in *Synagogues in Antiquity*, ed. A. Kasher et al. (Jerusalem: Yad Izhak ben Zvi, 1987), 205–12 (Hebrew).

42. See my "Temple and the Synagogue."

43. *Beraita de Nidda* also implies that ejaculants should not enter the synagogue because they too are impure; such a prohibition is endorsed by R. Saadia Gaon (tenth century) and is combatted by Maimonides. On R. Saadia see Moses Zucker, *Tarbiz* 33 (1963): 54; on Maimonides see *Qôbeṣ tĕšûbôt haRambam wĕ'igrôtāw*, ed. Abraham Lichtenberg (Leipzig, 1859), p. 25, col. b (Hebrew numeration), no. 140.

44. Most of the relevant material is assembled by Dinari, "The Violation of the Sacred by the Nidda."

45. See especially B. M. Lewin, ed., *Oṣār HaGĕônîm* Berakot, Tesubot, paras. 116–21, pp. 48–49. At the same time the custom arose that a menstruant pronounces the benediction upon her purification only after emerging from the water of immersion, not before (which had been the normal practice); see *Oṣār Ha-Gĕônîm* Pesahim, Teshubot, paras. 25–26, pp. 8–9.

46. *Sēper HaPardēs*, p. 3 Ehrenreich; cf. *Maḥzôr Vitry*, p. 606 Horovitz, and *Sēper Hā'ôrâ*, part 2, pp. 167–68 Buber. The reference to "touching a Hebrew book" in the *Sēper HaPardēs* is probably an interpolation; it is missing from the parallels in the other two texts (although it does appear in the version quoted by R. Moses ben Isaac of Vienna, *Or Zaru'a*, part 1, sect. 360, p. 48d), is awkwardly appended to the

sentence, and is ignored in the remainder of the paragraph (which addresses only the question of menstruants in synagogue). On the distinctions between Ashkenazim and Sephardim in the separation of menstruants from the sancta see H. J. Zimmels, *Ashkenazim and Sephardim* (London: Oxford University Press, 1958; reprinted London: Marla, 1976), 197–99, 228–29.

47. R. Eliezer ben Yoel HaLevi, *Sēper Rabya*, vol. 1, p. 45 Aptowitzer; cf. *Or Zaruʿa*, part 1, sect. 360, p. 48d. The meaning of the text is somewhat unclear, but I am not convinced by Dinari's exegesis ("Violation of the Sacred," 27–28).

48. *Oraḥ Ḥayyîm* 88. The point is confirmed by various *minhag* books of the sixteenth through eighteenth centuries, in both Hebrew and Yiddish.

49. Although some new customs arose: not to visit a cemetery, and not to look at the Torah scroll when it is being held aloft in synagogue. Contemporary Orthodox and Conservative rabbis still need to emphasize to their laity that the prohibition of touching a Torah scroll is based on custom, not law; see, for example, R. Avraham Weiss, "Women and Sifrei Torah," *Tradition*, Summer 1982, 106–18, and Shaye J. D. Cohen, "Purity and Piety: The Separation of Menstruants from the Sancta" (forthcoming).

50. R. Ovadyah Yosef, *Yĕḥaweh Daʿat* (Jerusalem, 1980), 3:27–33, no. 8.

51. Robert Parker, *Miasma: Pollution and Purification in Early Greek Religion* (Oxford: Clarendon Press, 1983), 100–103. It is striking, however, that some early Christian texts attack postmenstruation purifications as *pagan*, rather than *Jewish*: see Clementine Homilies 11:30 and 33, and especially *Apostolic Constitutions* 6.28.1 with Funk's note ad loc. (p. 375).

52. The prohibition is justified sometimes by appeal to Leviticus, sometimes by appeal to the likelihood that defective offspring will result from the union. See Funk's note on *Apostolic Constitutions* 6.28.8 (p. 379).

53. The earliest unambiguous references to separate seating in church are *Didascalia* chap. 12, in *The Didascalia Apostolorum in Syriac*, trans. Arthur Vööbus, Corpus Scriptorum Christianorum Orientalium 408, Scriptores Syri 180 (Louvain, 1979), 131–32; Eusebius, *Life of Constantine* 1.53.1 (Licinius ordains that men and women pray and receive catechism separately, a regulation that Eusebius finds ridiculous); *Testamentum Domini* 2.4, p. 117 Rahmani; Gregory of Nazianzus, *Palma de Seipso* 16:19–20 = *Patrologia Graeca* 37:1255 (virgins and matrons listen from an upper gallery); John Chrysostom, 73rd homily on Matthew, *Patrologia Graeca* 58:677 (a barrier between men and women in church); the "Clementine liturgy" in book 8 of the *Apostolic Constitutions* (separate doors for men and women). As far as I know, the only modern discussion of the subject is H. Selhorst, *Die Platzordnung im Gläubigenraum der altchristlichen Kirche* (Münster: Aschendorff, 1931), but Selhorst advances several unsubstantiated conjectures and too quickly sees Jewish influence on Christian practice; it is unfortunate that only part of Selhorst's dissertation was published. Jewish antiquity provides no archaeological or literary evidence for

separate seating in the synagogue; see S. Safrai, *Tarbiz* 32 (1962–63): 329–38, and Bernadette Brooten, *Women Leaders in the Ancient Synagogue* (Chico: Scholars Press, 1982), esp. 103–38. Separate seating for women in synagogues is not securely attested until the eleventh century.

54. Like the rabbis, Christian clerics, especially with the rise of monasticism and a celibate clergy, were more interested in the violation of the sancta by polluted men than by polluted women, but this is not the place for a full discussion.

55. *Apostolic Tradition* 20. See Gregory Dix, *The Apostolic Tradition of St. Hippolytus* (London: Society for the Promotion of Christian Knowledge, 1937; reprinted 1968), 32, and Bernard Botte, *La tradition apostolique de Saint Hippolyte* (Münster: Aschendorff, 1963), 42–43.

56. R. J. Z. Werblowsky explains that Hippolytus regards the menstruant as possessed by demonic powers and therefore ineligible for baptism and exorcism; I see no indication of this in the text of Hippolytus. See Werblowsky, "On the Baptismal Rite according to St. Hippolytus," *Studia Patristica* 2 (1957): 93–105, esp. 95–97.

57. *Patrologia Graeca* 10:1281; Charles L. Feltoe, *The Letters and Other Remains of Dionysius of Alexandria* (Cambridge: Cambridge University Press, 1904), 102–3. The responsum of Dionysius was adopted a century later by Timothy of Alexandria (*Patrologia Graeca* 33:1300). My attention was first directed to Dionysius by G. E. M. de Ste Croix, *The Class Struggle in the Ancient Greek World* (Ithaca: Cornell University Press, 1981), 109 and nn.

58. The menstruant was excluded only from "the holy and holy of holies" (the *naos*); I presume that she could stand in the narthex. Bruce Nielsen has brought to my attention that Origen too might have accepted the literalness of the Levitical purity rules; Origen writes that an ejaculant ought not to enter a church and partake of the Eucharist (*Patrologia Graeca* 13:793, commentary on Ezekiel 7:22).

59. Dionysius is following Matthew 9:20 (*hēpsato tou kraspedou tou himatiou autou*) against Mark 5:27 (*hēpsato tou himatiou autou*); the manuscripts offer various readings at Luke 8:44.

60. See Vööbus, p. 244 n. 229: "Since a deliberate change cannot come into account here we must reckon with an accidental loss of the missing part of the text." I disagree; the Syriac version fits the argument of the paragraph, the Latin does not. Contrast the note of R. H. Connolly ad loc. in his translation. It would be important to know the provenance of the Latin translation.

61. The separation of menstruants from the sancta has enjoyed remarkable persistence within the church. In the West the letter of Gregory the Great to Augustine of Canterbury (given in Bede, *History of the Church* 1.27, no. 8; and cf. no. 9) should have put an end to the notion of ritual or physical impurity, but it did not. Impurity caused by menstruation and ejaculation is prominent in the penitentials and is well attested in the Christianity of Merovingian and Carolingian

France; see Pierre J. Payer, *Sex in the Penitentials* (Ithaca: Cornell University Press, 1984), and *A History of Private Life* (Cambridge, Mass.: Belknap Press of Harvard University Press, 1987–), 1:527 and 535–36 (where the source of the belief is ascribed to paganism rather than to Leviticus and Judaism). The *purificatio post partum* ritual (later known as *Muttersegen* in German, and "the churching of women" in English) is first attested in the twelfth or thirteenth century. The idea that a menstruant or a parturient should not contaminate a church was widespread in European Christianity at least until the seventeenth century; see Patricia Crawford, "Attitudes to Menstruation in Seventeenth-Century England," *Past and Present* 91 (1981): 47–73 (a reference I owe to Sara Heller). Menstruation figures prominently in Caroline Walker Bynum, *Holy Feast and Holy Fast: The Religious Significance of Food to Medieval Women* (Berkeley and Los Angeles: University of California Press, 1987). In the east the canons of Dionysius and Timothy were verified by numerous church councils and are still to be found in *Pedalion: The Rudder of the Metaphorical Ship of the One Holy Catholic and Apostolic Church of the Orthodox Christians*, by the monks Agapius and Nicodemus (completed in 1798 and first published in 1800; English translation by D. Cummings, Chicago: Orthodox Christian Educational Society, 1957). As Father Theodore Stylianopoulos confirms for me, Greek Orthodox women in "the old country" attend church during their menstruation but do not partake of communion.

62. See, for example, Delaney, *The Curse*, 33–39 (a chapter entitled "Woman Unclean: Menstrual Taboos in Judaism and Christianity"), and the chapter by Léonie Archer in *Images of Women in Antiquity*, ed. Averil Cameron and Amélie Kuhrt (London: Croom Helm, 1983), 273–87, esp. 276–78. Contrast Paige and Paige, *Politics*, 211: "The menstrual taboos of the ancient Hebrews, described in the Old Testament, are often cited to illustrate extreme contempt for women; but similar menstrual taboos and postmenstrual purification rituals are the norm in world societies rather than the exception."

63. How Jewish women viewed and observed the menstrual rituals is a subject for future research. In some cultures women enjoy the freedom provided them by their menstrual impurity; see, for example, Martin, *Woman in the Body*, 97. Misogynism does not have any necessary connection with a belief in menstrual impurity; in fact most of the misogynistic statements in ancient Jewish texts have no bearing at all on the menstrual rules. See Max Küchler, *Schweigen, Schmuck und Schleier: drei neutestamentliche Vorschriften zur Verdrängung der Frauen auf dem Hintergrund einer frauenfeindlichen Exegese des Alten Testaments im antiken Judentum* (Freiburg: Universität, and Göttingen: Vandenhoeck & Ruprecht, 1986), a rich collection of material that completely ignores menstruation and menstrual impurity.

CONTRIBUTORS

MARY TALIAFERRO BOATWRIGHT, associate professor of classical studies at Duke University, teaches courses in Roman history, archaeology, Latin, and women's studies. She covers the same range and uses a similarly interdisciplinary approach in her articles and book, *Hadrian and the City of Rome* (1987). Her current projects include a study of elite women of the Roman Empire and a book on Roman provincial cities.

ELIZABETH CARNEY, an associate professor of history at Clemson University, has written on Macedonian political history, on Virgil, and on the role of women in ancient monarchy. She is currently at work on a monograph dealing with royal Macedonian women.

SHAYE J. D. COHEN is Shenkman Professor of History at the Jewish Theological Seminary in New York. He is the author of *From the Maccabees to the Mishnah* (1987) and other studies of Judaism in antiquity. After completing his current research on the history of conversion to Judaism, he hopes to write a history of the Jewish laws and customs regarding menstruation.

MIREILLE CORBIER is director of research at the Centre National de la Recherche Scientifique in Paris and a member of the Ecole Française de Rome. Her publications include *L'aerarium Saturni et l'aerarium militare: administration et prosopographie sénatoriale* (Paris, 1975), *Indulgentia Principis* (forthcoming), and articles on the family, literacy, food, public finance, and the economy of the Roman Empire.

LESLEY DEAN-JONES is assistant professor of classics at the University of Texas at Austin, where she teaches courses in Greek and Latin and on aspects of Greek literature, society, and medicine. She has published articles on Greek history and medicine and is currently completing a monograph, *Women's Bodies in Classical Greek Science*.

DIANA DELIA is assistant professor of history at Texas A&M University, where she teaches ancient history. She is the author of *Alexandrian Citizenship during the Roman Principate* and several articles on Hellenistic and

Roman Egypt. Currently she is preparing a social and political history of ancient Alexandria.

ANN ELLIS HANSON was associate professor of classics and humanities at Fordham University, Lincoln Center, and currently teaches in the Department of Classical Studies at the University of Michigan. She has written on both Greek papyrology and Graeco-Roman medicine and is bringing to completion an edition of Hippocrates' *Diseases of Women* 1 and 2.

NATALIE BOYMEL KAMPEN is professor of women's studies and art history at Barnard College. She has published books and articles on women in ancient art and on feminist methodology in the history of art. She is now preparing books on iconographies of Roman women and on historical relief sculpture in the Roman provinces.

CLAUDE MOSSÉ is professor of ancient history at the University of Paris VIII. She has written numerous papers and books on ancient Greek history and society, including *La femme dans la Grèce antique* (1983), *La Grèce archaïque d'Homère à Eschyle* (1983), *Le procès de Socrate* (1987), and most recently, *L'antiquité dans la Révolution française* (1989).

CYNTHIA B. PATTERSON is assistant professor of history and women's studies at Emory University. She has published a monograph on the Athenian citizenship law of 451/450 B.C.E. and articles on the practice of infanticide in ancient Greece, the citizen status of Athenian women, and the nature of bastardy in Athens. Her contribution to this volume is part of a longer, ongoing study, "Household and Community in the Greek Polis."

SARAH B. POMEROY is the author of *Goddesses, Whores, Wives, and Slaves: Women in Classical Antiquity* (1975; paperback, 1976), *Women in Hellenistic Egypt from Alexander to Cleopatra* (1984; paperback, 1989), *A Social and Historical Commentary on Xenophon's Oeconomicus* (forthcoming), and many articles of the social and intellectual history of classical antiquity. She is also an author of *Women's Realities, Women's Choices: An Introduction to Women's Studies* (1983). She is professor of classics and women's studies at Hunter College and the Graduate School of the City University of New York.

MARILYN B. SKINNER is associate professor of classics at Northern Illinois University, where she teaches both classical studies and women's studies courses. She has edited a special "Women in Antiquity" issue of the journal *Helios* and has also published numerous essays on Greek and Roman women. Her interest in the epigrammatist Nossis develops out of her current project, a book on the ancient Greek female poetic tradition.

JANE McINTOSH SNYDER is professor of classics at Ohio State University, where she chairs the Department of Classics. Her books include *Puns and Poetry in Lucretius' De Rerum Natura* (1980), *Stringed Instruments of Ancient Greece*, with Martha Maas (1989), and *The Woman and the Lyre: Women Writers in Classical Greece and Rome* (1989).

INDEX